African Christian Theology

Journal of the Association for Christian Theological Education in Africa

VOLUME 1
(2024)

ACTEA

NAIROBI | KINSHASA

Théologie Chrétienne Africaine

Revue de l'Association Chrétienne de Théologie et d'Éducation en Afrique

VOLUME 1
(2024)

ACTEA

NAIROBI | KINSHASA

Teologia Christã Africana

Revista da Associação Cristã de Teologia e Educação em África

VOLUME 1
(2024)

ACTEA

NAIROBI | KINSHASA

African Christian Theology
Théologie Chrétienne Africaine
Teologia Cristã Africana

*Journal of the Association for
Christian Theological Education in Africa
Revue de l'Association Chrétienne de
Théologie et d'Éducation en Afrique
Revista da Associação Cristã de
Teologia e Educação em África*

**Volume 1 • Nº 2
September / Septembre / Setembro 2024**

Published by / Publié par / Publicado por

Association for Christian Theological Education in Africa

Continental Office

6th Floor, AEA Plaza
Valley Road
Nairobi, Kenya

P.O. Box 49332-00100
Nairobi, Kenya

Francophone Office

Niveau 2, Local 6
Immeuble Rev Bokundoa
Av. Shaumba no. 13
Q/Haut Commandement
Kinshasa-Gombe, Rép. Dem. du Congo

ISSN: 3006-1768
e-ISSN: 3007-1771
ISBN: 979-8-3852-4077-7

Copyright © 2024 by the Association for Christian Theological Education in Africa (ACTEA)
Creative Commons Attribution 4.0 International (CC BY 4.0)

The open access pdf of this journal is distributed under the following conditions:
The pdf may not be sold or used for profit except with written consent. The pdf may be printed only for private or institutional use, not for profit. Outside of Africa, the only printed copies that may be used in public are those obtained from the licensed distributor, Wipf and Stock.

Le pdf en libre accès de ce journal est distribué sous les conditions suivantes :
Le pdf ne peut être vendu ou utilisé à des fins lucratives, sauf accord écrit. Le pdf ne peut être imprimé que pour un usage privé ou institutionnel, sans but lucratif. En dehors de l'Afrique, les seules copies imprimées qui peuvent être utilisées en public sont celles obtenues auprès du distributeur autorisé, Wipf et Stock.

O pdf de acesso livre desta revista é distribuído sob as seguintes condições:
O pdf não pode ser vendido ou utilizado com fins lucrativos, exceto com autorização por escrito. O pdf pode ser impresso apenas para uso privado ou institucional, sem fins lucrativos. Fora de África, as únicas cópias impressas que podem ser usadas em público são as obtidas do distribuidor licenciado, Wipf e Stock.

Published outside of Africa by / Publié en dehors de l'Afrique par/ Publicado fora de África por

WIPF and STOCK Publishers
199 West 8th Avenue • Eugene OR 97401
wipfandstock.com

To order hard copies outside of Africa, contact orders@wipfandstock.com

EDITORIAL TEAM / ÉQUIPE ÉDITORIALE / CONSELHO EDITORIAL

Managing Editors / Directeurs-Éditeurs / Gestores-Editores

Joshua Robert BARRON	Research & Publications, ACTEA, Nairobi, Kenya
Wanjiru M. GITAU	Assistant Professor of Practical Theology and World Christianity, Palm Beach Atlantic University, Florida, USA
Martin MUNYAO	Senior Lecturer, Peace and International Studies, Daystar University, Nairobi, Kenya
Tom Joel OBENGO	Vice-Principal for Academic Affairs, Moffat Bible College, Kijabe, Kenya

Regional Editors / Éditeurs Régionaux / Editores Regionais

Ezekiel A. AJIBADE	Rector, Baptist College of Theology, Lagos, Nigeria
Chammah J. KAUNDA	Assistant Professor of World Christianity and Mission Studies, Yonsei University, South Korea
Fohle LYGUNDA LI-M	Manager for Africa, Theology and Network Engagement, TearFund
Marilyn NAIDOO	Professor of Practical Theology, University of South Africa, Pretoria, South Africa

EDITORIAL BOARD MEMBERS
MEMBRES DU COMITÉ REDACTION
MEMBROS DO CONSELHO EDITORIAL

Esther ACOLATSE (Ghana)	*Garrett-Evangelical Theological Seminary, Evanston, Illinois, USA*
John AZUMAH (Ghana)	*The Sanneh Institute, Accra, Ghana*
Nadine BOWERS DU TOIT (South Africa)	*Stellenbosch University, Stellenbosch, South Africa*
Joel A. CARPENTER (USA)	*Calvin University, Grand Rapids, Michigan, USA*
Sophia CHIRONGOMA (Zimbabwe)	*Midlands State University, Gweru, Zimbabwe*
Ini Dorcas DAH (Burkina Faso)	*Universität Münster, Münster, Deutschland*
Hervé DJILO KUATE (Cameroun)	*Université Protestante d'Afrique Centrale, Yaoundé, Cameroun*
Graham DUNCAN (South Africa)	*University of Pretoria, Pretoria, South Africa*
Bosela E. EALE (République Démocratique de Congo)	*ACTEA, Kinshasa, DR Congo*
Luc ELOMON (Côte d'Ivoire)	*Institut Theo-Strategique de Développement, Côte d'Ivoire*
Youdit Tariku FEYESSA (Ethiopia)	*Ethiopian Graduate School of Theology, Addis Ababa, Ethiopia*

Dion FORSTER (South Africa)	*Vrije Universiteit Amsterdam, Amsterdam, Nederland; Stellenbosch University, Stellenbosch, South Africa*
Sara J. FRETHEIM (Canada)	*Universität Münster, Münster, Deutschland*
Julius GATHOGO (Kenya)	*Kenyatta University, Nairobi, Kenya*
Riad Ibrahim GHOBRIAL (Egypt)	*Orthodox Coptic Center Cairo, Cairo, Egypt*
Paul GUNDANI (Zimbabwe)	*Zimbabwe Open University, Harare, Zimbabwe*
Hani HANNA (Egypt)	*Langham Literature, Cairo, Egypt*
Stan Chu ILO (Nigeria)	*DePaul University, Chicago, Illinois, USA*
Frederick KAKWATA (DR Congo)	*North-West University, Potchefstroom, South Africa*
Médine Moussounga KEENER (Congo-Brazzaville)	*Asbury Theological Seminary, Wilmore, Kentucky, USA*
Mookgo Solomon KGATLE (South Africa)	*University of South Africa, Pretoria, South Africa*
Roberta R. KING (USA)	*Fuller Theological Seminary, Pasadena, California, USA*
Joseph KOECH (Kenya)	*Moi University, Eldoret, Kenya*
Hoyce Jacob LYIMO-MBOWE (Tanzania)	*Mindolo Ecumenical Foundation, Ktiwe, Zambia*
Elizabeth MBURU (Kenya)	*Africa International University, Nairobi, Kenya*

Justine NABUSHAWO (Uganda)	*Moi University, Eldoret, Kenya*
Emioloa NIHINLOLA (Nigeria)	*Nigerian Baptist Theological Seminary, Ogbomoso, Nigeria*
Mbengu David NYIAWUNG (Cameroon)	*Presbyterian Theological Seminary, Kumba, Cameroon*
Emmanuel OYEMOMI (Nigeria)	*Baptist College of Theology Lagos, Nigeria*
Alfred SEBAHENE (Tanzania)	*St John's University of Tanzania, Dodoma, Tanzania*
Michèle SIGG (USA)	*Journal of African Christian Biography; Dictionary of African Christian Biography* (DACB) / *Dictionnaire Biographique des Chrétiens d'Afrique* (DIBICA)
Tite TIÉNOU (Burkino Faso)	*Trinity Evangelical Divinity School, Deerfield, Illinois, USA*
Abeneazer G. URGA (Ethiopia)	*Evangelical Theological College, Addis Ababa, Ethiopia*
Gerald O. WEST (South Africa)	*University of KwaZulu-Natal, Pietermaritzburg, South Africa*
Serge-Armand YAO (Côte d'Ivoire)	*l'Université de l'Alliance Chrétienne d'Abidjan, Abidjan, Côte d'Ivoire*

Editorial Policy

The articles in *African Christian Theology (ACT)* reflect the opinions of the authors and reviewers and do not necessarily represent those of the Editors or of ACTEA.

All submissions are subject to double-blind peer review. Unsolicited submissions are welcome, though not guaranteed of publication in the journal. Manuscripts and reviews may be sent to submissions@AfricanChristianTheology.org. Queries and other communications may be addressed to the managing editors at Editors@AfricanChristianTheology.org

Politique éditoriale

Les articles de *Théologie Chrétienne Africaine (TCA)* reflètent les opinions des auteurs et des évaluateurs et ne représentent pas nécessairement celles des rédacteurs ou d'ACTEA.

Toutes les soumissions font l'objet d'un examen par les pairs en double aveugle. Les soumissions spontanées sont les bienvenues, mais leur publication dans la revue n'est pas garantie. Les manuscrits et les critiques peuvent être envoyés à submissions@AfricanChristianTheology.org. Les questions et autres communications peuvent être adressés aux Directeurs-Éditeurs à l'adresse suivante :
Editors@AfricanChristianTheology.org

Política editorial

Os artigos da *Teologia Cristã Africana (TCA)* reflectem as opiniões dos autores e revisores, porém, não representam necessariamente os pensamentos dos editores ou da ACTEA.

Todas as submissões estão sujeitas a uma revisão por pares em dupla ocultação. As submissões não solicitadas são bem-vindas, embora não seja garantida a sua publicação na revista. Os manuscritos e as recensões podem ser enviados para submissions@AfricanChristianTheology.org. As questões e outras comunicações podem ser dirigidas aos Gestores-Editores para: Editors@AfricanChristianTheology.org

African Christian Theology is the academic journal of the Association for Christian Theological Education in Africa (ACTEA). The mission of ACTEA is to strengthen theological education through accreditation, scholarship, and support services to serve the church and transform society. The journal is one way in which ACTEA engages theological educators and church leaders in addressing relevant issues facing the church and society in Africa. *African Christian Theology* serves the whole of Africa and provides a venue for conversations between different regions of Africa, as well as an organ through which African voices can address World Christianity at large. Following in the footsteps of Kwame Bediako, Byang Kato, Kä Mana, Lamin Sanneh, Andrew F. Walls, and Isaac Zokoué, the journal promotes World Christianity perspectives through deep engagement with African contextual realities. Articles are published in English, French, and Portuguese; each article has a trilingual abstract in those languages.

ACTEA was founded in 1976 by the Theological and Christian Education Commission of the Association of Evangelicals in Africa (AEA). Under its continued sponsorship, ACTEA operates with internal autonomy in the accreditation of programmes of theological education throughout Africa, in order to stimulate the improvement and standardization of such programmes, and in order to secure academic recognition for such programmes wherever possible, especially among the constituencies of these institutions in Africa and among similar institutions and their constituencies overseas. ACTEA is a founding and constituent member of the International Council for Evangelical Theological Education (ICETE). ACTEA maintains offices in Nairobi and Kinshasa and can be found online at acteaweb.org. For further information on any aspect of ACTEA, please email the Executive Administrator at admin@acteaweb.org and copy the Executive Director at director@acteaweb.org.

The colours of ACTEA's logo are blue, red, and gold. Blue signifies royalty and speaks to ACTEA's efforts in raising a royal priesthood of God's servants throughout Africa. Red is the colour of blood and symbolises the redemptive act of Christ on the cross. Gold represents the preciousness of God's Word and the work which God's people do. Gold also reflects ACTEA's mission of prophetic proclamation of glorious hope in Christ, to African peoples first and then to the world, through theological education.

https://africanchristiantheology.org/

Théologie Chrétienne Africaine est la revue scientifique de l'Association Chrétienne de Théologie et d'Éducation en Afrique (ACTEA). La mission d'ACTEA est de renforcer l'éducation théologique par l'accréditation, la recherche et les services de soutien afin de servir l'église et de transformer la société. La revue est l'un des moyens par lesquels ACTEA stimule et implique les enseignants en théologie et les responsables d'église à aborder les questions pertinentes auxquelles sont confrontées l'église et la société en Afrique. *Théologie Chrétienne Africaine* est au service de l'ensemble de l'Afrique et constitue un lieu de dialogue entre les différentes régions d'Afrique. Elle sert ainsi d'organe par lequel les voix africaines peuvent s'adresser au christianisme mondial (« World Christianity ») dans son ensemble. Suivant les traces de Kwame Bediako, Byang Kato, Kä Mana, Lamin Sanneh, Andrew F. Walls, et Isaac Zokoué, la revue promeut les perspectives du christianisme mondial à travers un engagement profond avec les réalités contextuelles africaines. Les articles sont publiés en anglais, en français, et en portugais ; chaque article est accompagné d'un résumé trilingue dans ces langues.

ACTEA a été fondée en 1976 par la Commission d'Éducation Théologique et Chrétienne de l'Association des Évangéliques en Afrique (AEA). Sous le parrainage continu de l'AEA, ACTEA opère avec une autonomie interne dans l'accréditation des programmes d'éducation théologique à travers l'Afrique, afin de stimuler l'amélioration et la normalisation de ces programmes, et d'assurer la reconnaissance académique de ces programmes partout où cela est possible, notamment parmi les circonscriptions de ces institutions en Afrique et parmi les institutions similaires et leurs circonscriptions à l'étranger. ACTEA est un membre fondateur et constitutif du Conseil International pour l'Éducation Théologique Évangélique (en anglais, International Council for Evangelical Theological Education ou ICETE). ACTEA a des bureaux à Nairobi et à Kinshasa et peut être contactée en ligne à l'adresse suivante : acteaweb.org. Pour plus d'informations sur n'importe quel aspect d'ACTEA, veuillez envoyer un courriel au Directeur Francophone à directeur.francophone@acteaweb.org et une copie au Directeur Exécutif à director@acteaweb.org.

Les couleurs du logo d'ACTEA sont le bleu, le rouge, et l'or. Le bleu signifie la royauté et évoque les efforts d'ACTEA pour élever un sacerdoce royal de serviteurs de Dieu à travers l'Afrique. Le rouge est la couleur du sang et symbolise l'acte rédempteur du Christ sur la croix. L'or représente la valeur de la Parole de Dieu et le travail accompli par le peuple de Dieu. L'or reflète également la mission d'ACTEA, celle de la proclamation prophétique de l'espérance glorieuse en Christ, aux peuples africains d'abord et au monde ensuite, par le biais de l'éducation théologique.

https://africanchristiantheology.org/

Teologia Cristã Africana é a revista académica da Associação Cristã de Teologia e Educação em África (ACTEA). A missão da ACTEA é reforçar a educação teológica através de acreditação, pesquisa e serviços de apoio para servir a igreja e transformar a sociedade. A revista é uma das formas através das quais a ACTEA envolve educadores teológicos e líderes da igreja na abordagem de questões relevantes que a igreja e a sociedade em África enfrentam. A *Teologia Cristã Africana* serve toda a África e proporciona um local para conversas entre diferentes regiões de África, bem como um órgão através do qual as vozes africanas podem participar no diálogo de assuntos do cristianismo mundial ("World Christianity"). Seguindo os passos de Kwame Bediako, Byang Kato, Kä Mana, Lamin Sanneh, Andrew F. Walls, e Isaac Zokoué, a revista promove as perspectivas do cristianismo mundial através de um profundo envolvimento com as realidades contextuais africanas. Os artigos são publicados em inglês, francês e português; cada artigo tem um resumo trilingue nessas línguas.

A ACTEA foi estabelecida em 1976 pela Comissão de Educação Teológica e Cristã da Associação de Evangélicos em África (AEA). Sob o seu patrocínio contínuo, a ACTEA opera com autonomia interna na acreditação de programas de educação teológica em toda a África, a fim de estimular a melhoria e a padronização de tais programas, e a fim de assegurar o reconhecimento académico de tais programas sempre que possível, especialmente entre os stakeholders destas instituições em África e entre instituições semelhantes e os seus stakeholders no estrangeiro. A ACTEA é um membro fundador e constituinte do Conselho Internacional para a Educação Teológica Evangélica (ICETE). A ACTEA tem escritórios em Nairobi e Kinshasa e pode ser encontrada online em acteaweb.org. Para mais informações sobre qualquer aspeto da ACTEA, envie um e-mail para o Administrador Executivo em admin@acteaweb.org com cópia para o Diretor Executivo em director@acteaweb.org.

As cores do logótipo da ACTEA são o azul, o vermelho e o dourado. O azul significa realeza e fala dos esforços da ACTEA para erguer um sacerdócio real dos servos de Deus em toda a África. O vermelho é a cor do sangue e simboliza o ato redentor de Cristo na cruz. O ouro representa a preciosidade da Palavra de Deus e o trabalho que o povo de Deus realiza. O ouro também reflete a missão da ACTEA de proclamação profética da gloriosa esperança em Cristo, primeiro aos povos africanos e depois ao mundo, através da educação teológica.

https://africanchristiantheology.org/

Cover art created by Wexer Creative, Nairobi and Mombasa, Kenya and © 2024 by ACTEA. The building silhouettes are of the Basilica of Our Lady of Peace in Yamoussoukro, Côte d'Ivoire, the largest church building in the world, the Kenyatta International Convention Centre in Nairobi, Kenya, and Nigeria's National Theatre in Lagos. The symbols, including the acacia tree and the Ethiopian cross, represent the journal's commitment to all regions of Africa, urban and rural, anglophone, francophone, and lusophone (as well as arabophone), and to all African Christian traditions — Protestant, Roman Catholic, Orthodox, Pentecostal, and AICs. The cross in the center of Africa, designed from a photograph of an Ethiopian cross displayed in the home of one of our managing editors, conveys both the journal's central evangelical commitment and its commitment to Africanity.

(AICs refers to African Indigenous Churches, African Initiated Churches, and/or African Independent Churches.)

La couverture a été créée par Wexer Creative, Nairobi et Mombasa, Kenya et © 2024 par ACTEA. Les silhouettes des bâtiments représentent la Basilique Notre-Dame de la Paix à Yamoussoukro, en Côte d'Ivoire, le plus grand bâtiment d'église du monde, le Kenyatta International Convention Centre à Nairobi, au Kenya, et le Théâtre National du Nigeria à Lagos. Les symboles, dont l'acacia et la croix éthiopienne, représentent l'engagement de la revue envers toutes les régions d'Afrique, urbaines et rurales, anglophones, francophones, et lusophones (ainsi qu'arabophones), et envers toutes les traditions chrétiennes africaines, protestantes, catholiques romaines, orthodoxes, pentecôtistes et EIAs. La croix au centre de l'Afrique, conçue à partir d'une photographie d'une croix éthiopienne exposée chez l'un de nos rédacteurs en chef, traduit à la fois l'engagement évangélique central de la revue et son engagement en faveur de l'africanité.

(EICs est un anacronyme anglais qui désigne Églises indépendantes africaines, églises indigènes africaines, églises initiées africaines, et/ou églises indépendantes africaines.)

Arte da capa criada por Wexer Creative, Nairobi e Mombasa, Quénia e © 2024 pela ACTEA. As silhuetas dos edifícios são da Basílica de Nossa Senhora da Paz em Yamoussoukro, na Côte d'Ivoire, a maior edifício da igreja do mundo, e o Centro Internacional de Convenções Kenyatta em Nairobi, Quénia, e do Teatro Nacional da Nigéria, em Lagos. Os símbolos, incluindo a acácia e a cruz etíope, representam o compromisso da revista para com todas as regiões de África, urbanas e rurais, anglófonas, francófonas e lusófonas (bem como arabófonas), e para com todas as tradições cristãs africanas, protestantes, católicas romanas, ortodoxas, pentecostais e IIAs. A cruz no centro de África, concebida a partir de uma fotografia de uma cruz etíope exposta na casa de um dos nossos redactores-gerais, transmite tanto o compromisso evangélico central da revista como o seu compromisso com a africanidade.

(IIAs é um anacrónimo que se refere a igrejas indígenas africanas, igrejas iniciadas em África e/ou igrejas independentes africanas.)

The specialist review journal, *BookNotes for Africa*, published from 1996–2019, offered short academic reviews of recent Africa-related publications relevant for informed Christian reflection in Africa. Because of its importance, ACTEA was happy to promote *BookNotes for Africa* to its constituent schools. In 2018, the over 1,200 reviews published in issues 1–30 were published by Langham Global Library in a permanent reference collection, *Christian Reflection in Africa: Review and Engagement*, edited by Paul Bowers. A second enlarged edition including reviews from issues 31–40 together with a number of more recent reviews is forthcoming.

Inspired by the legacy of *BookNotes for Africa*, the editors hope that the book review section of *African Christian Theology* will be as robust and as helpful. This section of the journal includes both critical review essays and short book note style reviews. While the majority of books reviewed have been published recently, as is customary, we will sometimes publish retrospective reviews of older texts.

La revue spécialisée, *BookNotes for Africa*, ('Notes de Livres pour l'Afrique'), publiée de 1996 à 2019, proposait courtes critiques académiques de publications récentes liées à l'Afrique et pertinentes pour une réflexion chrétienne éclairée en Afrique. En raison de son importance, ACTEA a été heureux de promouvoir *BookNotes for Africa* auprès de ses écoles constitutives. En 2018, les plus de 1 200 comptes rendus publiés dans les numéros 1 à 30 ont été publiés par Langham Global Library dans une collection de référence permanente, *Christian Reflection in Africa : Review and Engagement*, sous la direction de Paul Bowers. Une deuxième édition révisée comprenant les comptes rendus des numéros 31 à 40 ainsi qu'un certain nombre de comptes rendus plus récents est à venir.

Inspirés par l'héritage de *BookNotes for Africa*, les éditeurs espèrent que la section des critiques de livres de *Théologie Chrétienne Africaine* sera aussi solide et utile. Cette section de la revue comprend à la fois des essais critiques et de courts comptes-rendus sous forme de notes de lecture. Bien que la majorité des livres analysés aient été publiés récemment, nous publierons parfois des analyses rétrospectives de textes plus anciens.

A revista especializada, *BookNotes for Africa* ('Notas de Livro para África'), publicada de 1996 a 2019, oferecia pequenas recensões académicas de publicações recentes relacionadas com África, relevantes para uma reflexão cristã informada em África. Devido à sua importância, a ACTEA teve o prazer de promover a BookNotes for Africa junto das escolas que a constituem. Em 2018, as mais de 1.200 recensões publicadas nos números 1–30 foram publicadas pela Langham Global Library numa coleção de referência permanente, *Christian Reflection in Africa: Review and Engagement* ('Reflexão Cristã em África: Recensão e Engajamento'), editada por Paul Bowers. Está a ser preparada uma segunda edição alargada que inclui as recensões dos números 31–40, bem como algumas recensões mais recentes.

Inspirados pelo legado da *BookNotes for Africa*, os editores esperam que a secção de recensões de livros da *Teologia Cristã Africana* seja tão robusta e útil. Esta secção da revista inclui ensaios de recensão crítica e pequenas recensões de livros. Embora a maioria dos livros recenseados tenha sido publicada recentemente, como é habitual, publicaremos por vezes recensões retrospectivas de textos mais antigos.

Table of Contents
Table des Matières
Índice

Editorial / Éditorial:
African Voices 208

Vozes Africanas 210

Voix Africaines 212
Joshua Robert Barron

**La Théologie de James H. Cone,
un Lieu de Libération pour l'Afrique** 215
Rodrick Kapwa Ilunga

**Completing the Circle: Treks, Trends, and Trajectory
of Circle Theology** 232
Esther Mombo & Jackline Makena

**The Rain Reveals the Leaks: How the Vulnerability of the
"Least of These" Reveals the Vulnerabilities in our
Own Hearts and Systems** 251
Ruth Barron

**Africa's Aquifers: Reflections on John S. Mbiti's Contributions
to African Christian Spirituality** 272
Diane B. Stinton

**Women, Leadership, and Ordination in the Anglican Church
in Nigeria: Debating 1 Corinthians 14:26–40** 291
Mercy U. Chukwuedo

**Diversity of Eucharistic Ritual in COVID-2019 Context:
A comparative study of CITAM Valley Road and
PCEA St. Andrews in Nairobi Kenya** 318
Samwel Kiuguini Nduati & Linda Ochola-Adolwa

Frank Weston of Zanzibar: An Assessment and Appreciation
of an "Apostle to Africans" 335
Maimbo W. F. Mndolwa, Fergus J. King, & Joshua Robert Barron

Book Reviews / Évaluations des Livres / Avaliações de Livros:
BOOK REVIEW ESSAYS
ESSAIS CRITIQUES DU LIVRE
ENSAIOS CRÍTICOS SOBRE O LIVRO

Finding the Kingdom of God in Africa
    SHAW, Mark, and Wanjiru M. GITAU.
    The Kingdom of God in Africa: A History of African Christianity 362
Christine Chemutai Chirchir

La « contextéisation » théologique :
Le nouveau paradigme en théologie contextuelle
    LYGUNDA LI-M, Fohle. *Contextualisation aujourd'hui :*
    Questions approfondies en théologie contextuelle 369
Lessi Traoré

Theological 'Contexted-ization':
A New Paradigm in Contextual Theology
    LYGUNDA LI-M, Fohle. *Contextualisation aujourd'hui :*
    Questions approfondies en théologie contextuelle ['Contextualization
    Today: In-Depth Questions on Contextual Theology'] 382
Lessi Traoré

Peregrinatio: Migrants and Migration in Christian History
    HANCILES, Jehu J. *Migration and the Making of Global Christianity* 394
Joshua Robert Barron

Contemporary Christology in Africa: Evangelical Perspectives
    REED, Rodney L., and David K. NGARUIYA, eds..
    Who Do You Say That I Am? Christology in Africa 400
Diane Stinton

Division and Unity
    KALU, Ogbu U. *Divided People of God: Christian Union Movement*
    in Nigeria: 1875–1966 408
Okuchukwu Venatus Akpe

Experiencing Salvation in Africa
REED, Rodney L., and David K. NGARUIYA, eds.
Salvation in African Christianity 412
Raphael Akhijemen Idialu

Women in Ordained Ministry
NKESIGA, Diana Mirembe. *Woven in Spirals: The Journey of an African Woman to the Priesthood* 430
Francis Omondi

Calls for Papers and Conference Announcements
Appels à Contributions et Annonces de Conférences
Convites de Artigos e Anúncios de Conferências
    Nicaea at 1700: Roots and Branches in African Christianity 435
    Nicée à 1700 ans : Racines et Branches dans le Christianisme Africain 436
    Nicéia a 1700 anos: Raízes e Ramos do Cristianismo Africano 437

    The Bible, African Spirituality, and Post-Modernity 438

    Yale-Edinburgh Conference: Christianity, Democracy, and Nationalism 439
    Conferência Yale-Edimburgo: Cristianismo, Democracia, e Nacionalismo 440

Book Reviews / Évaluations des Livres / Avaliações de Livros:
'BOOK NOTE' SHORT REVIEWS
BRÈVES CRITIQUES DU LIVRE
BREVE RESENHA DO LIVRO

    AMENVENKU, Frederick MAWUSI, and Isaac BOAHENG.
    Biblical Exegesis in African Context 441
Anthony Smith

    KIGAME, Reuben. *Essays in African Christianity and Theology* 443
Francis Omondi

    AYUK, Ayuk Ausaji. *African Theology of Missions* 446
Kent Michael I

EDITORIAL
African Voices

Joshua Robert BARRON

ORCID: 0000-0002-9503-6799
ACTEA, Enoomatasiani, Kenya
Joshua.Barron@ACTEAweb.org

African Christian Theology exists in part as a platform to highlight African voices. This issue succeeds at that task. Our lead article, demonstrating our pan-African commitment, is in French rather than English. Rodrick Kapwa Ilunga (DR Congo) applies the liberation theology of James Cone to contexts on the African continent. Because *birds have two wings* and *a one-winged bird cannot fly*, and too often the female wing of the Church is silenced, the editors rejoice that 78% of this issues articles have been contributed by women. Their voices need to be heard. In the second article, Esther Mombo and Jackline Makena (Kenya) explore the legacy and prospects of the theology of the Circle of Concerned African Women Theologians. Next, curriculum developer and victim advocate Ruth Barron (Kenya) draws on indigenous Maasai knowledge to challenge the Church to confront abuse. In the fourth article, Diane B. Stinton (Canada) reflects on John S. Mbiti's contributions to African Christian spirituality. Next Mercy U. Chukwuedo (Nigeria) examines 1 Corinthians 14:26–40 in the context of Igbo traditional culture and religion and the ongoing debate over the ordination of women in the Anglican Church of Nigeria. In the sixth article, Samwel Kiuguini Nduati and Linda Ochola-Adolwa (Kenya) examine the effect of the recent pandemic on Eucharistic practice in two denominations in Kenya. Finally, Anglican Archbishop Maimbo W. F. Mndolwa (Tanzania) joins Fergus J. King to offer, with some assistance from myself, an assessment of the legacy of an "Apostle to Africans," Bishop Frank Weston of Zanzibar (1871–1924).

Six books are evaluated with full-length review essays. Christine Chemutai Chirchir (Kenya) examines *The Kingdom of God in Africa* by Mark Shaw (USA / Kenya) and Wanjiru M. Gitau (Kenya). Lessi Traoré (Burkina Faso) offers a review — first in French, and then in English — of Fohle Lygunda Li-M's important text *Contextualisation aujourd'hui* ('Contextualization today'), and explores Lygunda's (DR Congo) seminal idea, *contextéisation* ('contextedization'). We customarily feature a book review written by one of our editors, and so I have reviewed *Migration and the Making of Global Christianity*, a magisterial work by Jehu J. Hanciles (Sierra Leone / USA). Next, Diane Stinton

Joshua Robert Barron, *managing co-editor*
Editorial: African Voices

reviews volume 6 in the ASET (Africa Society of Evangelical Theology) Series, *Who Do You Say That I Am?* In 1978, Ogbu U. Kalu (Nigeria) published *Divided People of God: Christian Union Movement in Nigeria.* Okuchukwu Venatus Akpe (Nigeria) has reviewed the recent reprint edition. *Salvation in African Christianity*, ASET Series 8, is reviewed by Raphael Akhijemen Idialu (Nigeria). Finally, Canon Francis Omondi reviews *Woven in Spirals: The Journey of an African Woman to the Priesthood* by Diana Mirembe Nkesiga (Uganda).

We are honored to share three Calls-For-Papers. The first, "Nicaea at 1700: Roots and Branches in African Christianity" is for a themed issue of this journal (September 2025), marking the 1700th anniversary of the Council of Nicaea in 325. We solicit submissions in English, French, and Portuguese. A conference on "The Bible, African Spirituality, and Post-Modernity" will be held at the West African Advanced School of Theology in Owerri, Nigeria in December 2024; submissions in English are welcome. Finally, the 2025 Yale-Edinburgh Conference — held for the first time in the Global South, in Brazil — seeks submissions of abstracts on the theme of "Christianity, Democracy, and Nationalism." Submissions will be accepted in English, Portuguese, and Spanish.

Finally, we have three 'Book Note' short reviews. Anthony Smith (USA / northeast Africa) reviews *Biblical Exegesis in African Context* by Frederick Mawusi Amevenku and Issac Boaheng (Ghana). Francis Omondi (Kenya) reviews *Essays in African Christianity and Theology* by Reuben Kigami (Kenya). Kent Michael I (USA) reviews *African Theology of Missions* by Ayuku Ausaji Ayuk (Nigeria / Philippines).

This issue offers voices from eight countries in Africa — Burkina Faso, DR Congo, Ghana, Kenya, Nigeria, Uganda, Sierra Leone, Tanzania. If your country is not represented, then we encourage you to consider writing for us in future issue. But for now — *tolle lege*, 'take and read.'

EDITORIAL
Vozes Africanas

Joshua Robert BARRON

ORCID: 0000-0002-9503-6799
ACTEA, Enoomatasiani, Kenya
Joshua.Barron@ACTEAweb.org

Teologia Christã Africana existe, em parte, como uma plataforma para destacar as vozes africanas. Esta edição é bem-sucedida nessa missão. O nosso artigo principal, que demonstra o nosso empenhamento pan-africano, está escrito em francês e não em inglês. Rodrick Kapwa Ilunga (RD Congo) aplica a teologia da libertação de James Cone aos contextos do continente africano. Porque *os pássaros têm duas asas* e *um pássaro com uma só asa não pode voar*, e que muitas vezes a asa feminina da Igreja é silenciada, a equipa editorial regozijam-se com o facto de 78% dos artigos desta edição terem sido escritos por mulheres. As suas vozes devem ser ouvidas. No segundo artigo, Esther Mombo e Jackline Makena (Quénia) exploram o legado e as perspectivas da teologia do Circle of Concerned African Women Theologians ('Círculo de Mulheres Africanas Teólogas Preocupadas'). Depois, Ruth Barron (Quénia), criadora de currículos e defensora das vítimas, baseia-se no conhecimento indígena Maasai para desafiar a Igreja a enfrentar os abusos. No quarto artigo, Diane B. Stinton (Canadá) reflecte sobre as contribuições de John S. Mbiti para a espiritualidade cristã africana. De seguida, Mercy U. Chukwuedo (Nigéria) examina 1 Coríntios 14:26–40 no contexto da cultura e religião tradicionais Igbo e o debate em curso sobre a ordenação de mulheres na Igreja Anglicana da Nigéria. No sexto artigo, Samwel Kiuguini Nduati e Linda Ochola-Adolwa (Quénia) examinam o efeito da recente pandemia na prática eucarística em duas denominações do Quénia. Finalmente, o Arcebispo anglicano Maimbo W. F. Mndolwa (Tanzânia) junta-se a Fergus J. King para oferecer, com alguma ajuda da minha parte,, uma avaliação do legado de um "apóstolo dos africanos", o Bispo Frank Weston de Zanzibar (1871–1924).

Seis livros são avaliados através de ensaios exaustivos. Christine Chemutai Chirchir (Quénia) analisa o livro *The Kingdom of God in Africa* ('O Reino de Deus em África') de Mark Shaw (EUA/Quénia) e Wanjiru M. Gitau (Quénia). Lessi Traoré (Burkina Faso) apresenta uma recensão — primeiro em francês, depois em inglês — do importante texto de Fohle Lygunda Li-M (RD Congo),

Joshua Robert Barron, *gestore-co-editore*
Editorial: Vozes Africanas

Contextualisation Aujourd'hui ('Contextualização Hoje'), e explora a ideia seminal de *contextéisation*[1] de Lygunda. Normalmente, apresentamos uma recensão de um livro escrita por um dos nossos editores, por isso escrevi uma recensão de *Migration and the Making of Global Christianity* ('Migração e a Construção do Cristianismo Global'), uma obra magistral de Jehu J. Hanciles (Serra Leoa / EUA). Em seguida, Diane Stinton analisa o volume 6 da série ASET (*Africa Society of Evangelical Theology* ou Sociedade Africana de Teologia Evangélica), *Who Do You Say That I Am?* ('Quem Dizeis Que Eu Sou?'). Em 1978, Ogbu U. Kalu (Nigéria) publicou *Divided People of God: Christian Union Movement in Nigeria* ('Povo de Deus dividido: Movimento da União Cristã na Nigéria') Okuchukwu Venatus Akpe (Nigéria) analisou a recente reimpressão da edição. *Salvation in African Christianity* ('A salvação no cristianismo africano'), volume 8 da Série ASET, é analisado por Raphael Akhijemen Idialu (Nigéria). Por fim, o Cónego Francis Omondi comenta *Woven in Spirals: The Journey of an African Woman to the Priesthood* ('Tecido em espiral: a viagem de uma mulher africana ao sacerdócio') de Diana Mirembe Nkesiga (Uganda).

Temos o prazer de anunciar três convites de artigos. O primeiro, "Niceia em 1700: raízes e ramos do cristianismo africano," destina-se a um número temático desta revista (setembro de 2025), assinalando o 1700º aniversário do Concílio de Niceia em 325. Os trabalhos são apresentados em inglês, francês e português. Uma conferência sobre "A Bíblia, a espiritualidade africana e a pós-modernidade" terá lugar na West African Graduate School of Theology em Owerri, Nigéria, em dezembro de 2024; são bem-vindas contribuições em inglês. Finalmente, a Conferência Yale-Edimburgo 2025 — que se realizará pela primeira vez no Sul Global, no Brasil — está a convidar à apresentação de resumos sobre o tema "Cristianismo, Democracia e Nacionalismo." Os trabalhos serão aceites em inglês, português e espanhol.

Por fim, temos três breves resenhas do livro. Anthony Smith (EUA/Norte de África Oriental) publicou uma resenha de *Biblical Exegesis in African Context* ('A Exegese Bíblica no Contexto Africano'), de Frederick Mawusi Amevenku e Issac Boaheng (Gana). Francis Omondi (Quénia) publicou uma resenha de *Essays in African Christianity and Theology* ('Ensaios sobre o cristianismo e a teologia em África'), de Reuben Kigami (Quénia). Kent Michael I (EUA) publicou uma resenha de *African Theology of Missions* ('Teologia africana das missões'), de Ayuku Ausaji Ayuk (Nigéria/Filipinas).

---

[1] Esta é uma nova palavra que o professor Fohle criou em francês. Ele tratou o substantivo *contexto* e tratou-o como um verbo, colocou-o no pretérito perfeito e depois, como sufixo, acrescentou -ização.

Joshua Robert Barron, *gestore-co-editore*
Editorial: Vozes Africanas

Esta edição apresenta as vozes de oito países africanos: Burkina Faso, a República Democrática do Congo, o Gana, o Quénia, a Nigéria, o Uganda, a Serra Leoa, e a Tanzânia. Se o seu país não estiver representado, encorajamo-lo a considerar escrever para nós numa edição futura. Mas por agora — *tolle lege*, "pegue e leia."

ÉDITORIAL
Voix africaines

Joshua Robert BARRON

ORCID: 0000-0002-9503-6799
ACTEA, Enoomatasiani, Kenya
Joshua.Barron@ACTEAweb.org

Théologie Chrétienne Africaine existe en partie en tant que plateforme pour mettre en valeur les voix africaines. Ce numéro remplit cette mission avec succès. L'article principal, qui témoigne de notre engagement panafricain, est rédigé en français plutôt qu'en anglais. Rodrick Kapwa Ilunga (RD Congo) applique la théologie de la libération de James Cone aux contextes du continent africain. Parce que les *oiseaux ont deux ailes* et qu'*un oiseau à une aile ne peut pas voler*, et que trop souvent l'aile féminine de l'Église est réduite au silence, la rédaction se réjouit que 78% des articles de ce numéro aient été rédigés par des femmes. Leurs voix doivent être entendues. Dans le deuxième article, Esther Mombo et Jackline Makena (Kenya) explorent l'héritage et les perspectives de la théologie du Cercle des théologiennes africaines concernées. Ensuite, Ruth Barron (Kenya), conceptrice de programmes d'études et avocate des victimes, s'appuie sur le savoir indigène des Maasai pour inciter l'Église à lutter contre les abus. Dans le quatrième article, Diane B. Stinton (Canada) réfléchit aux contributions de John S. Mbiti à la spiritualité chrétienne africaine. Ensuite, Mercy U. Chukwuedo (Nigeria) examine 1 Corinthiens 14 : 26–40 dans le contexte de la culture et de la religion traditionnelles Igbo et du débat actuel sur l'ordination des femmes dans l'Église anglicane du Nigeria. Dans le sixième article, Samwel Kiuguini Nduati et Linda Ochola-Adolwa (Kenya) examinent l'effet de la récente pandémie sur la pratique eucharistique dans deux confessions au Kenya. Enfin, l'archevêque anglican Maimbo W. F. Mndolwa (Tanzanie) se joint à Fergus J. King pour proposer, avec mon aide, une évaluation de l'héritage d'un « apôtre des Africains », l'évêque Frank Weston de Zanzibar (1871–1924).

Six livres sont évalués à l'aide d'essais complets. Christine Chemutai Chirchir (Kenya) examine *The Kingdom of God in Africa* ('Le Royaume de Dieu en Afrique') de Mark Shaw (USA / Kenya) et Wanjiru M. Gitau (Kenya). Lessi Traoré (Burkina Faso) propose une revue — d'abord en français, puis

Joshua Robert Barron, *co-directeur-éditeur*
Éditorial : Voix Africaines

en anglais — de l'important texte de Fohle Lygunda Li-M (RD Congo), *Contextualisation aujourd'hui*, et explore l'idée séminale de Lygunda, la *contextéisation*. Nous avons l'habitude de présenter une critique de livre rédigée par l'un de nos rédacteurs, et c'est pourquoi j'ai rédigé une critique de *Migration and the Making of Global Christianity* ('La Migration et Christianisme Mondial'), un ouvrage magistral de Jehu J. Hanciles (Sierra Leone / États-Unis). Ensuite, Diane Stinton examine le volume 6 de la Série ASET (*Africa Society of Evangelical Theology* ou Société Africaine de Théologie Évangélique), *Who Do You Say That I Am ?* ('Qui Dites-Vous Que Je Suis ?'). En 1978, Ogbu U. Kalu (Nigeria) a publié *Divided People of God : Christian Union Movement in Nigeria* ('Le Peuple Divisé de Dieu : Le Mouvement de l'Union Chrétienne au Nigeria') Okuchukwu Venatus Akpe (Nigeria) a examiné la récente édition réimprimée. *Salvation in African Christianity* ('Le Salut dans le Christianisme Africain'), le volume 8 de la Série ASET, est commenté par Raphael Akhijemen Idialu (Nigeria). Enfin, le chanoine Francis Omondi commente *Woven in Spirals : The Journey of an African Woman to the Priesthood* ('Tissé en Spirales : l'itinéraire d'une femme africaine vers la prêtise') de Diana Mirembe Nkesiga (Ouganda).

Nous avons l'honneur de vous faire part de trois appels à contributions. Le premier, « Nicée en 1700 : Racines et branches du christianisme africain » est destiné à un numéro thématique de cette revue (septembre 2025), marquant le 1700e anniversaire du Concile de Nicée en 325. Nous sollicitons des propositions en anglais, en français, et en portugais. Une conférence sur « La Bible, la spiritualité africaine et la postmodernité » se tiendra à l'École supérieure de théologie d'Afrique de l'Ouest à Owerri, au Nigéria, en décembre 2024 ; les contributions en anglais sont les bienvenues. Enfin, la Conférence Yale-Edinburgh 2025 — organisée pour la première fois dans le Sud global, au Brésil - sollicite des soumissions de résumés sur le thème « Christianisme, Démocratie et Nationalisme ». Les soumissions seront acceptées en anglais, portugais et espagnol. Les soumissions seront acceptées en anglais, portugais, et espagnol.

Enfin, nous avons trois brèves critiques du livre. Anthony Smith (États-Unis / Afrique du Nord-Est) a publié un compte rendu de *Biblical Exegesis in African Context* ('L'Exégèse biblique dans le contexte africain') de Frederick Mawusi Amevenku et Issac Boaheng (Ghana). Francis Omondi (Kenya) a publié un compte rendu de *Essays in African Christianity and Theology* ('Essais sur le christianisme et la théologie en Afrique') de Reuben Kigami (Kenya). Kent Michael I (États-Unis) a publié un compte rendu de *African Theology of Missions* ('Théologie Africaine des Missions') d'Ayuku Ausaji Ayuk (Nigéria / Les Philippines).

Joshua Robert Barron, *co-directeur-éditeur*
Éditorial : Voix Africaines

Ce numéro présente les voix de huit pays d'Afrique : Burkina Faso, la République démocratique du Congo, le Ghana, le Kenya, le Nigeria, l'Ouganda, la Sierra Leone et la Tanzanie. Si votre pays n'est pas représenté, nous vous encourageons à envisager d'écrire pour nous dans un prochain numéro. Mais pour l'instant — *tolle lege*, « prenez et lisez ».

La Théologie de James H. Cone, un Lieu de Libération pour l'Afrique

Rodrick Kapwa Ilunga
Faculté de Théologie Protestante, Université Méthodiste de Kolwezi,
Kolwezi, République Démocratique du Congo
rodrickkapwailunga@gmail.com

Résumé

Comme pour la plupart de crise contemporaine, la crise africaine est née d'une société dont les déséquilibres méritent d'être étudiés. Le néocolonialisme, l'oppression, la disette traduit au mieux la structure actuelle de l'Afrique. Dès lors le souci de lutte et de libération économique, social et politique semble inévitable. Ainsi le présent article postule la théologie de la libération de James H. Cone (1938–2018) et son ecclésiologie, comme voie de libération pour l'Africain.

Abstract

As with most contemporary crises, the African crisis is born of a society whose imbalances deserve to be studied. Neo-colonialism, oppression, and famine are the best expression of Africa's current structure. The need for economic, social and political struggle and liberation seems inevitable. The present article postulates the liberation theology and ecclesiology of James H. Cone (1938–2018) as a path to liberation for the African.

Resumo

Como a maioria das crises contemporâneas, a crise africana nasce de uma sociedade cujos desequilíbrios merecem ser estudados. O neocolonialismo, a opressão e a fome são a melhor expressão da estrutura atual de África. A partir daí, a necessidade de luta e de libertação económica, social e política parece inevitável. Este artigo toma a teologia da libertação de James H. Cone (1938–2018) e a sua eclesiologia como caminho para a libertação dos africanos.

Mots-clés

Théologie de la libération, James H. Cone, Afrique, ecclésiologie

---

Publié avec licence par ACTEA | DOI: https://doi.org/10.69683/mqh5qx42
© Rodrick Kapwa Ilunga, 2024 | ISSN: 3006-1768 (imprimé); 3007-1771 (en ligne)
Ceci est un article en libre accès distribué selon les termes de la licence CC BY 4.0.

Rodrick Kapwa Ilunga
**La Théologie de James H. Cone,
un Lieu de Libération pour l'Afrique**

Keywords

Liberation theology, James H. Cone, Africa, ecclesiology

Palavras-chave

Teologia da libertação, James H. Cone, África, eclesiologia

Introduction

L'histoire de l'émancipation des noirs en Amérique continue à passionner plusieurs scientifiques et historiens. Elle est l'une des révolutions de plus inspirantes de l'histoire de l'humanité. Nous sommes d'accord qu'après plusieurs siècles, le racisme est toujours déploré aux États-Unis mais il est tout à fait clair que depuis l'époque d'Anthony Benezet (1713-1784) jusqu'à l'avènement du *Black Lives Matter* ['Les Vies des Noirs Comptent'], les conditions de vie de noirs se sont considérablement améliorées.

La lutte afro-américaine n'a pas été le fruit d'une seule personne, elle est une lutte qui a vu la contribution de plusieurs couches de la société américaine. Parmi lesquelles, une figure tend à sortir du lot la lutte pour les droits des noirs dans un cadre théologique non encore utilisé jusqu'à son époque. James H. Cone, est un Afro-américain né à Fordyce en Arkansas en 1938. Il concilia la lutte noire et la théologie en Amérique. Pendant toute son enfance, il a souffert du racisme et des inégalités sociales dûs à sa couleur de peau noire. Il est l'un de premiers théologiens nord-américains à élaborer une théologie centrée sur la libération des noirs. Il publia en mars 1969 son premier essai *Black Theology and Black Power* ['La Théologie Noire et le Pouvoir Noir'] où se font sentir les influences de Martin Luther King, Malcolm X et Paul Tillich.[1] Selon Péter Gaál-Szabó la construction théologique de Cone serait fortement ancrée dans le bouleversement politique des années 1950 et 1960 et en tirerait son énergie.[2] Il est vrai qu'avant Cone il existait déjà des consciences religieuses noires en Amérique, mais sa pensée aurait tracé une ligne conjoncturelle dans le monde de l'après-seconde guerre mondiale. Il élabora une théologie noire de la libération dans un contexte historique de la souffrance des noirs et de la domination blanche aux Etats-Unis en la présentant comme une réponse corrective à la théologie blanche qui restait silencieuse sur la douleur et la souffrance des noirs.[3]

---

[1] Serge MOLLA, « James H. Cone, théologien noir américain », p. 219.
[2] Péter GAÁL-SZABÓ, « James Cone's Theology of Culture in *Black Theology of Liberation* », p. 143.
[3] Celucien L. JOSEPH, « James H. Cone : The Vocation of Christian Theology and the Christian Church Today », p. 9.

Rodrick Kapwa Ilunga
**La Théologie de James H. Cone,
un Lieu de Libération pour l'Afrique**

Selon Cone, l'insertion et la particularité historique noires ne devraient pas conduire à penser que tout processus de libération se limite au conflit racial nord-américain. Il estime qu'elle concerne aussi les relations entre nations riches et pauvres dans le tiers-monde. C'est ainsi que dans le cadre de cette étude, il sera question de revisiter la théologie de Cone tout en la liant au contexte actuel de l'Afrique. Nous partirons donc de l'interrogation suivante : Comment la théologie de Cone peut-elle constituer un lieu de discours de libération pour l'Afrique ? Pour bien assurer le cheminement de notre étude, le présent article s'articule en trois points : l'influence et la théologie de Cone, le contexte socio-politique de l'Afrique contemporaine, et enfin l'ecclésiologie dans la théologie de Cone comme voie de libération.

I. Influence et théologie de James H. Cone

I. 1. Influence

La théologie de Cone se trouve fortement enracinée dans l'expérience de sa vie en tant que noir. À Bearden, en Arkansas, où il passa son enfance, Cone gouta comme pour les noirs de son époque, aux traumatismes d'une société ségréguée et raciste qui déshumanisait les noirs, diabolisait les femmes noires en les privant de justice politique et de droits humains. Cette condition le poussa à développer très tôt une conscience de son identité en tant que personne noire. Il trouva aussi une conscience sociopolitique et un éveil théologique dans l'Église noire qu'il fréquentait avec sa famille. L'Église épiscopale méthodiste africaine macédonienne a aidé Cone à acquérir les ressources nécessaires à la lutte sociopolitique et au soulagement du peuple noir. A son époque l'Église noire était symbole de la résistance noire à l'injustice blanche et à la terreur raciale.[4]

Il trouva notamment un langage et une théologie dans la religion des esclaves noirs exprimée dans les *Negro spirituals* ['Spirituels Nègres']. Dans son ouvrage *The Spirituals and the Blues* ['Les Spirituels et le Blues'], il fait remonter l'origine de la théologie noire à l'esthétique des *spirituals* et des *blues*. Il postule l'idée selon laquelle les *Negro spirituals* sont une source de théologie noire qui décrit l'expérience collective de la population noire asservie aux Etats-Unis[5]. James Weldon Johnson et J. Rosamond Johnson rejoignent Cone que, les *Negro spirituals* « étaient un ensemble de chants exprimant toutes les vertus cardinales du christianisme — patience — tolérance — amour — foi — et espoir — à travers une forme nécessairement modifiée de musique africaine primitive. Les Noirs se réfugièrent complètement dans le christianisme, et les *spirituals*. »[6]

---

[4] Celucien L. Joseph, « Theodicy and Black Theological Anthropology in James Cone's Theological Identity », pp. 83–88.
[5] C. L. Joseph, « Theodicy and Black Theological Anthropology », p. 89.
[6] James Weldon Johnson et J. Rosamond Johnson, *The Book of American Negro Spirituals*, p. 20.

Rodrick Kapwa Ilunga
**La Théologie de James H. Cone,
un Lieu de Libération pour l'Afrique**

Cone fut aussi grandement influencé par Martin Luther King et Malcolm X. Dans son livre *Martin & Malcolm & America : A Dream or a Nightmare* ['Martin & Malcolm & l'Amérique : Rêve ou Cauchemar'], il les hisse au rang des « deux maîtres critiques du christianisme américain. »[7] Il évoque que la société contemporaine doit retenir de King et de Malcom le fait que le christianisme public inclut leur activité féroce pour contester le système américain d'inégalité et d'injustice de leurs vigoureuses campagnes contre la structure raciste du christianisme américain.[8] Pour Cone, King, et Malcolm sont des ingrédients nécessaires à la lutte Afro-Américaine. A cet effet, il objecte face à ceux qui tendent à opposer les deux figures en ces termes : « Malcolm empêche Martin de devenir un héros américain inoffensif. Martin empêche Malcolm d'être un héros noir ostracisé. »[9]

C'est à partir de ces différentes jointures que Cone développa sa théologie, et deviendra par ce fait le théologien noir-américain le plus important et le plus controversé du 20ème siècle.[10]

I. 2. La théologie de James D. Cone

Dans ses œuvres qui servent de jalons à sa théologie, Cone montre de façon surprenante combien l'évangile est indissociablement lié à l'affranchissement des pauvres de toute oppression. Pour lui le christianisme est d'abord et avant tout « une religion de libération » et le rôle de sa théologie est d'analyser le sens de la libération des opprimés et de les rendre conscients de la légitimité scripturaire de leur lutte.[11] Aussi soutient-il que la lutte pour la libération n'est pas extrabiblique. L'évangile, c'est d'abord la libération de ceux qui sont opprimés, car lorsque l'évangile ne parvient pas à faire émerger des communautés des opprimés, il cesse d'être évangile. Le souci de Cone fut de trouver à la fois une solution théologique et une réponse morale au problème du mal et de la souffrance dans la communauté noire. Il n'a pas seulement donné naissance à la théologie noire en Amérique mais il a également lutté pour libérer la théologie chrétienne de son époque de la suprématie blanche et de l'hégémonie théologique blanche.[12] La question de la libération des opprimés de la société est devenue le centre de l'existence de Cone :

> « Je suis revenu voir Philander Smith avec un enthousiasme accru. Mais qu'avaient à voir Barth, Tillich et Brunner avec les jeunes filles et garçons noirs venus des champs de coton de l'Arkansas, du Tennessee et du Mississippi cherchant à se forger un nouvel

---

[7] James H. CONE, *Martin & Malcolm & America : A Dream or Nightmare*, p. 295.
[8] C. L. JOSEPH, « James H. Cone : Vocation », p. 37.
[9] J. H. CONE, *Martin & Malcolm & America*, p. 316.
[10] C. L. JOSEPH, « Theodicy and Black Theological Anthropology », p. 83.
[11] Serge MOLLA, « James H. Cone, théologien noir américain », p. 221.
[12] C. L. JOSEPH, « Theodicy and Black Theological Anthropology », p. 86.

Rodrick Kapwa Ilunga
**La Théologie de James H. Cone,
un Lieu de Libération pour l'Afrique**

avenir ? C'était pour moi la question majeure. Et cela a été encore intensifié par la lutte pour les droits civiques. La contradiction entre la théologie entant que discipline et la lutte pour la liberté des noirs dans la rue ont été vécues au plus profond de mon être. Comment allais-je le résoudre ? »[13]

Tourmenté par la complicité de la théologie blanche, Cone s'évertua à construire une théologie de la libération des noirs et centra la pertinence de cette théologie sur deux questions majeures : comment est-il possible d'articuler l'expérience libératrice de la foi, une foi qui permet aux gens d'aimer leur noirceur, d'endurer de terribles épreuves et de résister à la douleur sans perdre la raison dans la lutte pour la liberté ? Comment construire une théologie qui permette aux gens de survivre et de lutter pour un changement libérateur ?[14] La théologie de la libération de Cone développe un christocentrisme, surtout dans sa manière d'exprimer la lutte pour la libération des noirs. Il déclare : « L'arbre à lyncher symbolisait le pouvoir blanc et la "mort noire", mais la croix symbolisait le pouvoir divin et la "vie noire" — Dieu triomphant du pouvoir du péché et de la mort créée par l'arbre du lynchage. »[15] Cone utilise le lynchage comme métaphore pour décrire le malheur des noirs en Amérique. Pour lui, chaque fois que des gens sont privés d'emplois, d'assurance-maladie, de logement, et du minimum pour exister ils sont lynchés. Les gens sont lynchés quand ils crient pour être reconnus comme des êtres humains et que la société les ignore. Pour Cone l'arbre à lyncher devient aussi le chemin par lequel les noirs s'identifient aux souffrances du Christ. La croix fut pour les esclaves enchaînés un pouvoir spirituel de résister à ce qui leur arrivait. Jésus fut alors le premier à être lynché, mais sa situation n'a pas été sans issue car après cela il a triomphé de la croix montrant que la mort et la souffrance n'avaient pas le dernier mot sur sa vie. Ainsi pour les noirs opprimés, Cone affirme que l'arbre à lyncher n'aura pas le dernier mot. Tout comme Christ, le salut leur est offert en Dieu, un salut qui triomphe de l'oppression.

Son ouvrage, *God of the Oppressed* [littéralement, 'Le Dieu des Opprimés'], traduit en français sous le titre *La noirceur de Dieu*, exprime la liberté comme n'étant pas au pouvoir des hommes. La liberté s'identifie à un don divin accordé à ceux qui luttent dans la foi contre la violence et l'oppression.[16] La libération sans engagement révolutionnaire contre l'injustice, l'esclavage et l'oppression n'est pas possible car la liberté n'est pas simplement l'idée que nous avons mais

---

[13] James H. Cone, *My Soul Looks Back*, pp. 38–39.
[14] Leslie R. James, « James Cone's Theology of Culture in *Black Theology of Liberation* », p. 91.
[15] James H. Cone, « 'Personne ne sait le malheur que j'ai vu' : La croix et l'arbre à lyncher dans l'expérience afro-américaine », p. 311.
[16] James H. Cone, *La noirceur de Dieu*, pp. 167–168.

aussi et surtout un mouvement socio-historique d'un peuple en marche contre l'oppression. Cone insiste donc sur le caractère visible du salut. Chaque fois que Jésus guérissait les malades, nourrissait les affamés et rendait la vue aux aveugles, il démontrait ainsi que le salut n'était pas quelque chose d'abstrait, ni une idée spirituelle ou un sentiment du cœur. Le salut pour Jésus fut la restauration de l'intégrité physique au sein même de l'affliction et de la souffrance. Dans cette logique, nous pouvons déduire que la liberté dont le christianisme prône n'est pas seulement liée à l'esclavage du péché, à Satan, à la domination, à la convoitise des passions ou encore aux désirs immodérés. La liberté chrétienne est également celle qui considère l'esclavage et l'oppression comme contraire à la volonté divine (Luc 4. 18–19).[17]

> « Dieu nous rencontre dans la situation humaine, non pas comme une idée ou un concept dont la véracité est évidente. Dieu nous rencontre dans la condition humaine en tant que libérateur des pauvres et des faibles, leur donnant les moyens de lutter pour la liberté parce qu'ils sont faits pour cela. »[18]

Pour Cone, le message de Christ n'est pas une abstraction ni une simple théorisation théologique. Le message dont Christ fut porteur est celui de la libération et l'évangile prouve que ce dernier a apporté la victoire ultime, un espoir concret et une émancipation pratique pour ceux qui souffraient et qui étaient soumis à la victimisation et à la subjectivité humaine.

Il en ressort donc que la théologie de la libération de Cone s'exprime en faveur des opprimés. Le christianisme ne doit pas oublier la dimension présente de l'homme. La théologie chrétienne doit donner une réponse à ces jeunes vivants dans l'incertitude, sans emploi et sans projet d'avenir. Elle doit donner une réponse à ces enfants qui restent orphelins à cause d'une guerre injuste. Elle doit être un lieu de consolation et d'espoir pour la société actuelle. Elle doit être un moyen de lutter, tel que Jésus qui a fait sien le combat de prophètes contre les fausses répartitions des biens et contre l'inégalité des droits dans la société de leur temps. Elle doit lutter pour une société équitable. C'est aux chrétiens que revient le devoir de fonder une solidarité nouvelle pour sortir de la misère, et de refuser des structures d'exploitation et d'oppression des pauvres. C'est dans cette visée que s'articule la théologie de la libération de Cone.

II. Le contexte socio-politique de l'Afrique contemporain

Rappelons que Cone décrit les souffrances des noirs en Amérique par la métaphore de « l'arbre à lyncher ». Cette métaphore semble décrier la situation présente de l'Afrique. La pratique du lynchage fut instaurée par Charles Lynch et elle consistait à rendre justice sans procès. Les coupables étaient exécutés

---

[17] J. H. CONE, *La noirceur de Dieu*, pp. 182–183.
[18] James H. CONE, *A Black Theology of Liberation*, p. 19.

Rodrick Kapwa Ilunga
**La Théologie de James H. Cone,
un Lieu de Libération pour l'Afrique**

généralement par pendaison. Le lynchage en Amérique devint après la guerre de sécession une arme de répression contre les Afro-Américains. Beaucoup des groupes antinoirs comme le *Ku Klux Klan* ont utilisé cette pratique pour jeter la peur de l'émancipation chez les gens des couleurs.

Comme pour les Afro-Américains pendus sur l'arbre à lyncher, l'Afrique devient chaque jour qui passe une terre de désolation avec des multiples questionnements. Comme Kä Mana l'évoque, l'Afrique distingue deux formes des paradoxes : « un paradoxe central qui traverse de part en part notre existence et des paradoxes plus spécifiques liés à des domaines précis de la vie de notre continent. »[19] Le misérabilisme africain est devenu une réalité collective et une vérité de la vie quotidienne. Malgré des décennies depuis la vague des « indépendances », l'Afrique peine toujours à se lever. Le continent se trouve toujours dans un grand dilemme. Dans les lignes qui suivent nous donnerons un aperçu du contexte de l'Afrique contemporaine.

II. 1. Le continent africain ou « l'indépendance du drapeau »[20]

Si l'Afrique est la mère du monde, si sa civilisation a été la première et l'origine de la civilisation moderne, et si les noirs ont été les premiers en tout, pourquoi sont-ils aujourd'hui les derniers qui souffre le plus, étant mal développé et démunis?, s'interroge Tshilenga Kabala.[21]

Il est vrai que depuis le début des années 1950 et la fin des années 1960, plusieurs pays africains ont accédé à leur indépendance. Pour beaucoup, l'indépendance fut l'aboutissement des luttes sanglantes et populaires. Pour les noirs, l'indépendance fut synonyme d'un nouveau départ où les oppressés d'autrefois seraient devenus maîtres de leur propre destin. L'Africain voyait enfin le bout du tunnel, après plusieurs décennies de colonisation ou d'esclavage. Les Africains ce sont mis de nouveau à rêver et à s'imaginer un lendemain prometteur. Malheureusement l'extase n'a pas été de longue durée. Durant les années qui suivirent la vague des indépendances, plusieurs pays se retrouvèrent dans le chaos. Pour d'autres, ce fut une série des coups d'État et des soulèvements populaires. Pour d'autres encore, ce fut une difficulté à se trouver une nouvelle identité entant qu'État. Cette réalité poussa Masanja à observer que « les mouvements de libération nationale des années cinquante étaient anticoloniaux et anti-impérialistes ; le principal slogan, c'était l'indépendance, mais on n'avait aucune idée claire ni de formulation du genre de société qui

---

[19] KÄ Mana, *L'Afrique va-t-elle mourir ? Bousculer l'imaginaire africain. Essai d'éthique politique*, pp. 31–32.
[20] Terme employé par Patrick MASANJA, « Néo colonisation et révolution en Afrique », pp. 12–23.
[21] Emmanuel TSHILANDA KABALA, « A collective sin in Africa : A missiological approach to the African crisis », p. 147.

émergerait après l'indépendance politique ».[22]

Les calamités postcoloniales ont ouvert les yeux à l'Afrique qui n'a pas cessé de s'interroger sur son sort. Fort malheureusement le constat est qu'en réalité, l'indépendance africaine ne fut qu'un leurre. L'impérialisme avait abandonné la formule démodée de l'occupation coloniale. Les métropoles ont eu recours au système néocolonial dans lequel les pays s'affirmaient comme indépendants avec tous les signes extérieurs (hymne national, drapeau, constitution, etc.), tandis qu'économiquement et politiquement ces pays sont restés liés aux pays impérialistes et asservis par eux. Ce fut l'indépendance du drapeau.[23] « L'histoire secrète des pseudo-indépendances et des coups d'Etat qui ont liquidé les pères de ces pseudo-indépendances nous révèle que civils et militaires à la haute magistrature des pays africains étaient tous des parrainés, des instruments entre les mains des puissances coloniales ».[24] Achille Mbembe souligne que l'acceptation de la décolonisation par les métropoles fut une affaire internationale. Les principales métropoles n'acquiescèrent à la question de l'indépendance que du bout des lèvres. Beaucoup opposèrent un refus parfois militant à la décolonisation de l'Afrique et des pays du tiers-monde.[25] Il souligne les causes principales qui ont fait de l'indépendance des pays africains un mirage :

> « Il y a deux raisons à cela : d'une part, les conditions historiques dans lesquelles se sont effectués la décolonisation et le régime des capitations qu'ont cimentées les accords inégaux "de coopération et de défense" signés dans les années 1960 ; d'autre part, l'infirmité révolutionnaire, l'impotence et l'inorganisation des forces sociales internes. Les accords secrets- dont certaines clauses touchaient au droit de propriété sur le sol, le sous-sol et l'espace aérien des anciennes colonies — n'avaient pas pour objectif de liquider le rapport colonial, mais de le contractualiser et de le sous-traiter à des fondés de pouvoir indigènes ».[26]

Les anciennes colonies ont hérité d'une économie liée aux puissances coloniales et aidée par elles en matière d'administration et de travaux publics. Ces structures avaient déjà avant l'indépendance des germes du mal développement, et les colonisateurs ont abandonné les colonies avant que ces problèmes ne se manifestent. La situation catastrophique actuelle était déjà ensemencée mais peu s'en sont rendu compte, ni les Africains, remplis de la joie de l'indépendance, ni

---

[22] P. MASANJA, « Néo colonisation et révolution », p. 17.
[23] P. MASANJA, « Néo colonisation et révolution », p. 13.
[24] Félix MUTOMBO-KUKENDI, *La théologie politique en Afrique : Exégèse et histoire*, p. 155.
[25] Achille MBEMBE, *Sortir de la grande nuit : Essai sur l'Afrique décolonisée*, p. 25–26.
[26] A. MBEMBE, *Sortir de la grande nuit*, p. 26.

les puissances coloniales dans leur fuite.[27]

Le néocolonialisme prend des formes variées suivant les États et cette différence se justifie dans la diversité économique et sociale des pays africains. Mais toutes ces formes conservent néanmoins un modèle fondamentalement uniforme : la domination et l'oppression demeurent le dominateur commun des forces impériales. La colonisation a été et est pour l'Afrique une option qui a privé et qui continue de priver le continent noir de son autonomie.[28] Le néocolonialisme se définit comme un esclavage moderne, tout comme les Afro-Américains dans les plantations des colons, les Africains vivent dans une politique d'exploitation. Le néocolonialisme en Afrique demeure la source principale de la pauvreté et de malheur pour la population. Certains dirigeants africains à la solde de cette idéologie continuent à renforcer l'oppression et la domination contre tous ceux qui osent contester. Dans d'autres pays les puissances impériales maintiennent et alimentent des guerres interethniques et le terrorisme dans le but de garder une main mise sur les ressources de ces pays. L'un des exemples typiques est la R.D. Congo et le Soudan. Ces pays sont en proie à des guerres et des troubles depuis plusieurs décennies, et les conséquences sont dévastatrices tant sur le plan politique qu'humanitaire. Beaucoup des gens sont privés des soins appropriés, des jeunes et des enfants dans des zones des conflits n'ont pas accès aux écoles ou aux universités, sans parler des femmes et des filles violées ainsi que du nombre pharamineux de décès.

II. 2. *L'Afrique, un géant qui ne veut pas naître ?*

En dehors du néocolonialisme se trouve aussi un autre facteur qui maintient l'Afrique dans le sous-développement. Dans son ouvrage, *Et si l'Afrique refusait le développement*, Axelle Kabou avance une autre raison du sous-développement de l'Afrique. Elle affirme que « l'Afrique ne se meurt pas : elle se suicide dans une sorte d'ivresse culturelle pourvoyeuse de seules gratifications morales. »[29] La colonisation et l'impérialisme étaient connus en Afrique, en Asie et en Amérique, mais comment pouvons-nous justifier que beaucoup de pays de l'Asie et de l'Amérique ont pu émerger contrairement à nombreux pays africains. Comment justifier cette dichotomie ?

Les résultats des recherches sur les causes du sous-développement en Afrique ne pointent pas du doigt seulement les forces extérieures mais aussi des forces internes. Le constat est que la majorité des pays africains « sont mal partis ». Les gouvernements africains ne doivent pas seulement évoquer des faits extérieurs (domination, dépendance, fluctuation des cours des produits de base

---

[27] E. Tshilanda Kabala, « A collective sin in Africa », p. 157.
[28] Boubacar Barry, « Regards croisés sur la crise africaine », p. 118.
[29] Axelle Kabou, *Et si l'Afrique refusait le développement ?*, p. 27.

sur les marchés mondiaux, la crise de l'énergie etc.) car ceux-ci ne servent que d'échappatoire. La lutte pour la liberté de l'Afrique n'est pas seulement contre les multinationales étrangères, mais aussi contre leurs alliés africains qui constituent les classes dominantes locales. Il y a donc lieu d'emprunter les mots de Patrick Mansaja : « La lutte exige l'affaiblissement des puissances impérialistes qui exploitent et dominent le Tiers Monde, mais la lutte doit aussi affaiblir ces forces du Tiers Monde qui favorisent ce système d'exploitation internationale. »[30] Les métropoles ont bâti et laissé sur le continent africain une classe privilégiée. C'est pourquoi la majorité de classes dirigeantes après l'indépendance ne fut pas issue des sociétés africaines traditionnelle. Elles furent plutôt le produit de l'école coloniale. Cette élite n'a aucun intérêt au développement d'une classe forte d'entrepreneurs urbains ou ruraux.[31]

Dans beaucoup d'États africains où la misère se vit, on peut remarquer un fait similaire : l'enrichissement d'une certaine classe d'individus qui détiennent le pouvoir politique, des grands capitaux ainsi que le monopole de plusieurs marchés. Quand on étudie de près ces classes, on déniche qu'elles ne sont qu'un allongement du pouvoir impérial. Beaucoup d'Africains sont prêts à lyncher leurs frères africains au profit du pouvoir et des richesses. C'est l'une de cause interne du sous-développement en Afrique. Certains fils et filles du continent servent de ponts aux impérialistes qui continuent à opprimer et ruiner la population africaine.

Dans une autre mesure, le problème interne africain se situe au niveau de la mentalité. Les africains sont largement convaincus que leur destin doit être pris en charge par des étrangers. « Dès lors, les aider à se développer, c'est d'abord les encourager à créer les conditions psychologiques de réceptivité au changement ; c'est favoriser l'émergence d'un vaste débat résolument décomplexé sur leur volonté de développement. »[32] L'idéologie du messianisme utopique pousse beaucoup des jeunes africains à déserter leur continent, contre vent et péril, pour rejoindre l'occident. Lutter contre le sous-développement en Afrique, c'est briser le mur psychologique et bâtir une idéologie d'auto-prise en charge.

Aujourd'hui plus que jamais, c'est au niveau de l'homme africain lui-même qu'il faut maintenant s'interroger. Le comportement des dirigeants africains ne permet plus de rendre la colonisation responsable du manque de développement en Afrique. Au-delà des cataclysmes naturels, des crises géologiques, écologiques ou climatiques, il est un domaine où les dirigeants africains d'aujourd'hui auraient dû prendre en main le destin de l'Afrique. Bien

---

[30] P. Masanja, « Néo colonisation et révolution », p. 23.
[31] René Dumont cité par E. Tshilanda Kabala, « A collective sin in Africa », p. 153.
[32] A. Kabou, *Et si l'Afrique refusait*, p. 27.

que la ressource humaine soit l'élément clé du développement, mais fort malheureusement, c'est cet aspect qui semble être le moins pris en compte en Afrique.[33]

Il est impérieux de considérer le nombre d'années que les Etats africains ont cumulées après leurs indépendances. Les africains ont eu près de la moitié d'un siècle pour panser leur plaie et redonner vie au continent. Mais comme insiste Diakite, une blessure qui ne s'améliore pas en l'espace d'un quart de siècle est une blessure mal soignée, ou pas soignée du tout, et par conséquent qui peut être fatale. Il est temps que l'Afrique se mire, et qu'elle arrête de condamner les autres pour ses propres erreurs.[34]

La lutte pour le développement et l'affranchissement de l'Afrique doit partir donc de deux pôles (une autodétermination contre le néocolonialisme et un éveille de la conscience des Africains). L'Afrique doit impérativement mettre ses batteries en marche pour quitter sa zone de confort afin d'accéder à la vraie liberté. Dans cette lutte nous devons comprendre que les puissances impérialistes n'ont pas seulement fait usage de force physique ; ils ont beaucoup plus utilisé des instruments idéologiques sous diverses formes : supériorité raciale, libéralisme, marginalisation. La résistance pour l'indépendance et l'autonomie africaine doit partir de la sphère idéologique.[35]

Puisque l'Église est une institution culturelle et idéologique, elle a l'obligation de montrer le chemin vers la vraie liberté. L'Église africaine a aujourd'hui le choix entre faire partir des forces d'oppression et d'aliénation, d'une part, et faire partir des forces de transformation sociale, d'autre part.[36] Si la réponse en toute nature est celle de la lutte pour la transformation, un préalable s'impose, celle de conformer le devenir de l'Église africaine aux réels besoins d'affranchissement. Là se situe le point de jointure de la théologie de Cone et le combat pour la libération en Afrique. Cone considère l'Église comme le lieu de résistance contre l'oppression. C'est l'un des points centraux de sa théologie.

III. L'ecclésiologie dans la théologie de Cone comme voie de libération

L'ecclésiologie occupe une place privilégiée dans la théologie de Cone. Elle constitue le socle de l'herméneutique théologique et de la lecture des actions libératrices de Dieu parmi son peuple. Pour Cone, l'Église est plus qu'un lieu de rencontres hebdomadaires pour les offices religieux. Il envisage l'Église comme un amplificateur des cris des opprimés. Bien avant d'entrer dans le fond de la

---

[33] Tidiane DIAKITE cité par E. TSHILANDA KABALA, « A collective sin in Africa », p. 173.
[34] Tidiane DIAKITE cité par E. TSHILANDA KABALA, « A collective sin in Africa », p. 173.
[35] P. MASANJA, « Néo colonisation et révolution », p. 23.
[36] P. MASANJA, « Néo colonisation et révolution », p. 23-24.

considération ecclésiologique de Cone, voyons d'abord ce à quoi ressemble l'ecclésiologie africaine aujourd'hui.

Le champ religieux en Afrique constitue un horizon inéliminable. Il est donc incontournable dans l'analyse et la compréhension des sociétés actuelles[37]. La croyance ou le spiritisme occupe une place importante dans l'anthropologie africaine. Ce phénomène a permis une croissance rapide du christianisme en Afrique.

> « Selon le centre d'études du christianisme mondial à la faculté de théologie de *Gordon-Conwell* en 2018, l'Afrique a dépassé l'Amérique du Sud [et serait devenue le continent avec un plus grand nombre de chrétiens,] soit 631 millions. Elle représenterait 26 % de tous les chrétiens du monde. ... Selon le *Pew Research Center*, le nombre de chrétiens européens est en déclin, et d'ici 2060 l'Allemagne disparaîtrait, avec la Chine et la Russie, de la liste des 10 pays comptant le plus de chrétiens. La Tanzanie, l'Ouganda et le Kenya les remplaceraient. Puisque la RDC, le Nigeria et l'Éthiopie se retrouvent déjà au sein du classement ... »

Donc sur dix pays au monde avec plus des chrétiens, l'Afrique en comptera six.[38]

Malgré cette forte présence du christianisme en Afrique, l'Église en Afrique serait passive dans son rôle primordial. Les rites, les dévotions, les actes de piété, les prières, les processions seraient encore insuffisants, selon la grande partie de l'ecclésiologie africaine, pour instruire une intelligence et une pratique de la foi affrontée aux défis de l'Afrique contemporaine[39]. Elle est devenue, comme l'évoque Félix Mutombo-Mukendi, un centre de distribution des miracles, de prospérité à sens unique et surtout une dangereuse agence de voyage vers le ciel de toutes les utopies terrestres.[40] Cet entendement de la foi chrétienne plonge la foi africaine dans une complicité avec le pouvoir oppressif. En absence du mieux, on peut nommer cette attitude, une « ecclésiologie négative ». Les chrétiens africains doivent savoir que l'apolitisme de l'Église est impossible car là où il est brandi par les pasteurs et les leaders, il est l'expression d'alignement politique, il est facteur du totalitarisme, il est la politique du pire ![41]

La réflexion théologique doit être toujours liée à un contexte de vie des théologiens. Tout en parlant de Dieu, l'Église parle aussi aux êtres humains[42]. Dès lors que notre foi d'Église ignore la situation présente de ses fidèles, la foi

---

[37] Achille MBEMBE, *Afrique indociles : Christianisme, pouvoir et Etat en société postcoloniale*, p. 18.
[38] « L'Afrique s'impose au sein de l'Église catholique. »
[39] A. MBEMBE, *Afrique indociles*, p. 17.
[40] F. MUTOMBO-KUKENDI, *La théologie politique en Afrique*, p. 116.
[41] F. MUTOMBO-KUKENDI, *La théologie politique en Afrique*, p. 115.
[42] S. MOLLA, « James H. Cone, théologien noir américain », p. 257.

réelle restera difficile à enraciner. Cone souligne que « pendant longtemps, et souvent inconsciemment, la théologie s'est faite la complice d'attitudes et de structures oppressives, racistes, sexistes, conduisant à des prises de pouvoir économique, politique, et même religieux. » Engelbert Mveng voit cela dans le même angle : « On entend souvent répéter de nos jours, dans les milieux d'hommes d'Église, des slogans qui disent : "L'Église n'as pas été envoyée pour fonder des écoles et des hôpitaux, tracer des routes, construire des ponts et nourrir les foules. L'Église a été envoyée pour prêcher l'Evangile !' »[43]

L'Église africaine ne doit pas continuer à se retirer sur la montagne pour prier, abandonnant la foule en détresse, dans les villages disséminés par les guerres, les terrorismes et les injustices sociales. Elle ne doit pas abandonner les paysans qui sont chassés de leurs terres sous prétexte d'une modernisation qui ne profite qu'aux classes les plus élevées. Au contraire l'Église africaine doit s'affirmer au sein de la population car, se retirer équivaut à nier sa vocation à participer à la libération divine. L'Église ne doit pas abandonner les pauvres, elle ne doit pas renier sa mère l'Afrique au motif qu'elle est pauvre. Elle ne doit pas abandonner ses malades aux commerçants de la santé ; elle ne doit pas livrer la jeunesse à la fumée des idéologies, elle ne doit pas fermer ses écoles parce qu'il n'y a plus d'argent ; elle ne doit pas chasser de la maison de Dieu les pauvres qui l'implorent.[44] L'Église africaine doit braver la peur et dénoncer le néocolonialisme ainsi que l'aliénation idéologique, elle doit être un lieu de refuge. L'Église comme une ville refuge (Deut 4. 41–43), doit manifester l'évidence de la nature gracieuse et indulgente de Dieu, même face à l'imperfection et à l'échec africaine.

Dans sa grammaire, Cone fournit une base solide de l'ecclésiologie de la libération. Pour lui, le but de l'Église est de créer une nouvelle communauté de liberté et de nouvel humanisme dans laquelle les pauvres pourraient expérimenter leur plein potentiel. Elle est le témoin fidèle de la bonté de Dieu et du mouvement émancipateur dans la société. A cet effet, une Église fidèle est celle qui opère une rupture avec la société en lançant une attaque véhémente contre les maux.[45] L'Église est un lieu de refuge pour les pauvres, contre les riches et les puissants. L'objectif de l'Église, comme postule Tshilenda, s'identifie dans une double vision : celle de transformer et de reformer. Par transformation, on entend le changement de culture et de situation sociale. La reforme quant à elle implique le changement de structure et de système.[46]

« L'ecclésiologie négative » a longtemps été complice de l'aliénation

---

[43] Engelbert MVENG, *L'Afrique dans l'Église : Paroles d'un croyant*, p. 212.
[44] E. MVENG, *L'Afrique dans l'Église*, p. 213.
[45] C. L. JOSEPH, « James H. Cone : Vocation », p. 41.
[46] E. TSHILANDA KABALA, « A collective sin in Africa », p. 224.

idéologique africaine. La vraie foi est celle qui met tous les hommes créés à l'image de Dieu sur un même niveau de considération sociale. Comme le disait Anthony Burns, cité par Cone, au sujet des esclaves noirs, « Dieu a fait de moi un homme, non un esclave, et m'a donné le même droit d'être homme qu'à celui qui m'a volé ce droit. »[47] Aujourd'hui plus que jamais l'Église d'Afrique doit briser son silence, elle ne doit pas continuer à se prosterner devant le veau d'or, ni devant l'encensoir des grands prêtres, ou des pharisiens, ni devant l'intimidation des suppôts de César, ni devant les mirages trompeurs des pompes anachroniques. Le temps est venu pour l'Église africaine de rendre à l'homme africain sa dignité, son identité, sa liberté, et sa présence dans le monde.[48]

Ainsi l'Église africaine doit épouser l'actualité du continent pour bâtir son expression. Ela rejoint Cone sur ce point : « En d'autres termes il faut faire une théologie à "ras de terre". C'est à partir des problèmes africains qu'il faut prêcher le salut en Jésus-Christ ».[49] Notre théologie ne pourrait pas être celle de Karl Rahner, ni celle de Yves Congar, ni celle de Hans Küng, mais elle devrait commencer à penser notre réalité quotidienne.[50] La vocation de l'Église en Afrique postcoloniale, devrait inclure une campagne vigoureuse en faveur d'une meilleure théologie de la justice sociale, de formes équitables de justice économique et de la réduction de la pauvreté et de la faim sur le continent.[51] Comme l'évoque Jose Camblin, la vérité de la théologie réside dans son combat, et le but de ce combat est la libération de l'intelligence humaine. C'est là la mission de la théologie. Si la théologie ne libère pas les gens, elle a perdu sa raison d'être. Une des caractéristiques de la théologie moderne est son sens du combat.[52]

La réflexion théologique de Cone dégage l'idée d'une « ecclésiologie positive ». La structure théologique de Cone, s'enracine dans le vécu de la foi quotidienne en tant que telle. Elle n'est pas politique, ni de tendance socialiste, mais elle se centre sur la révélation de Dieu en Christ. Les souffrances de Jésus à la croix n'ont pas été seulement ses souffrances mais étant Dieu et homme à la fois ses souffrances ont aussi été les souffrances de Dieu. Ainsi comme Dieu qui souffrit en Christ pour nous délivrer du péché, nous croyons que nos

---

[47] E. Tshilanda Kabala, « A collective sin in Africa », p. 168.
[48] E. Mveng, *L'Afrique dans l'Église*, p. 212.
[49] Gabriel Tchonang, « Brève histoire de la théologie africaine », p. 181; citant Jean-Marc Éla, *Le cri de l'homme africain* (Paris : Éditions L'Harmattan, 1980);   J-M. Éla, *Ma foi d'Africain* (Paris : Éditions Karthala, 1985); et J-M. Éla, *Repenser la théologie africaine : Le Dieu qui libère* (Paris : Éditions Karthala, 2003).
[50] S. Molla, « James H. Cone, théologien noir américain », p. 235.
[51] C. L. Joseph, « James H. Cone : Vocation », p. 44.
[52] José Camblin cité par E. Tshilanda Kabala, « A collective sin in Africa », p. 236.

souffrances actuelles étant qu'Africains sont aussi les souffrances de Dieu. Et l'Église qui est le reflet de l'amour de Dieu dans le monde se doit de lutter contre toute structure oppressive en Afrique. L'Église en Afrique doit se lever contre l'impunité, elle doit s'ériger contre le système impérial, elle doit dire non au semblant hypocrite des puissances d'oppression, elle doit tirer la sonnette d'alarme pour éveiller la conscience collective.

Conclusion

« L'ecclésiologie positive » qui se dégage de la théologie de Cone et vers laquelle doit migrer l'Église africaine est celle qui a pour projet de libérer l'homme africain. Le libérer du néocolonialisme et de la mentalité qui obstrue l'épanouissement. L'Église doit prendre au sérieux sa mission prophétique ; celle d'annoncer le salut aux âmes perdues et celle de dénoncer le mal. Car une Église prophétique est une Église en action émancipatrice et une communauté chrétienne revitalisante dans laquelle ses membres assument leurs rôles de leadership dans la transformation de la culture d'oppression et de désespoir en une culture d'optimisme qui contribue largement à l'émancipation des pauvres. Les Églises contemporaines en Afrique doivent comprendre que tout dans la société a une dimension politique et qu'il existe une dimension politique de la foi qui devrait contraindre les disciples du Christ à ne pas rester indifférents à la souffrance des pauvres et déshérités.[53]

La libération que prône la théologie de Cone se fonde sur l'acte de Dieu en Jésus-Christ qui est la conséquence logique de toute théologie chrétienne enracinée dans l'Écriture. Il n'y a donc pas de libération sans le Christ, Jésus-Christ est la source de la libération du genre humain. Il faut donc bannir une foi qui sépare le salut de la libération ou la liberté humaine indépendamment de la liberté divine.[54]

Bibliographie

« L'Afrique s'impose au sein de l'Église catholique ». Perspective Monde. 11 avril 2023.
https://perspective.usherbrooke.ca/bilan/servlet/BMAnalyse/3398

BARRY, Boubacar. « Regards croisés sur la crise africaine ». *Afrique et Développement* 19, n° 3 (1994) : 117–134.
https://www.journals.codesria.org/index.php/ad/article/view/2586

CONE, James H. *A Black Theology of Liberation*. Twentieth Anniversary Edition. Maryknoll, New York, États-Unis : Orbis Books, 1997.

---

[53] C. L. JOSEPH, « James H. Cone : Vocation », p. 45.
[54] J. H. CONE, *La noirceur de Dieu*, pp. 168–170.

Cone, James H. *Martin & Malcolm & America : A Dream or Nightmare.* Maryknoll, New York, États-Unis : Orbis Books, 1998.

———. *My Soul looks Back.* Maryknoll, New York, États-Unis : Orbis Books, 1986.

———. *La noirceur de Dieu.* Labor Et Fides. Genève : Evergreen, 1989.

———. « 'Personne ne sait le malheur que j'ai vu' : La croix et l'arbre à lyncher dans l'expérience afro-américaine ». *Études théologiques et religieuses* 86, n° 3 (2011) : 307–315. https://www.revue-etr.org/article/personne-ne-sait-le-malheur-que-jai-vu-la-croix-et-larbre-a-lyncher-dans-lexperience-afro-americaine/

Gaál-Szabó, Péter. « James Cone's Theology of Culture in *Black Theology of Liberation* ». *British and American Studies* 24 (2018) : 143-151.

James, Leslie R. « Cone and Cannon : Black Theology and Vision of Society ». *Journal of Black Religious Thought* 1, n° 1 (2022) : 88–100. https://doi.org/10.1163/27727963-01010005

Johnson, James Weldon, et J. Rosamond Johnson. *The Book of American Negro Spirituals.* New York : Viking Press, 1926.

Joseph, Celucien L. « James H. Cone : The Vocation of Christian Theology and the Christian Church Today ». *Africology : The Journal of Pan African Studies* 12, n° 7 (Décembre 2018) : 8–58. https://www.jpanafrican.org/docs/vol12no7/12.7-2-CLJoseph%20(1).pdf

———. « Theodicy and Black Theological Anthropology in James Cone's Theological Identity ». *Toronto Journal of Theology* 35, n° 1 (Spring 2019) : 83–111. https://doi.org/10.3138/tjt.2018-0133

Kä Mana. *L'Afrique va-t-elle mourir ? Bousculer l'imaginaire africain : Essai d'éthique politique.* Paris : Éditions du Cerf, 1991.

Kabou, Axelle. *Et si l'Afrique refusait le développement ?* Paris : Éditions L'Harmattan, 1991.

Masanja, Patrick. « Néo colonisation et révolution en Afrique », dans *Théologies du tiers monde : Du conformisme à l'indépendance : Le Colloque de Dar-es-Salaam et ses prolongements* (Colloque de Dar-es-Salaaam, août 1976), édité par Carols-H. Abesamis, 12–23. Traduit d'anglais et de l'espagnol par Pierre Buis et René Tabard. Christianisme au présent. Paris : Éditions L'Harmattan, 1977.

Mbembe, Achille. *Afrique indociles : Christianisme, pouvoir et État en société postcoloniale.* Paris : Éditions Karthala, 1988.

Mbembe, Achille. *Sortir de la grande nuit : Essai sur l'Afrique décolonisée.* Paris : Éditions La Découverte, 2010.

Molla, Serge. « James H. Cone, théologien noir américain ». *Revue de théologie et de philosophie*, troisième série, vol. 116, n° 3 (1984) : 217–239. https://www.jstor.org/stable/44355540

Mutombo-Kukendi, Félix. *La théologie politique en Afrique : Exégèse et histoire.* Paris : Éditions L'Harmattan, 2011.

Mveng, Engelbert. *L'Afrique dans l'Église : Paroles d'un croyant.* Paris : Éditions L'Harmattan, 1986.

Tchonang, Gabriel. « Brève histoire de la théologie africaine ». *Revue des sciences religieuses* 84, n° 2 (2010) : 175–190. https://doi.org/10.4000/rsr.344

Tshilanda Kabala, Emmanuel. « A collective sin in Africa : A missiological approach to the African crisis ». Thèse de doctorat. Pretoria, Afrique du Sud : University of Pretoria, 1999. http://hdl.handle.net/2263/62487

Completing the Circle
Treks, Trends, and Trajectories of Circle Theology

Esther MOMBO
ORCID: 0000-0002-7186-547X
Faculty of Theology, St Paul's University, Limuru, Kenya
emombo@spu.ac.ke

Jackline MAKENA
ORCID: 0009-0004-5202-6138
Faculty of Theology, St Paul's University, Limuru, Kenya
jacklinemakenamutuma7@gmail.com

Abstract

The Circle of Concerned African Women Theologians is celebrating thirty-five years of communal theology through research and writing and through intentional mentorship to increase the number of women in the pulpits and in academia. This is a milestone in the study of theology from the perspectives of women. This article ecords milestones of the Circle in achieving its mandate using a narrative methodology, reviewing the themes of Circle theology from what has been published. These themes are rooted in the lived realities of the women in living their faith. Like an expanding circle, the theology continues to expand as theology is not what we receive but what we struggle with.

Résumé

Le Cercle des Théologiennes Africaines Concernées célèbre trente-cinq ans de théologie communautaire par la recherche et l'écriture et par un mentorat intentionnel visant à augmenter le nombre de femmes dans les chaires et dans les universités. Il s'agit d'une étape importante dans l'étude de la théologie du point de vue des femmes. Cet article retrace les étapes franchies par le Cercle dans l'accomplissement de son mandat en utilisant une méthodologie narrative, en passant en revue les thèmes de la théologie du Cercle à partir de ce qui a été publié. Ces thèmes sont enracinés dans les réalités vécues par les femmes dans l'exercice de leur foi. Comme un cercle en expansion, la théologie continue de s'étendre car la théologie n'est pas ce que nous recevons mais ce avec quoi nous luttons.

Published with license by ACTEA | DOI: https://doi.org/10.69683/zqnhg303
© Esther Mombo & Jackline Makena, 2024 | ISSN: 3006-1768 (print); 3007-1771 (online)
This is an open access article distributed under the terms of the CC BY 4.0 license.

Esther Mombo & Jackline Makena
Completing the Circle
Treks, Trends, and Trajectories of Circle Theology

Resumo

O Círculo de Mulheres Africanas Teólogas Preocupadas está a celebrar trinta e cinco anos de teologia comunitária através da investigação e da escrita e através da orientação intencional para aumentar o número de mulheres nos púlpitos e no meio académico. Este é um marco no estudo da teologia a partir da perspetiva das mulheres. Este artigo regista os marcos do Círculo no cumprimento do seu mandato, utilizando uma metodologia narrativa, revendo os temas da teologia do Círculo a partir do que foi publicado. Estes temas estão enraizados nas realidades vividas pelas mulheres na vivência da sua fé. Como um círculo em expansão, a teologia continua a expandir-se, uma vez que a teologia não é o que recebemos mas aquilo com que lutamos.

Keywords

Circle theology, African women, African theology

Mots-clés

Théologie du Cercle, femmes africaines, théologie africaine

Palavras-chave

Teologia do Círculo, mulheres africanas, teologia africana

Mercy Oduyoye is calling to the Circle
After Many Publications
Many Celebrations
San wo ekyir, Sankofa [1]

More women at the pulpit
More women academics
Changing of legislations
Mainstreaming of gender [2]

The imagery of our title, *Completing the Circle*, is deliberately multivalent: it conveys that the circle continually expands to include everyone, symbolising the ongoing struggle for everyone to live a dignified life and the collective process of completion through solidarity and mutual support. From 1 to 5 July

---

[1] 'San we ekyir' is a Fante phrase; 'sankofa' is the anglicization of a Twi phrase; the phrases are synonymous (see the following paragraph below for a definition). Fante and Twi are both dialects of Akan. Some 80% of Ghanaians speak an Akan language as a first or second language.

[2] First two verses of the Circle's theme song.

Esther Mombo & Jackline Makena
Completing the Circle
Treks, Trends, and Trajectories of Circle Theology

2024, the Circle of Concerned African Women Theologians (henceforth Circle) undertook its first pilgrimage to its place of birth, Trinity Theological Seminary in Legon Ghana, for a Pan-African and African Diaspora conference on the theme of Mother Earth, Pandemics, Gender, and Religions / Culture / Ethics / Philosophy / African Literature to celebrate thirty-five years of writing theology since its inception in 1989. The word *Sankofa* comes from the Akan people of Ghana. It derives from an imperative Akan phrase, *san kɔfa!*, meaning "go back and get it!" One of the Adinkra symbols for Sankofa depicts a mythical bird flying forward with its head turned backward.[3] It therefore signifies revisiting one's roots in order to move forward.

Gold weight in form of Sankofa bird

In this article, we are reviewing the treks, trends, and trajectories of African women's theology, or Circle theology, in order to revisit the roots of the Circle story. We are also highlighting the contributions of African women theologians to the study of Theology in Africa in general. While the story of Circle theology begins officially in 1989 at a Conference in Ghana under the leadership of Mercy Amba Oduyoye, the roots of African Women's Theology go back to pre-colonial and colonial Africa. In pre-colonial Africa, Dona Beatriz Kimpa Vita (1684–1706) of the Christian kingdom of Kongo appropriated Christian doctrines within African sociocultural, religious and political contexts. She challenged the Portuguese colonial project of cultural imperialism, racism, and slavery.[4] In colonial Africa, Afua Kuma (1908–1987) of Ghana can be described as the first modern African modern oral theologian on the doctrine of christology. She used African idioms and social-cultural themes to talk about Jesus Christ.[5] The post-colonial period gave birth to

---

[3] Image courtesy of Arts of Africa collection of the Brooklyn Museum (New York City) and Wikimedia Commons, licensed under Creative Commons Attribution 3.0 Unported license, converted to grayscale with background digitally removed. Original image file available at https://commons.wikimedia.org/wiki/File:Brooklyn_Museum_45.11.5_Gold_Weight_in_Form_of_Sankofa_Bird.jpg

[4] For an overview, see John Thornton, *The Kongolese Saint Anthony: Dona Kimpa Vita and the Antonian Movement, 1684–1706.*

[5] Madam Kuma's oral theologizing has been transcribed and collected by others. Those who can read Twi, one of the literary dialects of Akan, should see her *Kwaebirentuw ase Yesu: Afua Kuma ayeyi ne mpaebo̱*. This is also available in English translation as *Jesus of the Deep Forest: Prayers and Praises of Afua Kuma*, a pdf of which has been made legally available on the website of *Dictionary of African Christian Biography* at https://dacb.org/resources/bio-pdfs/ghana/afua-e-read.pdf. More recently a new

Esther Mombo & Jackline Makena
Completing the Circle
Treks, Trends, and Trajectories of Circle Theology

African Theology which explicitly represented Africa's Christian voices. But for three decades, published written African theology was overwhelmingly articulated by males, until Mercy Amba Oduyoye's *Hearing and Knowing*, published in 1986, unmuted the voice of women to begin to articulate theology from their perspectives.[6]

Then in September 1989, the first meeting of the Circle took place, in Accra, Ghana, with a gathering of sixty-nine women. The papers presented were published in *The Will to Arise: Women, Tradition, and the Church in Africa* in 1992. In their introduction to that volume, Kanyoro and Oduyoye begin by observing that "as long as men and western strangers continue to write exclusively about Africa, African women will continue to be represented as if they were dead"[7] or absent. It was with that conviction that Oduyoye had earlier begun to look for her African sisters in churches and universities who had undertaken (or were undertaking) theological and religious studies, to initiate a programme of serious study, research, and publishing on religion and culture. It was from those efforts, with the support of those who shared her passion, that the idea of gathering a small group of African women theologians to launch an institute in religion and culture was conceived, leading to the formation of the Circle of Concerned African Women Theologians, an ecumenical and interfaith body of African women theologians who are concerned about interrogating the impact of religion and culture on African women.

Circle theology is characterized by themes captured in two key phrases. The first is the word spoken by Jesus to Jairus's dead daughter, whom Jesus raised from the dead (Mark 5:22–23, 35–43; Luke 8:41–42, 49–56): "*Talitha Koum!* ('Little girl, arise!')."[8] Applying this command to African Christian women,

---

collection of previously unpublished material has also been made available in English: Afua Kuma, *The Surprising African Jesus: The Lost Prayers and Praises of Afua Kuma*. See also Sara J. Fretheim's articles, "Afua Kuma," *Dictionary of African Christian Biography*; and "'Jesus! Say It Once Again and the Matter is Settled': The Life and Legacy of Oral Theologian Madam Afua Kuma of Ghana (1908–1987)."

[6] Mercy Amba Oduyoye, *Hearing and Knowing: Theological Reflections on Christianity in Africa*.

[7] Musimbi R. A. Kanyoro and Mercy Amba Oduyoye, "Introduction," in *The Will to Arise*, 1.

[8] The Aramaic phrase Jesus used, transliterated into the Greek New Testament Ταλειθά κούμ (*Taleithá koúm*; Greek: 'little girl, arise!' or 'little girl, get up!') in Mark 5:41 and often transliterated into English as either *Talitha qumi* or *Talitha cum*, has captured the imagination of African women, and is often used in works published by Circle members. See, e.g., Mercy Amba Oduyoye and Musimbi R. A. Kanyoro, eds., *Talitha, qumi! Proceedings of the Convocation of African Women Theologians, 1989*; and Nyambura Njoroge and Musa W. Dube, eds., *Talitha Cum! Theologies of African Women*.

Esther Mombo & Jackline Makena
Completing the Circle
Treks, Trends, and Trajectories of Circle Theology

Circle theology is about empowering women to tell their own faith stories rather than relying on others to write about them. The second phrase is "a one-winged bird cannot fly." Oduyoye compared then-current African theologies to a one-winged bird because the discipline was controlled and dominated by men. But Oduyoye and her colleagues recognized that "a bird with one wing cannot fly and that the foot that stays to crush another cannot move either."[9] The exclusion of women from theological education, scholarship, and institutional leadership was analogous to leaving one wing off a bird and still believing it could fly. Oduyoye asserted that for theology to fly, that is to be a thriving and living discipline, it must have the input of women. It must be a discipline with two healthy wings.

> Oduyoye notes that
> A Circle expands forever
> It covers all who wish to hold hands
> And its size depends on each other
> It is a vision of solidarity
> It turns outwards to interact with the outside
> And inward for self-critique
> A circle expands forever
> It is a vision of accountability
> It grows as the other is moved to grow
> A circle must have a center
> But a single dot does not make a Circle
> One tree does not make a forest
> A circle, a vision of cooperation, mutuality and care.[10]

The image of the circle is that of no beginning and no end, no front or back seat: the Circle of Concerned African Women Theologians and their theologizing is ever expanding, developing, and becoming. For generations, theological education was the exclusive province of males. When women were allowed to attend, they often were restricted to classes that taught them how to be good wives of clergymen and theologians. This exclusion was based on patriarchal values and economics. Patriarchal values dictated that formal education and theological leadership were male endeavors. From an economic perspective, the institutional church controlled theological education as well as any scholarship or church employment that would come from that education. Churches funded the schools and the candidates as well as prescribing the curriculum, which assumed male leadership. From the perspective of church leaders, money spent on theological education for women was money wasted as women could not be ordained or hold leadership positions in many churches and even when they

---

[9] Mercy Amba Oduyoye, *Introducing African Women's Theology*, 122.
[10] Mercy Amba Oduyoye, untitled poem.

could, it was the assumption of a patriarchal system that they would marry and move to their husbands' communities and churches.

To develop holistic theologies, African women theologians have worked to engender theological education. This process includes developing, critiquing, and implementing curricula for theological institutions with the goal of having gender sensitive curricula and the inclusion of women's voices and issues in theological training. Engendering theological education also includes advocating for the inclusion of women students and professors in those institutions and advocating for the ordination of women and placement of women in leadership roles that local churches and other religious institutions have often limited to men.[11]

The concept of a one-winged bird has also been applied within the workings of women's theological scholarship and community engagement. For example, African women theologians recognize the need for a second wing in biblical hermeneutics and encourage seeking the input of women who are not formal theologians but who are steeped in oral theology based on their experiences and on the experiences and teachings of their ancestors. The second wing of the bird also includes recognizing and finding value in differences among women in faith affiliation, tribal and cultural backgrounds, class, and marital status. For African women theologians, the incorporation of these different voices serves to advance not only their scholarly endeavors but their ability to speak to and act on issues that impact them personally as individuals and as part of their communities.

Methodologies of Circle Theology

Circle theology is not limited to a single theological methodology, as African women theologize from different perspectives. In reading Circle theology, one is presented with various ways of doing theology, the implementation of which relies heavily on the conditions or the context in which theology is applied, and the person or community involved. An important root common to many Circle writings is narrative theology. Related to this is paring theological scholarship with praxis. The aim of scholarship with praxis is to include all voices and to experience liberation of all in the community.

In *Introducing African Women's Theology*, Oduyoye offers an insightful overview of theology from the perspective of African women:

> In doing theology African women adopt a perspectival approach rather than analysis and critique of existing work. ... Rather, the approach is that of dialogue as women aim at affirmations, continued questioning of tradition in view of contemporary

---

[11] E.g., see Esther Mombo and Heleen Jozisses, eds., *If You Have No Voice, Just Sing!*

challenges, and as they struggle with making their own contribution to the creation of theologies that respond to the demands of spirituality. There is very little refutation and apologetic to be gleaned from African women's theology. What is present are statements of faith and the basis for such affirmations.[12]
She emphasizes the importance of storytelling — "the approach to theology, that has characterized women, is to tell a story and then to reflect upon it."[13] Reflection on the Bible is foundational in African women's theologies. But all such reflection necessarily takes place within a given context and culture. Aware of this, Circle theology emphasizes context(s) and culture(s). From such sources, theologians like Oduyoye have reflected on theology, e.g. "women's words about God": christology, Christian anthropology, ecclesiology, Christian life (e.g. hospitality and spirituality), and eschatology.[14] These and others are themes covered in the writings of Circle Women theologians.

Like the African worldviews it addresses, Circle theology is holistic and is interested in more than theory. Thus, Sarojini Nadar observes that "African feminist theologians therefore do not find it helpful to draw harsh distinctions between activism and academia. These two areas in the life and work of African feminist theologians are not mutually exclusive — they are simply a continuous never-ending spiral of action and reflection."[15] Similarly, Teresia Mbari Hinga describes African women's theology as being "primarily concerned with concrete issues of life as experienced."[16] She proposes that the church should not impose inculturation but should allow "inculturation from below."[17] Both Nadar and Hinga straightforwardly and yet gently bring awareness to the unnecessary and often harmful duality that is brought to theological scholarship and to religious practice. Theology, and even at times liturgy, becomes separated from the lives of individuals, especially individuals who are not connected with the academy and/or the institutional church hierarchy.

Theological themes

Bible and cultural hermeneutics

Due to the significant influence of religious texts in shaping the worldviews of adherents, which in turn affects the status of women within faith communities, the Circle of Concerned African Women Theologians engages in

---

[12] Oduyoye, *Introducing African Women's Theology*, 11.
[13] Oduyoye, *Introducing African Women's Theology*, 11.
[14] Oduyoye, *Introducing African Women's Theology*, 20.
[15] Sarojini Nadar, "Feminist Theologies in Africa," 276.
[16] Teresia Mbari Hinga, *African, Christian, Feminist: The Enduring Search for What Matters*, 6.
[17] Hinga, *African, Christian, Feminist*, 67.

the study and interpretation of the Bible. This includes a critical analysis of the hidden gender-oppressive scripts in the Bible, as well as the ways in which biblical texts have been (mis)used to subjugate women. Circle theologians like Musa Dube and Madipoane Masenya notes that the translation of the Bible into local languages led to the massive expansion of Christianity in Africa.[18] It is also through these translations that some African Instituted Churches were founded. However, adopting a hermeneutic of suspicion in interpreting scripture, Dube and Masenya highlight that biblical texts were often read through the lenses of missionary and colonial positions and in a gendered way.

The Circle has employed alternative methods of reading the Bible that reveal how centuries of patriarchal interpretation have left the plight of African women unresolved. These methods interrogate and challenge the underlying patriarchal tendencies that have attempted to explain or justify texts that appear to sanction the oppression of women. In rejecting models of interpretation that are not liberating, Circle theologians have been creative and versatile, employing methods such as hermeneutics of suspicion, cultural hermeneutics, and postcolonial hermeneutics to read the Bible. For Circle members, biblical studies have shifted from historical exegesis to contextual reading and interpretation. This shift signifies that women are no longer primarily interested merely in reconstructing the original text of the Bible but in finding meaning, guidance, and empowerment within the biblical narrative for their present-day lives. Musimbi Kanyoro articulates the premises of African women theologians that the Bible itself is not inherently an instrument of women's oppression; rather, it is the biased interpretation of the Bible, often vested with ulterior motives, that has led to such oppression. Therefore, women do not require liberation from the Bible itself but rather from the oppressive interpretations that have historically been imposed upon it.[19]

For members of the Circle, their hermeneutics are deeply informed by the context in which they live and work, a context that includes survival in harsh conditions of oppression, exploitation, and male dominance. In this environment, a reader-centered approach to scripture is more appropriate than the "historical-critical method," which is often seen as suited to "white, male, and middle-class academics" who "can afford to be 'impartial'" — impartiality here meaning non-committal.[20] African women theologians have audaciously reclaimed the power to reinterpret scriptures and assert their right to read, interpret, and listen to the scriptures through their own eyes and ears, in ways

---

[18] E.g., Musa W. Dube, "Consuming a Cultural Bomb: Translating *Badimo* into 'Demons' in the Setswana Bible (Matthew 8.28–34; 15.22; 10.8."

[19] Musimbi Kanyoro, *Introducing Feminist Cultural Hermeneutics: An African Perspective*, 13–15.

[20] Kwok Pui-lan, "Racism and Ethocentrism in Feminist Biblical Interpretation," 103.

that are life-affirming for all human beings, both women and men. Writing about feminist interpretations in Africa, Teresa Okure notes that African women's distinctive approach to biblical interpretation involves doing theology from a women's perspective.[21] This approach is characterized by inclusiveness; it considers both men and women in interpreting scripture and includes scholars and non-scholars, the rich and the poor. It also embraces diverse methodologies, including scientific, creation-centered, and popular methods.

One significant contribution to this field is the edited volume entitled *Other Ways of Reading*,[22] which exemplifies how women chose to interpret biblical texts using communal and narrative methods. These methods include reason, tradition, cultural and historical conditions, and lived experiences to unveil the cultural baggage hidden in scriptures that emphasizes the subordination of women. The narrative methodology is particularly resonant with African communities, where storytelling is a vital means of re-enacting communal history, instilling moral discipline, and passing on information. Storytelling, a method primarily used by women, also serves as a way for individuals to identify themselves, to think, and represent their realities.

Musimbi Kanyoro has significantly contributed to the development of feminist cultural hermeneutics. Her work emphasizes the importance of interpreting the Bible through the lens of African culture, recognizing the pivotal role that cultural context plays in shaping religious experiences and understanding. Exploring the African context and the reading of the Bible together, she argues that cultural hermeneutics is essential because it empowers unheard women and men to speak out, providing an opportunity for their questions and perspectives to contribute to understanding what God is communicating through scripture.[23] Kanyoro sets out the context of her hermeneutical method in experiences of rural women in Bware, Kenya and their interpretation of the book of Ruth.[24] It is in this context that she concludes that the dialogue between culture and the bible and the question of priority and allegiance highlights a perennial problem faced by many African Christians which Kanyoro describes as "one foot in African religion and culture and another in the church and western culture."[25]

Kanyoro's cultural hermeneutics is a method that closely aligns with the lived realities of African women. It interrogates the ways in which cultural practices and biblical interpretations have been used to justify the subordination

---

[21] Teresa Okure, "Epilogue: The Will to Arise: Reflections on Luke 8:40–56," 229.
[22] Musa W. Dube, ed., *Other Ways of Reading: African Women and the Bible*.
[23] Kanyoro, *Introducing Feminist Cultural Hermeneutics*, 1–12.
[24] Kanyoro, *Introducing Feminist Cultural Hermeneutics*, 32–57.
[25] Kanyoro, *Introducing Feminist Cultural Hermeneutics*, 13.

of women. She advocates for an approach that is not only critical of oppressive traditions but also seeks to reclaim cultural elements that affirm life and dignity. For Kanyoro, cultural hermeneutics involves reading the Bible alongside African cultural folktales, as both forms of narrative are significant in African women's liberation. She notes that all questions regarding the welfare and status of women in Africa are often explained within the framework of culture. Thus, cultural hermeneutics allows African women to engage with scripture in ways that are deeply connected to their cultural identities.[26]

Teresa Okure further elaborates on the distinction between the timeless truths of the Bible and its cultural underpinnings. She argues that rereading the Bible as a patriarchal text demands sustained efforts to discern between the divine and the human elements within it. While the divine embodies timeless truths essential for salvation, the human elements reflect socio-cultural practices that are conditioned by time and place and are, therefore, not universally applicable.[27] In their publications, Circle writers have focused on reading the Bible using cultural lenses. By doing so, they have been able to provide new insights that challenge traditional interpretations and offer life-affirming readings of scripture. These readings empower African women to see themselves in the biblical narrative, not as passive recipients of oppressive traditions but as active agents of their own liberation. Through cultural hermeneutics and the hermeneutics of suspicion,[28] Circle theologians continue to challenge oppressive interpretations of the Bible and offer alternative readings that affirm the dignity, agency, and worth of African women.

Musa Wenkosi Dube writes from a post-colonial perspective employing the decolonial theory. She has emphasized the use of indigenous hermeneutics, which are interpretive frameworks rooted in the cultural and spiritual traditions of African and other colonized peoples. These hermeneutics prioritize indigenous knowledge systems and ways of understanding the world. The decolonial reading is also concerned with healing and restoration. She seeks to heal the wounds inflicted by colonialism on the identities, cultures, and spiritualities of colonized peoples. This involves reinterpreting the Bible in ways that affirm the dignity and worth of indigenous peoples and their cultures.[29]

Christology

Christology is a major theme in Circle theology; Mercy Amba Oduyoye,

---

[26] Kanyoro, *Introducing Feminist Cultural Hermeneutics*, 13.
[27] See Teresa Okure, "Enkindling Fire in the Mission: Spirit and Scope of the BISAM Project."
[28] Mercy A. Oduyoye, "African Women's Hermeneutics," 362.
[29] Musa W. Dube, *Postcolonial Feminist Interpretation of the Bible*; Dube, "*Talitha Cum* Hermeneutics: Some African Women's Ways of Reading the Bible."

Esther Mombo & Jackline Makena
Completing the Circle
Treks, Trends, and Trajectories of Circle Theology

Elisabeth Amoah, Teresia Hinga, and Ann Nasimiyu Wasike are among the significant contributors on this topic. In 1988, Amoah and Oduyoye published an article titled "The Christ for African Women," in which they contended that, despite the dehumanizing challenges women face — culturally, economically, socially, and religiously — Jesus Christ serves as their liberator and savior from oppression. He empowers them in situations of powerlessness and stands as their friend and ally in the face of alienation and suffering.[30]

Christ, therefore, becomes the voice of the voiceless, the power of the powerless. Jesus becomes an African woman. Building on this theme of liberation, Teresia Hinga's work, particularly her chapter "Jesus Christ and the Liberation of Women in Africa,"[31] offers a critical perspective on traditional christology. Hinga critiques the received theology in which Christ is presented as the primordial scapegoat, arguing that this interpretation is not liberating but rather perpetuates the oppression of women. She contends that emulating Christ as a scapegoat could reinforce the role of women as victims and scapegoats within their cultures — roles that they are already compelled to play. Hinga's christology calls for a reimagining of Jesus not as a figure of passive suffering but as an active liberator who challenges and dismantles structures of oppression.[32]

Ann Nasimiyu's christology emphasizes Jesus as a protector and nurturer of life. In her article "Christology and African Women's Experience," Nasimiyu highlights the redemptive incarnation of Jesus, which unites his humanity with every other human being, thereby granting dignity and justice to all.[33] She argues that following the way of Jesus entails a deep commitment to caring for the suffering neighbor, critiquing and calling for changes in systems that cause suffering, and working to uncover the logic that perpetuates oppressive situations. She argues for a holistic approach to Jesus' ministry, one that integrates spiritual, social, and political liberation.

In African women's Christologies, the narrative method is central. Narration brings to the forefront the everyday experiences, faith encounters with Jesus Christ, and the ideas and practices of women. This highlights the importance of life stories, testimonies, and songs as channels for understanding the meaning of Jesus and the Christ-event from women's perspectives. Unlike many African male theologians who often use titles drawn from African cultural contexts, such as Jesus as Ancestor, female African theologians are cautious

---

[30] Elisabeth Amoah and Mercy Amba Oduyoye, "The Christ for African Women."
[31] Teresia M. Hinga, "Jesus Christ and the Liberation of Women."
[32] See Teresia M. Hinga, "Women Liberation in and through the Bible: The Debate and the Quest for a New Feminist Hermeneutics."
[33] Anne Nasimiyu-Wasike, "Christology and an African Woman's Experience."

about employing such images. These cultural titles derived from a patriarchal system do not fully resonate with their lived experiences as women of the saving presence of Jesus Christ.[34] Nasimiyu and Hinga advocate for a christology that affirms the dignity of African women and empowers them to challenge and transform oppressive structures in church and society. By presenting Jesus as a liberator, friend, protector, and nurturer, they offer a Christological vision that is deeply rooted in the realities of African women's lives, calling for a faith that is both life-affirming and liberating.

Circle Theology: Advocacy and Activism

Health and Healing

As well as theological themes, the Circle has been engaged in themes of theological advocacy because of combining scholarship and advocacy.[35] In terms of the story of the Circle, each period has had a special focus in the advocacy role. From 1989–2002, as the Circle was building its foundations, the themes interrogated how religions/cultures were constructed and their impact on women. Then from 2002–2019, the Circle focused on religion and culture with a very special focus on HIV/AIDS and the issues which HIV exposed such as Gender Based Violence. This was because of the magnitude of the impact of HIV on society in general and on women in particular. As noted above, Circle theology combines theological scholarship with praxis and that is why theological advocacy is part and parcel of doing theology. In affirming this, Hinga notes that a recognition of "the practice of injustices in church and society as a sinful betrayal of the vision of Jesus . . . African Christian women see their task as a prophetic one of unmasking and challenging such sinful practices and structures of injustices."[36] The primary concern of Circle theology is to nurture life affirming theologies amid death-dealing, hope-sapping, and life-denying forces. These forces include the outbreak of pandemics, climate change, war, global economic injustices, gender-based violence, etc. In response,

> Circle theology has engaged with embodied liberation in different themes, centering healing and health as significant for women and society as well. The onslaught of the HIV epidemic steered the Circle to devote time and resources into researching and publishing

---

[34] "Heleen" Leuntje Jannetje Joziasse, "Women's Faith Seeking Life: Lived Christologies and the transformation of gender relations in two Kenyan churches," 264–265.

[35] For the mutual engagement of scholarship and advocacy, see Frans Wijsen, Peter Henriot, and Rodrigo Mejía, eds., *The Pastoral Circle Revisited: A Critical Quest for Truth and Transformation*; and Maria Cimperman, *Social Analysis for the 21st Century: How Faith Becomes Action*.

[36] Hinga, *African, Christian, Feminist*, 8

on health and healing with a special focus on HIV and AIDS for about nineteen years.[37]

During the global COVID-19 crisis, Circle theologians continued to engage with the questions raised by this pandemic and its impact on those on the margins. Chisale, for example, writes about COVID-19 and women with disabilities, observing that

> as the COVID-19 pandemic spreads across the globe, particularly in Africa, women and girls with disabilities become vulnerable to sexual and gender-based violence, highlighting that the home is no longer a safe space for the vulnerable.[38]

COVID-19 exacerbated existing challenges such as hunger, poverty, and high unemployment, particularly affecting women. The Circle's theology on COVID-19 is captured in two volumes that reflect on the multiple vulnerabilities of women through their lived experiences. The book *COVID-19: African Women, and the Will to Survive* is a testament to women's resilience in navigating the numerous challenges arising from the virus and the measures taken to combat it, including lockdowns.[39] The other text, *A Time Like No Other*,[40] presents women's stories during the pandemic, highlighting their fears of violence, illness, and death, as well as the profound loss of loved ones. These stories make clear that poor women have suffered the effects of the pandemic most severely.

Gender-Based Violence

Another area of theological advocacy and activism is in the area of Gender-Based Violence (GBV), particularly Sexual and Gender-Based Violence (SGBV). In 2002, Isabel Apawo Phiri authored an article asking a heart wrenching question, "Why does God allow our husbands to hurt us?"[41] Similarly Dennis Ackerman observed that "there are two pressing issues at present that should be central to women doing theology in our part of the world, the first is the endemic nature of sexual violence against women and children. A war is being waged against bodies of women and children in this country."[42] The two

---

[37] Esther Mombo, "African Women's Theology," 33.
[38] Sinenhlanhla S. Chisale, "COVID-19 and Ubuntu Disruptions: Curbing the violence against Women and Girls with Disabilities through African Women's Theology of Disability," 1.
[39] Helen A. Labeodan, Rosemary Amenga-Etego, Johanna Stiebert, and Mark S. Aidoo, eds, *COVID-19: African Women and the Will to Survive*.
[40] Nontando Hadebe, Daniela Gennrich, Susan Rackoczy, and Nobesuthu Tom, eds., *A Time Like No Other Covid-19 in Women's Voices*.
[41] Isabel A. Phiri, "'Why Does God Allow Our Husbands to Hurt Us?' Overcoming Violence against Women."
[42] Denise A. Ackerman, "Forward from the Margins: Feminist Theologies for life," 67.

statements echo the realities confronting all Circle members doing theology in their different places. The theme of GBV and SGBV has cut across all the writings of the Circle as is apparent in the aforementioned brief bibliographical survey.[43] In the writings on Gender-Based Violence, it is noted that this practice is rooted in patriarchalist structures of society which value maleness as normative. There are cultural practices that marginalize women, making them vulnerable within society. Unfortunately, the texts show that the religious spaces are not immune to the same. Some teachings appear to condone GBV in theses such as gendered perseverance, which Esther Mombo has called "*vumilia* (perseverance) theology."[44]

Mother Earth

One of the current struggles experienced by people and nature is climate change. The theme of the Circle's 2019 conference was "Mother Africa: Mother Earth and Religion / Theology / Ethics / Philosophy." After having focused on Religions/Theology and HIV/AIDS from 2002–2019, at the end of the 2019 conference, the Circle adopted the themes of "Religions/Theology, the Environment and Sustainable Development Goals."[45] The image "Mother Earth" is derived from the connection between the violation of women's rights and the degradation of the Earth, which is usually described using feminine terms. There seems to be an unholy alliance of climate change crisis, the marginalization of women, the degradation of other life forms, and the degradation of the earth. Even if the Psalmist reminds us that "the earth is the Lord's and all that is in it" (Psa 24:1), the human beings have assumed that they are only the owners of the land, forgetting they are also stewards (Gen 1:28). The failure of being stewards has led to exploitation and plundering of the very earth they are expected to tend. The results of this are experienced in long drought, cyclones, floods and pollution. Those who suffer more from these changes are the poor and the marginalized and women are among these groups. The Circle writings on climate change are intersectional, approaching the issues through the lenses of the Bible, Gender, Culture, and Economics. This approach is formulated in view of challenging the Anthropocene views of human society that are causing harm to the whole creation. Several publications on climate change and mother earth are a testimony to the Circle's theology of advocacy and activism. So far, eight books have been published, or are in production, from this one conference, but the theme of mother is ongoing as women interrogate the connection.

---

[43] Mombo, "African Women's Theology," 33.
[44] Esther Mombo and Heleen Joziasse, "Deconstructing Gendered *vumilia* (perseverance) Theology in times of the Gender-based Violence Pandemic."
[45] "History of the Circle."

Esther Mombo & Jackline Makena
Completing the Circle
Treks, Trends, and Trajectories of Circle Theology

Collaboration with other feminist theologies

Sarojini Nadar provides a helpful overview of the basic differences between African women's theologies and other feminist theologies, which we will summarize as follows. The main difference between African women's theologies and feminist theologies . . . lies in the emphasis each wishes to place on particular issues, rather than on an inherent difference in ideologies. . . . the defining focus of feminist theologies in Africa has been on culture. This focus on culture has not been in opposition to issues of gender, race, and class, but in addition or as complementary to these important factors. It is important, therefore, not to draw false dichotomies between feminist theologies in Africa and feminist theologies in the Global North, this false dichotomy usually being understood in terms of African feminist theologies being "softer" and more "conservative."[46]

Conclusion

In this essay, we have tried to tell *her story* (the Circle theology story). We have named some of the features and themes of her story. We have also named the major methodology employed in Circle writing. This story of the Circle is not complete but continues. Mercy Oduyoye pointed out as an analogy of theology in Africa that as a one-winged bird cannot fly, African theology that only includes the voices of men is a one-winged theology.[47] Circle theology is the other wing so that theology can grow. The Circle has served as a vehicle for African women theologians to dialogue with and mentor other women theologians, to write and publish on issues pertinent to women. It has also created space for connecting and collaborating with other national and international organizations addressing related concerns. In supporting and nurturing women theologians, the Circle has helped the voices, perspectives, and visions of women to be heard in theological education and scholarship, and in the teachings and practices of local religious institutions. Circle theology is not complete, but a bird that continues to fly defining and redefining theology in the changing contextual realities.

Bibliography

ACKERMAN, Denise A. "Forward from the Margins: Feminist Theologies for life." *Journal of Theology in Southern Africa* 99 (1997): 63–67.
AMOAH, Elisabeth, and Mercy Amba ODUYOYE. "The Christ for African Women." Chapter 4 in *With Passion and Compassion: Third World*

---

[46] Nadar, "Feminist Theologies in Africa," 272.
[47] See especially Mercy Amba Oduyoye, "The Search for a Two-Winged Theology," 43.

Women Doing Theology: Reflections from the Women's Commission of the Ecumenical Association of Third World Theologians, edited by Virginia Fabella and Mercy Amba Oduyoye, 35–46. Maryknoll, New York, USA: Orbis Books, 1988.
NB: A reprint edition of *With Passion and Compassion* is still in print — Eugene, Oregon: Wipf & Stock, 2006.

BERMAN, Sidney K., Paul L. LESHOTA, Ericka S. DUNBAR, and Musa W. DUBE, eds. *Mother Earth, Mother Africa and Biblical Studies: Interpretations in the Context of Climate Change*. BiAS – Bible in Africa Studies 29. Bamberg, Germany: University of Bamberg Press, 2021.

CHIRONGMA, Sophia, and Scholar Wayua KIILU, eds. *Mother Earth, Mother Africa: World Religions and Environmental Imagination*. Stellenbosch, South Africa: SUN MeDIA, 2022.

CHIRONGOMA, Sophia, and Esther MOMBO, eds. *Mother Earth, Postcolonial and Liberation Theologies*. Foreword by Denise Ackermann. London: Lexington Press / Fortress Academic, 2021.

CHISALE, Sinenhlanhla S. "COVID-19 and Ubuntu Disruptions: Curbing the violence against Women and Girls with Disabilities through African Women's Theology of Disability." *Journal of International Women's Studies* 24, no. 4 (2022): Article #3, 13 pages. https://vc.bridgew.edu/jiws/vol24/iss4/3/

CHISALE, Sinenhlanhla, and Rozelle Robso BOSCH, eds. *Mother Earth, Mother Africa and Theology*. HTS Religion and Society 10. Cape Town: AOSIS, 2021.

CIMPERMAN, Maria. *Social Analysis for the 21st Century: How Faith Becomes Action*. Maryknoll, New York: Orbis Books, 2015.

DANIEL, Seblewengel, Mmapula Diana KEBANEILWE, and Angeline SAVALA, eds. *Mother Earth, Mother Africa and Mission*. Stellenbosch, South Africa: SUN PReSS, 2021.

DUBE, Musa W. "Consuming a Cultural Bomb: Translating *Badimo* into 'Demons' in the Setswana Bible (Matthew 8.28–34; 15.22; 10.8)." *Journal for the Study of the New Testament* 21, no. 73 (1999): 33–58.[48] https://doi.org/10.1177/0142064X9902107303

———, ed. *Other Ways of Reading: African Women and the Bible*. Atlanta/Geneva: Society of Biblical Literature / WCC Publications, 2001.

---

[48] Editors' note: Recently republished as "Consuming a colonial cultural bomb: Translating *Badimo* into 'demons' in the Setswana Bible (Matthew 8.28–34; 15.22; 10.8),"chapter 10 in *[Re]Gained in Translation II: Bibles, Histories, and Struggles for Identity*, edited by Sabine Dievenkorn and Shaul Levin, 251–277, TRANSÜD: Arbeiten zur Theorie und Praxis des Übersetzens und Dolmetschens 134 (Berlin: Frank & Timme, 2024), https://doi.org/10.57088/978-3-7329-9175-4_11

Esther Mombo & Jackline Makena
Completing the Circle
Treks, Trends, and Trajectories of Circle Theology

DUBE, Musa W. *Postcolonial Feminist Interpretation of the Bible*. St. Louis, Missouri, USA: Chalice Press, 2000.

———. "Talitha Cum Hermeneutics: Some African Women's Ways of Reading the Bible." In *The Bible and the Hermeneutics of Liberation*, edited by Alejandro F. Botta and Pablo R. Adiñach, 133–146. Society of Biblical Literature Semeia Studies 59. Atlanta: Society of Biblical Literature, 2009.

FRETHEIM, Sara J. "Afua Kuma." *Dictionary of African Christian Biography*, n.d., https://dacb.org/stories/ghana/afua-kuma/

———. "'Jesus! Say It Once Again and the Matter is Settled': The Life and Legacy of Oral Theologian Madam Afua Kuma of Ghana (1908–1987)." *Journal of African Christian Biography* 5, no. 3 (2020): 18–38. https://dacb.org/resources/journal/5-3/5-3-July2020-JACB-ejournal.pdf (link to entire issue)

HADEBE, Nontando, Daniela GENNRICH, Susan RACKOCZY, and Nobesuthu TOM, eds. *A Time Like No Other: Covid-19 in Women's Voices*. n.p.: Circle of Concerned African Women Theologians – South Africa, 2021. https://jliflc.com/resources/a-time-like-no-other-covid-19-in-womens-voices/

HINGA, Teresia Mbari. *African, Christian, Feminist: The Enduring Search for What Matters*. Maryknoll, New York: Orbis Books, 2017.

———. "Jesus Christ and the Liberation of Women." Chapter 11 in *The Will to Arise: Women, Tradition, and the Church in Africa*, edited by Mercy Amba Oduyoye and Musimbi R. A. Kanyoro, 183–194. Maryknoll, New York: Orbis Books, 1992.

———. "Women Liberation in and through the Bible: The Debate and the Quest for a New Feminist Hermeneutics." *African Christian Studies* 6, no. 4 (1990): 33–49.

"History of the Circle." Circle of Concerned Women Theologians – South Africa, n.d., https://circle.org.za/about-us/history-of-the-circle/

JOZIASSE, "Heleen" Leuntje Jannetje. "Women's Faith Seeking Life: Lived Christologies and the transformation of gender relations in two Kenyan churches." PhD dissertation, Universiteit Utrecht, 2020. https://doi.org/10.33540/98

KANYORO, Musimbi R. A. *Introducing Feminist Cultural Hermeneutics: An African Perspective*. Introductions in Feminist Theology 9. New York: Sheffield Academic Press, 2002.

KANYORO, Musimbi R. A., and Mercy Amba ODUYOYE, "Introduction." In *The Will to Arise: Women, Tradition, and the Church in Africa*, edited by Mercy Amba Oduyoye and Musimbi R. A. Kanyoro, 1–6. Maryknoll, New York: Orbis Books, 1992.

KUMA, Afua. *Jesus of the Deep Forest: Prayers and Praises of Afua Kuma*. Translated by Jon Kirby. Accra, Ghana: Asempa Publishers, 1981.

Esther Mombo & Jackline Makena
Completing the Circle
Treks, Trends, and Trajectories of Circle Theology

KUMA, Afua. *Kwaebirentuw ase Yesu: Afua Kuma ayeyi ne mpaebo*. Accra, Ghana: Asempa Publishers, 1980.

———. *The Surprising African Jesus: The Lost Prayers and Praises of Afua Kuma*. Translated by Jon P. Kirby. Transcribed by Joseph Kwakye. Foreword by Stephen Bevans. Preface and Introduction by Jon P. Kirby. Eugene, Oregon, USA: Wipf and Stock, 2022.

KWOK Pui-lan. "Racism and Ethocentrism in Feminist Biblical Interpretation." Chapter 7 in *Searching the Scriptures*, vol. 1: *A Feminist Introduction*, edited by Elisabeth Schüssler Fiorenza with Shelly Matthews, 101–116. New York: Crossroad, 1993. Reprint edition: London: SCM Press, 1994.

LABEODAN, Helen A., Rosemary Amenga-Etego, Johanna Stiebert, and Mark S. Aidoo, eds. *COVID-19: African Women and the Will to Survive*. Bible in Africa Studies (BiAS) 37 / Exploring Religion in Africa 8. Bamberg: University of Bamberg Press, 2021. https://doi.org/10.20378/irb-51639

MATHOLENI, Nobuntu Penxa, Georgina Kwanima BOATENG, and Molly MANYONGANISE, eds. *Mother Earth, Mother Africa, & African Indigenous Religions*. Stellenbosch, South Africa: SUN PReSS, 2020.

MOMBO, Esther. "African Women's Theology." Chapter 2 in *Ford's The Modern Theologians: An Introduction to Christian Theology since 1918*, edited by Rachel Muers and Ashley Cocksworth with David F. Ford, 28–38. Introduction by Rachel Muers and Ashley Cocksworth. 4th edition. The Great Theologians. Chichester, West Sussex, UK: Wiley Blackwell, 2024.

MOMBO, Esther, and Heleen JOZISSES. "Deconstructing Gendered *vumilia* (perseverance) Theology in times of the Gender-based Violence Pandemic." *Journal of International Women's Studies* 24, no. 4 'Violence against Women and Girls in Africa in the absence of Ubuntu' (2022): Article #14, 17 pages. https://vc.bridgew.edu/jiws/vol24/iss4/14

MOMBO, Esther, and Heleen JOZISSES, eds. *If You Have No Voice, Just Sing! Narratives of Women's lives and Theological Education at St. Paul's University*. Limuru, Kenya: Zaph Chancery, 2011.

NADAR, Sarojini. "Feminist Theologies in Africa." Chapter 18 in *The Wiley-Blackwell Companion to African Religions*, edited by Elias Kifon Bongmba, 269–278. Foreword by Jacob K. Olupona. Oxford: Wiley-Blackwell, 2012.

NASIMIYU-WASIKE, Anne. "Christology and an African Woman's Experience." Chapter 5 in *Faces of Jesus in Africa*, edited by Robert J. Schreiter, 70–81. Faith and Culture Series. Maryknoll, New York, USA: Orbis Books, 1991.

NJOROGE, Nyambura, and Musa W. DUBE, eds. *Talitha Cum! Theologies of African Women*. Pietermaritzburg, South Africa: Cluster Publications, 2001.

ODUYOYE, Mercy Amba. "African Women's Hermeneutics." In *Initiation into Theology: The Rich Variety of Theology and Hermeneutics*, edited Simon Maimela and Adrio König, 359–371. Pretoria: J. L. van Schaik, 1998.

Oduyoye, Mercy Amba. *Hearing and Knowing: Theological Reflections on Christianity in Africa.* Maryknoll, New York, USA: Orbis Books, 1986.

———. *Introducing African Women's Theology.* Introductions in Feminist Theology. Sheffield, England: Sheffield Academic Press, 2001.

———. "The Search for a Two-Winged Theology." Chapter 2 in *Talitha Qumi! Proceedings of the Convocation of African Women Theologians, 1989*, edited by Mercy Amba Oduyoye and Musimbi R. A. Kanyoro, 31–56. Ibadan, Nigeria: Daystar Press, 1990. Reprint edition: Accra-North, Ghana: SWL Press, 2001.

———. Untitled poem. In *Hope Abundant: Third World and Indigenous Women's Theologies*, edited by Kwok Pui-lan, 17. Maryknoll, New York, USA: Orbis Books, 2010.

Oduyoye, Mercy Amba, and Musimbi R. A. Kanyoro, eds. *Talitha Qumi! Proceedings of the Convocation of African Women Theologians, 1989.* Ibadan, Nigeria: Daystar Press, 1990. Reprint edition: Accra-North, Ghana: SWL Press, 2001.

Oduyoye, Mercy Amba, and Musimbi R. A. Kanyoro, eds. *The Will to Arise: Women, Tradition, and the Church in Africa.* Maryknoll, New York: Orbis Books, 1992.

Okure, Teresa. "Enkindling Fire in the Mission: Spirit and Scope of the BISAM Project." Chapter 1 in *To Cast Fire upon the Earth: Bible and Mission Collaborating in Today's Multicultural Global Context*, edited by Teresa Okure, 2–31. Pietermaritzburg, South Africa: Cluster, 2000.

———. "Epilogue: The Will to Arise: Reflections on Luke 8:40–56." In *The Will to Arise: Women, Tradition, and the Church in Africa*, edited by Mercy Amba Oduyoye and Musimbi R.A. Kanyoro, 221–230. Maryknoll, New York: Orbis Books, 1992.

Phiri, Isabel A. "'Why Does God Allow Our Husbands to Hurt Us?' Overcoming Violence against Women." *Journal of Theology for Southern Africa* 114 (November 2002): 19–30.

Thornton, John. *The Kongolese Saint Anthony: Dona Kimpa Vita and the Antonian Movement, 1684–1706.* Cambridge: Cambridge University Press, 1998.

Wijsen, Frans, Peter Henriot, and Rodrigo Mejía, eds. *The Pastoral Circle Revisited: A Critical Quest for Truth and Transformation.* Maryknoll, New York, USA: Orbis Books, 2005.

The Rain Reveals the Leaks
How the Vulnerability of the "Least of These" Reveals the Vulnerabilities in our Own Hearts and Systems [1]

Ruth BARRON

ORCID: 0009-0002-0768-6925
MissionStream and Africa Inland Church, Enoomatasiani, Kenya
renb2357@gmail.com

Abstract

When we consider the issue of vulnerability in the context of sexual abuse, we think of the vulnerable as those who have been victimized by abuse, and there is truth in this view. However, it is also important to recognize the vulnerability that abuse exposes in our own hearts and systems. It is easy, when the rains are far away, to assume our roofs are well-built and secure, but it is when the rain begins pouring over our own houses that the leaks become obvious. When we see only the vulnerability within the victims of sexual abuse, we too often blame the victims for their weakness and insist that if they strengthened themselves, the problem of sexual abuse would be resolved. However, if a child lives in a leaky house, teaching them to hold an umbrella over their head will not solve the problem. We must pay attention to the cries of the vulnerable to find and repair the hidden leaks in our systems, but we must also examine what the needs of the vulnerable reveal in our own hearts. As Christ teaches us in the parable of the sheep and the goats, it is how we respond to the cries of the vulnerable and not how many great deeds we claim to perform in the name of Christ which determines whether we are aligned with the Spirit of Christ or another spirit. An examination of pastoral responses to abuse, academic abuse research, and the Scriptures clearly demonstrate that there are severe 'leaks' in the 'roof' of the Church which we must address.

---

[1] An earlier version of this article was presented as an invited lead paper (plenary presentation) on 17 October 2023 at the International Academic Conference of Baptist College of Theology, Oyo (17–19 October 2023) in Oyo, Nigeria; it will appear in the next issue of *Baptist Journal of Theology* (the Journal of the Baptist College of Theology, Oyo). The conference theme was "Vulnerability, Molestation and Church's Response."

Published with license by ACTEA | DOI: https://doi.org/10.69683/93skxp79
© Ruth Barron, 2024 | ISSN: 3006-1768 (print); 3007-1771 (online)
This is an open access article distributed under the terms of the CC BY 4.0 license.

Ruth Barron
The Rain Reveals the Leaks: How the Vulnerability of the "Least of These" Reveals the Vulnerabilities in our Own Hearts and Systems

Résumé

Lorsque nous examinons la question de la vulnérabilité dans le contexte des abus sexuels, nous pensons que les personnes vulnérables sont celles qui ont été victimes d'abus, et il y a du vrai dans ce point de vue. Cependant, il est également important de reconnaître la vulnérabilité que les abus révèlent dans nos propres cœurs et systèmes. Il est facile, lorsque la pluie est loin, de penser que nos toits sont bien construits et sûrs, mais c'est lorsque la pluie commence à tomber sur nos propres maisons que les fuites deviennent évidentes. Lorsque nous ne voyons que la vulnérabilité des victimes d'abus sexuels, nous leur reprochons trop souvent leur faiblesse et insistons sur le fait que si elles se renforçaient elles-mêmes, le problème des abus sexuels serait résolu. Cependant, si un enfant vit dans une maison qui prend l'eau, lui apprendre à tenir un parapluie au-dessus de sa tête ne résoudra pas le problème. Nous devons prêter attention aux cris des personnes vulnérables pour trouver et réparer les fuites cachées dans nos systèmes, mais nous devons également examiner ce que les besoins des personnes vulnérables révèlent dans nos propres cœurs. Comme le Christ nous l'enseigne dans la parabole des brebis et des boucs, c'est la manière dont nous répondons aux cris des personnes vulnérables, et non le nombre de grandes actions que nous prétendons accomplir au nom du Christ, qui détermine si nous sommes alignés sur l'Esprit du Christ ou sur un autre esprit. Un examen des réponses pastorales aux abus, de la recherche universitaire sur les abus et des Écritures démontre clairement qu'il y a de graves "fuites" dans le "toit" de l'Église et que nous devons y remédier.

Resumo

Quando consideramos a questão da vulnerabilidade no contexto do abuso sexual, pensamos nos vulneráveis como aqueles que foram vitimados pelo abuso, e há verdade nesta visão. No entanto, também é importante reconhecer a vulnerabilidade que o abuso expõe nos nossos próprios corações e sistemas. É fácil, quando as chuvas estão longe, assumir que os nossos telhados estão bem construídos e seguros, mas é quando a chuva começa a cair sobre as nossas próprias casas que as infiltrações se tornam óbvias. Quando vemos apenas a vulnerabilidade das vítimas de abuso sexual, muitas vezes culpamos as vítimas pela sua fraqueza e insistimos que, se elas se fortalecessem, o problema do abuso sexual estaria resolvido. No entanto, se uma criança vive numa casa com infiltrações, ensiná-la a segurar um guarda-chuva sobre a cabeça não resolverá o problema. Temos de prestar atenção aos gritos dos vulneráveis para encontrar e reparar as fugas escondidas nos nossos sistemas, mas também temos de examinar o que as necessidades dos vulneráveis revelam nos nossos próprios corações. Tal como Cristo nos

Ruth Barron
The Rain Reveals the Leaks: How the Vulnerability of the "Least of These" Reveals the Vulnerabilities in our Own Hearts and Systems

ensina na parábola das ovelhas e dos cabritos, é a forma como respondemos aos gritos dos vulneráveis e não o número de grandes acções que afirmamos realizar em nome de Cristo que determina se estamos alinhados com o Espírito de Cristo ou com outro espírito. Uma análise das respostas pastorais aos abusos, da investigação académica sobre abusos e das Escrituras demonstra claramente que há graves "fugas" no "telhado" da Igreja, que temos de resolver.

Keywords

vulnerability, abuse, church response to abuse

Mots-clés

vulnérabilité, abus, réponse de l'église aux abus

Palavras-chave

vulnerabilidade, abuso, resposta da igreja ao abuso

My children have a book entitled *Lazy Lion* by Mwenye Hadithi and Adrienne Kennaway. In the book, Lazy Lion sees the clouds appear in the sky and declares, "The Big Rain is coming. I will need a roof to keep me dry. And since I am the King of Beasts, I will order a fine house to be built."[2] He orders a succession of other animals to build houses for him, but he is dissatisfied with every house. The White Ants build him a majestic termite mound like a palace, but Lazy Lion refuses to live in the dirt. The Weaver Birds build him a large nest, but Lazy Lion won't live in a tree. The Ant Bear, the Honey Badger, and the Crocodile also fail to please Lazy Lion. When the clouds finally burst, all the animals rush into the houses they had offered Lazy Lion and find shelter from the rain, but Lazy Lion has no house to shelter in. To this day, Lazy Lion endures the rains without shelter.

This children's story is built upon the truth that a house is meant to provide shelter when the rains arrive, yet sometimes even houses can fail to shelter those inside because they have leaks. In 2008, a Maasai neighbor invited me to help her repair the roof of her traditional house in preparation for the rains. As we worked together, she taught me an important concept: *It is the rain which reveals the leaks.* It is tempting for us to blame the leaks on the rain itself. If there were no rain, there would be no leaks, but the holes in the roof through which the leaks pour during the rains had already been developing throughout the dry season. The rain does not cause the leaks; it reveals the leaks which are already present. One of the jobs of a Maasai woman is to tend the roof before

---

[2] Mwenye Hadithi and Adrienne Kennaway, *Lazy Lion*, 1.

Ruth Barron
**The Rain Reveals the Leaks: How the Vulnerability
of the "Least of These" Reveals the Vulnerabilities in our Own Hearts and Systems**

the rains arrive so that when the rains do come, her family will have shelter, and then she is to watch attentively when the rains begin, to ensure that she has not missed any holes.

Meteorologists tell us that we are currently in an El Niño weather season,[3] with record heat waves in parts of the world while other parts are expecting extreme rainfall and flooding. It is a time to be indoors, sheltering from the heat and the rains, but unfortunately many houses are not the shelter they should be. Some houses are built like ovens, designed to keep heat inside. Others are leaky or vulnerable to collapsing in the floods. What are we to do when our places of shelter actually increase our vulnerability rather than offering us safety? We must repair or rebuild our houses. Similarly, we are amid a global El Niño event regarding sexual abuse. The Joshua Center on Child Sexual Abuse Prevention states, "Though it is underreported and under-recorded, child sexual abuse [CSA] is a widespread global issue experienced by up to 31% of girls and 17.6% of boys."[4] The Journalist's Resource reports that the highest rates of CSA are in Africa, with especially high rates in South Africa.[5] Here in Nigeria, human rights groups have alerted the country to rapidly rising rates of CSA.[6] Similarly, End Violence states that online CSA is increasing and citing a survey by WeProtect, which found that "57% of the surveyed girls and 48% of the surveyed boys reported "at least one online sexual harm, with some regions — like North America, Australasia, and Western Europe — being even higher."[7] There is nowhere on the globe where our children are safe from sexual abuse. We are clearly in an El Niño event regarding CSA, with rising floodwaters across the globe. Our children need shelter, and we, as the Church, should be a house which offers children refuge from the rains and floods.

Unfortunately, the rains have revealed widespread leaks in the Church and in the hearts of its leaders and members. These leaks leave children in danger of CSA even within the Church itself, and it is on this topic that I will focus in this paper. Too often, church leaders have presumed the Church universal, or their own denominations or individual congregations, to be impervious to sexual abuse scandals, and, because of this presumption, they have failed to maintain the integrity of their roofs. This presumption has two parts. First, there are church leaders who believe that the Church itself is, for the most part, immune to sexual abuse. Because they consider the church immune, they do

---

[3] When the paper was presented in October 2023.
[4] "On Child Sexual Abuse | Joshua Center on Child Sexual Abuse."
[5] John Wihbey, "Global Prevalence of Child Sexual Abuse."
[6] E.g., see Victor Ifeanyi Ede and Dominic Zuoke Kalu, "Child Abuse in Nigeria: Responses of Christian Churches and the Way Out."
[7] End Violence Against Children, "Global Threat Assessment 2021 Shows Dramatic Increase in Online Child Sexual Exploitation & Abuse | End Violence."

Ruth Barron
The Rain Reveals the Leaks: How the Vulnerability of the "Least of These" Reveals the Vulnerabilities in our Own Hearts and Systems

not take any precautions to prevent abuse, and they disbelieve the victims who cry out about abuse. Second, these scandals have revealed that many church leaders knew that sexual abuse was taking place within their churches but believed that they could and should *prevent scandal* by silencing, blaming, and further abusing the victims rather than by addressing the scandal, which has already occurred, by rightly addressing the abuse. Thus, by church leaders either refusing to inspect the roof to prevent and repair leaks and/or silencing those on whom the leaks have fallen, the church's roof has become riddled with leaks, as with the church building in Alan Paton's powerfully prophetic book, *Cry, the Beloved Country*.[8] It is beyond the space allowed for this article to explore specific — and necessary! — questions of the nature and parameters of accountability and justice. My focus, in the context of abuse 'leaking' (or pouring) into the church, is on identifying the *source* of those leaks so that we know where to focus our efforts on 'repairing the roof' and preventing further leaks. The conference at which an earlier version of this article was presented was on the theme "Vulnerability, Molestation and Church's Response," so, for the purposes of this article, I use the term *vulnerability* throughout to describe the source of these leaks.[9]

In 2021, I shared a meme on Facebook which asked a question: "Why does the church ask the victim, 'did you forgive?' instead of asking the perpetrator, 'did you repent?'" One pastor replied, "my sermons as I preach are much more focused on forgiveness, because that's who's in my congregation. And I'd say most congregations. I think both questions are valid. I think a reason why perpetrators are not asked the questions as much and it seems off balance is because they are not the people in the churches" (5 May 2021). This response reveals how a pastor's presumptions regarding the nature of his own congregation as well as the nature of the church as a whole drive his preaching decisions, but his presumptions are only possible if he denies the validity of the multitudes of reports revealing widespread sexual abuse in the church. The reports are clear. Abusers are in our churches. Abuse is rampant in our

---

[8] Chapter 32 in Alan Paton, *Cry, the Beloved Country*, first published in 1948.
[9] There is a danger of confusion when talking about *vulnerability* in the context of abuse. The bottom line is that victims need support while perpetrators need accountability. When we focus on the vulnerability of the victim to abuse, we often respond by holding the victim accountable to become less vulnerable instead of offering much needed compassionate support to the victim. However, when we focus on the vulnerability of sinful desires within the perpetrator, we often shift our response from accountability to support, viewing the desire to harm another person as too difficult for the perpetrator to resist without sympathetic support. Note that in the section in which I direct our focus toward the vulnerability, or culpability, of the perpetrator, I still maintain that the appropriate and necessary response is on accountability — abusers *must* be held accountable; see Matthew 18:6–9.

churches.

Rather than acknowledge the truth, church leaders choose to believe the church is exceptional. Sexual abuse happens elsewhere, not in our churches. Unfortunately, church abuse statistics demonstrate just how false these claims are. As Boz Tchividjan, founder of GRACE (Godly Response to Abuse in the Christian Environment) and grandson of Billy Graham, wrote, citing a US based study,

> It is critical to note that this abuse is no less prevalent within the faith community. In fact, there are studies that demonstrate that the faith community is even more vulnerable to abuse than secular environments. The Abel and Harlow study revealed that 93% of sex offenders describe themselves as "religious" and that this category of offender may be the most dangerous. Other studies have found that sexual abusers within faith communities have more victims and younger victims.[10]

Akani's research in Nigeria suggests the same: when analyzing crime data for Christian and Muslim clergy, "the rate appears higher among Christian clerics."[11] *We must assess our churches, and we must listen to the reports of those who have assessed our churches.* We must learn the wisdom of the Maasai and pay heed to what the rains are revealing regarding the Church. From the foundation of the Church, there has been sexual abuse within its walls. In 1 Corinthians 5:1-2, Paul writes, "It is actually reported that there is sexual immorality among you, and of a kind that even pagans do not tolerate: A man is sleeping with his father's wife. And you are proud!"[12] Note Paul's words, "of a kind that even pagans do not tolerate," are echoed in the statistics quoted above, which reveal that the church is "even more vulnerable to abuse than secular environments." The Apostle Paul listened to and believed the reports of sexual immorality within the church. The Apostle Paul acknowledged that the problem was actually worse in the church than outside it. We must as well.

The presumption of the church's invulnerability to abuse has created the very conditions necessary to ensure that abuse thrives within the Church. As one minister/perpetrator told psychologist Anna Salter:

> I considered church people easy to fool... they have a trust that comes from being Christians. . . . They tend to be better folks all around. And they seem to want to believe in the good that exists in all people. . . . I think they want to believe in people. And because

---

[10] Boz Tchividjian, "Startling Statistics: Child Sexual Abuse and What the Church Can Do About It."

[11] Abdul Hakeem A Akanni, "Evil Men in the House of God: An Analytical Study of the Involvement of Christian and Muslim Clerics in Crime in Nigeria," 259.

[12] All Scripture quotations are from NIV (2011).

Ruth Barron
The Rain Reveals the Leaks: How the Vulnerability of the "Least of These" Reveals the Vulnerabilities in our Own Hearts and Systems

of that, you can easily convince, with or without convincing words.[13]

Nigerian scholars Adesanya Ibiyinka Olusola and Clement Ogunlusi write, "An important thing that the Church needs to admit is that child rape happens and that it happens among its own members."[14] Child sexual abuse happens. It happens in the church. It happens among its own members, and worse, it happens among its own leaders. A. A. Akanni's research found that Christian and Muslim clergy are involved in crime in Nigeria "just like any other person." He adds that "sexual immorality of all sorts tops the list" of crimes they commit.[15] The phrase "just like any other person" is a key point. We must stop assuming that our churches, members, and leaders are exceptional, as in the pastor's statement above: "they are not the people in the churches." This is directly countered by Scriptural testimony, academic research, and the great multitude of media reports from around the globe. In Hosea 4:6, God declares, "my people are destroyed from lack of knowledge." We must do the work to gain the knowledge we need. The data is available to us if we will look for it.

Let us consider a parable. A Maasai man owned a flock of sheep. He lived in the village he had inherited from his father. He knew his father had built a good fence and a strong sheepfold. He decided that it would be dishonoring of his father to inspect and maintain the walls surrounding his village and his sheepfold. He also decided that it would be dishonoring of his father to guard the sheep within those walls. His father was a wise man who did excellent work. The walls he built must therefore be the best and safest walls anyone could build. He must trust his father's work. Because he presumed the sheep were secure within his father's walls, the man did not count the flock morning and night. He did not take them out to graze. Instead, he fed them grain in the sheepfold. There was not enough food for the sheep, so the stronger sheep began to butt away the weaker sheep, but the man did not notice. He spent his days raiding to find new sheep.

Unfortunately, leopards found the man's home. They did not have the same assumptions as the man. They could hear the bleating of sheep. They could smell the tasty flock. They tested the security of the walls by leaping them. And they met no guards. The leopards were wiser than the shepherd. They assessed the walls and found them unprotected. The walls, in the absence of guards, did not protect the sheep but rather trapped the sheep. There was nowhere for the sheep to hide from the leopards. The leopards began to live in

---

[13] Anna C. Salter, *Predators: Pedophiles, Rapists, and Other Sex Offenders; Who They Are, How They Operate and How We Can Protect Ourselves and Our Children*, 29.

[14] Adesanya Ibiyinka Olusola and Clement Ogunlusi, "Recurring Cases of Child Rape in Nigeria: An Issue for Church Intervention," 63.

[15] Akanni, "Evil Men in the House of God," 259.

Ruth Barron
The Rain Reveals the Leaks: How the Vulnerability of the "Least of These" Reveals the Vulnerabilities in our Own Hearts and Systems

the trees surrounding the fence. Whenever they were hungry, they would leap the fence and take a sheep. The man never noticed the missing sheep.

Lions, too, found the walls, but they decided to live in the sheepfold itself. The lions were also wiser than the man. They assessed the flock. They noticed which sheep the stronger sheep pushed away from the food and targeted those weaker sheep. The stronger sheep didn't protest. Fewer sheep meant more food for the rest. When the Maasai man saw the lions, he was not disturbed. He saw their presence as proof of the power of his father's walls. Most of the sheep seemed unafraid of the lions, so he concluded the walls had transformed the predators into friends of sheep. The lions were big cats, and like any cat, they enjoyed playing with their prey before eating. They would pounce and claw, then let their prey go; pounce again and gnaw, then let it go; over and over. When the prey bleated in pain and terror, the man came, but rather than protecting the targeted sheep, he beat it for bleating. The man thought, "The lions clearly hadn't meant to hurt the sheep; after all, the sheep isn't dead. It is only scratched. The lions are clearly trying to learn how to be gentle with their claws and teeth, but they make mistakes. The sheep needs to be understanding of the lions' rougher nature and learn to live at peace with them like all the other sheep." Eventually, the lions would kill and eat their prey. The man never missed it. He was only relieved that it had stopped bleating.

The weaker sheep were also wiser than the man. They saw that the sheepfold wasn't safe. They began to stay near the doors, waiting for the man to enter. When the door opened, they would dart through it to escape to safety. They knew they would be safer outside the sheepfold. They knew they would find grass to eat and bushes to hide in. When the man saw them flee, he only shook his head and called them foolish. Only a foolish sheep would flee the safety of the sheepfold his father had built. He decided they were unworthy sheep. He saw that the stronger sheep were not fleeing and decided they were worthy sheep. He was not concerned that his flock was shrinking as the vulnerable sheep fled. He did not go after the fleeing sheep to protect and help them. Instead, he determined to go raiding again in hopes of finding more worthy sheep to fill his sheepfold.

The other Maasai men were wiser than him, and they criticized the man's careless shepherding, but he replied that his shepherding demonstrated his deep honor for his father and his love for the sheep. He told them that he knew his father was the greatest and wisest father. He insisted that this meant that his father's walls were truly the best and safest walls, and that all sheep would be safest within his father's walls rather than within the walls of other sheepfolds. He accused the other Maasai men of hating his father for holding him accountable for his failure to protect the sheep. Yet the man's father had indeed been a very wise man, who had taught his son how to inspect and repair the walls

Ruth Barron
**The Rain Reveals the Leaks: How the Vulnerability
of the "Least of These" Reveals the Vulnerabilities in our Own Hearts and Systems**

and how to shepherd wisely and provide for and protect the sheep. It was the son who despised and neglected the teaching of his father, and the wise counsel of the other Maasai men was that he should follow his father's teachings. Yet the man called their wisdom foolishness and his own foolishness wisdom, and thus he made the sheepfold his wise father had built a destroyer of sheep rather than a protector of sheep.

What is the greatest vulnerability in this parable? There are many vulnerabilities. There are the "weaker sheep." Will strengthening these sheep protect the flock from predators? No. The predators will only target different sheep. There is the inadequate supply of food, causing the sheep to compete for food. Will providing more food protect the flock from predators? No. The culture of the strong taking from the weak will remain. There are the leopards and lions living with the flock. Will removing individual predators protect the flock? Not fully. Other predators will still enter the sheepfold. The single greatest vulnerability in the parable is the man's own assumptions, and the single greatest step that could be taken to protect the flock would be for the man to question his assumptions and to assess for vulnerabilities within his own walls and his own shepherding system. The same is true in the church. "The biggest and most costly mistake church leadership can make related to child sexual abuse is assuming 'it can't happen here.'"[16] In my work urging the Church to address abuse, I have found that church leaders consistently rely on their own assumptions, but this tendency is not found only in individual leaders. Christian institutions and entire denominations live as the foolish shepherd in my parable does, as one leader told me when I urged for an assessment to be made: "I just don't think our denomination struggles with abuse like other denominations do." It is essential that we understand that the primary vulnerability of the church regarding molestation is our unwillingness to examine our walls and to admit the truth of what such an analysis reveals.

The Broken Silence report calls for pastoral "awareness" of the issue, finding that "an overwhelming majority" of the Christian faith leaders who responded to their survey (74%) "underestimate the level of sexual and domestic violence experienced within their congregations."[17] 65% of the respondents reported that they address sexual or domestic violence from the pulpit at most one time a year, with 10% reporting they never address it.[18] Additionally, 62% reported that they have offered couple marriage counseling to the batterer and spouse when responding to sexual or domestic violence within their congregations. Broken Silence noted that this is alarming: "a potentially dangerous or even potentially

---

[16] Floyd, "Child Sexual Abuse and the Church."
[17] "Broken Silence: A Call for Churches to Speak Out."
[18] "Broken Silence: A Call for Churches to Speak Out."

lethal response."[19] The Faith Trust Institute policy statement regarding domestic violence states that "Couple counseling is not a viable therapeutic tool for use in violent family relationships."[20] Again, we see that pastoral presumptions shape their regular preaching as well as their responses to specific abuse cases and that these presumptions lead to increased risk for church members who are already experiencing violence. I believe we must go beyond pastoral awareness. Every member of our congregations must become more aware of these issues. Jeff Vines, who was mentored by apologist Ravi Zacharias, addressed the need for church members to be watchful in the aftermath of the revelations that Zacharias had been a serial sexual predator. "Those of us in leadership who are on the wrong path are depending on the fact that you don't want to know about it. Any organization in this day and age that does not create systems of accountability will eventually come to ruin." He stressed that we must stop giving our leaders "the ultimate benefit of a doubt."[21] Every member of our churches must become more educated and watchful regarding sexual abuse.

How do these presumptions affect our responses to the threat of molestation? A few years ago, a friend told me that while visiting another family, a man was ogling her teenage daughter. The two mothers pulled the daughter aside and urged her to add extra covering to her body, even though she was already dressed modestly. This is a very common response, but does changing clothing protect girls and women from sexual assault? Jen Brockman and Dr. Mary Wyandt-Hiebert's 2013 art exhibit at the University of Arkansas entitled "What Were You Wearing? Survivor Art Installation" featured sexual assault victim's clothing to show how flawed this presumption is.[22] Since then, many eponymous exhibits have opened. In their online exhibit, the Dove Center urges visitors to challenge our "own long-held beliefs about sexual assault that are, in reality, myths and stereotypes that can aid perpetrators of crime in avoiding accountability for their choices."[23] Speaking at the opening of the UN headquarters exhibit in New York in 2022, Deputy Secretary-General of the United Nations Amina Mohammed stated that the clothing in the exhibit "demonstrate[s] more clearly than any legal argument could that women and girls are attacked regardless of what they were wearing. The power of some of

---

[19] "Broken Silence: A Call for Churches to Speak Out."
[20] Phyllis B. Frank and Beverly D. Houghton, "A Policy Statement on Domestic Violence Couples Counseling."
[21] Daniel Silliman, "Missions Organizations Urged to Assess Abuse Accountability."
[22] "What Where You Wearing?" (WWYW) Installation.
[23] "'What Were You Wearing?' Exhibit — DOVE Center of St. George Utah."

these clothes lies in their ordinariness."[24] She called on the UN to place the blame for sexual violence on "gender inequality" and on "patriarchal structures in our societies."[25] Sexual molestation is not caused by the victim's clothing.

In Matthew 5:28 Jesus says, "I tell you that anyone who looks at a woman lustfully has already committed adultery with her in his heart." He tells those who lust, "If your right eye causes you to stumble, gouge it out and throw it away. It is better for you to lose one part of your body than for your whole body to be thrown into hell" (v. 29). This concept is so important that he repeats it nearly verbatim, "And if your right hand causes you to stumble, cut it off and throw it away. It is better for you to lose one part of your body than for your whole body to go into hell" (v. 30). We can see the truth of this teaching in the story of David and Bathsheba. David was walking on his roof and chanced to see Bathsheba bathing, which led him to send for her and then rape her. We can infer that David saw parts of Bathsheba's body which were erotic to him, yet God does not place the blame on Bathsheba for tempting David with her exposed skin. In his parable, Nathan displays Bathsheba as an innocent lamb, and lays the blame fully on David, "Why did you despise the word of the LORD by doing what is evil in his eyes?" (2 Sam 12:7, 9). God did not blame David's crime on the body of Bathsheba but on the wickedness in David's own heart; David's culpability is his heart vulnerability. Even if a man sees a woman or child naked, he is still accountable for his own lustful thoughts and actions. Victims are not responsible for abuse; the perpetrator is.[26]

---

[24] "What Were You Wearing? UN Exhibit Demands Justice for Survivors of Sexual Violence | Spotlight Initiative."

[25] "What Were You Wearing? UN Exhibit Demands Justice."

[26] There is a dangerous trend which works very hard to blame Bathsheba and to exonerate, or at least excuse, David. See, for example, Randall C. Bailey, *David in Love and War: The Pursuit of Power in 2 Samuel 10-12*, Journal for the Study of the Old Testament Supplement Series 75 (Sheffield, England: JSOT Press, 1990), 86; Cheryl A. Kirk-Duggan, "Slingshots, Ships, and Personal Psychosis: Murder, Sexual Intrigue, and Power in the Lives of David and Othello," in *Pregnant Passion: Gender, Sex, and Violence in the Bible*, Semeia Studies 44 (Atlanta: Society of Biblical Literature, 2003), 59; Lillian R. Klein, *From Deborah to Esther: Sexual politics in the Hebrew Bible* (Minneapolis, Minnesota: Fortress, 2003), 56; and Nigerian scholar Honor Sewapo, "Seduction of Leadership Success: A Reconsideration of King David and Bathsheba Seductive Practice," *Insight: Journal of Religious Studies* 10 (2014): 51-66. All such treatments are guilty of eisegesis. In both the Hebrew MT and the Greek LXX, the biblical text only blames David and refers to Bathsheba as "a lamb," both innocent and the victim.

For responsible exegesis of this narrative, see Jennifer I. Andruska, "'Rape' in the syntax of 2 Samuel 11:4," *Zeitschrift für die alttestamentliche Wissenschaft* 129, no. 1 (2017): 103–109; Richard M. Davidson, *Flame of Yahweh: Sexuality in the Old*

Ruth Barron
The Rain Reveals the Leaks: How the Vulnerability of the "Least of These" Reveals the Vulnerabilities in our Own Hearts and Systems

Kgaugelo Lekalakala researched the justifying narratives given by perpetrators of child sexual abuse in South Africa. She found two main rationales. First, there was childhood adversity, accentuated by dissatisfaction in adulthood with their relationships with women.[27] This justification gives context for molestation, but it cannot be an explanation, because, as many scholars and lay people have observed, this does not account for the existence of the many people who face childhood adversity and struggle with dissatisfaction in adult relationships who do *not* go on to commit child sexual abuse. Second, her research revealed "pro-abusive attitudes to women and young children" in the justifications offered by the perpetrators.[28] Their narratives demonstrated the ways in which "socio-cultural factors including patriarchal notions of manhood, mainly a belief in sexual entitlement, are used to justify CSA."[29] She concluded that these factors led to a failure to accept responsibility and to victim-blaming.[30] As we discussed above, God confronts the heart vulnerability of the powerful regarding their assaults on the physical vulnerability of the weak, calling them toward ownership of responsibility for their own sinful actions, and we see this in the parable the prophet Nathan told David. Nathan tells David, "You are the man!" (2 Sam 12:7), indicating that David is the guilty party in the rape of Bathsheba and murder of Uriah. God held David accountable for his sins against both Uriah and Bathsheba, and we see David taking responsibility for his sinful actions in Psalm 51: "For I know my transgressions, / and my sin is always before me."

However, Nathan's parable also reveals a sense of entitlement in David. The parable describes David as a wealthy man with many sheep, who, when an unexpected guest arrives, steals a poor man's beloved only sheep. David's power and wealth led to his failure to esteem the humanity of those less powerful, which led him to rape and murder. God urges David to recognize this vulnerability within his heart. However, David's confession in Psalm 51 reveals that, while David accepted responsibility for his sinful actions, he continued to dismiss the inherent worth of his fellow human beings as demonstrated in verse 4: "Against you, you only, have I sinned / and done what is evil in your sight; / so you are right in your verdict / and justified when you judge." David failed to

---

Testament (Peabody, Massachusetts: Hendrickson, 2007), 523–532; David E. Garland and Diana R. Garland, "Bathsheba's Story: Surviving Abuse and Devastating Loss," Chapter 6 in *Flawed Families of the Bible: How God's Grace Works through Imperfect Relationships*, 153–177 (Grand Rapids, Michigan: Brazos, 2007); and Nigerian scholar Solomon O. Ademiluka, "Interpreting the David–Bathsheba narrative (2 Sm 11:2–4)."

[27] Kgauhelo Lekalakala, "The Use of Patriarchy and a Sense of Entitlement in Justifying Gender-Based Violence Including Sexual Abuse of Young Children."

[28] Lekalakala, "The Use of Patriarchy and a Sense of Entitlement."

[29] Lekalakala, "The Use of Patriarchy and a Sense of Entitlement."

[30] Lekalakala, "The Use of Patriarchy and a Sense of Entitlement."

Ruth Barron
The Rain Reveals the Leaks: How the Vulnerability of the "Least of These" Reveals the Vulnerabilities in our Own Hearts and Systems

recognize the humanity of Uriah and Bathsheba. As Nathan prophesied, that heart cause, the unconquered vulnerability of the powerful despising the humanity of the less powerful, continued to wreak destruction in the lives of his descendants. Keltner states that "contexts of unchecked power make many of us vulnerable to, and complicit in, the abuse of power," as we saw in King David.[31] Keltner argues that three things are needful to remedy this: 1) Even though the stories of the abused are overwhelming to hear, we must grow our capacity for distress and listen to these stories; 2) We need more women in positions of power; and 3) as has been noted above, we must challenge "the myths that sustain the abuses of power."[32] I believe these three remedies offer a special challenge to pastors to address in their preaching. As just one example, pastors must examine how they teach the David and Bathsheba story and David's confession in Psalm 51 to ensure they are not teaching in ways that perpetuate abuser justifications and victim blaming but rather preach in ways that challenge the powerful to recognize the full humanity of women and children.

Although the story of Cain and Abel is about murder rather than molestation, I believe it also offers wisdom for us as we consider vulnerability, molestation, and the church's response. Just before Cain murders his brother Abel, the Bible tells us that God pulled one of the brothers aside and warns him that he is vulnerable and in danger of being destroyed. Which brother does God warn? Abel, who is about to be murdered by Cain, is physically vulnerable, yet God confronts Cain regarding *his* vulnerability. God warns Cain that sin is seeking to dominate him and urges him to conquer the sin instead: "Why are you angry? Why is your face downcast? If you do what is right, will you not be accepted? But if you do not do what is right, sin is crouching at your door; it desires to have you, but you must rule over it" (Gen 4:6–7). God's choice is unsettling. Why didn't God warn Abel and send him away to preserve his life? The story focuses on Cain rather than Abel. Perhaps God did warn Abel, but Abel simply couldn't comprehend that a brother could actually kill a brother, and perhaps, like Cain, the idea of fleeing his community for safety felt like a certain death sentence. We can't argue from silence. What we are told is that God warned Cain that he was vulnerable. The abuser is vulnerable, and the abuser must be confronted. As illustrated in the story about my friend's daughter, we regularly choose ineffective strategies to prevent abuse and place burdensome demands on those who are physically vulnerable. Instead, we must confront the vulnerability in the hearts of the molesters. I ask us to consider ourselves in the position of the women. Would we have urged the daughter or the ogler to change their behavior? As the Dove Center suggests, we must hold

---

[31] Dagher Keltner, "What the Science of Power Can Tell Us About Sexual Harassment."
[32] Keltner, "What the Science of Power Can Tell Us."

the abusers themselves accountable. We must also address the harmful gendered biases and systems within our churches and societies and confront our own vulnerabilities evidenced in our failure to confront those who endanger women and children.

Noting the reality that victims of sexual assault experience the reporting process as an additional significant trauma, Nicole Bedera analyzed how one US university responded to abuse allegations.[33] Like churches, despite statistics showing that 1 in 5 women students will experience sexual assault, and 1 in 10 men students will *commit* at least one act of sexual assault during university, university leaders insist that *their* individual institutions are the exception, and that students at their schools neither experience nor commit sexual assault.[34] She notes that in justifying their refusal to respond appropriately to sexual violence, they relied on victim-blaming stereotypes[35] and "himpathy," a term coined by Manne to describe gendered sympathy, which prioritizes the narratives of men who perpetrate sexual assault over the experiences of their victims.[36] As one example, university staff justified their refusal to address sexual assault by citing concern that they might ruin the young man's career by holding him accountable. Yet they failed to acknowledge that their refusal to address assault greatly impacted the victim's studies and career. Gendered stereotypes allowed them to bypass the impact on the victims either by insisting that the victims had simply misunderstood the nature of their own assault due to hysteria or that the victims "were already damaged beyond repair" and could not be remedied by any action the university took.[37] Bedera notes that contrary to the claims of university staff, a positive outcome was of vital importance for victims, and adds that leaders "had the capacity to learn about the impact" their refusal to act had upon the victim, but instead, they insulated themselves from the victim's stories. She adds, "As a result, there was no tension in administrators' use of himpathy — their full attention was on the perpetrator."[38]

---

[33] Nichole Bedera, "I Can Protect His Future, but She Can't Be Helped: Himpathy and Hysteria in Administrator Rationalizations of Institutional Betrayal."

[34] Bedera, "I Can Protect His Future, but She Can't Be Helped," 1; citing Hayley Munguia, "College presidents appear to be delusional about sexual assault on their campuses," *FiveThirtyEight*, 13 March 2015, https://fivethirtyeight.com/features/college-presidents-appear-to-be-delusional-about-sexual-assault-on-their-campuses/

[35] Bedera, "I Can Protect His Future, but She Can't Be Helped," 4.

[36] Bedera, "I Can Protect His Future, but She Can't Be Helped," 3.

[37] Bedera, "I Can Protect His Future, but She Can't Be Helped," 18.

[38] Bedera, "I Can Protect His Future, but She Can't Be Helped," 20.

Psychologist Jessica Freyd coined the terms "institutional betrayal"[39] and "betrayal trauma"[40] to describe this phenomenon and its impact. As a result of her research, Freyd founded an organization called "Center for Institutional Courage." The Center's website acknowledges our dependence on organizations for our well-being. We need schools and hospitals and churches and other institutions, but often, these institutions fail us when we need them most deeply. "We are in a terrible bind: **we depend on institutions that betray us.**"[41] Yet institutions fail us out of fear of their own vulnerability. If they acknowledge and address the harm, they fear decreased profits or even the destruction of the organization itself. It seems better to sacrifice the victims than to risk harm to the organization and its mission. Yet, as the Center notes, institutional betrayal harms everyone involved, including the institution itself. Institutional betrayal *causes* the very harm it seeks to prevent. As a result, the Center calls for "institutional courage," which they define as:

> ... an institution's commitment to seek the truth and engage in moral action, despite unpleasantness, risk, and short-term cost. It is a pledge to protect and care for those who depend on the institution. It is a compass oriented to the common good of individuals, institutions, and the world. It is a force that transforms institutions into more accountable, equitable, effective places for everyone.[42]

Institutional courage is not, Freyd argues, a fixed resource which you either have or lack. Instead, it is a resource we must cultivate and grow. This is a helpful framework for the church as we seek to address sexual assault. As Danya Ruttenberg notes, demands for perfection can prevent us from acting at all.[43] I would also note that demands for perfection often lead to abuse.

In her book *On Repentance and Repair*, Ruttenberg argues that "institutional repentance" is necessary in the aftermath of institutional betrayal. This repentance must contain two elements: 1) It must address the acts of betrayal which have already occurred, and 2) it must ensure that the organization will take a different course of action the next time such situations arise. She found that when organizations do the first part well, the second will

---

[39] Danya Ruttenberg, *On Repentance and Repair: Making Amends in an Unapologetic World*, 105; citing Carly Parnitzke Smith and Jennifer J. Freyd, "Dangerous Safe Havens: Institutional Betrayal Exacerbates Sexual Trauma," *Journal of Traumatic Stress* 26, no. 1 (2013): 119–124.

[40] Jennifer J. Freyd, *Betrayal Trauma: The Logic of Forgetting Childhood Abuse*.

[41] Jennifer Freyd, "The Call to Courage."

[42] Jennifer Freyd, "The Call to Courage;" see also Ruttenberg, *On Repentance and Repair*, 107.

[43] Ruttenberg, *On Repentance and Repair*, 108.

naturally follow.[44] When an institution commits to address past harm by "transparent investigation, apology, and compensation," it meets the needs of both victims and institutions.[45] Often, institutions want to bypass step 1 and skip to step 2, as one pastor told me, "You are going about this wrong. Instead of focusing on the harms done in the past, just focus on putting better systems in place for the future." He told me that I would alienate people by pointing out the harm their actions have caused to victims in the past. But as Ruttenberg points out, it is this very process of examining the past which makes it possible for us to do better in the future.[46] Through investigation of our past mistakes, in which we truly listen to the victims' stories and study how we have failed them, we are enabled to do the work both to make the past harms right and to prevent future harm. As Ruttenberg notes, we often minimize the value of apology, but true victim-centered apologies combined with restitution are deeply healing to the victim and enable us to do better in the future.[47] Too often, as seen in David's confession in Psalm 51, our apologies and our efforts at change bypass the very people we have harmed. And as in David's story, this leads to the continuation of the same harmful and dehumanizing patterns.

One particular way in which churches prioritize the abuser over the victim is exemplified at the beginning of this paper. We emphasize a demand that victims forgive their abusers and shame victims for their on-going trauma while ignoring the need to hold abusers accountable so as not to shame them. This conveys the message that it is a worse sin to be a wounded victim than it is to harm another person. As I have examined our teachings on forgiveness, I have consistently found cognitively dissonant teachings. Cognitive dissonance is an important term, especially for those studying abuse and trauma. It refers to "the state of having inconsistent thoughts, beliefs, or attitudes, especially as relating to behavioral decisions and attitude change."[48] For example, Olusola and Ogunlusi spend one paragraph on the need for victim forgiveness. They begin with the thesis that forgiveness is important. Their first two subpoints, however, state that forgiveness teachings can be deeply hurtful to victims. Their third point suggests that the pastor assure the victim of God's love and God's assumption of the guilt of the abuser and the community's support. Their conclusion reiterates the importance of victim forgiveness.[49] I find it interesting that two of their three points undercut their thesis, yet they don't question that

---

[44] Ruttenberg, *On Repentance and Repair*, 97–114.
[45] Ruttenberg, *On Repentance and Repair*, 107.
[46] Ruttenberg, *On Repentance and Repair*, 108–109.
[47] Ruttenberg, *On Repentance and Repair*, 106–107.
[48] *New American Oxford Dictionary*, s.v. "Cognitive dissonance," (Oxford: Oxford University Press, 2022).
[49] Olusola and Ogunlusi, "Recurring Cases of Child Rape in Nigeria," 64.

thesis. I agree with them that rushing to forgiveness is harmful to victims. It takes responsibility away from the abuser who caused the harm and places it on the victim who received the harm. This places a heavy burden on the back of someone who has, essentially, been brutally whipped. Luke 17:3 states, "If your brother or sister sins against you, rebuke them; and if they repent, forgive them." Our first focus must be on abuser repentance and on teaching what true repentance looks like. As Ruttenberg noted above, if those who have caused harm truly take the time to hear the victim's story and examine their own sinful beliefs and actions and make restitution, then forgiveness will follow. After the healing process of justice, forgiveness will become an easy yoke to bear rather than a heavy burden on a bloody back.

Gerrie Snyman states, "a hermeneutic of vulnerability is imperative for a perpetrator in order to enable him or her to become more response-able and responsible to those who are still bearing the marks of apartheid."[50] The same is true of molestation. For both the molester and those who enabled the molester, the vulnerability of grief and shame for their harmful actions and dehumanizing attitudes is a necessary step toward wholeness. Too often in the church, we demand "grace" in response to molesters and their enablers, a grace that silences the victim and allows those who caused harm to bypass the harm they caused. I offer Zechariah 12:10 as a more righteous example of grace.

> And I will pour out on the house of David and the inhabitants of Jerusalem a spirit of grace and supplication. They will look on me, the one they have pierced, and they will mourn for him as one mourns for an only child, and grieve bitterly for him as one grieves for a firstborn son.

Zechariah promises those who have committed harm a "spirit of grace and supplication" which will enable them to look upon those they have harmed and overflow with grief. This is true grace. As Snyman explains, "as long as the latter remains ideologically committed to the victim's lack of humanity" the memory of the committed "atrocities will only keep on haunting the perpetrator."[51] We must realize that "release from guilt can be measured by a person's ability to bear the reality of victim's suffering. As long as the victim's humanity is denied, no release takes place."[52] We must not quench the work of the Holy Spirit in the hearts of those who have caused harm by offering them a grace which bypasses the harm they have caused, and which ignores the humanity and the needs of their victims.

As we have seen, our children need safety from the rains. The molestation of children is widespread around the world. Yet the church has no safety to offer

---

[50] Gerrie Snyman, "A Hermeneutic of Vulnerability: Redeeming Cain?," 636–637.
[51] Snyman, "A Hermeneutic of Vulnerability," 653.
[52] Snyman, "A Hermeneutic of Vulnerability," 653.

children because our roof is riddled with leaks. We have relied on the presumption that our roof is secure rather than regularly inspecting our churches both during the dry season, with a goal toward finding and addressing the holes which are developing before the rains arrive, and during the rainy season, with the goal of ensuring that we have done the work well. This failure to inspect the roof of the church has created the conditions necessary for abuse to flourish in our churches. Furthermore, when the rains have revealed the leaks we failed to repair, rather than addressing those leaks, the church has blamed the victims and placed the burden of preventing their own abuse on them, essentially handing them an umbrella and telling them to hold it over their heads. This is ineffective. Our children need true shelter. We have seen that we must address the vulnerabilities in both the hearts of the molesters themselves and in the hearts of those enabling the molesters. We must also address both the immediate sinful actions and the underlying dehumanizing attitudes which caused the actions. This requires accountability for the abusers and enablers and restitution for the victims. Key to this is truly facing the harm we have done to the victims.

I offer a parable intersecting Maasai and Israelite culture as a framework for accomplishing this. As I shared in my recently published piece, "Bitter Roots and Bitter Herbs,"[53] Jewish law commanded the Israelites to include bitter herbs in their Passover celebrations. These herbs were to serve as a remembrance of the bitterness of their captivity in Egypt. God called the Israelites to remember their own bitter captivity as a reminder that they must treat foreigners living among them as "native-born." The remembrance was to help them see the humanity of those who were easily "othered" in their midst. Maasai women mix bitter leaves with the mud they use to build their houses. These herbs are used to prevent termites from eating away at the wood which gives the house its strength. As we repair the roof of the church, we must be sure to include the bitter herbs of remembrance of the harm we have caused victims in our failure to address molestation and victim dehumanization.

Bibliography

ADEMILUKA, Solomon O. "Interpreting the David–Bathsheba narrative (2 Sm 11:2–4) as a response by the church in Nigeria to masculine abuse of power for sexual assault." *HTS Teologiese Studies/ Theological Studies* 77, no. 4 (2021): Article #5802, 11 pages. https://doi.org/10.4102/hts.v77i4.5802

---

[53] Ruth Barron, "Bitter Roots and Bitter Herbs."

AKANNI, Abdul Hakeem A. "Evil Men in the House of God: An Analytical Study of the Involvement of Christian and Muslim Clerics in Crime in Nigeria." *KIU Journal of Humanities* 5, no. 3 (October 30, 2020): 251–263. https://ijhumas.com/ojs/index.php/niuhums/article/view/1042

BARRON, Ruth. "Bitter Roots and Bitter Herbs." *Mutuality*, CBE International, 30 August 2023. https://www.cbeinternational.org/resource/bitter-roots-and-bitter-herbs/

BEDERA, Nicole. "I Can Protect His Future, but She Can't Be Helped: Himpathy and Hysteria in Administrator Rationalizations of Institutional Betrayal." *The Journal of Higher Education* 95, no. 1 (2023): 30–53. https://doi.org/10.1080/00221546.2023.2195771

"Broken Silence: A Call for Churches to Speak Out." Protestant Pastors Survey on Sexual and Domestic Violence. Washington, DC, USA: Sojourners, 2014. https://sojo.net/sites/default/files/Broken%20 Silence%20Report.pdf

EDE, Victor Ifeanyi, and Dominic Zuoke KALU. "Child Abuse in Nigeria: Responses of Christian Churches and the Way Out." *International Journal for Innovative Research in Multidisciplinary Field* 4, no. 4 (April 2018): 46–53. https://www.ijirmf.com/wp-content/uploads/IJIRMF201804008.pdf

End Violence Against Children. "Global Threat Assessment 2021 Shows Dramatic Increase in Online Child Sexual Exploitation & Abuse | End Violence." Accessed August 9, 2023. https://www.end-violence.org/articles/global-threat-assessment-2021-shows-dramatic-increase-online-child-sexual-exploitation

FLOYD, Scott. "Child Sexual Abuse and the Church: How Widespread Is the Problem?" *Baptist Standard*, 22 August 2018. https://www.baptiststandard.com/falling-seed/child-sexual-abuse-church-widespread-problem/

FRANK, Phyllis B., and Beverly D. HOUGHTON. "A Policy Statement on Domestic Violence Couples Counseling." In *Confronting the Batterer: A Guide to Creating the Spouse Abuse Educational Workshop*. Edited by Judi Fisher. New York: Volunteer Counseling Service of Rockland County, 1982. Excerpted by Faith Trust Institute, n.d., https://www.faithtrustinstitute.org/resources/articles/Policy-Statement-on-DV-Couples-Counseling.pdf

FREYD, Jennifer J. *Betrayal Trauma: The Logic of Forgetting Childhood Abuse*. Revised edition. Cambridge, Massachusetts: Harvard University Press, 1998.

———. "The Call to Courage." Center for Institutional Courage. n.d. https://www.institutionalcourage.org/the-call-to-courage

HADITHI, Mwenye, and Adrienne KENNAWAY. *Lazy Lion*. London: Hodder Children's Books, 2005.

KELTNER, Dagher. "What the Science of Power Can Tell Us About Sexual Harassment." Greater Good, 18 October 2017. https://greatergood.berkeley.edu/article/item/what_the_science_of_power_can_tell_us_about_sexual_harassment

LEKALAKALA, Kgauhelo. "The Use of Patriarchy and a Sense of Entitlement in Justifying Gender-Based Violence Including Sexual Abuse of Young Children." Presented at the 4th International Conference, SVRI Forum 2015, Innovation and Intersections, Stellenbosch, South Africa, 15 September 2015. https://www.svri.org/forums/forum2015/ presentations/Patriarchy.pdf

OLUSOLA, Adesanya Ibiyinka, and Clement OGUNLUSI. "Recurring Cases of Child Rape in Nigeria: An Issue for Church Intervention." *INSANCITA: Journal of Islamic Studies in Indonesia and Southeast Asia* 5, no. 1 (February 2020): 55–72. https://www.journals.mindamas.com/index.php/insancita/article/view/1331

"On Child Sexual Abuse | Joshua Center on Child Sexual Abuse." Joshua Center on Child Sexual Abuse Prevention. n.d. https://uwjoshuacenter.org/series/child-sexual-abuse

PATON, Alan. *Cry, the Beloved Country*. New York: Charles Scribner's Sons, 1948.

RUTTENBERG, Danya. *On Repentance and Repair: Making Amends in an Unapologetic World*. Boston: Beacon Press, 2022.

SALTER, Anna C. *Predators: Pedophiles, Rapists, and Other Sex Offenders: Who They Are, How They Operate and How We Can Protect Ourselves and Our Children*. New York: BasicBooks, 2004.

SILLIMAN, Daniel. "Missions Organizations Urged to Assess Abuse Accountability." News & Reporting, *Christianity Today*, 22 November 2021. https://www.christianitytoday.com/news/2021/november/missions-icom-ravi-zacharias-accountability-jeff-vines-cmfi.html

SNYMAN, Gerrie. "A Hermeneutic of Vulnerability: Redeeming Cain?" *Stellenbosch Theological Journal* 1, no. 2 (2016). https://doi.org/10.17570/stj.2015.v1n2.a30

TCHIVIDJIAN, Boz. "Startling Statistics: Child Sexual Abuse and What the Church Can Do About It." GRACE, 9 January 2014. https://www.netgrace.org/resources/startling-statistics

"'What Were You Wearing?' Exhibit - DOVE Center of St. George Utah," 25 April 2020. https://dovecenter.org/what-were-you-wearing-exhibit/

"What Were You Wearing? UN Exhibit Demands Justice for Survivors of Sexual Violence | Spotlight Initiative." Accessed 10 September 2023. https://spotlightinitiative.org/news/what-were-you-wearing-un-exhibit-demands-justice-survivors-sexual-violence

WIHBEY, John. "Global Prevalence of Child Sexual Abuse." Criminal Justice, Race & Gender. The Journalist's Resource. 15 November 2011. https://journalistsresource.org/criminal-justice/global-prevalence-child-sexual-abuse/

"What Were You Wearing?" (WWYW) Installation. Sexual Assault Prevention & Education Center, University of Kansas. Accessed 10 September 2023. https://sapec.ku.edu/wwyw

Africa's Aquifers
Reflections on John S. Mbiti's Contributions to African Christian Spirituality

Diane B. STINTON

ORCID: 0000-0003-0541-8863
Regent College, Vancouver, Canada
dstinton@regent-college.edu

Abstract

While John S. Mbiti (1931–2019) is highly acclaimed for his scholarly contributions to the fields of African religion and philosophy, little attention has been paid to his reflections on African Christian spirituality. Arguing vehemently against "imported Christianity," he contends that only a genuine encounter between African religiosity and the Christian faith will quench the spiritual thirst of African peoples. This essay identifies and explores a few key contributions Mbiti offers in this regard and outlines certain critiques of his work. The central argument is that like the tremendous resource of Africa's vast aquifers, African religiosity is a deep, enduring reservoir for enriching the understanding and experience of African Christian spirituality. Examples of the wellsprings of African religiosity that African Christian spirituality draws from include prayer, a unified worldview that does not erect dichotomies between the physical and spiritual realms, and a deeply communal orientation. Mbiti also underlines that certain elements within African religion require discernment in light of the gospel, so that Africans' prior religious experience might be transposed into the fullness of life in Christ. Thus, African Christian spirituality can enhance not only the faith experience of African believers, but also followers of Jesus throughout the world who seek to deepen their spiritual lives.

Résumé

Bien que John S. Mbiti (1931–2019) soit très apprécié pour ses contributions scientifiques dans les domaines de la religion et de la philosophie africaines, peu d'attention a été accordée à ses réflexions sur la spiritualité chrétienne africaine. S'élevant avec véhémence contre le "christianisme importé", il soutient que seule une rencontre authentique entre la religiosité africaine et la foi chrétienne pourra étancher la soif spirituelle des peuples africains. Cet essai identifie et explore quelques

Diane B. Stinton
Africa's Aquifers: Reflections on John S. Mbiti's Contributions to African Christian Spirituality

contributions clés de Mbiti à cet égard et présente certaines critiques de son travail. L'argument central est qu'à l'instar de l'énorme ressource que constituent les vastes aquifères de l'Afrique, la religiosité africaine est un réservoir profond et durable qui permet d'enrichir la compréhension et l'expérience de la spiritualité chrétienne africaine. Parmi les sources de la religiosité africaine dans lesquelles puise la spiritualité chrétienne africaine, on peut citer la prière, une vision unifiée du monde qui n'érige pas de dichotomie entre les domaines physique et spirituel, et une orientation profondément communautaire. Mbiti souligne également que certains éléments de la religion africaine nécessitent un discernement à la lumière de l'Évangile, afin que l'expérience religieuse antérieure des Africains puisse être transposée dans la plénitude de la vie en Christ. Ainsi, la spiritualité chrétienne africaine peut enrichir non seulement l'expérience de foi des croyants africains, mais aussi celle des disciples de Jésus du monde entier qui cherchent à approfondir leur vie spirituelle.

Resumo

Embora John S. Mbiti (1931–2019) seja muito aclamado pelas suas contribuições académicas para os campos da religião e da filosofia africanas, pouca atenção tem sido dada às suas reflexões sobre a espiritualidade cristã africana. Argumentando com veemência contra o "cristianismo importado", defende que só um encontro genuíno entre a religiosidade africana e a fé cristã poderá saciar a sede espiritual dos povos africanos. Este ensaio identifica e explora algumas das principais contribuições que Mbiti oferece a este respeito e apresenta algumas críticas ao seu trabalho. O argumento central é que, tal como o enorme recurso dos vastos aquíferos de África, a religiosidade africana é um reservatório profundo e duradouro para enriquecer a compreensão e a experiência da espiritualidade cristã africana. Entre os exemplos de fontes da religiosidade africana de que a espiritualidade cristã africana se alimenta contam-se a oração, uma visão unificada do mundo que não estabelece dicotomias entre os domínios físico e espiritual, e uma orientação profundamente comunitária. Mbiti também sublinha que certos elementos da religião africana requerem discernimento à luz do Evangelho, para que a experiência religiosa anterior dos africanos possa ser transposta para a plenitude da vida em Cristo. Assim, a espiritualidade cristã africana pode melhorar não só a experiência de fé dos crentes africanos, mas também dos seguidores de Jesus em todo o mundo que procuram aprofundar a sua vida espiritual.

Keywords

John S. Mbiti, African spirituality, African religiosity

Diane B. Stinton
Africa's Aquifers: Reflections on John S. Mbiti's Contributions to African Christian Spirituality

Mots-clés

John S. Mbiti, spiritualité africaine, religiosité africaine

Palavras-chave

John S. Mbiti, espiritualidade africana, religiosidade africana

> *Jesus said, "Anyone who drinks the water I give will never thirst — not ever. The water I give will be an artesian spring within, gushing fountains of endless life."*
>
> (John 4:13–14, The Message)

> *"The river swells with the contribution of the streams."*
>
> (Bateke proverb[1])

A decade ago, discoveries of Africa's aquifers — massive reserves of underground water — created a stir within and beyond Africa. Studies in Africa's geology found aquifers to be highly prevalent across the continent, even in some of the driest places such as the Turkana region in northwest Kenya and the Nubian Sandstone reservoir North Africa spanning Libya, Egypt, Sudan, and Chad. Water experts estimated that Africa's aquifers, filled with new or ancient rain, hold "more than 100 times the annual renewable freshwater resources in dams and rivers, and 20 times the freshwater stored in the Africa's lakes."[2] Despite the excitement at these enormous resources for easing water shortages, experts cautioned that the water quality within them was not always drinkable on account of the iron or saline content and other pollutants. Additional challenges in accessing the underground springs led to the conclusion that "they're not always going to help address water scarcity."[3]

Half a century ago, John S. Mbiti (1931–2019) created a similar stir within and beyond Africa with his fresh "discovery" of African religions. Against longstanding denigration of African religions by colonizers, anthropologists, and missionaries, Mbiti embarked upon extensive research of indigenous religions across the continent in attempt to rehabilitate African peoples' religious and cultural heritage. Moreover, he did so from the perspective of his Christian faith, despite strong criticism from both Christian scholars, suspecting

---

[1] The Bateke are a Bantu Central African ethnocultural group who live primarily in the Democratic Republic of Congo.
[2] Gaathier Mahed, "Africa's Aquifers Hold More than 20 Times the Water Stored in the Continent's Lakes, but They Aren't the Answer to Water Scarcity."
[3] Gaathier Mahed, "Africa's Aquifers."

Diane B. Stinton
Africa's Aquifers: Reflections on John S. Mbiti's Contributions to African Christian Spirituality

syncretism, and proponents of African religion, accusing him of misappropriating indigenous religion in the service of Christianity.

Through decades of scholarship, teaching, and pastoring, Mbiti became known to many as the father of modern African theology.[4] By 1979, he had gained "an international reputation as the leading African theologian."[5] Jesse N. K. Mugambi (b. 1947), another prominent African theologian, noted Mbiti's acclaim as "the most widely published and the most distinguished African scholar in the research fields of African expressions of Christianity and African religions and philosophy."[6] Henri Mbaya and Ntozakhe Cezula added that his place within these fields of study is "undoubtedly colossal."[7]

Mbiti's contributions have been rightly noted in these and other fields, including biblical studies and creative writing in European languages and in his own Kenyan mother-tongue, Kikamba. Surprisingly, however, very little attention has been given to date on his contributions to African Christian spirituality.[8] This oversight is even more striking given the tremendous surge of interest in Christian spirituality in recent decades and the relative lack of reflection on African resources. For example, in a 2001 historical survey, *The Story of Christian Spirituality: Two Thousand Years, from East to West*, the "story" of spirituality within twentieth-century Africa receives less than three pages out of a sixty-page summary of twentieth-century spiritualities, and out of the entire 367-page volume. Yet within those few pages, the author acknowledges that "on no continent did the Christian faith spread more rapidly in the twentieth century than in Africa.[9]

A further challenge, as Chioma Ohajunwa and Gubela Mji point out, is that "literature on spiritually has been historically permeated with Western understandings and definitions of spirituality . . . largely due to the influence of Christianity."[10] Reflecting on the Western missionary inheritance in Africa,

---

[4] E.g., in the DACB article on Mbiti, he is introduced as "generally acclaimed as the father of the Christian theology of African Traditional Religion (ATR) and of indigenous efforts for the inculturation of the Gospel on the continent." Francis Anekwe Oborji, "Mbiti, John Samuel."

[5] Adrian Hastings, *A History of African Christianity 1950–1975*, 232.

[6] Jesse N. K. Mugambi, "A Tribute to John S. Mbiti," 437.

[7] Henri Mbaya and Ntozakhe Cezula, "Contribution of John S Mbiti to the Study of African Religions and African Theology and Philosophy," 421.

[8] The only source I was able to find specifically on Mbiti's reflections on African Christian spirituality is Richard H. Schmidt, "John S. Mbiti: African Christian Spirituality."

[9] Bradley Holt, "Spiritualities of the Twentieth Century," 316.

[10] Chioma Ohajunwa and Gubela Mji, "The African Indigenous Lens of Understanding Spirituality: Reflection on Key Emerging Concepts from a Reviewed Literature," 2530.

Diane B. Stinton
Africa's Aquifers: Reflections on John S. Mbiti's Contributions to African Christian Spirituality

Mbiti repeatedly expresses appreciation for the sacrificial role of Western missionaries in proclaiming the Christian faith across the continent. Yet he famously declares, "The missionaries who introduced the gospel to Africa in the past 200 years did not bring God to our continent. Instead, God brought them."[11] Against the cultural imperialism that Africans often experienced within the Western missionary movement, Mbiti strongly contends that Christianity will only last in Africa through "a serious encounter of the Gospel with the indigenous African culture when the people voluntarily accept by faith the Gospel of Jesus Christ."[12] He is convinced that Africans have the resources to understand, articulate, and propagate the Christian faith, and he therefore argues vehemently against "imported Christianity":

> Until we can cultivate a genuine Christianity which is truly MADE IN AFRICA, we will be building on a shallow foundation and living on borrowed time. Let it be said once and for all, as loudly as technology can make it, that IMPORTED CHRISTIANITY WILL NEVER, NEVER QUENCH THE SPIRITUAL THIRST OF AFRICAN PEOPLES.[13]

Citing an African proverb, "that which comes from charity is never sufficient to fill the granary," Mbiti affirms that Africa desires and needs the gospel. However, he insists, it does not require imported Christianity "because too much of it will only castrate us spiritually or turn us into spiritual cripples."[14]

What, then, does Mbiti envision and advocate for African Christian spirituality? This essay identifies and explores a few key contributions which Mbiti offers in this regard. The central argument is that like the tremendous resource of Africa's vast aquifers, African religiosity is a deep, enduring reservoir for enriching the understanding and experience of African Christian spirituality. Following a brief introduction to the subject of African Christian spirituality, Mbiti's contributions and critiques of his work will be outlined before concluding reflections are offered.

African Christian Spirituality

If there is no word for "religion" in most African languages, as Mbiti points

---

[11] John Mbiti, "The Encounter of Christian Faith and African Religion," 818; emphasis original. This theological assumption remains contested, particularly among some evangelical scholars. For example, see Alistair I. Wilson, "'Missionaries Did Not Bring Christ to Africa – Christ Brought them' (Bediako/Mbiti)."
[12] John S. Mbiti, "Christianity and African Culture," 276.
[13] Mbiti, "Christianity and African Culture," 276; emphasis original.
[14] Mbiti, "Christianity and African Culture," 276.

Diane B. Stinton
Africa's Aquifers: Reflections on John S. Mbiti's Contributions to African Christian Spirituality

out,[15] there is also "no word . . . which denotes spiritual life or spirituality."[16] The reason, Mbiti explains and other scholars affirm, is that in Africa, "religion permeates into all departments of life so fully that it is not easy or possible always to isolate it. . . . Religion is in their whole system of being."[17] Indeed, Mbiti famously opened his early work, *African Religions and Philosophy* (1969), with the fundamental assertion that "Africans are notoriously religious . . . ."[18] In opposition to widespread views of African religion as paganism, animism, superstition, magic, fetishism, or ancestor worship, Mbiti sought to describe the beliefs and practices of hundreds of ethnic societies across Africa. In the process, he affirmed the validity and integrity of African religions that warrant study on par with other world religions. As Mugambi summarizes,

> Professor John Mbiti's research reconfirms that the African cultural and religious heritage is founded on God the Creator and Source of life, with many attributes, who has sustained the hope of African peoples across generations, in their sorrow and joy; in their suffering and celebration. This African religiosity underlines all expressions of faith among Africans in the continent and in the Diaspora.[19]

"African religiosity" is Mbiti's preferred term, for he notes that "spirituality is a difficult word to define."[20] Nonetheless, he explains in relation to African religion that "spirituality . . . refer[s] to those religious elements dealing with the direct relationship between human beings and the divine realm . . . including God, divinities, spirits and spiritual forces."[21] It is expressed through many avenues including prayers, symbols, rituals, dance and other art forms.

A major achievement in Mbiti's scholarship is his systematic analysis of the five-fold "religious ontology" of African peoples, including their apprehension of God, spirits, human beings, animals and plants, and inanimate objects and phenomena.[22] Yet his seminal contribution to African Christian theology lies in

---

[15] John S. Mbiti, *African Religions and Philosophy*, 2.
[16] Spirituality Department, "A Search for An Authentic African Christian Spirituality," 41–42.
[17] Mbiti, *African Religions and Philosophy*, 1, 3.
[18] Mbiti, *African Religions and Philosophy*, 1. Recently this claim has been rightly contested in view of the rapid rise of secularism in Africa. For example, see the chapters in Benno van den Toren, Joseph Bosco Bangura, and Richard E. Seed, eds., *Is Africa Incurably Religious? Secularization and Discipleship in Africa*. However, the assertion was apropos in its original context of examining African traditional religions before the colonial era.
[19] Jesse N. K. Mugambi, "Foreword to the Second Edition," 3.
[20] John S. Mbiti, *The Prayers of African Religion*, 23.
[21] John S. Mbiti, "African Religion," 514.
[22] Mbiti, *African Religions and Philosophy*, 16.

his assertion that the African religious and cultural heritage formed a *preparation evangelica*, or preparation for the gospel. He writes,

> It was in fact African religion more than anything else, which laid down the foundation and prepared the ground for the eventual rapid accommodation of Christianity in Africa, and for the present rapid growth of the Church in our continent. Without African religiosity, whatever its defects might be, Christianity would have taken much longer to be understood and accommodated by African peoples.[23]

Within his interpretive framework of the gospel being "the crowning fulfilment of African religiosity,"[24] Mbiti sets forth three fundamental convictions related to African Christian spirituality that become recurring themes throughout his writings. First, he insists that careful attention must be given to oral, as opposed to written, theology. As in the early church before the New Testament and other theological writings were produced, Mbiti underlines that much of the theological activity across Africa is expressed in the lived experience of believers: "It is theology in the open, from the pulpit, in the market place, in the home as people pray or read and discuss the scriptures."[25]

Therefore, in a seminal article in which Mbiti outlined recommended sources for the development of African theology, he identifies the Bible as the primary "pillar" and the theology of the older churches, especially Christian tradition in Europe, as the second. However, it is the third and fourth pillars which metaphorically allow the resources of Africa's aquifers — her religiosity — to emerge and engage with the Christian faith. Mbiti's third pillar is the traditional African world which must be taken seriously since "it is within the traditional thought-forms and religious concerns that our peoples live and try to assimilate Christian teaching."[26] His fourth pillar is the living experience of the church, or the actual life of African Christian communities reflected in their diverse forms of oral expression: worship, testimonies, sermons, prayers, blessings, rituals, etc. — all of which illuminate African Christian spirituality in dynamic expression.

Mbiti's second major conviction is based on his extensive research of over five hundred African societies, in particular their names for God and attributes describing him, with his theological conviction that God is one. He concludes:

> I have no doubt whatsoever that God the Father of our Lord Jesus

---

[23] John Mbiti, "African Indigenous Culture in Relation to Evangelism and Church Development," 86.

[24] The phrase is Kwame Bediako's, in his *Theology and Identity: The Impact of Culture upon Christian Thought in the Second Century and in Modern Africa*, 310.

[25] John S. Mbiti, *Bible and Theology in African Christianity*, 229.

[26] John S. Mbiti, "Some African Concepts of Christology," 52.

Diane B. Stinton
Africa's Aquifers: Reflections on John S. Mbiti's Contributions to African Christian Spirituality

> Christ is the same God who for thousands of years has been known and worshiped in various ways within the religious life of African peoples. He is known by various names, and there are innumerable attributes about him which are largely identical or close to biblical attributes about God.[27]

However, far from equating the biblical revelation of God with the knowledge of God derived from African religion, Mbiti states categorically:

> African Religion reflects God's witness among African peoples through the ages. It has been a valuable and indispensable lamp on the spiritual path. But however valuable this lamp has been, it cannot be made a substitute for the eternal Gospel which is like the sun that brilliantly illuminates that path. Yet it is a crucial stepping-stone towards that ultimate light. . . . The Gospel has come to fulfil and complete African religiosity.[28]

Third, Mbiti contends that the essence of the gospel is the person of Jesus Christ. He underlines that "the uniqueness of Christianity is in Jesus Christ. He is the stumbling block of all ideologies and religious systems; . . . His own Person is greater than can be contained in a religion or ideology." Mbiti therefore longs for genuine encounter between Africans, with all the riches of their indigenous spirituality, and Jesus Christ, so that their prior religious existence might be transposed to that existence brought about by Christ. In Mbiti's words, "The Gospel enabled people to utter the name of Jesus Christ[,] . . . that final and completing element that crowns their traditional religiosity and brings its flickering light to full brilliance. . . . Without Him, [i.e., Jesus Christ], the meaning of our religiosity is incomplete."

African Christian spirituality, then, may be interpreted as the inner springs of African believers' cultural identity and religiosity welling up within to deepen their understanding and experience of life in Christ. Mbiti insists that the gospel is not a set of beliefs and practices, but a way of life in which Jesus brings "the whole [person], . . . [one's] total existence, into a deep and intimate relationship with God the Father."[29] Although Mbiti does not employ the phrase, "African Christian spirituality," his writings are replete with the call for African followers of Christ to "drink from their own wells," to adapt the well-known phrase from Gustavo Gutierrez.[30] Mbiti is adamant that "African traditional religiosity can become an enrichment for Christian presence in Africa."[31]

---

[27] John Mbiti, "On the Article of John W. Kinney: A Comment," 68. This theological assumption remains contested, particularly among some evangelical scholars.
[28] John S. Mbiti, "Christianity and African Religion," 313.
[29] John S. Mbiti "Christianity and East African Culture and Religion," 4.
[30] Gustavo Gutiérrez, *We Drink from Our Own Wells: The Spiritual Journey of a People*.
[31] John S. Mbiti, "Christianity and Traditional Religions in Africa," 153.

Diane B. Stinton
Africa's Aquifers: Reflections on John S. Mbiti's Contributions
to African Christian Spirituality

Wells of African Christian Spirituality

Since spirituality encompasses every dimension of life, this essay reflects on a few aspects of Christian spirituality that may be enhanced by the deep, life-giving aquifers of African religiosity. The primary well drawn from is prayer, which Mbiti emphasizes as "the most intense expression of African spirituality"[32] and "the windows that open into people's deepest spirituality."[33] While prayer is undoubtedly a cultural universal, Mbiti emphasizes that "praying has always been the core of African religion."[34] In *The Prayers of African Religion* (1976), he collects and studies three hundred prayers from across the continent, most of which date from before Christianity penetrated deeply into the interior of Africa. As Kwame Bediako (1945–2008) observes, "The merit of this work lies in its character as a theological interpretation of the prayers used in African pre-Christian religious life, which transforms a work of compilation into a major account and presentation of African spirituality."[35]

Mbiti summarizes key elements of indigenous spirituality reflected in these prayers under the following headings: (a) holiness, purity, and cleanliness of heart; (b) humility, as "absolutely essential" in being "a posture of spiritual surrender";[36] (c) faith, trust, and confidence in the spiritual realm; (d) peace — a comprehensive peace encompassing individuals, the community, society, and nature — as the final end of prayer; (e) love, care, and gentleness; (f) praise, thanksgiving and joy; (g) blessings; and (h) spiritual wrestling with evil, including "moral evil, suffering, sickness, misfortunes, death, sorrow, separation, broken relationships, witchcraft, infertility, and so on."[37] Mbiti explains that "in traditional life, African peoples understand and practice prayer as a natural form of relating to spiritual realities," expressing "anxieties and gratitude, "fears and hopes," "confidence and assurance," "faith and intimacy."[38] He then notes,

> But people do not spend time theorizing about prayer, or analysing its academic meaning, or its form and structure. Praying is living spiritually just as walking or sleeping is living physically. Just as you live, so you pray, as an integral part of being a human being.[39]

Having brought to light the primacy and richness of prayer in African religiosity, Mbiti points out that African Christians have inherited the traditions

---

[32] John S. Mbiti, *The Prayers of African Religion*, 1.
[33] Mbiti, "Christianity and African Religion," 312.
[34] Mbiti, *The Prayers of African Religion*, 2.
[35] Kwame Bediako, "John Mbiti's Contribution to African Theology," 377.
[36] John S. Mbiti, *Prayer and Spirituality in African Religion*, 9.
[37] Mbiti, *Prayer and Spirituality in African Religion*, 13.
[38] Mbiti, *Bible and Theology*, 72.
[39] Mbiti, *Bible and Theology*, 72.

of both prayer in African religion and in biblical revelation, which are largely congruent in his estimation. As these two prayer traditions coalesce in the lives of African Christians, Mbiti highlights the interchange between them in animating African Christian spirituality.

Certainly, Christians build upon the foundation of African religiosity, "aided by the biblical revelation and faith in Jesus Christ."[40] Here Mbiti outlines new and distinctive contributions that the Christian faith offers, most obviously in the practice of praying in the name of Jesus. While traditional African prayers invoke and appeal to God, the use of God's name in these does not carry the type of authority that Jesus demonstrated and taught his followers. Mbiti underlines that for African Christians, the name of Jesus is not simply a distant, historical name but rather "a living experience" as "he is mediated to them first and foremost in and through prayer."[41] Drawing upon the well of African religiosity, "African Christians are reinvesting the name of Jesus Christ of Nazareth with the authority, the power, the force, the promise, the protection, the dynamism which it had in New Testament times. This is an extremely important christological emphasis in Christian prayer, at least as Africans are experiencing and promoting it."[42]

Other aspects of newness arising from Christian prayer include confession of wrongdoing, requesting forgiveness, and seeking absolution, said to be very rare in African religion.[43] In addition, there is further emphasis on praying personally in Christianity, as well as corporately. Moreover, Mbiti explains, it is rare in traditional African practice for someone to request prayer for another person, whereas prayer requests are common practice within African Christianity. And significantly, in contrast to prayer in African religions, Mbiti highlights "the ecumenicity of prayer" in Christianity in that believers pray across boundaries of race, religion, ethnicity, nationality, and denomination.[44]

Conversely, certain aspects of prayer in African religiosity potentially enhance prayer traditions within mission-planted churches in Africa. For example, women as well as men are priests in many African religions and there is no sex discrimination in performing religious functions including prayer.[45] Mbiti lamented that many churches in Africa have withheld leadership positions from women, a prohibition he hoped would change. Nonetheless, even if

---

[40] Mbiti, *Bible and Theology*, 88.
[41] Mbiti, *Bible and Theology*, 77.
[42] Mbiti, *Bible and Theology*, 77–78.
[43] Mbiti, *The Prayers of African Religion*, 131.
[44] Mbiti, *Bible and Theology*, 88.
[45] Mbiti, *Prayer and Spirituality in African Religion*, 3. Gender discrimination in many mission churches has contributed to the prevalence of women-founded, women-led independent churches.

Diane B. Stinton
Africa's Aquifers: Reflections on John S. Mbiti's Contributions to African Christian Spirituality

women in these churches do not pray publicly in church services, he underlined their freedom and spiritual force in praying with their families and women's groups.

Another aspect of prayer in African religiosity that enlivens African Christian spirituality lies in its relatively heightened awareness of spiritual realities. Mbiti observes, "Out of their traditional African background, Christians are sensitizing the church greatly to invisible and spiritual realities which have generally been forgotten or suppressed in the more technologically-oriented churches of the North."[46] In the interplay between African worldviews and the Christian faith, prayer affirms Jesus Christ as Lord over the principalities and powers and over any spiritual forces affecting people, thus making the ministry of healing prayer vitally important to evangelism and discipleship within African Christianity.

While far from exhaustive, this consideration of prayer within the coalescence of African religion and Christianity brings to light certain resources within African religiosity for vitalizing African Christian spirituality. Mbiti observes that millions of spontaneous prayers are uttered throughout Africa each day and each week. With very few of them recorded, their theological content cannot be ascertained precisely. Yet, Mbiti concludes, such prayers

> are, nevertheless, the bulwark of Christian spirituality in African circles; and they are the theological utterances by means of which Christians lift up their own beings towards God in private and public worship. They are based on scriptural passages, promises, insights and people's experiences; and others are based on the riches of African religiosity.[47]

He therefore urges the Church to draw upon crucial elements in the prayers of African religion, "to show people that by becoming Christian their prayer spirituality is fulfilled and enriched by the Gospel."[48]

A second wellspring of African religiosity that flows into African Christian spirituality is a worldview which reflects "a unified cosmic system" or "a sacramental universe" in which "there is no sharp dichotomy between the physical and the spiritual."[49] As Mbiti explains, "Because traditional religions permeate all the departments of life, there is no formal distinction between the sacred and the secular, between religious and non-religious, between the spiritual and the material areas of life."[50] He continues that wherever Africans

---

[46] Mbiti, *Bible and Theology*, 76.
[47] Mbiti, "'Cattle Are Born with Ears, Their Horns Grow Later,'" 24.
[48] Mbiti, "Christianity and African Religion," 312.
[49] Harold Turner, "The Primal Religions of the World and their Study," 32.
[50] Mbiti, *African Religions and Philosophy*, 2.

Diane B. Stinton
Africa's Aquifers: Reflections on John S. Mbiti's Contributions to African Christian Spirituality

are, there is their religion, whether in the fields, the beer party or funeral ceremony, the examination room at school or in the house of parliament. So intertwined are the physical and spiritual realms that "in effect the two worlds converge in the lives and experiences of the people."[51] Examples include a farmer dedicating seeds before sowing, a fisherman seeking permission from the river to fish, or a traveller entrusting personal safety to the spiritual realm. Mbiti explains,

> In this way, ... [humans are] treading on a path in which the physical and the spiritual intermingle. The prayers that [they] offer are the threads which interweave the two realms and [humans are], *ipso facto*, ... priest[s] of the universe around [them], rubbing the physical against the spiritual and the spiritual against the physical.[52]

In striking contrast to this unified worldview, Mbiti tells the story of an African who studied theology overseas, learning several biblical and European languages and eventually returning home with excess luggage containing works by major Western theologians. As his family and friends gather to celebrate his return, he struggles to speak his own language with them. Suddenly his older sister shrieks and falls to the floor; he rushes to her and urgently calls for them to take her to the hospital. The others are stunned, reminding him that the nearest hospital is fifty miles away with few buses that go there. The chief tells him, "You have been studying theology overseas for 10 years. Now help your sister. She is troubled by the spirit of her great aunt."[53] He carefully checks the index of Rudolf Bultmann's work to read about spirit possession in the New Testament and promptly insists that his sister is not possessed, for "Bultmann has demythologized demon possession."[54]

While Mbiti makes clear that the story is entirely fictional, it graphically conveys key challenges in the interplay between African Christianity and Western Christianity which, on account of the European Enlightenment, tends to erect a dichotomy between the natural and supernatural, or the physical and spiritual realms. Moreover, studies show the enduring impact of this 'enchanted' world as a predominant aspect of African Christianity today. Peter Nyende writes,

> There seems to be a revival, relatively speaking, of the traditional African worldview, contrary to the expectations that economic and social modernization following on the worldview of the European Enlightenment would eliminate it. This African worldview, in which we have a constant interaction of the physical and spiritual

---

[51] Mbiti, *Prayer and Spirituality in African Religion*, 2.
[52] Mbiti, *The Prayers of African Religion*, 68.
[53] Mbiti, "Theological Impotence and the Universality of the Church," 7–8.
[54] Mbiti, "Theological Impotence," 8.

Diane B. Stinton
Africa's Aquifers: Reflections on John S. Mbiti's Contributions to African Christian Spirituality

worlds, with the latter perceived to be heavily influencing the former, is a crucial part of the context of Christianity in Africa.[55] Consequently, this distinguishing feature of African religiosity feeds into African Christian spirituality, with potentially deepening and possibly distressing effects that call for careful discernment from biblical perspectives.

A third wellspring of African religiosity that enhances African Christian spirituality is its deeply communal orientation. In contrast to the strong individualism characteristic of Western Christianity, African religiosity is grounded in communal existence: "To be human is to belong to the whole community."[56] Mbiti's dictum is well-known: "The individual can only say: 'I am, because we are; and since we are, therefore I am'. This is a cardinal point in the understanding of the African view of [humanity]."[57] This notion is affirmed by other African scholars such as Laurenti Magesa (1946–2022), who writes, "Full personhood or humanity is made possible first and foremost by inter-subjectivity, meaning *insertion* into, connectivity to, and interaction within a community."[58] Magesa acknowledges the critique against Mbiti and others for romanticizing Africa's communalism at the expense of individualism's rightful place. However, he believes that the criticism is overdone and strives for an appropriate balance between the two, citing P. H. Coetzee and A. P. J. Roux: "The good life for an individual is conceived of as coinciding with the good life of the community, and a person's choice is highly or lowly ranked [that is, seen as moral or immoral] as it contributes to or detracts from the common good."[59]

Implications of this aspect of African religiosity for African Christian spirituality are manifold. Mbiti laments,

> Another example where African religiosity would have lent itself readily in Church development is its communality and corporateness. African Religion and social life lay great emphasis on communal welfare, values, concerns, and kinship, both horizontally and vertically (to include the departed). On the whole evangelism has presented Christianity on an individualist basis, making individualistic appeals, and the development of the Church has tended to ignore the communality dimensions of the Church's existence and concerns.[60]

---

[55] Peter Nyende, "An Aspect of the Character of Christianity in Africa," 43.
[56] Mbiti, *African Religions and Philosophy*, 2.
[57] Mbiti, *African Religions and Philosophy*, 108–109.
[58] Laurenti Magesa, *What Is Not Sacred? African Spirituality*, 46; emphasis original.
[59] P. H. Coetzee and A. P. J. Roux, eds., *The African Philosophy Reader,* 276.; cited in Magesa, *What Is Not Sacred?*, 47; inserted text is Magesa's.
[60] Mbiti, "African Indigenous Culture," 86.

Diane B. Stinton
Africa's Aquifers: Reflections on John S. Mbiti's Contributions to African Christian Spirituality

However, he notes that this oversight was beginning to be remedied, and certainly the vitality of African church life reflects many aspects of this feature of African Christian spirituality — in worship, ecclesiology, discipleship, service, and mission. etc.

Two features of African communal life that flow into African Christian spirituality are noteworthy. The first is the scope of the community in African understanding, which encompasses the living, the departed, and the unborn. Moreover, the well-being of the community is inextricably bound with the well-being of creation, so that "African Church life should lead the way, in exploring Christ's salvation as being not only personal, but also communal, corporate and cosmic."[61]

A second feature is the emphasis within African religion on celebrating life, marking key events in life and in the agricultural season with joyous religious activities. Mbiti comments, "If traditional life filled these moments with celebration and festivals, the Church should also fill these events with jubilation."[62] Certainly Mbiti's call is borne out in more recent reflections on African Christian spirituality. For example, Agbonkhianmeghe E. Orobator (b. 1967) states that its most significant aspect lies in being "a spirituality of life; it is a celebration of life in all its dimensions."[63] Even funerals are usually celebratory in marking the deceased's transition from this life to the next. Orobator further notes that worship, praise, and celebration form important elements of this spirituality as "Africans love to celebrate and express their faith in song and dance."[64] Indeed, a Western observer notes that African Christian spirituality "is a deep and lively spirituality for all who have the privilege of meeting it."[65]

For all the resources that African religiosity offers to African Christian spirituality, like the aquifers that hold impurities needing treatment to ensure drinkable water, so too, African wellsprings require testing to ensure clarity in Christian belief and practice. Mbiti clearly acknowledges that "within our culture, there are elements that may obscure the preaching or elucidation of the Gospel," which must be discerned and overcome by the power of the gospel.[66] This is undoubtedly a task for the entire African Church to undertake, not a single individual. Nonetheless, Mbiti has been critiqued for not adequately addressing certain aspects of African culture in light of the gospel. For example, despite his early call for re-examining culture and leadership regarding "such

---

[61] Mbiti, "Christianity and Culture in Africa," 277.
[62] Mbiti, "Christianity and African Religion," 311–312.
[63] Agbonkhianmeghe E. Orobator, *Theology Brewed in an African Pot*, 144.
[64] Orobator, *Theology Brewed*, 148.
[65] Holt, "Spiritualities of the Twentieth Century," 316.
[66] Mbiti, "Christianity and Culture in Africa," 279.

issues as hierarchy, respect, authority, human rights, role and dignity of women and children, etc.,"[67] he rarely addresses the plight of women in traditional African culture. For all his contributions in recovering African culture through proverbs, stories, and sayings, etc., he neglects the many cultural expressions that denigrate women. Furthermore, Esther Mombo (b. 1957) laments not only that "there is little about women and theology" in Mbiti's works, but also that he did not engage with the theology of the Circle of Concerned African Women Theologians.[68] Given the significance of the Circle since its founding in 1989, Mbiti might well have enriched his own reflections on African Christian spirituality through interacting with them.

Even more significantly, Mercy Amba Oduyoye (b. 1934), the mother of African theology and the founder of the Circle, incisively critiques Mbiti's treatment of marriage and procreation within traditional African cultures. In brief, Mbiti states that "for African peoples, marriage is the focus of existence," that "without procreation marriage is incomplete," and that "everybody, therefore, must get married and bear children" as a religious and ontological duty.[69] The stipulated reason: to ensure a person becomes immortalised by having offspring to remember one after death, so that one's existence is not extinguished. Surely if there are aspects of African religio-culture that must be evaluated, judged, and transformed by the gospel, as Mbiti advocates,[70] these fundamental beliefs must be among them. Hence Oduyoye questions Mbiti's assumption about "the necessity of linking immortality to procreation."[71] Instead, she posits "Christian immortality ... as identity with and in Christ," which does not require marriage or physical reproduction.[72] She and other theologians address additional aspects of African religio-cultures that are harmful to women, thereby demonstrating the need for certain elements of African religiosity to be purified by the gospel.

Conclusion

While Mbiti's contributions to the study of African religion, philosophy, and Christian theology are extensive and well-documented, viewing his work through the lens of African Christian spirituality further illuminates the significance of his scholarship. As early as 1980, he upheld the final communiqué from the conference of African theologians in Ghana, 1977: "The God of history speaks to all peoples in particular ways. In Africa the traditional

---

[67] Mbiti, "Christianity and Culture in Africa," 282.
[68] Esther Mombo, "Reflection on John S. Mbiti," 421.
[69] Mbiti, *African Religions and Philosophy*, 133–134.
[70] Mbiti, "Christianity and Culture in Africa," 281.
[71] Mercy A. Oduyoye, "A Critique of Mbiti's View on Love and Marriage in Africa," 348.
[72] Oduyoye, "A Critique of Mbiti's View," 347.

Diane B. Stinton
Africa's Aquifers: Reflections on John S. Mbiti's Contributions to African Christian Spirituality

religions are a major source for the study of the African experience of God. The beliefs and practices of the traditional religions can enrich Christian theology and spirituality."[73] He devoted his lifetime to demonstrating this conviction by elucidating African religiosity in relation to Christian faith. In sum, he concludes,

> African religiosity has indeed been a preparation for the gospel. It has provided the religious groundwork, religious vocabulary, religious insights, religious aspirations and direction for the gospel to find a hearing and an acceptance among African peoples. . . . Jesus Christ . . . colors the experience of Christians.[74]

Like the vast aquifers bringing life to African landscapes, African religiosity vitalizes African Christian spirituality through spiritual wells like prayer, holistic worldviews integrating the physical and spiritual realms, and the communal and celebratory dimensions of life. With appropriate discernment of African religiosity in light of the gospel, these resources can quench the spiritual thirst not only of African believers, but also followers of Jesus throughout the world who seek to deepen their understanding and experience of Christian spirituality. For as Glen Scorgie points out,

> Christianity has become a global religion. Consequently, no serious conversation about Christian spirituality can remain merely Western or otherwise parochially bounded, but now must include diverse and insightful voices from around the world. The globalization of Christianity also means that Christian spirituality is acquiring new faces as it becomes contextualized into various cultures.[75]

May we all drink from the wellsprings of African Christian spirituality, as one source through which Jesus offers an "artesian spring within, gushing fountains of endless life."

Bibliography

Bediako, Kwame. "John Mbiti's Contribution to African Theology." In *Religious Plurality in Africa: Essays in Honour of John S. Mbiti*, edited by Jacob K. Olupona and Sulayman S. Nyang, 367–390. Religion and Society 32. Berlin: Mouton de Gruyter, 1993.

———. *Theology and Identity: The Impact of Culture upon Christian Thought in the Second Century and in Modern Africa*. Oxford: Regnum Books, 1992.

---

[73] Cited in Mbiti, "The Encounter of Christian Faith and African Religion," 819.
[74] Mbiti, "On the Article of John W. Kinney," 68.
[75] Glen G. Scorgie, "Overview of Christian Spirituality," 29.

Diane B. Stinton
Africa's Aquifers: Reflections on John S. Mbiti's Contributions to African Christian Spirituality

Coetzee, P. H., and A. P. J. Roux, eds. *The African Philosophy Reader: A Text with Readings*. 2nd edition. Cape Town: Oxford University Press of Southern Africa, 2002.

Gutierrez, Gustavo. *We Drink from Our Own Wells: The Spiritual Journey of a People*. Translated by Matthew J. O'Connell. Maryknoll, New York: Orbis Books, 2003.

Hastings, Adrian. *A History of African Christianity 1950–1975*. African Studies Series 26. Cambridge: Cambridge University Press, 1979.

Holt, Bradley. "Spiritualities of the Twentieth Century." In *The Story of Christian Spirituality: Two Thousand Years, from East to West*, edited by Gordon Mursell, 305–365. Minneapolis, Minnesota: Fortress Press, 2001.

Magesa, Laurenti. *What Is Not Sacred? African Spirituality*. Maryknoll, New York: Orbis Books, 2013.

Mahed, Gaathier. "Africa's Aquifers Hold More than 20 Times the Water Stored in the Continent's Lakes, but They Aren't the Answer to Water Scarcity." *The Conversation*, 21 March 2023, https://theconversation.com/africas-aquifers-hold-more-than-20-times-the-water-stored-in-the-continents-lakes-but-they-arent-the-answer-to-water-scarcity-201704

Mbaya, Henri, and Ntozakhe Cezula. "Contribution of John S Mbiti to the Study of African Religions and African Theology and Philosophy." *Stellenbosch Theological Journal* 5, no. 3 (2019): 421–442.

Mbiti, John [S]. "African Indigenous Culture in Relation to Evangelism and Church Development." In *The Gospel and Frontier Peoples*, edited by R. Pierce Beaver, 79–95. South Pasadena, California: William Carey Library, 1973.

———. "African Religion." In *The Study of Spirituality*, edited by Cheslyn Jones, Geoffrey Wainwright, and Edward Yarnold, 513–516. London: SPCK, 1986.

———. *African Religions and Philosophy*. Nairobi: Heinemann, 1969.

———. *Bible and Theology in African Christianity*. Nairobi: Oxford University Press, 1999.

———. "'Cattle Are Born with Ears, Their Horns Grow Later': Towards an Appreciation of African Oral Theology." *Africa Theological Journal* 8, no. 1 (1979): 15–25.

———. "Christianity and African Religion." In *Facing the New Challenges: The Message of PACLA, December 9–19, 1976, Nairobi*, edited by Michael Cassidy and Luc Verlinden, 308–313. Kisumu, Kenya: Evangel Publishing House, 1978.

———. "Christianity and Culture in Africa." In *Facing the New Challenges: The Message of PACLA, December 9–19, 1976, Nairobi*, edited by Michael Cassidy and Luc Verlinden, 272–313. Kisumu, Kenya: Evangel Publishing House, 1978.

———. "Christianity and Traditional Religions in Africa." In *Crucial Issues in Missions Tomorrow*, edited by Donald A. McGavran, 144–158. Chicago: Moody Press, 1972.

———. *Concepts of God in Africa*. 2nd edition. Foreword by J. N. K. Mugambi. Nairobi: Acton Publishers, 2012.

———. "The Encounter of Christian Faith and African Religion." *The Christian Century* 97, no. 27 (27 August 1980): 817–220.

———. "On the Article of John W. Kinney: A Comment." *Occasional Bulletin of Missionary Research* 3, no. 2 (1 April 1979): 68.

———. *Prayer and Spirituality in African Religion*. The Charles Strong Memorial Lecture, Australia, Aug. 1978. Bedford Park: Australian Assoc. for the Study of Religions, 1978.

———. *The Prayers of African Religion*. Maryknoll, New York: Orbis Books, 1976.

———. "Some African Concepts of Christology." In *Christ and the Younger Churches*, edited by Georg F. Vicedom, 51–62. London: SPCK, 1972.

———. "Theological Impotence and the Universality of the Church." In *Mission Trends No. 3: Third World Theologies*, edited by Gerald H. Anderson and Thomas F. Stransky, 6–18. Grand Rapids, Michigan: Eerdmans, 1976.

Mombo, Esther. "Reflection on John S. Mbiti." Chapter 21 in *Who Do You Say That I Am? Christology in Africa*, edited by Rodney L. Reed and David K. Ngaruiya, 417–426. ASET Series 6. Carlisle, Cumbria, UK: Langham Global Library, 2021.

Mugambi, Jesse N.K. "A Tribute to John S. Mbiti." Chapter 23 in *Who Do You Say That I Am? Christology in Africa*, edited by Rodney L. Reed and David K. Ngaruiya, 437–440. ASET Series 6. Carlisle, Cumbria, UK: Langham Global Library, 2021.

———. "Foreword to the Second Edition." In *Concepts of God in Africa*, by John S. Mbiti, 2nd edition. Nairobi: Acton Publishers, 2012.

Nyende, Peter. "An Aspect of the Character of Christianity in Africa." *Journal of Theology for Southern Africa* 132 (November 2008): 38–52. https://www.academia.edu/10275756/

Oborji, Francis Anekwe. "Mbiti, John Samuel." Dictionary of African Christian Biography, n.d., https://dacb.org/stories/kenya/mbiti-johns/

Oduyoye, Mercy A. "A Critique of Mbiti's View on Love and Marriage in Africa." In *Religious Plurality in Africa: Essays in Honour of John S. Mbiti*, edited by Jacob K. Olupona and Sulayman S. Nyang, 341–365. Religion and Society 32. Berlin: Mouton de Gruyter, 1993.

Ohajunwa, Chioma, and Gubela Mji. "The African Indigenous Lens of Understanding Spirituality: Reflection on Key Emerging Concepts from a

Reviewed Literature." *Journal of Religion and Health* 57 (2018): 2523–2537. https://doi.org/10.1007/s10943-018-0652-9

Orobator, Agbonkhianmeghe E. *Theology Brewed in an African Pot.* Maryknoll, New York: Orbis Books, 2008.

Schmidt, Richard H. "John S. Mbiti: African Christian Spirituality." In *God Seekers: Twenty Centuries of Christian Spiritualities*, 338–349. Grand Rapids, Michigan: Eerdmans, 2008.

Scorgie, Glen G. "Overview of Christian Spirituality." In *Dictionary of Christian Spirituality*, edited by Glen G. Scorgie, 27–33. Grand Rapids, Michigan: Zondervan, 2011.

Spirituality Department, Catholic University of Eastern Africa (C.U.E.A.). "A Search for An Authentic African Christian Spirituality." *African Christian Studies* 10, no. 1 (March 1994): 38–56.

van den Toren, Benno, Joseph Bosco Bangura, and Richard E. Seed, eds. *Is Africa Incurably Religious? Secularization and Discipleship in Africa.* Regnum Studies in Mission. Oxford: Regnum, 2020.

Turner, Harold. "The Primal Religions of the World and Their Study." In *Australian Essays in World Religions*, edited by Victor Hayes, 27–37. Bedford Park, South Australia: The Australian Association for the Study of Religions, 1977.

Wilson, Alistair I. "'Missionaries Did Not Bring Christ to Africa – Christ Brought them' (Bediako/Mbiti): Christ's Lordship in Mission in African Theology." Chapter 17 in *Who Do You Say That I Am? Christology in Africa*, edited by Rodney L. Reed and David K. Ngaruiya, 319–338. ASET Series 6. Carlisle, Cumbria, UK: Langham Global Library, 2021.

Women, Leadership, and Ordination in the Anglican Church in Nigeria
Debating 1 Corinthians 14:26–40

Mercy Uwaezuoke CHUKWUEDO

Trinity Theological College, Umuahia, Nigeria
mercychukwuedo@gmail.com

Abstract

Paul's injunction in 1 Corinthians 14:26-40 has often been used to restrict women from holding certain leadership positions in the Church. This paper examines 1 Corinthians 14:26-40 in light of the female ordination debate in the Anglican Church in Nigeria. Through an exegetical study of the text, Paul's perspective on women is demystified. To understand the place of women in the Church using scriptural texts, this article examines the perspectives of egalitarian theory, complementarian theory, and liberation theology. The latter is included because it aims at interpreting biblical texts in a liberational way — Scripture is meant to deliver humans from all kinds of bondage and not to enslave. Exegesis is accompanyied by an examination of leadership roles of women in Igbo Traditional Religion, in which women are recognized as priestesses. The place of women in leadership in Igbo Traditional religion is pertinent to this work. Biblical texts are necessarily interpreted from the perspectives of human experience — including African women's experiences. This article discovers through exegetical study of 1 Corinthians 14:26–40 that Paul was correcting a problem in the Corinthian church rather than hindering women from participating in the worship service or serving as leaders in the church. The Church should thus stop using the text to silence women or restrict them from holding certain leadership positions.

Résumé

L'injonction de Paul dans 1 Corinthiens 14 :26–40 a souvent été utilisée pour empêcher les femmes d'occuper certains postes de direction dans l'Église. Cet article examine 1 Corinthiens 14 :26–40 à la lumière du débat sur l'ordination des femmes dans l'Église anglicane du Nigeria. Une étude exégétique du texte permet de démystifier le point de vue de Paul sur les femmes. Pour comprendre la place des femmes dans l'Église

Mercy Uwaezuoke Chukwuedo
Women, Leadership, and Ordination in the Anglican Church in Nigeria: Debating 1 Corinthians 14:26–40

à partir des textes bibliques, cet article examine les perspectives de la théorie égalitaire, de la théorie complémentariste et de la théologie de la libération. Cette dernière est incluse parce qu'elle vise à interpréter les textes bibliques d'une manière libératrice — l'Écriture est destinée à libérer les humains de toutes sortes d'esclavages et non à les asservir. L'exégèse s'accompagne d'une analyse des rôles de leadership des femmes dans la religion traditionnelle Igbo, dans laquelle les femmes sont reconnues comme prêtresses. La place des femmes dans le leadership de la religion traditionnelle Igbo est pertinente pour ce travail. Les textes bibliques sont nécessairement interprétés dans la perspective de l'expérience humaine — y inclus l'expérience des femmes africaines. Cet article conclut, à travers l'étude exégétique de 1 Corinthiens 14 :26–40, que Paul corrigeait un problème dans l'église de Corinthe et n'empêchait pas les femmes de participer au culte ou de servir en tant que responsables dans l'église. L'Église doit donc cesser d'utiliser ce texte pour réduire les femmes au silence ou les empêcher d'occuper certaines fonctions dirigeantes.

Resumo

Para compreender o lugar das mulheres na Igreja utilizando os textos bíblicos, este documento examina as perspectivas da teoria igualitária, da teoria complementariana e da teologia da libertação. Esta última é incluída porque tem como objetivo interpretar os textos bíblicos de uma forma — as Escrituras destinam-se a libertar os seres humanos de todos os tipos de escravidão e não a escravizar. Para compreender o lugar das mulheres na Igreja a partir dos textos bíblicos, este documento examina as perspectivas da teoria igualitária, da teoria complementariana e da teologia da libertação. Esta última é incluída porque tem como objetivo interpretar os textos bíblicos de uma forma libertadora — as Escrituras destinam-se a libertar os seres humanos de todos os tipos de escravatura, e não a escravizá-los. A exegese é acompanhada de uma análise dos papéis de liderança das mulheres na religião tradicional Igbo, na qual as mulheres são reconhecidas como sacerdotisas. O lugar das mulheres na liderança na religião tradicional Igbo é pertinente para este trabalho. Os textos bíblicos são necessariamente interpretados a partir das perspectivas da experiência humana — incluindo as experiências das mulheres africanas. Este artigo conclui, através do estudo exegético de 1 Coríntios 14:26–40, que Paulo estava a corrigir um problema na igreja de Corinto e não a impedir as mulheres de participarem no culto de adoração ou de servirem como líderes na igreja. A Igreja deve, portanto, parar de usar o texto para silenciar as mulheres ou restringi-las de ocupar certas posições de liderança.

Mercy Uwaezuoke Chukwuedo
Women, Leadership, and Ordination in the Anglican Church in Nigeria: Debating 1 Corinthians 14:26–40

Keywords

ordination, women in leadership, egalitarian theory, complementarian theory, liberation theology, priestess

Mots-clés

ordination, femmes dirigeantes, théorie égalitaire, théorie complémentariste, théologie de la libération, prêtresse

Palavras-chave

ordenação, mulheres na liderança, teoria igualitária, teoria complementariana, teologia da libertação, sacerdotisa

Introduction

There are various views concerning Paul's writings on women. He is seen both as a misogynist and a philogynist. When we look at Pauline texts on women, we are left with the notion that Paul was not against women leadership because he walked closely with some women. However, we can still not deny the fact that at some point his Jewish patriarchal culture may have affected him. Paul encouraged women to use their spiritual gifts for the edification of the Church. Pauline texts abound that describe women as active participants in ministry such as Romans 16:1-16, 1 Cor. 11: 4–16 and at the same time texts that advocate the silence of women such as 1 Timothy 2:11 and 1 Cor. 14:33–35. It is needful to enquire, does 1 Corinthians 14:26-40 advocate for complete silence of women? This text is used to subordinate women in some parts of Africa, including in the Anglican Communion. Various perspectives exist on how the text is being interpreted and applied. However, this paper seeks to exegete the text and find out Paul's intention for giving the order to the Corinthian Church.

This paper is focused on the Anglican Communion especially the Church of Nigeria because the Anglican Communion is divided on the debate on women ordination based on scriptural texts, tradition and reason. The Anglican Communion is a religious body of national, independent and autonomous Churches throughout the world that adhere to the teachings of Anglicanism and that evolved from the Church of England. In the Anglican Communion, a province is comprised of dioceses being headed by an Archbishop. It can be described as the smallest complete unit of the Anglican Church because it exists under a college of Bishops, each of whom with his clergy and laity is autonomous within a diocese. Many provinces ordain women to the three holy orders, viz; deacon, priest, and bishop. In some dioceses and provinces, women are ordained as deacons and priests and not as Bishops. Individual dioceses within provinces are left to decide into which order — the diaconate (deacons), the

Mercy Uwaezuoke Chukwuedo
Women, Leadership, and Ordination in the Anglican Church in Nigeria: Debating 1 Corinthians 14:26–40

presbytery (presbyters or priests), or the episcopacy (bishops) — women in the pastorate should be ordained.[1]

In the Church of Nigeria (Anglican Communion), women's ordination is yet to be accepted, except as deacons with limited responsibility. Ordination is the rite by which the Church sets apart ministers, people whom it believes are qualified for the ministry of the word and sacrament.[2] Sacraments are only administered by those who are ordained. Ordination is made through discernment by the Church that one is called. God's call and training for the ministry are prerequisites for ordination. In the course of my doctoral research on "The Place of Women in the Church of Nigeria (Anglican Communion)"[3] from 2014–2017, I carried out oral interviews to discover opinions of people concerning the ordination of women in the Church of Nigeria (Anglican Communion). I interviewed fifteen women and fifteen men. Only two persons supported the ordination of women. One is a priest and a lecturer, the other is a Lay Reader[4] and also a University lecturer. None of the women I interviewed support women ordination. This is a clear indication that ordination of women in the Church of Nigeria is not in the church's agenda now.[5] I discovered from my interactions with most of my respondents that the Bible and culture are tools used to exclude women from ordination. Most of my respondents are of the opinion that it is neither culturally nor biblically acceptable for a woman to lead men.[6] 1 Corinthians 14:33–34 is one of such texts quoted to defend the exclusion of women from ordination.

Research Tools

Different approaches have been used in studying matters relating to women such as different feminism theories, egalitarian and complementarianism theories. Complementarianism and egalitarianism theories are examined in this

---

[1] Esther Mombo, "The Ordination of Women in Africa: A Historical Perspective," 124.
[2] A. C. Krass, *Applied Theology 1: 'Go and Make Disciples'*, 3.
[3] Mercy U. Chukwuedo, "The Place of Women in the Church of Nigeria (Anglican Communion): Perspectives from 1 Corinthians 14:26-40."
[4] A Lay Reader in the Church of Nigeria (Anglican Communion) is a lay person licensed to preach, read Bible lessons, and conduct some religious services, but not licensed to celebrate the Eucharist. He or she is authorized by the bishop to lead certain services of worship. Lay Readers are formerly trained and admitted to the office but not ordained as priests. Within the Akoko Anglican Diocese of the Church of Nigeria, "most of the churches have only women lay readers." Sade Oluwakemi Ayeni, "Women in the Nigerian Church: A Stucy of the Akoko Anglican Diocese," 443.
[5] Mercy U. Chukwuedo, *African Women in Ministry, the Nigerian Experience: Perspectives from 1 Corinthians 14:26–40*, 96–106; Timothy Agbo, *Women Ordination in Nigeria: An Ecclesiological Analysis*, 54–77.
[6] Chukwuedo, *African Women in Ministry*, 108–111.

Mercy Uwaezuoke Chukwuedo
Women, Leadership, and Ordination in the Anglican Church in Nigeria: Debating 1 Corinthians 14:26–40

paper to interpret the views surrounding women's ordination. They give an understanding of different ways by which scholars and Christians generally view ordination of women. To have a better understanding of ordination and women leadership in Nigeria, the study also brings to light the place of women in spiritual leadership among the Igbos of Nigeria, such as female gods (goddesses) and priests (priestesses).

Complementarianism — a euphemism for what is actually *hierarchicalism* — affirms that women are allowed to teach other women and children. Some complementarians (but not all) further affirm that women can engage in certain forms of public ministry, such as teaching and evangelizing unbelievers in a public setting. However, women may talk with Christian men about the Bible and Christian doctrine only in a private context (see Acts 18:26).[7] Within complementarianism, women are frequently considered to be less rational, more gullible, and more susceptible to temptation, and thus are restricted not only from leadership in Church, but from any position of authority over any men in any sphere.[8] Contrary to these views, Christian egalitarianism considers that men and women are equally created in God's image, equally responsible for sin, equally redeemed by Christ, and equally gifted by God's Spirit for service to be key biblical principles.[9] Egalitarians do not believe that "gender differences have been abolished" but only that, building equally on the Creation narratives in Genesis and on New Testament passages such as Galatians 3:28, "being male or female does not bring any disadvantage."[10]

Liberation theologians claim that the truth of the Bible is manifested in its liberating potential and that this truth is to be enacted by Christians through political and social praxis (action). The end goal of liberation theology is the realization of full economic and social equality and participation of all peoples in a utopian, harmonic and peaceful society.[11] Liberation theology focuses on the biblical message of God's mission to set humans free from bondage. In the light of oppression experienced by women and third world people, it seeks to

---

[7] William G. Witts, *Icons of Christ: A Biblical and Systematic Theology for Women's Ordination*, 12.
[8] Witts, *Icons of Christ*, 146.
[9] Bob Edwards, *Let My People Go: A Call to End the Oppression of Women in the Church*, 21.
[10] Samuel Oluwatosin Okanlawon, "Galatians 3:28: a Vision for Partnership," 39. Okanlawon continues to note that "Paul's declaration that there is 'neither male and female' stands in marked contrast to commonly accepted patterns of privilege and prejudice in the ancient world. Women were considered inferior within both Jewish and Greek culture.... Hence, Paul is emphasizing in Galatians 3:26-28 that men and women enjoy a new, equal and exalted status before God," 40.
[11] Mary A. Kassian, *The Feminist Gospel: The Movement to Unite Feminism with the Church*, 53.

communicate the good news of liberation. Liberation theology also includes the call for the emancipation of women in all spheres of life, including Church leadership.

Paul's intent in writing 1 Corinthians 14:26–40 is uncovered through exegesis. Scholars have noted that the worldview of Africans play a major role in the understanding of the scripture. Religion is practiced within a culture. This shows that both religion and culture go hand in glove. Because we recognize that Africans have a religion before the inception of Christianity, I will also examine Igbo Traditional Religious belief and practice regarding female priests in order to draw an analogy and correlations between ordination of women in Christianity and Igbo Traditional Religion.

Women's Ordination Debate

Churches in Africa are divided on the debate of ordination of women. The issue of women's ordination has posed a problem in different denominations because of divergent interpretations of biblical texts.[12] Women are ordained in some of the African Indigenous Churches and Pentecostal Churches. Women are not restricted from ordination in the Methodist Church in Nigeria. A good number of women serve as deacons or priests and occupy other leadership positions. In the Church, every human person should be seen as an instrument for the accomplishment of the divine will no matter the gender.[13] This is the essence of the human creation. Much has been written on matters relating to gender inequality, social injustice, and marginalization of women in Church leadership.

The Anglican Communion is divided into forty-two different automous provinces. Globally, as of January 2021, seven Anglican provinces (approximately 3% of global Anglicanism) ordained only men to all three of the orders, two ordained both men and women as deacons, sixteen ordained both men and women as deacons and presbyters but not as bishops, and twenty-two (approximately two thirds of global Anglicanism) ordain both men and women into all three of the orders.[14] African provinces of the Anglican Communion

---

[12] E.g., see Frank B. Chirwa, *Mission in Progress: The Developing Role of Women in the Church: an SDA Perspective from Malawi*; Nancy Carol James, *The Developing Schism within the Episcopal Church: 1960–2010: Social Justice, Ordination of Women Charismatics, Homosexuality, Extra-territorial Bishops*; etc.; Hilfah F. Thomas and Rosemary Skinner Keller, eds., *Women in New Worlds: Historical Perspectives on the Wesleyan Tradition*.

[13] Anuli B. Okoli and Lawrence Okwuosa, "The Role of Christianity in Gender Issues and development in Nigeria," 8.

[14] Benjamin Knoll, "Women's Ordination in the Anglican Communion: the Importance of Religious, Economic, and Political Contexts."

which currently permit consecration of women as bishops include the Anglican Church of Southern Africa, the Episcopal Church of South Sudan, the Anglican Church of Angola and Mozambique, and the Anglican Church of Kenya.[15] As of November 2023, all Anglican provinces in Africa ordained women as deacons, and "many of Anglicanism's most theologically conservative provinces now ordain women to the priesthood, including Uganda, Kenya, South Sudan, Rwanda, Tanzania," and the 'Province of West Africa' (covering Cameroon, Cape Verde, Gambia, Ghana, Guinea, Liberaia, Senegal, and Sierra Leone).

Although an increasing number of women have been ordained in a number of Churches in various countries in the Western world and in Southern Africa, the case of the Church of Nigeria is still a subject under debate. The (Anglican) Church of Nigeria *does* ordain women as deacons, but reserves service in the diaconate and episcopacy to men.[16] The restriction of women from ordination in the Church of Nigeria (Anglican Communion) is premised on: Scripture, Church Tradition and Reason. On Church tradition, the ordination of women is seen as a deliberate violation of the tradition of the Church. Paul's teaching forbids women from exercising authority over men, it is argued, especially to be subordinate in things pertaining to liturgical teachings and expression of doctrine.

In 1992, a bishop from the Church of Nigeria (Anglican Communion), Herbert Haruna, ordained three women as deacons — Mrs Beatrice Aciwunaya, Mrs Hannah Bello and Mrs Abigail Akinwade. The Right Rev. Joseph Abiodun Adetiloye, second Primate of the Church of Nigeria (Anglican Communion) reacted to sharply, deeming the ordinations as irregular and nullifying them. Bishop Haruna faced disciplinary action and was retired compulsorily.[17] In 2003, female graduates from Immanuel College of Theology wrote to the Provincial standing committee of the Church of Nigeria challenging the refusal to ordain women "whether the unjust state of affairs in which women are denied ordination, simply because they are women, should be allowed to continue." They presented the criteria for ordination that the Church should consider: faith in the Triune God, confession of personal salvation, moral probity and integrity, maintenance of a stable Christian home, active membership of the Church, adequate theological training and evidence of God's call.[18] In 2010, Archbishop Nicholas Dikeriehi Orogodo Okoh, fourth Primate of the Church of Nigeria, "endorsed the ordination of women as deacons" but strictly limited their ecclesial service as deacons to "specific purposes like hospital work and school

---

[15] See Fredrick Nzwili, "Africa's six Anglican women bishops meet and issue call to combat Africa's 'triple threat'."
[16] Kirk Petersen, "Province of Central Africa Approves Ordination of Women."
[17] Agbo, *Women Ordination in Nigeria*, 47.
[18] Agbo, *Women Ordination in Nigeria*, 57.

services."[19] The Church in Africa has frequently been characterized as 'a church of women,'[20] because women not only provide the majority of church members but also do the most of the work. In the Church of Nigeria (Anglican Communion), today women serve as "wardens, evangelists, lay readers, choir directors, ... among other leadership roles."[21] Yet the Church of Nigeria has not as yet reconsidered its stand on the ordination of women.

The Female Ordination Debate: Theories and Theological Reflections

Different theories have been adopted in the study of women especially on the debate of female leadership. Two main opposing sides in the women ordination debate are complementarianism (i.e., hierarchicalism) and egalitarianism. Each present arguments from Theology, Religion, Sociology, Psychology, Philosophy, History, and Anthropology to elucidate their propositions.[22]

Complementarianism and Women's Ordination Debate

Complementarians are opposed to the notion of ordination of women.[23] Some Protestant Churches such as the Church of Nigeria (Anglican Communion) and others object the ordination of women on the grounds of biblical exegesis, Church tradition, culture, and/or reason. Complementarians use Scripture to exclude women from ordination and occupying some leadership positions in the Church. Complementarian theory holds that male and female were created by God as equal in dignity, value, essence, and human nature, but also distinct in role whereby the male was given leadership

---

[19] Odogwu Emeka Odogu, "Anglican Archbishop Okays Women's Ordination to the Diaconate."

[20] E.g., see Dorothy L. Hodgson, *The Church of Women*.

[21] Ayeni, "Women in the Nigerian Church," 428.

[22] Daniel Dei and Robert Osei-Bonsu, "The Female Ordination Debate: Theological Reflections," 31.

[23] In the debate of women's ordination and women in leadership, the leading voices among complementarians are all white men from the United States. E.g., see Wayne Grudem, *Evangelical Feminism and Biblical Truth: An Analysis of 118 Disputed Questions*; James B. Hurley, *Man and Woman in Biblical Perspective*; George W. Knight III, *The New Testament Teaching on the Role Relationship of Men and Women*. Evangelical theologian and biblical scholar Kevin Giles, an Anglican minister Australia, has cogently demonstrated that Grudem's book, which is representative of complementarian thought, is full of "erroneous arguments" and fails to engage with the evidence produced by long list of biblical scholars such as Gordon Fee, Phillip Payne, and Eldon Jay Epp. Giles further notes that Grudem (falsely) accuses a long list of "some of the most respected and godly evangelical leaders in the world" of denying the authority of Scripture when they are only denying the supposed authority of human interpreters of Scripture who share Grudem's complementarian commitment. Giles, "Book Review: Wayne Grudem's *Evangelical Feminism*."

responsibility of loving authority over the female, and the female was to offer willing, glad-hearted, and submissive assistance to the man. Genesis 1:26-27 makes clear that male and female are equally created as God's image, and are, by God's design, equally and fully human. But, as Genesis 2 bears out, their humanity would find expression differently in a relationship of complementarity, with female functioning in a submissive role under the leadership and authority of the male.[24]

The Roman Catholic Church and Church of Nigeria (Anglican Communion) are still not considering the ordination of women into priesthood.[25] On grounds of Church tradition, the contemporary Church cannot, it is argued, ordain women because there is a universal tradition against it. The argument from tradition is primarily a Catholic argument. They link ordination to a sacramental understanding of orders and sacraments that is connected to a particular understanding of apostolic succession. Contemporary ordinations are valid only if they can be traced through an unbroken chain all the way to the time of the apostles. Hence, an unbroken tradition is necessarily important because if someone is ordained invalidly, the chain of apostolic tradition is broken.[26]

The Catholic objections of the ordination of women is because to them "only a male priest can represent Christ in the celebration of the Eucharist. Specifically, presiding at the Eucharist, the priest acts 'in the person of Christ.' Since Jesus is male, only a male can play this representation role."[27] It is frequently argued that there is a strong connection between ordination of women and affirmation of male-male and female-female sexual practice. It is believed that one leads to the other and the Church should be cautious, never to give room to such. This 'slippery slope' argument, however, has little logical cogency and less evidence. As noted above, many of the Anglican Communion's most theologically conservative and evangelical provinces are Africa provinces which ordain women as presbyters.

The Seventh Day Adventists (SDAs) have "debated the issue of the ordination of women to the gospel ministry for over a hundred years." In time past, "the decision has not been in favor of women ordination." Throughout most of the 1990s, leadership of the SDA was of the opinion that there is no

---

[24] Chukwuedo, *African Women in Ministry*, 14–15.
[25] See Agbo, *Women Ordination in Nigeria*; Chukwuedo, *African Women in Ministry*, 14-15; Anthony B.C. Chiegboka, *Women Status and Dignity in the Society and the Church: A Perspective from Galatians 3: 26-29*, 112-11; Sara Butler, "Women's Ordination: Is it Still an Issue?"
[26] Witts, *Icons of Christ*, 20.
[27] Witts, *Icons of Christ*, 203.

"clear biblical basis" for the "support of the ordination of women."[28] They asserted that

- The Bible is the standard for the practice of Christian faith both in the past, present and will continue to be our guide.
- There is a clear indication in both Old Testament and New Testament that no women were ordained.
- Christ's model in the choosing the apostles provides the fundamental framework for ministry and its practice in the Christian Church within multicultural context of the expanding Church without introducing women's ordination. This serves as a good example to the present day Church.[29]

SDA leadership recommended that since there is no biblical support for the ordination of women pastors, then the ordination of women elders should also not be considered. That implies that as from the action date, women shall no longer serve as elders. This position is held by many churches which are opposed to women's ordination. In recent times, the Seventh Day Adventists have given room for the ministry of women, including within leadership positions. Several women have been ordained in the SDA since 2012 after the Columbia Union Conference approved the ordination of women.[30] The Anglican Communion, on the other hand, is still divided on this. However, all hope is not lost. The Methodist Church in Nigeria has given women acceptance in all spheres of Church leadership. The Church of Nigeria (Anglican Communion) may give consideration to the ordination of women in the near future.

Egalitarianism and Women's Ordination Debate

In practice, the hierarchical practice described above positions women as inherently inferior to men, contrary to scriptural teaching. Within Christianity, egalitarianism is a position based on the theological view that not only are all people equal before God in their personhood but there is no gender based limitations of what functions or roles each can fulfill in the home, the Church,

---

[28] "The Summary of SID BRC Position on the Ordination of Women."

[29] George W. Reid, "The Ordination of Women: A Review of the Principal Arguments for and against the Ordination of Women to the Gospel Ministry" (1985), 20–24. The SDA has made some adjustments to their stance on the ordination of women. The policies of the General Conference from 1990 and onwards allowed for ordination of women as church elders, employment of women as associates in pastoral care (if they were ordained as local elders), and also commissioning of women in pastoral types of ministry. In recent times, the SDA generally is not opposed to women's ordination. The General Conference has given room for the ordination of women as they affirm being part of the global Church and needing to listen to and be in harmony with the decision of the Church at large.

[30] Alberto R. Timm, "Seventh Day Adventists on Women's Ordination: A Brief Historical Overview," 30.

and society. Most egalitarians affirm ordination of women.[31] There is no valid biblical, theological, or traditional endorsement of the position to exclude women from the Gospel Ministry as ordained ministers.[32]

The Methodist Church and Baptist Church in Nigeria uphold this theory as women are not excluded from priestly office and ordination. They argue that God calls people to leadership roles in the Church without regard to class, gender or race and all have equal responsibility to use their gifts to obey their calling. It is very astounding the giant strides and achievements that have been recorded over the years by women in the Church and secular world. In the New Testament, not only were women the recipients of Jesus' ministry (Matt. 15:21-28; Mark 5:25-34; Luke 7:36-50; 13:10-17; John 4:7-30), but they also served Him and the disciples (Mark 15:40-41; Luke 8:1-3). Some have argued that the ordination of women is not rooted in the Scripture since Jesus did not call any female among the twelve apostles. He did not ordain any man either if we are to judge based on today's understanding of ordination.

From the various definitions of ordination, one could see that those who are called by God into the pastoral ministry have the right to be ordained. Women who have the personal knowledge and evidence of the call of God on their lives have the right to get ordained after passing through the Church's discernment and ordination process. Ordination should be open to all regardless of gender as can be seen from Galatians 3:28.

Exegesis of 1 Corinthians 14:26–40

It is important at this point to uncover the reasons behind Paul's injunction to the women of Corinth to be silent. Seeing that the understanding of this passage has posed a problem to some Christians and scholars, it is necessary to investigate the meaning and message of 1 Corinthians 14:26–40 to the present Church. Is this text meant to subordinate women universally or was Paul trying to correct an error in the Corinthian assembly?

This text introduces something that not only seems unlike Paul elsewhere but also seems to contradict what he assumed in 11:4–5 — that women prayed and prophesied in the assembly. Paul may have been influenced at one point or another as a Jew born into a patriarchal society. But 1 Corinthians 14 basically deals with confusion within the Corinthian assemblies. This confusion arose

---

[31] Notable egalitarian biblical scholars include Linda Belleville, Michael Bird, F. F. Bruce, Gordon D. Fee, Craig S. Keener, Howard I. Marshall, Scott McKnight, Leon Morris, Carol D. Osburn, Ben Witherington III, and N. T. Wright. John Stott was broadly egalitarian and encouraged women to serve in ministry positions, but opposed women serving in certain ministry leadership positions in some contexts.

[32] Dei and Osei-Bonsu, "The Female Ordination Debate," 31.

from chaotic exercise of the gift of tongues and prophecy. Paul offered guidelines for order in the worship meeting. 1 Corinthians 14:26–36 lists three groups of people who are disturbing the worship. These are as follows:

1. The prophets;
2. The speakers-in-tongues;
3. Married women who have Christian husbands in the Church. These are told: don't ask questions during the worship; don't chat during worship; ask your husbands questions at home and be silent in the church.

The bone of contention is found in verse 34. The Greek texts of this reads as follows:

αἱ γςναῖκερ ἐν ηαῖρ ἐκκληζίαιρ ζιγάηυζαν·
οὐ γἀπ ἐπιηπέπεηαι αὐηαῖρ λαλεῖν, ἀλλὰ ὑποηαζζέζθυζαν,
καθὼρ καὶ ὁ νόμορ λέγει.

In English, a word-for-word gloss gives

the women in the churches let them be silent: not indeed it is allowed to them to speak, but to be in submission, as also the law says.

Commenting on contemporary interpreters of 1 Corinthians 14:34–35 (both complementarian and egalitarian), Anna Sui Hluan has demonstrated that "it is clear that their presuppositions have infuenced their interpretations." She then argues that it is necessary for all of us to allow "the gospel to challenge one's presuppositions" and that interpreters of Scripture "must allow the gospel to challenge those influences that shape our understanding of Scripture."[33] The modern cultural readings which see in this text a biblical basis for woman's inferiority fit well with the prevailing culture. In patriarchal cultures, women are not seen as men's equal. The common belief in such cultures is that men are the peak of humanity, while women fall short. Today, those statements seem distasteful. This puts today's readers in a radically different place for interpreting passages like 1 Corinthians 14:34–35. There are many ways to read 1 Corinthians 14:26–40. However, the Church should not use any text of Scripture either to affirm or negate a position on any matter, unless it explicitly speaks to the proposed position. Implicit passages and those that do not clearly silence women should not be used to formulate doctrines. There are various arguments and interpretations on 1 Corinthians 14. Some of these arguments are really subordinating to women in the ministry of the Church. Other arguments speak a refreshing word of good news to women. This section examines these various interpretations.

---

[33] Anna Sui Hluan, *"Silence" in Translation: 1 Corinthians 14:34–35 in Myanmar and the Development of a Critical Contextual Hermeneutic*, 203, 204, 318.

Mercy Uwaezuoke Chukwuedo
Women, Leadership, and Ordination in the Anglican Church in Nigeria: Debating 1 Corinthians 14:26–40

1. Scribal Insertion

In Galatians 3:28, we see the yearning of Paul for all to be free from slavery and sexism. Paul cannot call for the liberation of all in that text and suddenly shift to enslaving and subordinating women in 1 Corinthians 14:34–35. Because this passage, taken at face value, seems to contradict so much of Paul's thought elsewhere in his corpus, a number of scholars have argued this passage was inserted by another writer later than Paul, possibly to conform to more conservative norms, such as might be expected in a Jewish synagogue. They also observe that in some manuscripts, verses 34–35 appear after verse 40. As a matter of fact, if verses 33b–36 are omitted (and even more so if 33b–38 are omitted), the thought moves smoothly from verse 33a to the conclusion in verses 39–40.[34]

2. Correction of Disorderliness

It is not unreasonable to think that this passage was written to combat some kind of disorder or a particular type of speaking; if original to Paul, this could refer to a local Corinthian problem in the first century or if a later insertion could be in response to a disturbance such as Montanism, in which women had a prominent role. However, a major objection to this assumption is that the troublesome passage occurs in all the manuscripts, even in those where it is displaced; and in the more reliable manuscripts, the order is what we have in the text above. Moreover, the passage is unlike that in 1 Timothy 2:11–15, which seemingly forbids women to teach in the Church.[35] It is more likely that Paul himself wrote or dictated this passage, perhaps after receiving a report of the disorderly and chaotic situation in Corinth. When we reconcile his statement that women should keep silent in the churches, for they are not allowed to speak, with 1 Corinthians 11:4–5, where they pray and prophesy, we understand it

---

[34] George T. Montague, *First Corinthians*, 255–256; Philip B. Payne, *Man and Woman, one in Christ: An Exegetical and Theological Study of Paul's Letters* (Grand Rapids: Zondervan, 2009), 217–267; Payne, "Vaticanus Distigme-obelos Symbols Marking Added Text, Including 1 Corinthians 14.34–5." Kirk R. MacGregor specifically refutes Payne in "1 Corinthians 14:33b–38 as a Pauline Quotation-Refutation Device." See also Payne's response to MacGregor, "Is 1 Corinthians 14:34–35 a Marginal Comment or a Quotation? A Response to Kirk MacGregor." Jerome Murphy-O'Connor offers an excellent review of the issues, "Interpolations in 1 Corinthians," 90–92.

[35] A discussion of 1 Timothy 2:11–15 is beyond the scope of this article, but I say "*seemingly* forbids" because the clarity of most English translations is misleading. E.g., see Linda L. Belleville, "Exegetical Fallacies in Interpreting 1 Timothy 2:11–15: Evaluating the text with contextual, lexical, grammatical, and cultural information"; Belleville, "Teaching and Usurping Authority: 1 Timothy 2:11-15"; Jamin Hübner, "Revisiting the Clarity of Scripture in 1 Timothy 2:12"; Craig S. Keener, "Interpreting 1 Timothy 2:8–15"; Cynthia Long Westfall, "The Meaning of αὐθεντέω in 1 Timothy 2.12."

better. Thus, he must be referring to speaking other than praying or prophesying. It is needful to ask; what kind of speaking would that be? The sequence about asking in their meeting gives a hint — several people speaking at once, speaking words that no one could understand.[36]

3. *Addressing Insubordination*

Why did Paul write to the Corinthians that women should keep silent in the Churches when he had just informed them that women prayed and prophesied in public (11:5)? What did he mean when he used the word 'to speak' (λαλεῖν / *laleĩn*)? What relationship is there between the word 'to speak' and the enquiries which they were to direct to their husbands at home? The verb σιγάω (*sigáō*, 'to keep silence' or 'to be silent') was not only meant for the women but was also used with reference to tongue speakers and others in exercising their spiritual gifts. Paul's usage of λαλέω (*laléō*), usually glossed simply as 'speak' in contemporary English, in context would mean disruptive chattering to the original readers (or listeners, as most of the recipients would have experienced Paul's letters by listening to them being read aloud). This approach is also given by Hurley, who suggests that since Paul commanded the prophets to evaluate their messages to make sure no false doctrine was present, and since women were among the prophets, then a problem of subordination to men arose.[37] Witt explains that women are the third group of people whom Paul told to keep silent within the short space between 14:28 and 14:34.[38] Paul makes use of the same word he used on tongue speakers as he does about women.[39]

4. *Inappropriate Evaluation of Prophetic Utterance*

Seemingly after the prophets spoke; other prophets would judge the utterance. If this position is correct, then women were disallowed this opportunity, for this would put them over the male prophets. One might counter that this would be in contradiction to 1 Corinthians 11:2–16, where Paul allowed women to pray and prophesy as long as their heads were covered. But in that passage the women were speaking divine utterances, whereas in 14:33b–36 they were not. Hurley opines that those who spoke under divine control were not expressing their own authority and so were not in violation of the Law. So then any public speaking other than a divine utterance would be in violation of Paul's prohibition in 1 Corinthians 14:33b–36.[40] From the various interpretations and arguments on the Pauline injunction to the Church and women, one

---

[36] Montague, *First Corinthians*, 255–256.
[37] Hurley, *Man and Woman in Biblical Perspectives*, 112–113.
[38] Witt, *Icons of Christ*, 149–150.
[39] Hurley, *Man and Woman in Biblical Perspectives*, 201.
[40] Hurley, *Man and Woman in Biblical Perspectives*, 127–128.

could say that Paul never intended to silence women but to caution those who were disorderly in the Church.

5. Quotation-Refutation Device

Alternatively, perhaps Paul is quoting and correcting a Corinthian approach to women. It is well-established that Paul at times will quote something his interlocutors have previously written and then give a refutation of their claim. In at least five other passages of 1 Corinthians (6:12–13; 7:1–2; 8:1, 8; 10:23), "Paul quotes a position from the Corinthians' letter with which he disagrees and then refutes it."[41] Peppiatt and MacGregor have independently argued that verses 14:33b–35 represent the incorrect position of the Corinthians and verses 36–38 are Paul's rebuke of their error.[42] If, as they have argued, this is another example of Paul correcting the faulty views of the recipients of his letter, then this

> reveals a great sense of harmony and coherence in this section, as well as demonstrating how it fits in with the letter as a whole. Not only does it rescue Paul from either gross misogyny or just strange and contradictory thinking, but it also gives us the key to understanding how 1 Corinthians 11–14 is entirely consistent with Paul's theology, with his views on the mutuality of relations between men and women expressed elsewhere, with his concern to look after the poor and the marginalized, and with his desire that all should be down decently and in order, which for Paul means with due consideration and care for the entire congregation.[43]

6. New Interpretations

In recent times, no longer does everything revolve around men. Coinciding with this shift, new interpretations of 1 Corinthians 14:26-40 have emerged. The best interpretations should make sense to both current readers and provide insight into how the original audience would have understood it. It's possible that Paul was addressing a specific local issue or applying a timeless principle to a local context in his writing to the Corinthians. Since many specific details about the Church in Corinth are no longer known, it is important to consider how Paul's original audience would have perceived his message, even if it seems confusing to later readers. Perhaps the words silencing women were not

---

[41] MacGregor, "1 Corinthians 14:33b–38," 25.
[42] MacGregor, "1 Corinthians 14:33b–38;" Peppiatt, *Women and Worship at Corinth*. Peppiatt argues throughout the book that "Paul was using a strategy throughout 1 Corinthians 11–14 where he cites his opponents views from their letter . . . in order to refute them" and does so "more than had previously been acknowledged," 4.
[43] Peppiatt, *Women and Worship at Corinth*, 135.

originally part of the letter.[44] Alternatively, as noted above, the Corinthians were silencing women and Paul was correcting that practice. Again, either of these makes Paul's actual letter intelligible to the Corinthians, and the cultural bias against women explains why a scribe felt the need to add words commanding their silence or why it was forgotten that Paul was arguing against the silencing of women.

Hence, proper exegesis and liberation theology play significant roles in the text to liberate the Church from misinterpretation of Bible text and re-interpreting to reflect God's plan of liberating humanity. "Theology of liberation attempts to reflect on the experience and meaning of faith based on the commitment to abolish injustice and to build a new society."[45] 1 Corinthians 14:26–40 is centred on orderliness. Paul enjoins the Corinthian Church to be orderly in the use of spiritual gifts. The gifts of the Spirit are not meant for public show but to edify the body of Christ. Based on this, he set out rules that should govern worshippers when they gather for worship which this study paraphrased thus:

Paul expected those exercising their spiritual gifts to be orderly.

Do not all speak at once.

Utterances should be one at a time.

As one speaks, the other should keep silent.

One should interpret.

If there is no interpreter, the speaker should keep quiet.

Two or three prophets should speak, and let others judge.

If anything is revealed to another who sits by, let the first keep silent.

The gifts of the Spirit are not for show off or personal aggrandizement but for the edification of the Church.

1 Corinthians 14:26–40 speaks volumes about Paul's intention for women when compared to other texts such as: Galatians 3:28 which says there is neither Jew nor Gentile, slave nor free, male nor female; for you are all one in Christ, Romans 16:1–15 gives a list of women whom Paul commended and referred to as co-workers, and in 1 Corinthians 11:2–16, Paul advised the women to cover their head when praying or prophesying. These texts give us a clue that Paul was only trying to correct anomalies in the Corinthian Church. Examining the entire corpus of Paul's writings reveals that "Paul was a proponent of women in ministries, spreading the good news of equality throughout the Empire. He

---

[44] Craig S. Keener, *Paul, Women and Wives: Marriage and Women's Ministry in the Letters of Paul*, 74.

[45] Letty M. Russell, *Human Liberation in a Feminist Perspective — A Theology*, 20.

modelled and supported equitable practices. He led the way for establishing a new kind of community where all were empowered to lead in God's Church."[46]

Background and Review of 1 Corinthians 14:26–40

A brief background of Corinth helps us to understand Paul and the Church in Corinth better. Contrarily to popular opinion, Paul's adherence to gender equity aligns with the gospel of freedom that he champions and preaches. The apostle is seen by many feminists as one who hates women, or at least as one who accepts their supposed inferiority. Others have perceived him to have been one attracted to women.

The city of Corinth was located on a narrow strip of land, called an isthmus. This isthmus connected Peloponnesus with Greece. Corinth was about 40 miles (64 kilometers) west of Athens; it was the capital of the province of Achaia with a population of 500,000. In the first century, Corinth was the crossroads of the commercial world. It had two seaports, one on each side of the narrow isthmus. Frequently, instead of sailing all the way around the landmass, ships would have their cargo carried overland from the Aegean Sea to the Gulf of Corinth.[47] The importance of Corinth as a city was its geography. It was situated between the harbours of Lechaion on the North and Cenchreae on the South-East. The location provided Corinth with a busy emporium. Corinth had numerous temples, shrines and theatres.[48]

Because of the commercial aspect of the city, Corinth had a lot of money and low morals. The city was known for its sensual pleasure. Even to the pagan world, Corinth was known for its moral corruption, so much so that in classical Greek κορινθιάζω (*korinthiázō* — literally, 'to behave like a Corinthian') came to represent gross immorality and drunken debauchery; in the middle voice (κορινθιάζομαι / *korinthiázomai*) the verb meant "to visit prostitutes."[49] On the highest hill of the city stood the temple of the Greek goddess Aphrodite. A thousand sacred prostitutes worked from this temple satisfying the sensual needs of the devotees. This background reveals why the Corinthian Church was faced with a lot of issues bordering on moral values to battle with which also informed the purpose of the letters the apostle Paul wrote to them. The inhabitants of Corinth with their Corinthian lifestyle came into the Church and were displaying their permissive lifestyles.

---

[46] Grace May, "Appreciating how the Apostle Paul Champions Women and Men in Church Leadership," 94.
[47] Danny McCain, *Notes on New Testament Introduction*, 217.
[48] Matthew R. Malcom, *The World of 1 Corinthians: An Annotated, Visual and Literary Source-Commentary*, xix.
[49] BrillDAG, s.v. "κορινθιάζω."

Paul addresses the problem of disorderliness in the worship assembly by saying in verse 35, "If they want to inquire about something, let them ask their own husbands at home" (NIV-1984). This implies that the problem in Corinth is concerning the asking of questions with a desire to learn something says Blomberg. The word translated as "inquire" in this verse (in the NIV) is μανθάνω (*manthánō*), which is usually translated as *learn*. Blomberg suggests that "perhaps the largely uneducated women of that day" who had a legitimate desire to *learn* "were interrupting proceedings with irrelevant questions that would be better dealt with in their homes."[50] Similarly Belleville states that the "their fault was not in the asking per se but in the inappropriate setting for their questions."[51] Keener advocates this as the primary problem — the women were speaking up, asking questions to learn what was going on during the prophecies or the Scripture exposition in church. They were also interrupting the Scripture exposition with questions. This would have caused an affront to more conservative men or visitors to the church, and it would have also caused a disturbance to the service due to the nature of the questions.[52] The major concern of Paul was to discourage both men and women from using their freedom in Christ as a license to behave indecently in the Church. This is the reason he rebuked the women who probably were calling out their questions across the Christian assembly.

Female Leadership Debate: Goddesses and Priestesses in Igbo Traditional Religion

It is relevant to state that in the traditional African society, women are not expected to play the roles of men. Generally, there are societal expectations associated with being male or female. Women are expected, traditionally in the African society to handle household chores and care giving. Based on this, one would have assumed that women cannot fit into the position of becoming priests. Women play the role of priestess in some parts of Africa, including in my Igbo tribe. The Igbo are found in the southeastern part of Nigeria.[53] In the

---

[50] Blomberg, *1 Corinthians*, 280.
[51] Linda L. Belleville, *Women Leaders and the Church: Three Crucial Questions*, 161.
[52] Keener, *Paul, Women and Wives*, 71–72.
[53] The Igbo speaking people share the same belief system no matter their location. The Igbos believe strongly in the Supreme Being — *Chi Ukwu* or *Chukwu*, both of which can be translated as 'God Almighty.' *Chi Ukwu* is also called *Chineke* (the Creator). John Mbiti reports that *Chukwu* (though he gives the spelling *Chuku*) "is derived from words (*Chi* and *uku*) that mean 'the Great Spirit'" and that "the Igbo believe God to be 'the Great First Cause', who continues to create more people and without whom they cannot be formed (born)." Mbiti, *Concepts of God in Africa*, 50, 57. Many Igbos are Christians, but before the introduction of Christianity, they practiced *Odinala* (Igbo Traditional Religion).

Igbo context, priestesses are authorized to perform sacred religious rites, especially as a mediatory agent between humans and deities. They also have the authority or power to administer religious rites; in particular, rites of sacrifice to, and propitiation of, a deity or deities. Their office or position is the priesthood, a term which also may apply to such persons collectively.[54] Historically, women served in these capacities as diviner, healer and priestess comfortably in the precolonial era before the inception of Christianity. However, these practices were challenged by the Church and seen as paganism, thereby producing a negative stereotype.

The goddesses are believed to exert great influence in the affairs of human beings.

> In African societies, deities, the most powerful of whom is the Great Creator God, serve as the true political heads or spiritual monarchs of their communities. Next in rank to God are the lesser gods and goddesses. Personifications of natural phenomena, the most influential are gendered females, deities in charge of the waters and the land. These deities are the moral judges of conduct and wield power indiscriminately. I center the leadership of (fe)male gendered spiritual forces such as goddesses, oracles, female medicines, and their human helpers (e.g., priestesses, diviners, spirit mediums, and prophetesses)—the real rulers of African kingdoms, paramount, towns, and communities.

In Igbo culture, women play a vital role in religious worship but are traditionally not permitted to enter the shrine. However, they can serve as priestesses for minor deities, such as the Ogbanje priestess, who represents the *chi* or personal spirit for women.

On 15 August 2023, in the Awgu Local Government Area of Enugu State, I was privileged to meet a beautiful woman who serves as *Eze-nwanyi* ('Priestess' or 'Queen mother'). She was not ashamed to identify herself as such, not minding how society and Christians look at the vocation. By Christians and Muslims, those who occupy the position of *Eze-nwanyi* are seen as idol worshippers and pagans. She bragged about her position as a worshipper and servant of the water goddess. According to her, she was chosen by the water goddess "mamiwater" (water spirit) to serve. In my interaction with her, she disclosed to me that she is serving God through the smaller deities he created. Those who have ailments, hard luck, and different challenges come to her to consult spirits and get quick answers to their problems. Not only do the spirits tell her the cause of the problems of her clients, she says, but they also give her a solution to the problem.

---

[54] Gladys I. Udechukwu, "Position of Women in Igbo Traditional Religion," 88.

Mercy Uwaezuoke Chukwuedo
Women, Leadership, and Ordination in the Anglican Church in Nigeria: Debating 1 Corinthians 14:26–40

This is a confirmation to Achebe's assertion that spirit mediums are believed to be embodiments of the spirits or the ancestors. It is a form of possession in which a person serves as an intermediary between the gods and the society.[55] This affirms that women occupy high ranking leadership positions even concerning spiritual matters. According to Achebe, "spirit medium societies provide women with the most direct avenues for active participation in politics and religious life. Spirit mediums can achieve measures of power that place them above men and mortals."[56]

We have complementarian (i.e., hierarchical) views among Igbo regarding the roles of priestesses in Igboland. Of this complementarian view, Udechukwu cites an informant who asserted that

> a woman cannot handle or be the chief priestess of a family or village deity. It is said in Igbo "Agwụ anaghi ama nwaanyi" (a woman cannot be a deity) which means that an oracle cannot suggest a woman as a legitimate person to handle "Isi Agwu" (the head deity). A woman cannot lead public worship in the presence of men. The "Isi Mmoo" (the spirit head) is meant for a man.[57]

When we compare the views concerning women as ministers in Christianity and women occupying spiritual positions in Igboland, we can see a correlation. Women occupy the position of *Eze-nwanyi* ('priestess'), which is a spiritual leadership position. They are recognized in most Igbo communities. There are still pockets of resistance against women taking up leadership positions in Igbo Traditional Religion and in the Church. Women are restricted from being in charge of the *ofo* ('staff') which stands for peace and justice. They cannot be in charge of the *obi* ('a space at the entrance of a compound where guests are welcomed').[58]

Significantly, the existence of goddesses and priestesses show that women are recognized in Igbo Traditional Religion. This could be a potential correlation with current-day policies and practices supporting gender balance, and Christian ethical standards. More teachings and enlightenment ought to be carried out because my observation as a leader in the Church shows that women are more in number in the Church and contribute more in the development of the Church and so their ordination and full participation in leadership should be encouraged.

---

[55] Achebe, *Female Monarchs and Merchant Queens in Africa*, 35.
[56] Achebe, *Female Monarchs and Merchant Queens in Africa*, 36.
[57] Udechukwu, "Position of Women," 89; citing p. 20 of an interview with U. Ikeokwu.
[58] The *obi* is a connection point in every Igbo home.

Conclusion

Women are enjoined in 1 Corinthians 14:26-40 to be orderly in the Church and not participate in a way that leads to confusion and disruption. Exegesis of the text shows that it is not a blanket ban on their active participation in the worship assembly. Women's contributions to Church growth and development in different denominations through the women's ministry is an affirmation that the ordination of women will bring about more records of progress. Paul's injunction to women in 1 Corinthians 14:26-40 should not be used to silence women since Paul had earlier said women prayed and prophesied in 1 Corinthians 11. It is clear looking at the pericope that the church in 1 Corinthians 14 was disorderly. Paul cautioned both men and women to exercise their spiritual gifts in such a way that promotes decorum. Liberation theology is a call to all despite gender, ethnicity, or nationality to serve God with an open mind and use the gifts bestowed by God to serve the people. God has liberated all through the death and resurrection of his son Jesus.

Paul was addressing a specific situation rather than making a general prohibition on women speaking in the Church. He intended to prohibit disruptive and disrespectful questions and comments that were observed in Corinthian meetings. These particular practices were coming from the women. Just as Paul told the disorderly tongue speakers and prophets to control themselves because God is not a God of disorder, he also told the women to control themselves because the law teaches self-control. If they want to learn anything, they can ask questions somewhere else. Only one person should speak at a time. Everyone else, whether male or female should be quiet for it is disgraceful for people in the audience to be talking while another is speaking to the group. Taking stance with the egalitarians, women can serve in all forms of Church leadership. As Cynthia Long Westfall has demonstrated,

> women should interpret and apply instructions to all believers with the same hermeneutics as men. The passages about determining the function of each believer in the church and the call to ministry are general instructions for all believers. The priesthood of the believer applies to all believers, so that the function, race, social status, physical condition, and gender of priests in the Old Testament are not requirements or prerequisites for any ministry in the Christian community. The Holy Spirit determines who gets what gift; a theological system that filters and restricts the gifts for a given group compromises the authority of the Holy Spirit.[59]

---

[59] Cynthia Long Westfall, *Paul and Gender: Reclaiming the Apostle's Vision for Men and Women in Christ*, 242.

Men and women are to diligently and whole heartedly develop their spiritual gifts for the edification of the Church and societal development.

Recommendations

As Paul advised, there should be orderliness in the Church. The local assembly should not be chaotic in the exercise of spiritual gifts. Women called to serve or allowed to serve should bring out their best and make an impact. The Church and society need more women to contribute to societal development and building of lives.

Ordination of women will enhance Church growth and enable women clergy to lead change in the society. It will also allow female voices to be heard concerning the challenges women face in different cultures.

Women are resilient and highly productive in any project they undertake. Therefore, the ordination of women is crucial in the Church based on the significant contributions they have made as educators, caregivers, counselors, prayer leaders, and more. This indicates that when given the opportunity, they can achieve even more.

Providing women with opportunities in leadership would offer additional personnel, especially in areas experiencing a shortage of ministers. In some parts of the country where there are few or no men in the Church, women can take on leadership roles. Therefore, there should be more openness to having women serve as pastors.

Bibliography

ACHEBE, Nwando. "Igbo Goddesses and the Priests and Male Priestesses who serve them." Chapter 2 in *Igbo in the Atlantic World: Origins and Diasporic Destinations,* edited by Toyin Falola and Raphael Chijioke Njoku, 28–45. Bloomington, Indiana, USA: Indiana University Press, 2016.

———. *Female Monarchs and Merchant Queens in Africa.* Ohio Short Histories of Africa. Athens, Ohio, USA: Ohio University Press, 2020.

AGBO, Timothy. *Women Ordination in Nigeria: An Ecclesiological Analysis.* Enugu, Nigeria: Snaap Press, 2003.

AYENI, Sade Oluwakemi. "Women in the Nigerian Church: A Stucy of the Akoko Anglican Diocese." *Anglican and Episcopal History* 92, no. 3 (2023): 427–244. https://www.jstor.org/stable/27241155

BELLEVILLE, Linda L. "Exegetical Fallacies in Interpreting 1 Timothy 2:11–15: Evaluating the text with contextual, lexical, grammatical, and cultural information." *Priscilla Papers* 17, no. 3 (2003): 3–11. PDF link to entire issue: https://www.cbeinternational.org/wp-content/uploads/2021/04/Silence_Summer-2003-Volume-17-Number-

3_PP17.3.pdf; link to article in html format: https://www.cbeinternational.org/resource/exegetical-fallacies-interpreting-1-timothy-211-15/

———. "Teaching and Usurping Authority: 1 Timothy 2:11-15." Chapter 12 in *Discovering Biblical Equality: Complementarity Without Hierarchy*, edited by Ronald W. Pierce and Rebecca Merrill Groothuis, with Gordon D. Fee, 205–223. 2nd edition. Downers Grove, Illinois, USA: IVP Academic, 2005.

———. "Teaching and Usurping Authority: 1 Timothy 2:11-15." Chapter 11 in *Discovering Biblical Equality: Biblical, Theological, Cultural & Practical Perspectives*, edited by Ronald W. Pierce and Cynthia Long Westfall, with Christa L. McKirland, 205–227. 3rd edition. Downers Grove, Illinois, USA: IVP Academic, 2021.

———. *Women Leaders and the Church: Three Crucial Questions*. Grand Rapids, Michigan, USA: Baker Books, 1999.

BLOMBERG, Craig L. *1 Corinthians*. NIV Application Commentary. Grand Rapids, Michigan, USA: Zondervan, 1994.

BUTLER, Sara. "Women's Ordination: Is it Still an Issue?" Arch Diocese of New York.[60] 7 March 2007. Archived at Pontificio Consiglio per i Laici [Italian: 'Pontifical Council for the Laity'], https://www.laici.va/content/dam/laici/documenti/donna/teologia/english/womens-ordination-still-an-issue.pdf

CHIEGBOKA, Anthony B. C. *Women Status and Dignity in the Society and the Church: A Perspective from Galatians 3:26–29*. Enugu, Nigeria: Pearl Functions Limited, 1997.

CHIRWA, Frank B. *Mission in Progress: The Developing Role of Women in the Church: An SDA Perspective from Malawi*. Mzuzu, Malawi: Mzuni Press, 2020.

CHUKWUEDO, Mercy U. *African Women in Ministry, The Nigerian Experience: Perspectives from 1 Corinthians 14:26-40*. Enugu, Nigeria: Rabboni Publishers, 2019.

———. "The Place of Women in the Church of Nigeria (Anglican Communion): Perspectives from 1 Corinthians 14:26-40." PhD Dissertation, Nnamdi Azikiwe University, Awka, Nigeria, 2018. https://phd-dissertations.unizik.edu.ng/onepaper.php?p=459

DEI, Daniel, and Robert OSEI-BONSU. "The Female Ordination Debate: Theological Reflections." *Asia-Africa Journal of Mission and Ministry* 11, no. 1 (2015): 31–62. https://dx.doi.org/10.21806/aamm.2015.11.02

---

[60] As of 20 August 2023, this paper was still available at the Arch Diocese's website at www.archny.org/seminary/st-josephs-seminary-dunwoodie/administration/sister-sara-butler/, but that link is now defunct.

EDWARDS, Bob. *Let My People Go: A Call to End the Oppression of Women in the Church*. Charleston, South Carolina, USA: Createspace, 2011.

GRUDEM, Wayne. *Evangelical Feminism and Biblical Truth: An Analysis of 118 Disputed Questions*. Sisters, Oregon, USA: Multnomah, 2004; reprint: Leicester, England: Inter-Varsity Press, 2005.

GILES, Kevin. "Book Review: Wayne Grudem's *Evangelical Feminism*." CBE International, 31 July 2008, https://www.cbeinternational.org/resource/book-review-wayne-grudems-evangelical-feminism/

HLUAN, Anna Sui. *"Silence" in Translation: 1 Corinthians 14:34–35 in Myanmar and the Development of a Critical Contextual Hermeneutic*. Carlisle, Cambria, UK: Langham Monographs, 2022.

HODGSON, Dorothy L. *The Church of Women: Gendered Encounters Between Maasai and Missionaries*. Bloomington, Indiana, USA: Indiana University Press, 2005.

HÜBNER, Jamin. "Revisiting the Clarity of Scripture in 1 Timothy 2:12." *Journal of The Evangelical Theological Society* 59, no. 1 (2016): 99–117.

HURLEY, James B. *Man and Woman in Biblical Perspectives*. Leicester, England: Inter-Varsity Press; Grand Rapids: Academie Books, 1981.

JAMES, Nancy Carol. *The Developing Schism within the Episcopal Church: 1960-2010: Social Justice, Ordination of Women Charismatics, Homosexuality, Extra-territorial Bishops; etc*. Lewiston, New York, USA: Edwin Mellen Press, 2010.

KASSIAN, Mary A. *The Feminist Gospel: The Movement to Unite Feminism with the Church*. Wheaton, Illinois, USA: Crossway Books, 1992.

KEENER, S. Craig. "Interpreting 1 Timothy 2:8–15." *Priscilla Papers* 12, no. 3 (1998): 11–13. PDF link to entire issue: https://www.cbeinternational.org/wp-content/uploads/2021/05/Summer-1998-Volume-12-Number-3-Paul-PP12.3.pdf; link to article in html format: https://www.cbeinternational.org/resource/interpreting-1-timothy-28-15/

———. *Paul, Women and Wives: Marriage and Women's Ministry in the Letters of Paul*, Peabody, Massachusetts, USA: Hendrickson, 1992.

KNIGHT, George W., III. *The New Testament Teaching on the Role Relationship of Men and Women*. Grand Rapids, Michigan, USA: Baker, 1977.

KNOLL, Benjamin. "Women's Ordination in the Anglican Communion: the Importance of Religious, Economic, and Political Contexts." Religion in Public. 25 January 2021. https://religioninpublic.blog/2021/01/25/womens-ordination-in-the-anglican-communion-the-importance-of-religious-economic-and-political-contexts/

KRASS, A. C. *Applied Theology 1: 'Go... And Make Disciples.'* TEF Study Guide 9. London: SPCK, 1974.

MALCOM, R. Matthew. *The World of 1 Corinthians: An Annotated, Visual and Literary Source-Commentary*. Milton Keynes, England: Paternoster, 2012.

MAY, Grace. "Appreciating How the Apostle Paul Champions Women and Men in Church Leadership." Chapter 7 in *The Quest for Gender Equity in Leadership: Biblical Teachings on Gender Equity and Illustrations of Transformation in Africa*, edited by Keumju Jewel Hyun and Diphus C. Chemorion, 77–95. Foreword by Joseph D. Galgalo. House of Prisca & Aquila Series. Eugene. Oregon, USA: Wipf & Stock, 2016.

MBITI, John S. *Concepts of God in Africa*. 2nd edition. Foreword by Jesse N. K. Mugambi. Nairobi: Acton Publishers, 2012.

McCain, Danny. *Notes on New Testament Introduction*. Bukuru, Nigeria: Africa Christian Textbooks, 2005.

MACGREGOR, Kirk R. "1 Corinthians 14:33b–38 as a Pauline Quotation-Refutation Device." *Priscilla Papers* 32, no. 1 (2018): 23–28. https://www.cbeinternational.org/wp-content/uploads/2019/01/Pauline-Quotation-Refutation-Device-PP321.pdf

MONTANARI, Franco. *The Brill Dictionary of Ancient Greek*. Edited by Madeleine Goh and Chad Schroeder. Leiden: Brill, 2015. (Abbreviated BrillDAG)

MOMBO, Esther. "The Ordination of Women in Africa: A Historical Perspective." Chapter 9 in *Women and Ordination in the Christian Churches: International Perspectives*, edited by Ian Jones, Janet Wootton, and Kirsty Thorpe, 123–143. T&T Clark Theology. London: T&T Clark, 2008.

MONTAGUE, George T. *First Corinthians*. Catholic Commentary on Sacred Scripture. Grand Rapids, Michigan, USA: Baker Academic, 2011.

MURPHY-O'CONNOR, Jerome. "Interpolations in 1 Corinthians." *The Catholic Biblical Quarterly* 48, no. 1 (1986): 81–94. http://www.jstor.org/stable/43719287

NZWILI, Fredrick. "Africa's six Anglican women bishops meet and issue call to combat Africa's 'triple threat'." Religion News Service. 19 January 2024. https://religionnews.com/2024/01/19/africas-six-anglican-women-bishops-meet-and-issue-call-to-combat-africas-triple-threat/

ODOGWU, Odogwu Emeka. "Anglican Archbishop Okays Women's Ordination to the Diaconate." *Daily Champion* (Lagos newspaper). 8 June 2010. Reprint: World-Wide Religious News, https://wwrn.org/articles/33610/

OKANLAWON, Samuel Oluwatosin. "Galatians 3:28: a Vision for Partnership." In *Co-Workers and Co-Leaders: Women and Men Partnering for God's Work*, edited by Amanda Jackson and Peirong Lin, 35–46. The WEA Global Issues Series. Bonn, Germany: Verlag für Kultur und Wissenschaft, 2021.

OKOLI, Anuli B., and Lawrence OKWUOSA. "The Role of Christianity in Gender Issues and Development in Nigeria." *HTS Teologiese Studies/Theological Studies* 76, no. 4 (2020): Article #6007, 8 pages. https://doi.org/10.4102/hts.v76i4.6007

PAYNE, Philip B. *Man and Woman, One in Christ: An Exegetical and Theological Study of Paul's Letters*. Grand Rapids, Michigan, USA: Zondervan, 2009.

———. "Vaticanus Distigme-obelos Symbols Marking Added Text, Including 1 Corinthians 14.34–5." *New Testament Studies* 63, no. 4 (2017): 604–625. https://doi.org/10.1017/S0028688517000121

PEPPIATT, Lucy. *Women and Worship at Corinth: Paul's Rhetorical Arguments in 1 Corinthians*. Foreword by Douglas Campbell. Eugene, Oregon, USA: Cascade Books, 2015.

PETERSEN, Kirk. "Province of Central Africa Approves Ordination of Women." The Living Church. 7 November 2023. https://livingchurch.org/news/province-of-central-africa-approves-ordination-of-women/

REID, W. George. "The Ordination of Women: A Review of the Principal Arguments for and against the Ordination of Women to the Gospel Ministry." Unpublished white paper, Seventh Day Adventist Church, Office of Archives, Statistics, and Research (Adventist Archives), January 1985. https://www.adventistarchives.org/the-ordination-of-women-a-review-of-the-principal-arguments.pdf

RUSSELL, Letty M. *Human Liberation in a Feminist Perspective — A Theology*. Philadelphia: Westminster Press, 1974.

"The Summary of SID BRC Position on the Ordination of Women." Seventh Day Adventist Church, Office of Archives, Statistics, and Research (Adventist Archives), n.d., https://www.adventistarchives.org/brc-southern-africa-indian-ocean-division-presentation.pdf

THOMAS, Hilfah F., and Rosemary Skinner KELLER, eds. *Women in New Worlds: Historical Perspectives on the Wesleyan Tradition*. Nashville, Tennessee, USA: Abingdon Press, 1982.

TIMM, Alberto R. "Seventh Day Adventists on Women's Ordination: A Brief Historical Overview." Unpublished paper submitted to the Theology of Ordination Study Committee, Columbia, Maryland, 21–25 January 2014. Seventh Day Adventist Church, Office of Archives, Statistics, and Research (Adventist Archives), https://www.adventistarchives.org/seventh-day-adventists-on-womens-ordination-a-brief-historical-overview.pdf

UDECHUKWU, Gladys I. "Position of Women in Igbo Traditional Religion." *Journal of Linguistics, Language and Culture* 4 (2017): 86–101. https://journals.ezenwaohaetorc.org/index.php/JoLLC/article/view/006-4-1-2017

WESTFALL, Cynthia Long. "The Meaning of αὐθεντέω in 1 Timothy 2.12." *Journal of Greco-Roman Christianity and Judaism* 10 (2014): 138–173. http://www.jgrchj.net/volume10/JGRChJ10-7_Westfall.pdf

———. *Paul and Gender: Reclaiming the Apostle's Vision for Men and Women in Christ*. Grand Rapids, Michigan, USA: Baker Academic, 2016.

WITTS, William G. *Icons of Christ: A Biblical and Systematic Theology for Women's Ordination*, Waco, Texas, USA: Baylor University, 2020.

Diversity of Eucharistic Ritual in COVID-2019 Context
A comparative study of CITAM Valley Road and PCEA St Andrew's in Nairobi, Kenya

Samwel Kiuguini NDUATI

ORCID: 0009-0009-3141-0057
Egerton University, Nairobi, Kenya
nduatisam1973@gmail.com

Linda OCHOLA-ADOLWA

ORCID: 0000-0003-0539-8989
International Leadership University,
Nairobi, Kenya
lindaochola@gmail.com

Abstract

Discussing diversity in the celebration of the Eucharistic ritual in COVID-2019 contexts, this is a comparative study of CITAM (Christ is the Answer Ministries) Valley Road assembly and St. Andrew's PCEA (Presbyterian Church of East Africa) in Nairobi, Kenya. COVID-2019 had a great impact on the order of worship in Christian churches across the world. Churches were closed down at times. Whereas CITAM Valley Road administered the Eucharist in the virtual space, St Andrew's PCEA did not adopt virtual Eucharist and had to wait until the lockdown prohibiting church meetings was lifted. This ethnographic study was carried out in Nairobi County at CITAM Valley Road and St. Andrew's PCEA over a period of six months from late 2021 to early 2022. The methodological approach taken by the researchers was a blend of ethnography and grounded theology. Data was collected through virtual ethnography, participant observation, interviews, and focus group discussions. Findings from the study demonstrated an emerging trend of administering the Eucharist digitally as the Church in Kenya navigated both continuity and change. The findings also revealed the fact that religious change advances not suddenly, or as a single complete change, but in specific expressions that are local and distinct. The researchers posit that in the PCEA, believers could not imagine themselves administering virtual Eucharist in their homes; in CITAM also some Christians felt that administering the Eucharist in the virtual space was different from when it was administered in the physical space.

Published with license by ACTEA | DOI: https://doi.org/10.69683/8ad96283
© Samwel Kiuguini Nduati & Linda Ochola-Adolwa, 2024
ISSN: 3006-1768 (print); 3007-1771 (online)
This is an open access article distributed under the terms of the CC BY 4.0 license.

Samwel Kiuguini Nduati & Linda Ochola-Adolwa
Diversity of Eucharistic Ritual in COVID-2019 Context: A comparative study of CITAM Valley Road and PCEA St. Andrew's in Nairobi, Kenya

Résumé

Cette étude comparative porte sur la diversité de la célébration du rituel eucharistique dans les contextes COVID-2019. Elle porte sur deux congrégations religieuses différentes, toutes deux situées à Nairobi, au Kenya : l'assemblée *CITAM* (*Christ is the Answer Ministries* ['Le Christ est la Réponse Ministères) qui se réunit sur la rue *Valley Road* et l'église de St André *PCEA* (*Presbyterian Church of East Africa* ['Église Presbytérienne d'Afrique du l'Est']. Le COVID-2019 a eu un impact considérable sur le déroulement du culte dans les églises chrétiennes du monde entier. Des églises ont parfois été fermées. Alors que le *CITAM Valley Road* a administré l'eucharistie dans l'espace virtuel, *PCEA* de St André n'a pas adopté l'eucharistie virtuelle et a dû attendre que la fermeture interdisant les réunions d'église soit levée. Cette étude ethnographique a été menée dans le comté de Nairobi au *CITAM Valley Road* et à *PCEA* de St André sur une période de six mois, de fin 2021 à début 2022. L'approche méthodologique adoptée par les chercheurs est un mélange d'ethnographie et de théologie ancrée. Les données ont été recueillies par le biais d'une ethnographie virtuelle, d'une observation participante, d'entretiens et de discussions de groupe. Les résultats de l'étude ont démontré l'émergence d'une tendance à administrer l'eucharistie numériquement alors que l'Église du Kenya naviguait à la fois dans la continuité et le changement. Les résultats ont également révélé le fait que le changement religieux ne se produit pas soudainement, ni comme un seul changement complet, mais dans des expressions spécifiques qui sont locales et distinctes. Les chercheurs avancent que dans le *PCEA*, les croyants ne pouvaient pas s'imaginer administrer l'eucharistie virtuelle dans leurs maisons ; dans le *CITAM* également, certains chrétiens estimaient que l'administration de l'eucharistie dans la salle de bain était une pratique qui ne pouvait pas se faire à l'extérieur de la maison.

Resumo

Discutindo a diversidade na celebração do ritual eucarístico em contextos COVID-2019, este é um estudo comparativo de duas congregações eclesiais diferentes, ambas em Nairobi, Quénia: a assembleia *CITAM* (*Christ is the answer ministries* ['Cristo é a Reposta Ministérios']) ue se reúne na estrada *Valley Road* e a igreja de St André *PCEA* (*Presbyterian Church of East Africa* ['Igreja Presbiteriana da África Oriental']. A COVID-2019 teve um grande impacto na ordem do culto nas igrejas cristãs de todo o mundo. Por vezes, as igrejas foram encerradas. Enquanto o *CITAM Valley Road* administrava a Eucaristia no espaço virtual, a *PCEA* de St André não adoptou a Eucaristia virtual e teve de esperar que o confinamento que proibia as reuniões da igreja fosse levantado. Este estudo etnográfico foi realizado no condado de Nairobi, no *CITAM Valley Road* e no *PCEA* de St André, durante um período de seis meses, entre o final de 2021 e o início de 2022. A abordagem metodológica adoptada pelos investigadores foi uma mistura de etnografia e teologia fundamentada. Os dados foram recolhidos através de etnografia virtual, observação participante, entrevistas e discussões em grupos de discussão. As conclusões do estudo demonstraram uma tendência emergente de administrar a Eucaristia digitalmente à medida que a Igreja no Quénia navegava tanto na continuidade como na mudança. Os resultados também revelaram o facto de que a mudança religiosa não avança subitamente, ou como uma única mudança completa, mas em expressões específicas que são locais e distintas. Os investigadores afirmam que, no *PCEA*, os crentes não se imaginavam a administrar a Eucaristia virtual nas suas casas; no *CITAM*, também alguns cristãos sentiam que administrar a Eucaristia nas casas de família era uma tarefa difícil.

Keywords

Eucharist, CITAM, COVID-2019, PCEA

Mots-clés

Eucharistie, CITAM, COVID-2019, PCEA

Palavras-chave

Eucaristia, CITAM, COVID-2019, PCEA

Introduction

The Eucharist — also known as Holy Communion, Lord's Supper, the Mass, and the Divine Liturgy — is a sacred time of fellowship with God and with one another, where believers remember the sacrifice of Jesus on the cross.[1] The Lord's Supper has always been and "remains the central Christian ritual. It celebrates the life, death and resurrection of Jesus Christ – whose death is at the heart of the gospel of salvation."[2] Jesus himself instituted Holy Communion, as seen in all three of the synoptic Gospels (Mathew, Mark, and Luke). In the Matthean account, Jesus instituted the Communion in the following way:

---

[1] Ralph N. McMichael, *Eucharist: A Guide for the Perplexed*, 2.
[2] Edison Muhindo Kalengyo, *Celebrating the Lord's Supper: Ending the Eucharistic Famine*, 4. Baptism, of course, is equally central to Christian faith and practice — but baptism is intended as a single event, whereas we are intended to partake of the Lord's Supper repeatedly.

Samwel Kiuguini Nduati & Linda Ochola-Adolwa
Diversity of Eucharistic Ritual in COVID-2019 Context: A comparative study of CITAM Valley Road and PCEA St. Andrew's in Nairobi, Kenya

Now as they were eating, Jesus took bread, and blessed, and broke it, and gave it to the disciples and said, "Take, eat; this is my body." And he took a cup, and when he had given thanks, he gave it to them, saying, "Drink of it, all of you; for this is my blood of the covenant, which is poured out for many for the forgiveness of sins. I tell you I shall not drink again of this fruit of the vine until that day when I drink it new with you in my Father's kingdom." (Matt 26:26–29, RSV).

Paul adds the following saying of Jesus from the tradition he had received: "This cup is the new covenant in my blood. Do this, as often as you drink it, in remembers of me" (1 Cor 11:25, RSV). Across Christian traditions, Holy Communion symbolizes Christ's death, participation in the benefits of Christ's death, spiritual nourishment, the unity of believers, the affirmation of Christ's love for Christians, Christ's blessings of salvation and the affirmation of a Christian's faith in Christ.[3]

Around the world, the pandemic had an immeasurable effect on ecclesial life, as has been widely studied.[4] Following the first reported case of the coronavirus epidemic in Kenya in March 2020, religious and other social gatherings were suspended to contain the spread of the virus. Where possible, social gatherings including churches, mosques, temples, weddings, and burials were discouraged. As an alternative, social media and virtual meetings were recommended as a way to maintain devotion and worship. The goal of this was that congregants were encouraged to pray and worship from their homes to prevent exposure to the virus. While many churches made technological adaptations to ecclesial life during the pandemic — some enthusiastically, others reluctantly — it is generally clear that "the use of technologies is not as much a new way of being church as an adaptive practice to maintain the connection."[5] The longterm impact, of course, remains to be seen. While there are many

---

[3] Wayne Grudem, *Systematic Theology: An Introduction to Biblical Doctrine*, 988.
[4] Articles are too numerous to list. Notable books specific to the impact of COVID-19 on Christian faith and practice specifically in Africa include, e.g., Mookgo Solomon Kgatle and Collium Banda, eds., *Pastoral Interventions During the Pandemic: Pentecostal Perspectives on Christian Ministry in South Africa*; Harvey C. Kwiyani and Joseph Ola, eds., *Wash and Pray: African Theological Discourse on COVID-19*; Martin Munyao, Joseph Muutuki, Patrick Musembi, and Daniel Kaunga, eds., *The African Church and COVID-19: Human Security, the Church, and Society in Kenya* [editors' note: this text was reviewd in vol. 1, no. 1 of this journal]; Emiola Nihinlola and Folashade Oloyede, eds., *The Church & the COVID-19 Pandemic*; and Owojaiye, Babatomiwa M. *Evangelical Response to the Coronavirus Lockdown: (Insights from the Evangelical Church Winning All)*.
[5] Geomon K. George et al., "Lament in the City," 45.

published studies regarding the the pandemic's impact on Christian faith and practice, its effects on participation in the Eucharist has received less attention.

Administering Eucharist Virtually at St. Andrew's PCEA during the Covid-19 Pandemic

During the lockdown of the churches in Kenya, the Presbyterian Church of East Africa did not administer Holy Communion for a period of several months. This was despite the fact that historically, the Presbyterian church of East Africa had celebrated Holy Communion once a month as corroborated in the earliest records of the St. Andrew's Church. The St. Andrew's church leadership noted that the impact of virtual meetings and the absence of the ritual of Holy Communion resulted in decreased emotional solidarity among church members. The youth service media team articulated similar views in a focus group discussion, noting that interaction with others in a virtual space was limited. As a result, the emotional solidarity or warmth experienced in gathering physically and in sharing rituals such as Holy Communion were all but non-existent. To assess the perceptions of the church members with regard to the impact of virtual services on the worship experience, the church members were asked which practices could not be substituted by the virtual space. One of the practices they highlighted was Holy Communion. They noted that the absence of Holy Communion from their experience affected their sense of belonging. The absence of the opportunity to gather and ask for God's forgiveness and to receive absolution in community as well as to pray together and to eat the bread and drink the wine seems to have impacted on the sense of belonging and communality experienced by the members of the church.

To compare the differences between the physical worship experience and the virtual worship experience, congregants were asked to indicate the degree of the emotional solidarity experienced in both. The respondents consistently noted that "it is hard to interact with others when one is watching virtually." Thus a common view among the interviewees was that community and fellowship would be lost if the church were to remain totally in the virtual space. A recurrent theme in the discussions was a sense that the beauty of fellowship and the warmth of the people that encouraged the faith of members to grow was missing from the virtual experience.

When the church reopened partially, allowing limited numbers to come to church services, the requirement to maintain social distancing affected the administration of communion. Contrary to expectations, there was no uniform way prescribed by the church in which communion should be administered. Kenya's Ministry of Health provided guidelines in consultation with religious institutions including the PCEA. Broadly, these guidelines included the wearing of masks in public space and the washing of hands with soap and running water.

Many churches including St. Andrew's Church provided these facilities. St. Andrew's and other churches also provided clearly demarcated seating spaces to enable the congregants maintain a physical distance of a meter from one another. The mode of administering communion also changed to accommodate COVID protocols of minimizing physical contact. The congregants at first had to pick the bread or wafers up with a spatula and dip the cup in a basin with water after partaking of the elements.

Administering Eucharist Virtually at CITAM Valley Road during the Covid-19 Pandemic

In a similar way, the COVID-19 pandemic caused a pastoral and theological challenge to CITAM (Christ is the Answer Ministries) congregation on Valley Road because of the containment measures which led to the closure of all physical gatherings at least for a time. CITAM Valley Road had to adopt new strategies to maintain a sense of community, whilst adhering to health protocols provided by the state. Besides the struggle to preach to and reach the congregants virtually, CITAM Valley Road Church also struggled with the administration of the sacrament of Holy Communion in the virtual space. In traditions such as CITAM Valley Road, where the altar and the clergy remained the focal point of worship, there were two main options. The first was to distribute the pre-blessed elements to the congregation the day before so that communicant members could receive them together in real time. This, however, posed health risks and severe legal repercussions based on the laws of the country. The second alternative, which was adopted by CITAM Valley Road Church and in which one of the researchers also participated, facilitated a virtual blessing of the bread and wine supplied by the households themselves.

Amidst the COVID-19 pandemic, the government in Kenya mandated that only "essential services" remain open. Worship was considered to be an essential service. This dealt an irreparable blow for churches and their leaders. Some pastors — especially Pentecostal ones — resisted this move by the Government. They met physically with congregants against the moratorium. Others, secretly hoping for things to return to normal in a few days, became complacent. In this latter group, the transition to an online format soon picked up as people became desperate for spiritual and clerical guidance. Even the most reluctant of pastors realized that this was no time for a sabbatical especially after noticing the rapid growth of online worship services.

St. Andrew's Church and CITAM Valley Road: Historical Comparison

There are important reasons for choosing St. Andrew's PCEA Church and CITAM Valley Road when researching the different ways in which churches addressed the administration of Holy Communion during the legal suspension of physical gatherings. One of these lies in the basic difference between St. Andrew's PCEA and CITAM Valley Road Church.

To begin with, the Presbyterian Church of East Africa is one of the four largest denominations in Kenya with about four million members in Kenya, Uganda, and Tanzana.[6] By 1929, the number of converts had risen to over 5,000. Since 1935, PCEA pastors have been trained at St. Paul's United College alongside Anglican and Methodist clergy. The PCEA has played and continues to play an important role in Kenya, having pioneered in educational and medical work. PCEA founded the first hospital in Kenya. The church currently sponsors over 700 primary and secondary schools across the country. In terms of its online presence, the Nairobi region has nine presbyteries. A total of fifty-seven parishes within these presbyteries have online services and only fifteen do not have an online service.

The Presbyterian Church of East Africa grew out of the work of the Church of Scotland starting in 1891.[7] Preston provides an in-depth analysis of the historical beginnings of the PCEA Church.[8] The first service connected with the Scots church was conducted in May 1908. The foundation stone of St. Andrew's church in Nairobi was laid in 1910 with the involvement of both the foreign mission and the colonial committee. The church continued to grow under its successive ministers even against the backdrop of the world war of 1939–1945. In its earlier years under the Rev. Howieson, the church grew both through missions to various parts of Kenya and Uganda as well as through monthly wireless broadcast services and by the congregational magazine which the minister edited. Whereas the Presbyterian Church of East Africa came into being as a mission church founded by the white settlers and reflects the liturgy and structures of the Church of Scotland, some aspects of members' African culture have been retained. These include the use of vernacular language for worship, the use of dance as an expression of worship, and the practice of communal eating and drinking, particularly in the context of the district fellowships, but also on special occasions in the congregation, to enhance the sense of community. Khasandi-Telewa notes that the Scottish missionaries embraced the use of the local vernacular to enable the new converts to read and understand the Bible clearly.[9] It is worth noting that for the PCEA in general, even though many years have passed, the use of vernacular is still a unique characteristic of the PCEA churches even in highly cosmopolitan urban areas,

---

[6] PCEA, "About Us," n.d., https://PCEA.or.ke/about-us/
[7] PCEA, "Our History," n.d., https://PCEA.or.ke/about-us/
[8] David Preston, *History of the Colonial Mission of the Church of Scotland*, 2.
[9] Vicky Khasandi-Telewa, "'She Worships at the Kikuyu Church': The Influence of Scottish Missionaries on Language in Worship and Education among African Christians."

such as Nairobi, where St. Andrew's Church is located. Whereas this team of researchers did not observe the use of vernacular language at PCEA St. Andrew's Church in particular, PCEA St. Andrew's predominantly remains the preserve a single community or language group, the Kikuyu. This means that the aspect of a shared way of life, shared values and obligations, shared meanings and understanding remains vibrant even the midst of the apparent formality of the church processes and procedures.

On the other hand, Christ is the Answer Ministries (CITAM) began about fifty years later, in 1959 when Nairobi Pentecostal Church (NPC) was founded as a multi-ethnic church grounded in the Word of God and sound doctrine.[10] The initial congregation which became CITAM was established as a ministry of the Pentecostal Assemblies of Canada (PAOC). In September 1960, the congregation moved to Valley Road where the present CITAM Valley Road campus is located. In 2003, Nairobi Pentecostal Church changed its name to Christ is the Answer Ministries (CITAM). By 2016, CITAM had a total of eighteen assemblies: seven located in Nairobi (Valley Road, Woodley, Parklands, Karen, Thika Road, Buru, and Embakasi), four within the environs of the greater Nairobi area (Ngong Town, Kiserian/Rongai, Athi River, and Thika Town), four in other towns (Kisumu, Nakuru, Eldoret, and Kapsabet), one in Namibia, and two outside of Africa (Romania and USA). Within Kenya, CITAM runs mission stations in Marsabit, Isiolo, and Turkana Counties, with additional outreach to the Rendille, Borana, Burji, Gabra, Elmolo, Samburu, and Turkana communities. CITAM Media comprises radio and TV stations which also stream online. The radio station, Hope FM, has become a premier station with a large listenership in Nairobi and its environs, Mombasa, Western Kenya, and streaming to other parts of the world. CITAM Valley Road church has grown from a small assembly with a morning service attendance of about twenty to thirty people in 1959 to an estimated attendance today of 45,000 and more than 250 regular staff.

The phenomenal growth of the Nairobi Pentecostal Church can be clearly seen. Among other factors, the growth of CITAM can be attributed to its focus on evangelism, which has been expressed through a variety of approaches including the adoption of cyberspace long before the advent of the COVID-19 pandemic. CITAM Valley Road in particular had already invested heavily in the equipment necessary to stream its content live through various social media platforms including Facebook, Twitter, Instagram, and Youtube. Consequently, the use of the virtual space to administer Holy Communion was embraced quickly by CITAM Valley Road which had already adopted online services long before the start of the COVID-19 pandemic. St. Andrew's Church however, like

---

[10] Christ is the Answer Ministries [CITAM], *2016–2015 Strategic Plan*, 4.

many other mainline Churches, found itself in a dilemma on how Holy Communion could be administered in the virtual space.[11] The PCEA primarily establishes new congregations in person. This strategy involves existing congregations starting new ones when there are enough potential members nearby.

St. Andrew's and CITAM Valley Road: Theological Similarities around the Eucharist

Nonetheless, there are enough similarities between St. Andrew's and CITAM Valley Road to warrant a worthwhile comparison. Both St. Andrew's and CITAM Valley Road share a common Protestant understanding of the Eucharist, based on a symbolic and spiritual presence of Christ. John Calvin and other reformers argued that the bread and wine of the Lord's Supper did not physically change into the body and blood of Christ (transubstantiation), nor did they somehow contain the body and blood of Christ. But they symbolized the body and blood of Christ, and they gave a visible sign of the fact that Christ Himself was truly present. Today most Protestants would say, in addition to the fact that the bread and the wine symbolize the body and blood of Christ, that Christ is also spiritually present in a special way as Christians partake of bread and wine.

Eucharist and Ritual theory

Ritual theories assert that focused interaction, which these theories refer to as ritual, is at the heart of all social dynamics.[12] Rituals generate group emotions which are linked to symbols. These symbols form the basis for beliefs, thinking, morality, and culture. People use the capacity for thought, beliefs, and strategy to create emotion, which in turn generates interactions in the future. This cycle

---

[11] It is important to note that across the PCEA as a denomination, there was no single prescribed way to administer Holy Communion after the church resumed physical gatherings. Once congregations began gathering again, the ministers exercised a lot of creativity around that time including pre-packed communion. Pre-packed communion as an approach has been preserved to this day due to the ease and efficiency, in spite of its greater expense. While the clergy were given a communication to administer communion in a way that ensures the health of the congregants, there was no one particular prescribed way. In addition, there was no communication forbidding virtual administration of the Holy Communion. Some congregations silently allowed the families to take communion. If a family took communion, no one chastised them or consider them to be out of order. Some families took communion by themselves but not officially. There were conversations around how long this could be continued. If COVID-19 had extended, how was this to happen?

[12] Erika Summers-Effler, "Ritual Theory," 135.

forms patterns of interaction over time. These patterns are the most basic structural force that organizes society.[13]

Durkheim was one of the first to put forward a strong theory of ritual and emotion, building his theory on ethnographic accounts of the ritual behavior of aborigines in central Australia.[14] Durkheim investigated the mechanisms that held society together from many angles, focusing on religious ritual, and ultimately arguing that ritual is the fundamental mechanism that holds a society together. He provided a powerful theory of the role of ritual in group life. He illustrated how religious ritual leads to increased interaction, especially focused, intense, and rhythmic interaction. Durkheim described how rituals generate emotional arousal, which he referred to as collective effervescence. Collective effervescence is experienced as a heightened awareness of group membership as well as a feeling that an outside powerful force has sacred significance.

We argue that the Eucharist fits into Durkheim's definition of a ritual, given that it is a focused interaction that lies at the heart of the social dynamics between Christian believers. In the celebration of the Eucharist, Christian group emotions are linked to the bread and wine as symbols, thereby forming the basis for beliefs, thinking, morality, and culture. In this way, Christians use their capacity for thought, beliefs, and strategy to create emotion-generating interactions in the future. During observance of the Eucharist, the Christian community gathers, asks God's forgiveness for its sins, and listens to readings from the Bible including a reading from one of the Gospels. A sermon or homily may be preached, and the community prays together. Bread and wine (or substitutionary elements) are brought to the table (called 'the altar' in some traditions), the celebrant prays a Eucharistic Prayer, and in some traditions everyone recites the Lord's Prayer together. The community then receives the consecrated bread and wine. At the end of the service, the community is sent out into the world as a 'living sacrifice' to live and work to God's praise and glory.

Given the historical and doctrinal significance of the Eucharist as the central ritual of the Church (along with Baptism), handed down by Christ himself, the difference in the responses of St. Andrew's PCEA church and CITAM Valley Road is particularly curious, especially given that they were each functioning in the same geographical context of Nairobi and were facing the same global challenges as other churches across the world. We explored the concerns behind their different responses as we sought to understand the emerging trends in the administration of the Eucharist during the COVID-19 pandemic.

---

[13] Summers-Effler, "Ritual Theory," 135.
[14] Emile Durkheim, "The elementary forms of religious life."

Samwel Kiuguini Nduati & Linda Ochola-Adolwa
Diversity of Eucharistic Ritual in COVID-2019 Context: A comparative study of CITAM Valley Road and PCEA St. Andrew's in Nairobi, Kenya

Findings

Two issues were identified arising from the divergent positions adopted by CITAM Valley Road and the St. Andrew's Church, PCEA. The first was the question of distinguishing between communicants and the non-communicants. The PCEA does not celebrate an open Holy Communion table. St. Andrew's Church offers communion exclusively for confirmed members. From the 1950s, participation in Holy Communion was restricted to a specific group called communicants. Data from archival records point out that a period of instruction was undertaken for adults as well as for young people in several high schools including the Kenya High School for girls, among others. Thereafter, an application for admission to become communicants was made. Once the minister was satisfied with the knowledge and professions of the applicants, prescribed questions were put to the applicants and upon satisfactory answers, the applicants were confirmed in their baptism through prayer and in the name of the kirk session and admitted to communion.[15] These early records indicate that the process by which individuals were admitted to the church was quite clearly laid down. Similarly, the early records of St. Andrew's Church indicate that the practice of the church was to prepare and update a roll of members and adherents. The roll was to be updated by a committee composed of the moderator and two others. To accommodate the growth of the church, it became necessary to separate the rolls of each district, overseen by an elder. In the past, the practice was to make the communion roll available for members to scrutinize and to make changes in case of mistakes. The absence of communion during COVID may be explained by the fact that in a virtual service, there would be no easy way to distinguish between those confirmed and those not confirmed and no easy way to hold services for communicants alone. It would have been possible for anyone from among those following on YouTube, Facebook, and the church hub, to participate in Holy Communion — not all of whom were necessarily communicants. Although the respondents acknowledged that church was not limited to a physical building or the physical gathering of its members, those interviewed specifically noted that some of the practices that could not be substituted in virtual forms included weddings, confirmation, baptisms, and Holy Communion. Despite the fact that the members of St. Andrew's Church who participated in the research felt that the virtual church met the spiritual needs in the same way as the physical service, nevertheless given that they could not access Communion except through i- person presence in church services, they also acknowledged that certain elements that would be lost if the church were to totally remain in the virtual space including Confirmation and Communion. In the course of the research period, one

---

[15] David Preston, *History of the Colonial Mission of the Church of Scotland*, 74. Note that 'kirk' is the Scots English word for 'church.'

ordained minister remarked: "Imagine, we have not had Communion since last year April!"

CITAM Valley Road took a different position and opted to administer Holy Communion virtually. Most Protestants agree that only those who believe in Christ should participate in it,[16] and many Protestants also argue that only those who have been baptized should participate in the Lord's Supper. However, some churches practice what is called *open communion* while others practice a 'members only' *closed communion*. Because they practice closed communion, PCEA congregations bar a visiting Roman Catholic from the Table and Roman Catholic congregations bar visiting Christians who are not Roman Catholic from participating in Holy Communion.[17] While most who practice open communion only limit communion to the baptized, others object to such restriction advancing an argument that 'genuine believers' should be allowed to participate in the Lord's Supper whether baptized or not.[18] CITAM Valley Road made the decision to practice open communion, leaving the choice of whether or not to participate virtually in communion in the hands of those participating, without being concerned as to whether participants were CITAM members or even whether they had been baptized.

A second emerging issue was the question of who should administer the Eucharist. Some recognize that scripture gives no explicit teaching about who should administer communion and therefore conclude that there is freedom to decide on what will benefit the believers in the Church.[19] To guard against abuse, some who take this view assume that a responsible leader ought to oversee the administering of the Lord's Supper. However, there is no reason other believers cannot assist the leader to distribute the elements. This was the view espoused by CITAM Valley Road in its decision to administer Holy Communion virtually. Other traditions limit the role of presiding over the Table to particular ordained individuals.

At St. Andrew's Church, as well as the Presbyterian church of East Africa in general, the administration of the Holy Communion requires the elders or presbyters. It is the elders who prepare the communion and then pass it on to

---

[16] Grudem, *Systematic Theology*, 996.
[17] Historically, in the Presbyterian tradition the practice of closed communion was referred to as 'fencing the Table.'
[18] The question as to whether someone who has refused baptism can nonetheless be a 'genuine believer' is beyond the scope of this article. Furthermore, many congregegations — whether practicing closed communion or open communion — operate under a *de facto* 'don't ask, don't tell' policy, and announce that communion is only for members or only for the baptized but then will serve anyone who wants to be served.
[19] Grudem, *Systematic Theology*, 998.

the members. The role of supporting the minister in the administration of the Holy Communion is one of the reasons why elders are ordained. Uncertainty around the question of whether a member of the church alone could expressly take communion without the presence of an elder was the principal concern for PCEA leadership. The challenge was more ecclesiastical and traditional than theological as theologically the minister can offer communion without assistance. In church practice, the PCEA minister administers communion with the support of an elder under normal circumstances. This is similar to baptism, during which a minister is also paired with an elder. In traditional PCEA practice, Holy Communion is a sacrament administered by an elder and minister together. That is the order. During the pandemic shutdowns, it was difficult to find a way to administer communion since the minister was not in the same place as the members. In the practice of the St. Andrew's Church and the PCEA as a whole, the minister can double as an elder, so he is not limited in terms of administering communion if there is no elder present. Conversely however, although the minister is sufficient by himself, the PCEA elders cannot offer communion on their own. For example, the district fellowships in the past have been one of the contexts within which Holy Communion can be administered in the presence of a minister and an elder. In this regard, the question arose as to whether the head of a family could stand in for an elder in the absence of the elder or whether the faith of a believer could suffice in the absence of an elder.

One important question still remains to be answered. Given that there was no evidence of members missing a particular grace while they did not access communion for several months, what is the value of communion for PCEA members? What then is the necessity of Holy Communion, given that during the COVID-19 pandemic church members did not access Holy Communion for several months? What was the efficacy of Holy Communion if people went on with their lives and missed no grace in the months when no communion was taken? Was it just a ritual whose value could be mediated in another way if it could not be done?

Perhaps, the critical question is the conceptualization of administering Eucharist in the virtual space. What was the perception of Christians on the virtual administration of Eucharist? The evidence from this study suggests that some Christians (from St. Andrew's PCEA) were completely disoriented when they stayed for some months without partaking of the Holy Communion. This study has raised an important question on whether the urgency to receive or administer the elements in isolation concealed an even greater pursuit, namely, the search for God-with-us. This question suggests that if Christians see God as not dwelling in a building, then everything is understood as sacramental. In this sense, he is deeply immersed within the realm of human and cosmic beings.

There is great need therefore to have a renewed understanding of sacrament and especially in the administration of Eucharist. While some may have temporarily experienced a pandemic-induced "eucharistic famine", perhaps others did not 'miss' participation in Holy Communion due to "a general ignorance of its importance and its benefits" among many Africans.[20]

Although the current study is based on a relatively short period of study within the two churches, between October 2021 and March 2022, it has shown that CITAM Valley Road and St Andrew's Church, PCEA adopted different approaches to the administration of Holy Communion when physical contact became untenable as a result of the containment measures introduced by the governments of the World. These included physical closure of religious institutions. This paper contributes to our understanding of the impact of the adoption of virtual church services on the unchangeable constants of Christian worship.

The pandemic lockdowns brought about an onslaught on a global scale triggering a universal revolution with reference to social and ecclesial norms. Aiava asserts that they

> prompted a retrospective turn to 'what was' as the 'new normal' had become overrun by physical isolation. Things formerly taken for granted, for instance, communal worship, face-to-face learning, or even simple things like shaking hands, stimulated an inevitable rethinking of normalcy in both public and private spheres. Even for countries and cultures like those in the Pacific, where subsistence living is predominant, a ripple effect was clearly visible. Some more than others had finally realized how far ecology had been enslaved by the economy and worse, how far the Christian faith had been systemically isolated from both.[21]

Administration of Holy Communion was greatly affected despite its place as a venerated sacrament in a Christian life. Its role in the Christian life is vital:

> The sacrament of Holy Communion is a foundational resource for the life of faith, an imperative of our Lord, and one of the key ways in which our belonging within the body of Christ is affirmed. It also plays a pivotal part in shaping the church's mission and witness in the world, by calling members of the body of Christ to the daily practice of sacramental living.[22]

---

[20] Kalengyo, *Celebrating the Lord's Supper*, 3.
[21] Faafetai Aiavā, "Pacific Christianity online or on the line? Renewing church, sacrament and worship amidst the pandemic," 129.
[22] Wessel Bentley, "Celebrating the sacrament of Holy Communion during COVID-19: A Methodist perspective," 129.

The proper way to take part in that Holy Communion is to receive the Body and Blood of Christ in the Eucharistic Bread and Wine both *spiritually* (in faith) and *physically* (with the body), *oraliter* (with one's mouth), as some reformers put it the latter dimension. The COVID-19 pandemic would not allow this to continue. However, the use of technology helped the Churches to appeal to the virtual space. Virtual spaces became innovative places of worship and as Aiava (2022) posits, it became apparent that if interpersonal communication through virtual spaces can communicate God's grace and compassion to others, then it too can be a place of worship.[23] Administering Eucharist as a Christian Sacrament had to have a new meaning in the virtual space. 'Sacrament' is frequently glossed as "an outward and visible sign of an inward and invisible grace."[24] According to Aiava, this "Augustinian formula ... has served the church for eons" and "in the context of ecclesiology," Christians seldom negate this teaching.[25]

Conclusion

We set out to study the emerging trends of the Eucharist and its administration in two faith communities in Kenya. Given the impact of the containment measures of COVID-19, we have discussed the fact that this fellowship among believers was not available during the covidian lockdown of churches, which resulted in divergent approaches to addressing the issue. We have shown that there are differences in terms of the adoption of virtual services on the worship of PCEA and CITAM amidst the COVID-19 pandemic. These distinctives find their basis in the differing ecclesiologies and sacramental theologies held by the PCEA, is a historic mission church, and CITAM, a Pentecostal church. These case studies may indicate that it was easier for a Pentecostal church, which shares many characteristics with AICs, to inculturate ecclesial practice to a new situation, while a mission church was more bound by its inherited tradition.

Bibliography

AIAVĀ, Faafetai. "Pacific Christianity online or on the line? Renewing church, sacrament and worship amidst the pandemic." Chapter 11 in *Christianity and COVID-19: Pathways for Faith*, edited by Chammah J. Kaunda, Atola Longkumer, Kenneth R. Ross, and Esther Mombo, 129–139. Routledge New Critical Thinking in Religion, Theology and Biblical Studies. London: Routledge, 2021.

---

[23] Aiavā, "Pacific Christianity online or on the line?," 136.
[24] E.g., so Bruce Milne, *Know the Truth: A Handbook of Christian Belief*, 285.
[25] Aiavā, "Pacific Christianity online or on the line?," 131.

BENTLEY, Wessel. "Celebrating the sacrament of Holy Communion during COVID-19: A Methodist perspective." *HTS Teologiese Studies/Theological Studies* 77, no. 3 (2021): Article #6741, 8 pages. https://doi.org/10.4102/hts.v77i3.6741

Christ is the Answer Ministries [CITAM]. *2016–2015 Strategic Plan.* Nairobi: Christ is the Answer Ministries [CITAM], n.d. https://www.citam.org/wp-content/uploads/2019/02/CITAM-Strategic-Plan.-2016-2025-rvsd-1.pdf

COLLINS, Randall. *Interaction Ritual Chains.* Princeton Studies in Cultural Sociology. Princeton, New Jersey, USA: Princeton University Press, 2004.

Congregational Health Messages on COVID – 19: For Use By Religious Leaders. Nairobi, Kenya: Ministry of Health, 2020. https://nsdcc.go.ke/wp-content/uploads/2020/11/FAITH-SECTOR-COVID-19-MESSAGES.pdf

DURKHEIM, Emile. "The Elementary Forms of Religious Life." Chapter 4 in *Social Theory Re-Wired: New Connections to Classical and Contemporary Perspectives,* edited by Wesley Longhofer and Daniel Winchester, 52–67. 2nd edition. London: Routledge, 2016.

GEORGE, Geomon K., Reji GEORGE, Sarah Gerth VAN DEN BERG, Mark R. GORNIK, Adebisi OYESILE, and Afia Sun KIM. "Lament in the City." Chapter 3 in *World Christianity and Covid-19: Looking Back and Looking Forward,* edited by Chammah J. Kaunda, 25–46. Cham, Switzerland: Palgrave Macmillan, 2023. https://doi.org/10.1007/978-3-031-12570-6_3

GRUDEM, Wayne A. *Systematic theology: An Introduction to Biblical Doctrine.* 2nd edition. Grand Rapids, Michigan, USA: Zondervan Academic, 2020.

KALENGYO, Edison Muhindo. *Celebrating the Lord's Supper: Ending the Eucharistic Famine.* Foreword by Alfred Olwa. Bukuru, Nigeria: HippoBooks, 2018.

KGATLE, Mookgo Solomon, and Collium BANDA, eds. *Pastoral Interventions During the Pandemic: Pentecostal Perspectives on Christian Ministry in South Africa.* Cham, Switzerland: Palgrave Macmillan, 2022.

KHASANDI-TELEWA, Vicky. "'She Worships at the Kikuyu Church': The Influence of Scottish Missionaries on Language in Worship and Education among African Christians." Chapter 13 in *Africa in Scotland, Scotland in Africa: Historical Legacies and Contemporary Hybridities,* edited by Afe Adogame and Andrew Lawrence, 287–306. Africa-Europe Group for Interdisciplinary Studies 14. Leiden: Brill, 2014.

KWIYANI, Harvey C., and Joseph OLA, eds. *Wash and Pray: African Theological Discourse on COVID-19.* Liverpool: MissioAfricanus, 2023.

MACQUARRIE, John. *Principles of Christian Theology.* New York: Charles Scribner's Sons, 1966.

McMichael, Ralph N. *Eucharist: A Guide for the Perplexed.* T&T Clark Guides for the Perplexed. London: T&T Clark, 2010.

Milne, Bruce. *Know the Truth: A Handbook of Christian Belief.* Downers Grove, Illinois, USA: IVP Academic, 2009.

Munyao, Martin, Joseph Muutuki, Patrick Musembi, and Daniel Kaunga, eds. *The African Church and COVID-19: Human Security, the Church, and Society in Kenya.* Lanham, Maryland: Lexington Books, 2022.

Nihinlola, Emiola, and Folashade Oloyede, eds. *The Church & the COVID-19 Pandemic.* Ogbomoso, Nigeria: The Nigerian Baptist Theological Seminary, 2020.

Owojaiye, Babatomiwa M. *Evangelical Response to the Coronavirus Lockdown: (Insights from the Evangelical Church Winning All).* Bloomington, Indiana, USA: WestBow Press, 2020.

PCEA. "About Us." n.d. https://PCEA.or.ke/about-us/

PCEA. "Our History." n.d. https://PCEA.or.ke/about-us/

Preston, David. *History of the Colonial Mission of the Church of Scotland.* Unpublished manscript, 1978.[26]

Summers-Effler, Erika. "Ritual Theory." Chapter 6 in *Handbook of the Sociology of Emotions*, edited by Jan E. Stets and Jonathan H. Turner, 135–154. Handbooks of Sociology and Social Research. New York: Springer, 2006.

---

[26] A photocopy of the manuscript is held at the Kenya National Archives in Nairobi.

Frank Weston of Zanzibar
An Assessment and Appreciation of an "Apostle to Africans" [1]

Maimbo W. F. MNDOLWA

ORCID: 0009-0002-4252-3179
Archbishop, Anglican Church of Tanzania
maimbo1969@gmail.com

Fergus J. KING

ORCID: 0000-0001-6822-1529
Trinity College Theological School,
Victoria, Australia
fergusk@trinity.unimelb.edu.au

Joshua Robert BARRON

ORCID: 0000-0002-9503-6799
ACTEA, Enoomatasiani, Kenya
Joshua.Barron@ACTEAweb.org

Abstract

On 2 November 1924, Bishop Frank Weston died at Hegongo, in what is now Tanzania. He was a significant theologian and controversialist, defending an Anglicanism rooted in Chalcedonian theology and episcopal ecclesiology. He rejected modernist theology not least because it implied that African Christians had to adopt European liberalism to understand the gospel. He lambasted German and British colonial administrations as disingenuous and inhumane. His commitment to orthodox theology, social justice, and rejection of claims for European superiority, remain relevant in a world still marred by injustice and neocolonial matrices which would seek to diminish the people of Africa.

Résumé

Le 2 novembre 1924, l'évêque Frank Weston est décédé à Hegongo, dans l'actuelle Tanzanie. Théologien et controversiste important, il défendait un anglicanisme enraciné dans la théologie chalcédonienne et l'ecclésiologie épiscopale. Il rejetait la théologie moderniste, notamment parce qu'elle impliquait que les chrétiens africains devaient adopter le libéralisme européen pour comprendre l'Évangile. Il a critiqué les administrations coloniales allemandes et britanniques en les qualifiant

---

[1] Christopher Byaruhanga, "Weston, Frank."

Published with license by ACTEA | DOI: https://doi.org/10.69683/dwjqv631
© Maimbo W. F. Mndolwa, Fergus J. King, & Joshua Robert Barron, 2024
ISSN: 3006-1768 (print); 3007-1771 (online)
This is an open access article distributed under the terms of the CC BY 4.0 license.

Maimbo W. F. Mndolwa, Fergus J. King, & Joshua Robert Barron
**Frank Weston of Zanzibar:
An Assessment and Appreciaiton of an "Apostle to Africans"**

de malhonnêtes et d'inhumaines. Son engagement en faveur de la théologie orthodoxe, de la justice sociale et du rejet des prétentions à la supériorité européenne reste d'actualité dans un monde encore marqué par l'injustice et les matrices néocoloniales qui chercheraient à diminuer les peuples d'Afrique.

Resumo

A 2 de novembro de 1924, o Bispo Frank Weston morreu em Hegongo, na atual Tanzânia. Foi um importante teólogo e polémico, defendendo um anglicanismo enraizado na teologia calcedoniana e na eclesiologia episcopal. Rejeitou a teologia modernista, sobretudo porque esta implicava que os cristãos africanos tinham de adotar o liberalismo europeu para compreender o Evangelho. Criticou as administrações coloniais alemã e britânica, considerando-as desonestas e desumanas. O seu compromisso com a teologia ortodoxa, a justiça social e a rejeição das reivindicações de superioridade europeia continuam a ser relevantes num mundo ainda marcado pela injustiça e por matrizes neocoloniais que procurariam diminuir o povo de África.

Keywords

African Christian history, Tanzania, Frank Weston, African agency

Mots-clés

Histoire chrétienne africaine, Tanzanie, Frank Weston, Agence africaine

Palavras-chave

História cristã africana, Tanzânia, Frank Weston, agência africana

Introduction

The late Lamin Sanneh challenged his readers to resist a simplistic reading of Christianity as a sanctified servant of the colonial enterprise.[2] This is not to say that there was no collaboration between mission and colonialism, but rather to note that this description is not appropriate universally. One of those who resists the easy identification, in Sanneh's opinion, was David Livingstone, whose preaching in the universities of Oxford and Cambridge would inspire the foundation of the Universities' Mission to Central Africa (UMCA), an Anglican

---

[2] For example, Lamin Sanneh, *Encountering the West: Christianity and the Global Cultural Process: The African Dimension*, 102–106.

Maimbo W. F. Mndolwa, Fergus J. King, & Joshua Robert Barron
Frank Weston of Zanzibar:
An Assessment and Appreciaiton of an "Apostle to Africans"

High Church mission identified linked strongly to the Oxford Movement.[3] Interestingly, UMCA's first missionary endeavours took place in territories which were not part of existing colonial regimes. Based first at the Zambezi delta, the rate of attrition due to climate and illness forced a relocation to Zanzibar, at that stage a Sultanate, technically independent of European colonial regimes, even if becoming increasingly a client state in a shifting political and economic landscape.

After the notorious Berlin Conference of 1884–1885, much of the area in which the UMCA worked, essentially moving from the coast up the existing trading routes to the interior, were under British or German administration as in the 1913 map. Thus, missionary and colonial activities were not always synchronous. Nor were they always sympathetic to the political activities of existing regimes: UMCA was committed to an eradication of the slave trade, a significant part of the Zanzibari economy. The eventual achievement of this goal, though not entirely the work of the society, is still visible today in Anglican Cathedral at Mkunazini, in the old Stone Town of Zanzibar, which is built on the site of the former slave market. To the Anglican missionaries, "government must constantly be tested against the ideals of Christianity. If it failed them it must be condemned, publicly and with authority."[4] Importantly, the UMCA was also committed to producing "an African clergy as early as possible."[5] This is the environment into which Frank Weston (13 September 1871 – 2 November 1924) would work, first as a missionary priest and educator, and later as the Bishop of Zanzibar. His own political and theological views would also shape a distinctive theological and political programme which challenged the conventional orthodoxies of his day. These, however, are also products of the environments — African, ecclesial, and political — in which Weston operated.

Biography

At 4:30 am on the morning of All Souls' Day, 2 November 1924, Bishop Frank Weston, after being anointed and receiving the last rites, died at Hegongo, in the Tanga Region of Tanganyika, now the United Republic of Tanzania. He is laid to rest there, in a place which was central to his life, mission, and commitment to Africa and its peoples.

Frank Weston was born on 13 September 1871. He was educated at Dulwich College and Trinity College, Oxford, graduating with a first class degree in

---

[3] A. E. M. Anderson-Morshead, *The History of the Universities' Mission to Central Africa*, Vol.1: *1859-1909*, 1–9; A. G. Blood, *The History of the Universities' Mission to Central Africa, Vol. 2: 1907-1932*, 1–4.
[4] John Iliffe, "The Spokesman: Martin Kayamba," 69.
[5] Terence O. Ranger, "The Apostle: Kolumba Msigala," 13.

Maimbo W. F. Mndolwa, Fergus J. King, & Joshua Robert Barron
**Frank Weston of Zanzibar:
An Assessment and Appreciaiton of an "Apostle to Africans"**

Theology in 1893. He was ordained Deacon in 1894 and Priest in 1895. He served two curacies at St John's Stratford East, (1894–1896) and St Matthews, Westminster (1896–1898). He joined the Universities' Mission to central Africa in 1898 and served as Chaplain, St Andrew's Training College, Kiungani (1898–99), St Mark's Theological College (1899–1901), Principal, St Andrew's Training College, Kiungani (1901–1908), Principal/Rector, St Mark's Theological College (1906–1908). He was consecrated Bishop, Zanzibar, 1908–1923. During the First World War, he served in the British Army's Carrier Corps, reaching the rank of Major.[6]

Weston was a leading light in the Anglo-Catholic movement of the 1920s,[7] praised for his oratory, and his personality. He was not tolerant of ecumenism and opposed the proposals of the Kikuyu Missionary Conference of 1913[8] for an ecclesiastical federation and inter-communion, even if this would have taken place under Anglican leadership.[9] His theological interests were varied. They included a significant theological study, *The One Christ*,[10] which has been highly praised:

- A "truly great book,"[11]
- "which scholars were still debating seventy years later."[12]
- "One of the most neglected of all books on the person of Christ," it is "simple and plausible", "maintain[ing] its value and

---

[6] According to Bengt Sundkler and Christopher Steed, "for his efforts the Bishop was awarded `the local rank of Major (but never gazetted)'." *A History of the Church in Africa*, 612.

[7] Sundkler and Steed describe him as "the living embodiment of the Anglo-Catholic movement." *A History of the Church in Africa*, 878.

[8] For an overview of the Conference, see Julius Gathogo, "The early attempts at ecumenical co-operation in East Africa: the case of the Kikuyu Conference of 1913" and Christopher Byaruhanga's discussion in "Nineteenth Century Missionary Enterprise in East Africa," chapter 3 in his *The History and Theology of the Ecumenical Movement in East Africa*.

[9] The Kikuyu Conference was born out of a spirit of ecumenicity and a hope for renewed ecclesial unity, or at least cooperation. But such early initiatives for cooperation in East Africa largely failed because they were primarily attempts at cooperation between missionary societies rather than between churches and also because they excluded African Christians, with the result that "the missing African dimension . . . meant that [African Christians] had no influence over the form of the future Christian church in Africa." Sam Kobia, "Denominationalism in Africa: The Pitfalls of Institutional Ecumenism," 302. Sundkler and Steed lament that "no African was invited to the negotiations, despite the fact that they were the ones concerned." *History of the Church in Africa*, 561.

[10] Frank Weston, *The One Christ: An Enquiry into the Manner of the Incarnation*.

[11] Donald M. MacKinnon, *Borderlands of Theology and Other Essays*, 112.

[12] John S. Peart-Binns, *Herbert Hensley Henson: A Biography*, 115.

relevance through to the present day in relation to those Christologies which start from the standpoint of Chalcedonian doctrine."[13]

His other writings engaged with issues of ecclesiology, mission, and political theology. His remarks remain pertinent today. The Anglican Communion is still grappling with issues he discusses in his more provocative, controversial, and polemic texts. Yet, for all that he may seem a difficult opponent, he could work constructively with those who held views deeply critical of his Anglo-Catholic theology and practice. His critique of colonial practice, aimed both at German and British administrations, would provoke reviews and changes in government policy.[14] Weston's rejection of colonialism is just one example of what Lamin Sanneh has identified as problematic: the simplistic notion that Christianity and Christian missions were always the handmaid of colonialism. Borrowing one of the oldest stories from European culture, he could say that:

> The missionary movement turned colonial empires into cathedrals of variety, difference, and irony, making religion in the empire a Trojan horse. The idea that Europe could take other lands and impose its own ideas and standards on the people was abandoned in deference to local realities for long-term security and stability.[15]

Or was it? Unfortunately, even today, the imposition of Eurocentric patterns on non-Western cultures and peoples persists. Weston, as shall be seen, would have no truck with such conceits.

For the purposes of this essay, Weston's legacy will be examined under some of those headings, and provide primary materials, as well as comment on them, to allow his thoughts to be heard addressing his own contexts, as well as their enduring significance, particularly for those who would wish to identify with his legacy. Christopher Byaruhanga, an Anglican theologian and churchman from Uganda, identifies two particular concerns which emerged from what might be termed Anglican "comprehensiveness":

> Although Weston was a great missionary scholar, administrator, and preacher, the undue relaxation of historic teaching and discipline in the name of "comprehensiveness" by the Anglican Communion often gave him cause for anxiety. This troubling trend exhibited itself at the 1913 Kikuyu Conference and in a collection

---

[13] Brenda C. Cross, "The Christology of Frank Weston: A Reappraisal," 73.
[14] Andrew Porter, "The Universities' Mission to Central Africa: Anglo-Catholicism and the Twentieth Century Colonial Encounter," 88; James Tengatenga, *The UMCA in Malawi: A History of the Anglican Church 1861-2010*, 227.
[15] Lamin Sanneh, *Disciples of All Nations: Pillars of World Christianity*, 149.

of essays called "the Foundations."[16]
This provides a neat set of categories to explore Weston's theological work.

Foundations and Christology

Weston held a deep commitment to the traditional and credal formulations of the church. As noted, his *The One Christ* is rooted firmly within the tradition of Chalcedon.[17] His starting point is that "the Person who became incarnate is purely divine":[18] an "Alexandrine" and "God-centred" perspective.[19] Identified as the divine Logos, this person is unlimited in ability on a cosmic level, but limited in the Incarnation to "manhood's capacity to mediate divine power."[20] In a kenotic theology, the Logos chooses to take on the limits demanded by the Incarnation: self-limitation.[21] Brenda C. Cross comments that Weston's "great contribution to Christological thought is his central conception of the Logos self-restrained within the limits of manhood."[22] With this, "he would seem to preserve in his basic theory of the self-restrained Logos the best of Antiochene and Alexandrine thought."[23] This allows Weston to maintain the humanity and divinity of the Incarnate Logos, but also to say that they are somehow one: "There is an essential (but not existential) relationship between the divine and human natures, and there is a moral identity of will (in terms of result). If we are to keep within the bounds of Chalcedon, the incarnate is one person but two natures."[24] This limitation which allows this is vital for the Incarnation to be real rather than illusory, and does not occur only within the Incarnation, but within the eternal dimensions and activities of the Logos.[25] Yet, one problem remains. Whilst Weston made great emphasis of limitation, he struggled to accept that this might imply limitations in the extent of Jesus' knowledge:

> This Weston refused to acknowledge. The infallibility of Christ and his Messianic vocation were inviolate. Here the discussion turns on what we consider the extent of the divine influence, or to put it another way, in Weston's terms, their capacity of the manhood for giving and receiving knowledge, and of what kind this knowledge would be. But, in one sense, we cannot blame Weston for not

---

[16] Byaruhanga, "Weston, Frank."
[17] Cross, "The Christology of Frank Weston," 74.
[18] Weston, *The One Christ*, 149.
[19] Cross, "The Christology of Frank Weston," 73.
[20] Cross, "The Christology of Frank Weston," 73.
[21] For Weston's critique of varieties of kenosis and their resolution in self-limitation, see *The One Christ*, 117–199.
[22] Cross, "The Christology of Frank Weston," 76.
[23] Cross, "The Christology of Frank Weston," 86.
[24] Cross, "The Christology of Frank Weston," 89.
[25] Cross, "The Christology of Frank Weston," 77–78.

'thinking through' to the logical end of his ideas. He had by nature a conservative mind and biblical criticism was anathema if it meant questioning the infallibility of Christ.[26]

There is an irony here: his own explorations of self-limitation would have logically allowed such a conclusion, but his unflinching orthodoxy could not bring him to say as much.

He rejected wholeheartedly modern theology's rejections of ancient standards. A particular focus of his wrath was the volume *Foundations: A Statement of Christian Belief in Terms of Modern Thought*.[27] In his critique, *Ecclesia Anglicana*, Weston presents a brutal polemic and binary opposition of the modern perspective which places orthodoxy in a strict opposition to many of the claims of that volume's biblical scholarship. Subsequent scholarly debate which has moved beyond the "faith vs. history" dichotomy allows more validity to some of the points made by modern biblical scholarship than Weston did. It may well be that Weston would have rejoiced to see later generations of biblical scholars and theologians revive and endorse the central claims of the Bible which he saw removed by the writers of *Foundations*, whose position he summarized as:

(a) that the Old Testament is the record of the religious experiences of holy men who lived roughly from 800 B.C. onwards; some of whom wrote the so-called historical books in order to shew how, in their view, God acted in circumstances that quite possibly, and in many cases probably, never existed;

(b) that the Christ's historic life opens with His baptism, at which He suddenly realized a vocation to be the last of the Jewish Prophets;

(c) that Christ did not come into the world to die for us; but having come, He died because of the circumstances of the case;

(d) that Christ was mistaken in what He taught about His Second Advent, thinking that the world would not outlast St. John;

(e) that therefore He did not found a Church, nor ordain Sacraments;

(f) that His body has gone to corruption;

(g) that there is no Authority in the Church beyond the corporate witness of the Saints, many of whom are now unknown, to the spiritual and moral value of the Christian religion.

---

[26] Cross, "The Christology of Frank Weston," 80.

[27] B. H. Streeter et al., *Foundations: A Statement of Christian Belief in Terms of Modern Thought By Seven Oxford Men*.

Thus it is allowed by the Seven to any priest to deny the Trustworthiness of the Bible, the Authority of the Church, and the Infallibility of Christ.[28]

More recent scholars would point out that claims for historicity and theological truth in biblical narratives are again more recognized now than in the liberal scholarship of Weston's time,[29] and point to the recovery of both high christological,[30] and proto-trinitarian[31] readings of the NT, the continued development of thinking about atonement,[32] eschatology, church, mission,[33] and sacraments.[34] Most of these were set aside in the modernist readings of Weston's period. These fashions, however, would prove short-lived. The warning signs were already present when Weston wrote. Albert Schweitzer's monumental *The Quest of the Historical Jesus*,[35] first published in German in 1906, had laid bare the shortcomings of the new Higher Criticisms.[36]

---

[28] Frank Weston, *Ecclesia Anglicana: For What Does She Stand?: An Open letter to the Right Reverend Father in God Edgar, Lord Bishop of St. Albans*, n.p.

[29] Consider the resurgence of interest in the Gospel of John as historically plausible, which is widely at odds with the prevalent modern view in Weston's time, that Mark was the most reliable source, and all the others were infected by greater intrusions of dogmatism.

[30] E.g., Larry Hurtado, *Lord Jesus Christ: Devotion to Jesus in Earliest Christianity*.

[31] E.g., Matthew W. Bates, *The Birth of the Trinity in the New Testament: Jesus, God, and Spirit in New Testament and Early Christian Interpretations of the Old Testament*.

[32] E.g., Hans Boersma, *Violence, Hospitality, and the Cross: Reappropriating the Atonement Tradition*.

[33] For the discussion of Jesus's eschatology as more than a simple choice between imminent or late, and the related founding of a movement, see Dale C. Allison, *Constructing Jesus: Memory, Imagination, and History*, 67–76.

[34] This is in part due to the recovery of interest in Paul and the gospel of John. Donald MacKinnon long ago suggested that both may be "far nearer to the Jesus of history than is normally allowed" by "the ruling reconstruction of the development of primitive Christianity." MacKinnon, *Borderlands of Theology*, 55.

[35] Albert Schweitzer, *The Quest of the Historical Jesus: A Critical Study of its Progress from Reimarus to Wrede*.

[36] Weston, though, would not have agreed with the results, as Schweitzer's work effectively ended for a generation claims within the academy to identify the historical Jesus, whom Weston identified wholly with the witness preserved in the Scriptures and subsequent apostolic and episcopal tradition. The blunt instruments of the early twentieth century debate would receive modification. Not least, the refining of a crude "history vs. faith" distinction has rendered the crude opposition of Weston's time obsolete; Sandra M. Schneiders, *The Revelatory Text: Interpreting the New Testament as Sacred Scripture*, 97–111. Indeed, the aspirations of modernism to claim scientific, objective, and universal analyses have been found equally wanting. For example,

The nub of the matter is found in that last sentence of Weston's. There is a fundamental *a priori* decision about whether the tradition is trustworthy or not which needs to be made. This does not deny critical enquiry, or even the use of critical tools and methods of reading which are always capable of drawing fresh insights from the material under examination, but it does imply an attitude that the tradition is trustworthy. This, of course, aligns well with the pivotal New Testament concept *pístis* (traditionally translated as 'faith', 'trust', or 'belief') which embraces all of faith, trust, and allegiance rather than pure reason or rationality.[37] Weston's debate with the modernists takes us into territory in which we might ask what basic attitude shapes the way we read: trust, suspicion, or even paranoia.[38] He believed that faith and truth are to be found in Bible, Church, and Christ, rather than modern thought:

> It is easy to see the method of the thorough-going Modernist: he is a "modern thinker" and frankly throws over faith for reason, keeping just so much of what corporate faith has stored up for him as approves itself to his moral and spiritual measures. But these experiments of the younger men neither start from faith nor finish in pure reason; they are themselves the measures of individual readiness to sacrifice the past for the sake of the present: whereas all that really matters is the future.[39]

His comments anticipate what the later developments revealed: that "modern thinking" was not some better way to truth than faith. Nor, indeed, would the kinds of historical truth which modernism claimed to rescue from dogmatic corruption provide the answer. Confirmation of a significant foundational role for faith rather than history is rehearsed by MacKinnon, whose praise for Weston's thinking has already been noted:

> Yet faith is most certainly not another name for historical certainty, nor does the achievement of a greater measure of such certainty make faith itself less a problem and a mystery. *Faith is something which goes before historical reconstruction, and is something which*

Michael Polanyi, whose *Personal Knowledge: Towards a Post-Critical Philosophy* showed the extent to which hard scientific studies depend on consensus and lack objectivity (150–160), and Thomas Nagel, who rejected the concept of an objective, scientific "view from nowhere" (*The View from Nowhere*), have further laid bare such pretensions.

[37] Matthew W. Bates, *Salvation by Allegiance Alone: Rethinking Faith, Works and the Gospel of Jesus the King*; Teresa Morgan, *Roman Faith and Christian Faith: Pistis and Fides in the Early Roman Empire and Early Churches*.

[38] Fergus J. King, "More Than a Vapid Sound: The Case for a Hermeneutic of Resonance," 91–92.

[39] Weston, *Ecclesia Anglicana*, n.p.

even conditions its most radical exercise, relating it to its own intense and searching discipline.[40]

It is Weston's particular articulation of faith which puts him at odds with his opponents, Protestant or modern. The question his legacy leaves is this: to trust in the faith of the church as preserved and transmitted in the episcopal tradition, or to trust rather to our own intellectual abilities and the spirit of the age or place. In Weston's view, only that received episcopal tradition with its already visible catholic[41] ability to transcend fashion and geography would do.

The Kikuyu Controversy and Ecclesiology

Weston's deep commitment to episcopacy would further manifest itself in resistance to the increasingly ecumenical thrust of global mission in which comity agreements between different denominations and churches began to as fundamental questions about the necessary structures of the church: did, for example, they need to include the historic episcopate, or were alternatives structures such as the congregational and presbyterian varieties of Western Christianity[42] equally valid expressions of church.

The Kikuyu Controversy — called the Westonian controversy by some[43] — of 1913 revealed Weston to be as deeply opposed to non-catholic forms of Protestantism as to modernism. The Kikuyu Missionary Conference was held in June of that year in Kikuyu in British East Africa[44] (now Kikuyu Town in Kenya). It was the last of a series of meetings, started in 1904, of representatives of different church mission bodies in East Africa, both Anglican and Protestant, was presided over by the Anglican bishops of Uganda and Mombasa and set on "an ecclesiastical federation and intercommunion under Anglican leadership."[45] Weston was not in attendance, but objected vigorously — going so far as indicting "his fellow [Anglican] Bishops of Mombasa and Uganda for heresy

---

[40] MacKinnon, *Borderlands of Theology*, 79. Italics added for emphasis.

[41] For Weston, and for Anglo-Catholics generally, *catholic* is not synonymous with *Roman Catholic* and thus does not refer to the denomination led by the Roman Catholic pope. Rather, it literally means ecclesially *catholic* or 'universal' — that which the Church has always and everywhere believed and practiced. We maintain this usage in this article and will specific *Roman Catholic* when that denomination is meant.

[42] In should be remembered that these, with few exceptions, are forms of church government which emerged primarily in Western Europe at the time of the Reformation. Eastern and Oriental Orthodoxies (including the Coptic Orthodox Church of Egypt and the Orthodox Tewahedo Church of Ethiopia) , as well as the Church of the East and ancient Indian churches, maintained their episcopal forms.

[43] Gathogo, "Early attempts at ecumenical co-operation," 80–85.

[44] Mark Chapman, "The 1913 Kikuyu Conference, Anglo Catholics and the Church of England," 121.

[45] Porter, "The Universities' Mission," 87.

Maimbo W. F. Mndolwa, Fergus J. King, & Joshua Robert Barron
Frank Weston of Zanzibar:
An Assessment and Appreciaiton of an "Apostle to Africans"

because of their participation in a joint communion service" following that Conference,[46] accusing them of "propagating heresy and committing schism" in a letter he sent to the Archbishop of Canterbury.[47] The ecumenical acceptance of non-conformist ecclesiastical structures which would be implied by intercommunion was, for him, tantamount to declaring the episcopate a matter of choice rather than necessity, and threatened its status as the legitimate continuation of the authority of Christ and the guarantor of orthodoxy. The ecumenical drive for comprehensiveness within the Anglican Communion resulted, Weston believed, in an "undue relaxation of" the Church's "historic teaching and discipline,"[48] making the disagreement a matter of obedience to Christ. He thus saw a distinct schism between what he would deem catholic[49] and protestant ecclesiologies and orthodoxies:

> The differences between the catholic and protestant interpretations of the formulas of the Church are so well known to us that we hardly need explain them. As was said above, the *Ecclesia Anglicana* has always desired to find room for those who otherwise must pass into schism, and their translation of privilege into right has so far been accepted popularly in England that we, who claim the older interpretation as true, have suffered much at their lips. To-day we are justified. For in British East Africa and Uganda the protestantizing party has developed itself with a grim logic, in warm-hearted love of souls, and at Kikuyu announced clearly the Deposit that it was prepared to make over to the new African Church.
>
> Let us for a moment consider the negative side of the Deposit:
> (a) It does not contain the Creed commonly called the Creed of St. Athanasius.
> (b) It does not contain the Rite, or Sacrament, of Confirmation.
> (c) It does not contain the Rite, or Sacrament, of Absolution.
> (d) It does not contain Episcopacy.
> (e) It does not provide a Priest for the Celebration of the Holy Communion.
> (f) It does not contain a rule of Infant Baptism,
> (g) It does not know the Catholic Church, or the

---

[46] Kevin Ward, "The First World War and Mission in the Anglican Communion," 108.
[47] Chapman, "The 1913 Kikuyu Conference," 127.
[48] Christopher Byaruhanga, "The Legacy of Bishop Frank Weston of Zanzibar 1871–1924 in the Global South Anglicanism," 257.
[49] Remembering that for Weston, "catholic" did not mean Roman Catholic, but the church of the conciliar and patristic eras.

Communion of Saints, except in such a general sense as is already admitted by the four protestant bodies that have joined the Federation.[50]

The list makes obvious Weston's commitment to the faith and practice of conciliar Christianity as necessary for the shaping of the church in marked contrast to positions which would be well described as *sola Scriptura* (Latin: 'Scripture alone'), based on the Bible alone. It also reveals his view that episcopacy is an *esse* ('an essential requirement'), not a *bene esse* ('an option or preference') for what he considered the true church:[51]

> This doctrinal difference is *episcopacy*, which for Weston is not a doctrine a denomination may or may not choose as it sees fit, but is *absolutely essential* to the Christian faith. Consequently, the issue raised by the Kikuyu Conference is 'whether life in fellowship with the Episcopate be, or be not, the evident condition of retaining a full membership in the Catholic Church, and, therefore, of approach to the altar of that Church. All else is beside the point.'

The key issue, then, is whether episcopacy is a *sine qua non* for the

---

[50] Weston, *Ecclesia Anglicana*, n.p.

[51] The Latin term *esse* literally means 'to be'; sixteenth century Anglican divine Richard Hooker (c. 1554 – 1600) used the term to refer to whatever belongs to the essence of Christianity, distinguishing between *esse*, i.e., what is essential to the Christian faith, and *bene esse* (literally 'to be well'), i.e., that which is not essential yet is beneficial to the life of the Church. Richard Bancroft (1544–1610), Archbishop of Canterbury (1604–1610) borrowed the language and "held that bishops were of the *esse* of the Church." Horton Davies, *Worship and Theology in England*, Part 3, *From Watts and Wesley to Maurice, 1690–1850*, 262.

The Chicago-Lambeth Quadrilateral, adopted by the bishops of the Anglican Communion in 1888, listed four essential elements on which Anglican churches could not compromise: 1) "the Holy Scriptures of the Old and New Testaments are the revealed Word of God" and, as such, contain everything necessary for salvation, 2) the Nicene Creed is "the sufficient statement of the Christian Faith," 3) the centrality of the two Sacraments, "Baptism and the Supper of the Lord", and 4) "the Historic Episcopate, locally adapted . . . "to the varying needs of the nations and peoples called of God." For the Anglican Communion to contemplate communion with Christians of another tradition, the other church must affirm all four of these. But at the Kikuyu Missionary Conference, Anglican bishops communed (shared the Sacrament of the Supper of the Lord) with Christians who did not accept the historic episcopate as essential, thereby in effect challenging the Lambeth Quadrilateral. That is why Weston protested so vigorously.

For an analysis of the Quadrilateral's understanding of episcopacy as essential to the nature and life of the Church, see Ansley Tucker, "The Historic Episcopate in Anglican Ecclesiology: The *Esse* Perspective."

Church of England or an optional extra.⁵²

Weston petitioned the Archbishop of Canterbury to resolve the issue, warning that a failure to affirm the necessity of the episcopate would effectively mean that the church was no longer the church. The debate was aired in public letters and correspondence. The final result saw Weston vindicated. The proposal for intercommunion with nonconformists was shelved. The consequences of the controversy would echo for decades. When the united Churches, such as those of North India and South India, emerged, they would adopt an episcopal form of government. Still, more recently, Anglicans have found it easier to enter into agreements about intercommunion, such as the Porvoo agreement (1992), with churches which have maintained episcopal forms of government.

Weston's resistance to Kikuyu provoked hostile assessments of his character. Thus, Herbert Hensley Henson, then Dean of Durham, commented that he "discloses a temper which is no longer normal among religious people."⁵³ More recently he has been described as "impetuous and emotional" and "a man of single-minded devotion in whom the passion for souls burned fiercely": in regard to Kikuyu, "his fury was frenzied."⁵⁴

It would be possible to conclude that Weston was a formidable controversialist, but this would not be the whole picture. It is true that his reaction to Henson's appointment as Bishop of Hereford was equally spectacular. He viewed Henson's acceptance of liberal theologians like B.H. Streeter as intolerable, and declared that he was no longer in communion with Hereford.⁵⁵ For all that, Henson's assessment of Weston damned with faint praise:

> in my belief he was a very good unselfish Christian, with all a fanatic's injustice, but by nature entirely lovable. It was impossible not to feel his charm even when one execrated his bigotry. . . . His practical sagacity was quite conspicuously great whenever his fanaticism did not influence his judgement.⁵⁶

For all their differences, the Lambeth Conference of 1920 would see both collaborate to produce one of the key documents ("An Appeal to All Christian People") to emerge: "the 'Appeal' . . . would never have been brought to fruition

---

⁵² David R. Law, "Frank Weston, the Kikuyu Controversy, and the Necessity of Episcopacy," 220.
⁵³ Law, "Frank Weston," 227; citing H. Hensley Henson, "The Issue of Kikuyu," *The Edinburgh Review* 448 (1914): 257–283, 280.
⁵⁴ Peart-Binns, *Herbert Hensley Henson*, 115.
⁵⁵ Peart-Binns, *Herbert Hensley Henson*, 116. Weston's views are set out in *The Christ and the Critics*, of which more below.
⁵⁶ Quoted in Peart-Binns, *Herbert Hensley Henson*, 116.

without the co-operative draftsmanship of Weston and Henson working together in the Library or in the Chaplain's room between the formal sittings."[57]

Not all were as hostile. Bishop Gore of Oxford wrote of *Ecclesia Anglicana* that:

> The Bishop of Zanzibar has certainly succeeded in raising in an acute form the question of the coherence of the Church of England and of the Anglican Communion generally. I cannot but think that, at least in this general sense, he has done us a great service. We Church people have of recent years shown ourselves unmistakably anxious to avoid questions of principle. We have let ourselves drift.[58]

There was, indeed, more to Weston than a contrary Catholicism. However expressed his Catholic sensibility was profound, and not just intellectual. It was founded on a deep sense of justice. His remarks to the Anglo-Catholic Conference of 1923, a gathering which might have been tempted to adopt a triumphalist ritualism given the advances made in recovering Catholic expressions of worship within the Church of England, cautioned:

> … when you come out from before your tabernacles, you must walk with Christ, mystically present in you, through the streets of this country, and find the same Christ in the people of your cities and villages. You cannot claim to worship Christ in the tabernacle if you do not pity Jesus in the slum. … It is folly, it is madness, to suppose that you can worship Jesus in the sacrament and on the throne of glory when you are sweating Him in the bodies and souls of his children. … You have your Mass, you have your altars, you have begun to have your tabernacles. Now go out into the highways and hedges, and look for Jesus in the ragged and the naked, in the oppressed and the sweated, in those who have lost hope and in those who are struggling to make good. Look for Jesus in them; and when you find Him, gird yourselves with His towel of fellowship, and wash His feet in the person of His brethren.[59]

Thus, his theology and understanding of the sacraments connect with a profound political sensibility. The political dimensions are less well known. Some of these include comments which appear in a work from a few years later, his pamphlet, *The Serfs of Great Britain*, which contains the vestiges of his ongoing differences with some of his fellow missionaries. At the end of his impassioned condemnation of British colonial administration, he notes that "the Memorandum signed by the Bishops of Mombasa and Uganda, and by Dr.

---

[57] Peart-Binns, *Herbert Hensley Henson*, 117.
[58] Blood, *The History of the Universities' Mission*, 70.
[59] Frank Weston, *In Defence of the English Catholic*, 30.

Arthur of the Church of Scotland, ... admits that pressure must be used to obtain labour in East Africa, much as they regret the need."[60] Weston was again out of step, concluding his diatribe:

> It is necessary to allude to this Memorandum because many people have taken Lord Milner's line of quoting these leaders of the Kikuyu Alliance of East Africa Missionary Societies as a sufficient justification of Forced Labour. I wish to make it clear that some of us who are missionaries will not agree to any such policy. We regard forced labour, apart from war, as in itself immoral; and we hold that forcing Africans to work in the interests of European civilization is a betrayal of the weaker to the financial interests of the stronger race.[61]

Weston's words here should not be construed as claims for European superiority. He is careful to stress the appropriation of the Memorandum by the colonial establishment, noting, in fact, its preferences about "'encouragement' to work on plantations" with a degree of choice in the potential place where "forced labour" might be undertaken, and its ideal that "all labour should be voluntary."[62] However, his real scorn had been poured out on the British government in a classic *praeteritio*[63] at the beginning of the piece: "I do not pause to remark upon the utter callousness of the government, its broken pledge, or its hypocritical invocation of God's name . . . ."[64] There was no doubt about where the fault truly lay. Christianity is not always the ally of colonialism. That he not only critiques the colonial structures of the day, but also rejects claims for European superiority, can be further seen in his views of about mission. Details of his ministry and practice will reveal the high regard he had for African agency, not least in their crucial role in designing and implementing rituals which would integrate Christian faith and liturgy with traditional practices. They have been anticipated in his comments on the *Foundations*, and his wholesale rejection of the conceit that African Christians should adopt modalities of European thought.

Mission

Weston's views on episcopacy also informed his thinking about mission.

---

[60] Frank Weston, *The Serfs of Great Britain: Being a Sequel to* The Black Slaves of Prussia, 11–12.
[61] Weston, *The Serfs of Great Britain*, 12.
[62] Weston, *The Serfs of Great Britain*, 12.
[63] *Praeteritio*, a Latin rhetorical term, refers to calling attention to an issue by seeming to disregard it; the Greek term *paralipsis* (sometimes anglicized as 'paralipse') is a synonym.
[64] Weston, *The Serfs of Great Britian*, 3.

Maimbo W. F. Mndolwa, Fergus J. King, & Joshua Robert Barron
**Frank Weston of Zanzibar:
An Assessment and Appreciaiton of an "Apostle to Africans"**

He considered it to preserve reliably the full unbroken teaching and intention of Jesus of Nazareth. He was able to see how other cultural, social, and political factors might compromise that body of faith and its spread. Indeed, they might be seem as limiting, if not choking, the potential propagation of the gospel into new cultures. His writings reveal his struggles with Anglican missionary strategies which were based in the northern hemisphere:

> I and my people constitute a missionary diocese: we have no regular diocesan organization beyond a Synod of Priests and a Cathedral Chapter: the Bishop has no seat in a Provincial Synod, nor is he given any canonical position in the counsels of his Metropolitan. We come from Canterbury, we lean on Canterbury, we are subject to the judgement of the Bishops of the Province of Canterbury: yet Canterbury as a Province knows us not, and gives us no share in deliberations over matters that affect us vitally, as part of the Province.[65]

There is a critical edge, we would suggest, to his words — an implication of dissatisfaction. The remarks which follow this imply a desire to see the establishment of an African church, presumably with an African leadership:

> That is to say, we are missionaries, we have been sent, and here we are. If we ask for what we have been sent, we are told that we are here to found and edify a church of Africans who shall be in communion with Canterbury, giving them the Deposit of Faith to which the *Ecclesia Anglicana*, in common with all catholic Christendom, bears its witness.[66]

These words, published in 1914, which hint at African ecclesial leadership, began to be realized shortly after the end of the War, as Weston then "ordained seven [African] priests, after an accelerated track" of training through the diaconate.[67] With deeper vision "than most," Weston reminded the missionaries under his authority "that 'the African and not we are the permanent leaders of the African church'."[68]

His work as a theological educator on Zanzibar reveals Weston "had a vision of a vigorous and self-correcting African Church with her own theology,"[69] but such a reality would not emerge until the second half of the twentieth century. A number of factors contributing to this may be identified:

---

[65] Weston, *Ecclesia Anglicana*.
[66] Weston, *Ecclesia Anglicana*.
[67] Morgan J. Robinson, *A Language for the World: The Standardization of Swahili*, 90.
[68] Sundkler and Steed, *History of the Church in Africa*, 614; the authors quote Weston but do not provide a citation.
[69] Byaruhanga, "The Legacy of Bishop Frank Weston," 256; see also Byaruhanga, "Weston, Frank."

an apparent resistance to indigenous leadership across mission agencies at the time (seen in the virulent reaction to Roland Allen's prescient writings such as *Missionary Methods: St Paul's or Ours?*, first published in 1912), language (the privileging of Kiswahili might lead to a concomitant loss of ability in English which would hamper participation in what was essentially a diocese of the Church of England), and the Eurocentric processes for the appointment of bishops.[70] That said, Weston may have considered London-based appointments as embodying sound episcopal practice in the circumstances.[71] He also may have stymied his own pro-African feelings by an increased recruitment of expatriate personnel: a move driven by fears that high expectations of clergy discipline might not be met (despite his recognition of "most zealous and able ministers"), and also by a comparative dearth of vocations.[72] In spite of his early support for African ecclesial leadership, in 1908 he "publicaly called for increased European supervision," feeling that it would be "two or three generations" more before "the native ministry" would be sufficiently mature for the task.[73]

Nonetheless, Weston was determined that missionary work from Europe should not simply transport European categories into African contexts, pointing towards a body of faith which he viewed as capable of different cultural presentations:

> [The missionary bishop] is then Catholic rather than English, and aims at becoming an African Catholic, and the leader of African Catholics. That is to say, he desires to present the one unchangeable truth to Africa in such a way as to make it hereafter easy of interpretation by African thought, in African language. So far from looking forward to the day when Africans will mould the Revelation to their own minds, he would bring their minds into captivity to Christ, and it is his duty to make clear to them, once and for all, the meaning and scope of the authority in virtue of which he demands the response of their minds and hearts to their Saviour and his.
>
> Thus inevitably the nature and office of the College of Bishops must be made clear to Africans; and it is impossible to hide from them that certain Christian bodies have rejected this catholic authority, some in favour of European non-Episcopal ministries,

---

[70] Maimbo W. Mndolwa and Fergus King, "In Two Minds? African Experience and Preferment in the UMCA and the Journey to Independence in Tanganyika," 332–335.
[71] Porter, "The Universities' Mission,",89.
[72] Porter, "The Universities' Mission," 92–93, quotation from 93.
[73] Ranger, "The Apostle: Kolumba Msigala," 16.

some out of exaggerated loyalty to a European Papalism.[74]

Linked to this was his bitter opposition to what he identified as "modern thought." He had no time for theological strategies which would demand that African Christians had to adopt the philosophical presuppositions of European thought, or the attendant claims for intellectual superiority which they entailed:

> You will bear me out that Gethsemane and Calvary are most real in Africa; that Christ is brutally crucified here, crucified in the persons of Africans, by his professing followers… God in manhood, God on the Cross, God of the empty tomb. Now into the glory of our Calvary breaks the voice of prelatical and priestly liberalism. And its message, what is it? It is that Africans cannot possibly understand the Gospels, Church or sacraments until they re-interpret them in the light of modern European thought! Poor Africans: not yet among the wise of European thought.[75]

Again, this may stem from what he considers to be the foundations of faith, which he roots in life and its experience, not ratiocination.

He was further deeply concerned that such attitudes also implied worldly standards at the criteria for correct theology:

> We appear to forget that our essential relation with eternal love is through the Response of Love incarnate, Jesus, the coloured-man of Nazareth. Moreover we ignore our relation with the poor Man of Galilee, the naked Christ of Calvary. And we allow ourselves to be, almost entirely, dominated by standards of wealth and caste the world about us approves … Eternal love, when He takes flesh, comes as a poor, coloured Man, whereas we dislike poverty and despise colour! How then can we preach love incarnate?[76]

Here may be seen a hermeneutic which is grounded in a deep morality and sense of justice. It was also rooted in a profound love for those amongst whom he lived.

---

[74] Frank Weston, *The Case against Kikuyu: A Study in Vital Principles*, 40–41. By "against Kikuyu," Weston was referring to the ecumenicity of the Kikuyu Conference, which Weston felt necessarily attacked the importance of the episcopacy, not to the Agĩkũyũ people of Kenya. Note that missionaries such as those influenced by Henry Venn of the Church Missionary Society shared similar aspirations; Peter Williams, "'Not Transplanting': Henry Venn's Strategic Vision," 148; Stanley, "The CMS and the Separation of Anglicanism from 'Englishness'," 349–350. Similar strategies underpinned the practice advocated later by John V. Taylor, and recognised by Jesse N. K. Mugambi: Mugambi, "Introduction," xii–xiii.

[75] Weston, *The Christ and the Critics*, 68–69.

[76] Weston, *The Revelation of Eternal Love*, 157.

Maimbo W. F. Mndolwa, Fergus J. King, & Joshua Robert Barron
Frank Weston of Zanzibar:
An Assessment and Appreciaiton of an "Apostle to Africans"

Canon Kolumba Yohana Msigala, born as Lisapulu in what is now southeastern Tanzania, was an effective evangelist who was ordained as a deacon in 1901[77] and eventually served as a priest and then as a canon in the Anglican Church.[78] He left a record of Weston's practice:

> Every month he found opportunity to ask about the homes of these students, their customs and the state of the Christians where they lived, the best way to bring them up, and the state of advance of the Church at that time. There was indeed a period every month for students of each tribe and in this way he got at the heart of Africans, by being taught by his charges, the students who explained to him the act of shepherding the inhabitants of their different parts.[79]

A second unnamed African writer who served in the Carrier Corps, the military unit Weston established in the First World War, gave the following assessment:

> The bishop loved the souls of his men, and knew all their weakness". (*sic*) Again, it was "his custom to walk last [though he sometimes led the column], lest he should lose even one man on the way through weariness, or finding his load too heavy, or through sickness." And the account ends thus: "On the whole expedition all the men obeyed every word of his without question not because they were afraid or forced [though the Bishop's disciple was very strict and his punishment of offenders drastic], but because they realized that they must obey every word because of the way the Lord Bishop treated them, as a father and his children."[80]

Weston, although obviously strict and firm in his opinions, left a legacy in which his respect and love for others was palpable, and has been manifested in those who followed him in ministry such as the late John Acland Ramadhani, another bishop, rooted in the UMCA tradition, whose love for those in his care was legendary.[81] Weston bequeathed not just liturgy and theology, but an ethos.

Legacy in Tanganyika/Zanzibar/Tanzania

In the years of Weston's episcopate, the diocese of Zanzibar was the single episcopal see in what are now identified as the *Pwani* (Coastal) or UMCA

---

[77] Anderson-Morshead, *The History of the Universities' Mission to Central Africa*, Vol.1: *1859-1909*, 423.

[78] For details of Msigala's biography and career as an evangelist, see Ranger, "The Apostle: Kolumba Msigala."

[79] Quoted in Anne Marie Stoner-Eby, "African Clergy, Bishop Lucas and the Christianizing of Local Initiation Rites: Revisiting 'The Masasi Case'", 179. See Kolumba Msigala, "Canon Kolumba's Reminiscences."

[80] Quoted in Tengatenga, *The UMCA in Malawi*, 190-191.

[81] Patrick Bendera, Maimbo W. F. Mndolwa, and Fergus J. King, "John Acland Ramadhani."

dioceses within the Anglican Church of Tanzania. Devoted to his vocation and to those within the territory assigned to him, in July 1922 he recorded that he had walked a thousand miles (1,609 km) since mid-December 1921.[82] The second oldest diocese, Masasi, was not founded until 1926, two years after his death. Thus, Weston's legacy includes the establishment of a number of parishes and institutions across what is now mainland Tanzania. During his episcopate, churches were established at Pemba Island, Masasi, Majembe, and Makonde, and the church at Mkomaindo rededicated.[83] Schools were also founded at Kwa Magome, Mpundu (Ruvuma), Kwitonji, Luatala,[84] and a hospital at Mkuzi.[85] He also founded Holy Water Point, currently a tourist attraction in Nilo Natural reserve.

The foundation of a theological college at Hegongo would increase the numbers of African clergy: by 1924, there were 21 African priests and eight deacons in the diocese.[86] That same year, Weston encouraged Kolumba Msigala to accept a call to go "as an apostle" with ecclesial authority over a large area, and that "without local white supervision."[87] There was also growth in the provision of secondary schooling and teacher training at Kiungani and, later, Minaki.[88] A further educational legacy was Kiwanda Vocational Training Center. In this, he originated vocational education in Tanzania. Preparations were also started which would allow the subsequent foundation of the Diocese of Masasi.[89]

He developed a firm liturgical legacy. *Kitabu cha Sala za Kanuni Ilivyo Desturi ya Kanisa la Unguja* (Swahili: 'The Book of Common Prayer according to the Usage of the Church in Zanzibar') first appeared in 1919, and has been often reprinted. It is a decidedly Anglo-Catholic in ethos. It includes the Eucharist, Offices, a Calendar and hymns. Later versions would include occasional services for baptisms, marriage, confession, and burial services.[90] These rites continued to be used in some of the UMCA dioceses.

---

[82] Adrian Hastings, *The Church in Africa 1450–1950*, 422; citing H. Maynard Smith, *Frank, Bishop of Zanzibar*, 276.
[83] Blood, *The History of the Universities' Mission*, 16, 19, 50, 154.
[84] Blood, *The History of the Universities' Mission*, 19, 20, 51.
[85] Blood, *The History of the Universities' Mission*, 43.
[86] Blood, *The History of the Universities' Mission*, 119, 162
[87] Ranger, "The Apostle: Kolumba Msigala," 19.
[88] Blood, *The History of the Universities' Mission*, 167–168.
[89] Blood, *The History of the Universities' Mission*, 157.
[90] For example, *Kitabu Cha Ibada Za Kanuni na Kuhudumu Sakramenti Pamoja Na Kawaida Za Kanisa Ilivyo Desturi Ya Kanisa La Unguja* ('The Prescribed Rites for Worship and the Administration of the Sacraments according to the Practice of the

Maimbo W. F. Mndolwa, Fergus J. King, & Joshua Robert Barron
Frank Weston of Zanzibar:
An Assessment and Appreciaiton of an "Apostle to Africans"

In 1913, the first Christian *jando la kikristo* (Christian initiatory rites for boys) were held in Masasi;[91] equivalents for girls, *malango ya kikristo* (Christian initiatory rites for girls), would follow in 1922.[92] There rites meant that Anglican Christians might engage in a rite of passage in which catechetics and preparation for Confirmation replaced traditional religious beliefs, which were often animist, and ethics. Whilst their development has often been attributed to Vincent Lucas, who would become bishop of Masasi in 1926,[93] the dates here suggest that Weston would also have had a prior responsibility for their adoption, as the process started in 1907.[94] William Wynn Jones from Kongwa, in the low church evangelical tradition, was also privy to these developments.[95] However, the prime movers in any such process must be those African Christians who would both have identified the need and used their wisdom to formulate appropriate rituals and practices, as Anne Marie Stoner-Eby recognizes whilst also detailing the role of the missionaries.[96] The development of these rites potentially reveals both Weston's respect for African people and culture and, again, his ability to work with Anglicans from a different tradition, just as did his work with Bishop Hensley Henson.

He was also responsible for the foundation of the religious life[97] within the Diocese of Zanzibar. Sister Margaret Anne (Cameron) from the Community of

---

Church in Zanzibar'); *Unguja* is the proper name of the largest island of the Zanzibar archipelago.

[91] Stoner-Eby, "African Clergy," 181.
[92] Blood, *The History of the Universities' Mission*, 154–157.
[93] Stoner-Eby, "African Clergy," 172.
[94] Stoner-Eby, "African Clergy," 178–184.
[95] Canon Hugh Prentice kindly supplied this information. Further evidence of Weston's flexibility in dealing with CMS colleagues is provided in an anecdote recorded by Maynard Smith:

"He was ready to celebrate in churches of many types, and was scrupulous in conforming to their respective usages. One of his staff who travelled with him to Africa in 1920 tells me that there were several C.M.S. missionaries on board the ship. When Sunday came round they proposed that there should be two services, but Frank would not hear of it. He celebrated himself and in such a way that the most prejudiced C.M.S. clergyman was not shocked. He preached at the official service and attended the C.M.S. prayer meetings. Before the ship reached Mombasa, he and the C.M.S. missionaries were friends.

"He could always get on with devout evangelicals, for he was so essentially evangelical himself." H. Maynard Smith, *Frank, Bishop of Zanzibar*, 280.

[96] Stoner-Eby, "African Clergy," 178–184; 201, footnotes 51–56; 202, footnotes 71–72.
[97] Here "religious life" is used in the precise sense of communities of men or women who live together under a shared rule, usually monastic in nature. Members of such religious communities are often lay people. Before the coming of women's ordination,

Maimbo W. F. Mndolwa, Fergus J. King, & Joshua Robert Barron
**Frank Weston of Zanzibar:
An Assessment and Appreciaiton of an "Apostle to Africans"**

St Margaret of Scotland (Aberdeen) was seconded for five years to be the first Mother of the Order. On May 29, 1910, the first sisters of what would become the Community of the Sacred Passion (CSP) arrived on Zanzibar. In 1911, Sr Frances was elected Superior and Sr Margaret Anne returned to Scotland.[98] Whilst the Community of the Sacred Passion is no longer active in Tanzania, it, in turn, seeded the *Chama cha Mariamu Mtakatifu* ('Society of St Mary' or *CMM*) which now has eleven houses throughout Tanzania and in Zambia.[99] CSP would have houses in Masasi, Njwara, Chiwata, Newala and Saidi Maumbo: some operated dispensaries.[100] Members of *CMM* describe Weston affectionately as their grandfather. Male religious life was realized with the foundation of the Priory of St. Peter at Mkuzi.[101] He was also responsible for the founding of the Scouts in Tanzania through St. Mary's and St. Martin's schools at Magila in 1917.

Concluding Remarks [102]

Bishop Frank Weston made a significant contribution to the church in his own time: as both a theologian, and a bishop. He was a key personality in the Anglo-Catholic movement of his time. His legacy has persisted. His famous remarks reminding the Anglo-Catholics of the need for social justice as well as a sacramentalism adorned many parish walls. Weston condemned "publicly both the German and the British governments in Tanganyika for their exploitation of African labour."[103] He transformed British colonial administration. The development of liturgy and education set in place the necessary components for an independent African church to emerge. In Tanzania, he left a legacy both of church growth, and a significant theological ethos in which Anglo-Catholicism was never an empty

Bishop Frank Weston

Anglican female religious would all have been lay women. Sometimes, male religious might have been ordained as deacons or priests.
[98] Blood, *The History*, 15, 40–41.
[99] African Sisters of St Mary (CMM) Support Group, https://www.africansisters.org.uk
[100] Blood, *The History of the Universities' Mission*, 158–160
[101] Blood, *The History of the Universities' Mission*, 46.
[102] Accompanying public domain image available at https://anglicanhistory.org/weston/ and https://commons.wikimedia.org/wiki/File:Weston_Zanzibar.jpg
[103] Iliffe, "The Spokesman: Martin Kayamba," 69–70.

ritualism or formalism, but to be accompanied by firm faith, and deep discipline. His disdain for European claims of privilege anticipated and continue to resonate with the rejection of Eurocentric theologies and practice.[104] His memory is one which we neglect to our own detriment.

Bibliography

ALLEN, Roland A. *Missionary Methods: St Paul's or Ours?* Grand Rapids, Michigan, USA: Eerdmans, 1962.

ALLISON, Dale C. *Constructing Jesus: Memory, Imagination, and History.* Grand Rapids, Michigan: Baker Academic, 2010.

ANDERSON-MORSHEAD, A. E. M. *The History of the Universities' Mission to Central Africa*, Vol.1: *1859–1909*. London: The Universities' Mission to Central Africa, 1955.[105]

BATES, Matthew W. *The Birth of the Trinity in the New Testament: Jesus, God, and Spirit in New Testament and Early Christian Interpretations of the Old Testament.* Oxford: Oxford University Press, 2015.

———. *Salvation by Allegiance Alone: Rethinking Faith, Works and the Gospel of Jesus the King.* Grand Rapids, Michigan, USA: Baker Academic, 2017.

BENDERA, Patrick, Maimbo W. F. MNDOLWA, and Fergus J. KING. "John Acland Ramadhani." In *Anglican Theology: Postcolonial Perspectives*, edited by Stephen Burns and James Tengatenga, 165–177. London: SCM Press, 2024.

BLOOD, A. G. *The History of the Universities' Mission to Central Africa*, Vol. 2: *1907-1932*. London: The Universities' Mission to Central Africa, 1957.

BOERSMA, Hans. *Violence, Hospitality, and the Cross: Reappropriating the Atonement Tradition.* Grand Rapids, Michigan, USA: Baker Academic, 2004.

BYARUHANGA, Christopher. "The Legacy of Bishop Frank Weston of Zanzibar 1871–1924 in the Global South Anglicanism." *Exchange* 35, no. 3 (2006): 255–269. https://doi.org/10.1163/157254306777814373

———. *The History and Theology of the Ecumenical Movement in East Africa.* Kampala, Uganda: Fountain Publishers, 2015.

———. "Weston, Frank." *Dictionary of African Christian Biography.* n.d. https://dacb.org/stories/tanzania/weston-frank/

CHAPMAN, Mark D. "The 1913 Kikuyu Conference, Anglo-Catholics and the Church of England." Chapter 5 in *Costly Communion Ecumenical Initiative and Sacramental Strife in the Anglican Communion*, edited by Mark D.

---

[104] E.g., see, Robert E. Hood, *Must God Remain Greek? Afro-Cultures and God-Talk*; Willie James Jennings, *The Christian Imagination: Theology and the Origins of Race.*

[105] A digitized copy is available at https://dn790002.ca.archive.org/0/items/historyofunivers00ande/historyofunivers00ande.pdf

Chapman and Jeremy Bonner, 121–144. Anglican-Episcopal Theology and History 4. Leiden: Brill, 2019. https://doi.org/10.1163/9789004388680_007

Cross, Brenda C. "The Christology of Frank Weston: A Reappraisal." *Journal of Theological Studies* 21, no. 1 (1970): 73–90.

Davies, Horton. *Worship and Theology in England.* Vol. 2: *From Watts and Wesley to Martineu, 1690–1900.* Grand Rapids, Michigan, USA: Eerdmans, 1996.[106]

Gathogo, Julius. "The early attempts at ecumenical co-operation in East Africa: The case of the Kikuyu Conference of 1913." *Studia Historiae Ecclesiasticae* 36, no. 2 (2010): 73–93.

Hastings, Andrian. *The Church in Africa 1450–1950.* Oxford History of the Christian Church. Oxford: Clarendon Press, 1994, 2004.

Hood, Robert E. *Must God Remain Greek? Afro-Cultures and God-Talk.* Minneapolis, Minnesota, USA: Fortress Press, 1990.

Hurtado, Larry. *Lord Jesus Christ: Devotion to Jesus in Earliest Christianity.* Grand Rapids, Michigan, USA: Eerdmans, 2003.

Iliffe, John. "The Spokesman: Martin Kayamba." Chapter 4 in *Modern Tanzanians: a volume of biographies*, edited by John Iliffe, 66–94. Nairobi: East African Literature Bureau, for The Historical Association of Tanzania, 1972.

Jennings, Willie James. *The Christian Imagination: Theology and the Origins of Race.* New Haven, Connecticut, USA: Yale University Press, 2010.

King, Fergus J. "More Than a Vapid Sound: The Case for a Hermeneutic of Resonance." *Journal for Theology in Southern Africa* 148 (2014): 83–98.

Kitabu Cha Ibada Za Kanuni na Kuhudumu Sakramenti Pamoja Na Kawaida Za Kanisa Ilivyo Desturi Ya Kanisa La Unguja. London: Society of Ss. Peter and Paul, 1927.

Kitabu cha Sala za Kanuni Ilivyo Desturi ya Kanisa la Unguja: Swahili. London: SPCK, 1950.

Kobia, Sam. "Denominationalism in Africa: The Pitfalls of Institutional Ecumenism." *The Ecumenical Review* 53, no. 3 (2001): 295–305.

Law, David R. "Frank Weston, the Kikuyu Controversy, and the Necessity of Episcopacy." *International Journal for the Study of the Christian Church* 15, no. 3 (2015): 214–243.

MacKinnon, Donald M. *Borderlands of Theology and Other Essays.* Philadelphia: Lippincott, 1968.

---

[106] *Worship and Theology in England* was first published by Princeton University Press (1970–1965) in five volumes. In the Eerdmans reprint edition, volumes 1 and 2 of the first edition were printed in a single volume, and volumes 3 and 4 of the first edition were printed together as volume 2 of the Eerdmans edition.

SMITH, H. Maynard. *Frank, Bishop of Zanzibar.* London: SPCK, 1926.

MNDOLWA, Maimbo W., and Fergus KING. "In Two Minds? African Experience and Preferment in the UMCA and the Journey to Independence in Tanganyika." *Mission Studies* 53, no. 3 (2016): 327–335. https://doi.org/10.1163/15733831-12341466

MORGAN, Teresa. *Roman Faith and Christian Faith: Pistis and Fides in the Early Roman Empire and Early Churches.* Oxford: Oxford University Press, 2015.

MSIGALA, Kolumba. "Canon Kolumba's Reminiscences." Unpublished archive collection. Box D1(2). UMCA Archives.

MUGAMBI, Jesse N. K. "Introduction." In *Christian Presence amid African Religion*, by John V. TAYLOR, xi–xxxv. Nairobi: Acton, 2001.

NAGEL, Thomas. *The View from Nowhere.* Oxford: Oxford University Press, 1986.

PEART-BINNS, John S. *Herbert Hensley Henson: A Biography.* Cambridge: Lutterworth, 2013.

POLANYI, Michael. *Personal Knowledge: Towards a Post-Critical Philosophy.* London: Routledge, 1962.

PORTER, Andrew. "The Universities' Mission to Central Africa: Anglo-Catholicism and the Twentieth Century Colonial Encounter." Chapter 14 in *Missions, Nationalism, and the End of Empire*, edited by Brian Stanley with Alaine Low, 79–107. Studies in the History of Christian Mission. Grand Rapids, Michigan, USA: Eerdmans, 2003.

RANGER, Terence O. "The Apostle: Kolumba Msigala." Chapter 1 in *Modern Tanzanians: a volume of biographies*, edited by John Iliffe, 1–26. Nairobi: East African Literature Bureau, for The Historical Association of Tanzania, 1972.

ROBINSON, Morgan J. *A Language for the World: The Standardization of Swahili.* New African Histories. Athens, Ohio, USA: Ohio University Press, 2022. https://library.oapen.org/bitstream/handle/20.500.12657/86094/external_content.pdf

SANNEH, Lamin O. *Encountering the West: Christianity and the Global Cultural Process: The African Dimension.* World Christian Theology Series. London: Marshall Pickering, 1993.[107]

———. *Disciples of All Nations: Pillars of World Christianity.* Oxford Studies in World Christianity. Oxford: Oxford University Press, 2008.

SCHNEIDERS, Sandra M. *The Revelatory Text: Interpreting the New Testament as Sacred Scripture.* Collegeville, Minnesota, USA: Liturgical Press, 1999.

---

[107] A reprint edition was made available for North American markets the same year — *Encountering the West: Christianity and the Global Cultural Process: The African Dimension.* World Christian Theology Series. Maryknoll, New York, USA: Orbis Books, 1993.

SCHWEITZER, Albert. *The Quest of the Historical Jesus: A Critical Study of its Progress from Reimarus to Wrede*. Translated by W. Montgomery. 3rd Edition. London: SCM, 1981.

STANLEY, Brian. "The CMS and the Separation of Anglicanism from 'Englishness'." Afterword in *The Church Mission Society and World Christianity, 1799–1999*, edited by Kevin Ward and Brian Stanley, 344–352. Studies in the History of Christian Mission. Grand Rapids, Michigan, USA: Eerdmans, 2000.

STONER-EBY, Anne Marie. "African Clergy, Bishop Lucas and the Christianizing of Local Initiation Rites: Revisiting 'The Masasi Case'." *Journal of Religion in Africa* 38, no. 2 (2008): 171–208. https://doi.org/10.1163/157006608X289675

STREETER, B. H., R. BROOK, A. E. J. RAWLINSON, W. H. MOBERLY, N. S. TALBOT, R. G. PARSONS, and W. TEMPLE. *Foundations: A Statement of Christian Belief in Terms of Modern Thought By Seven Oxford Men*. London: Macmillan, 1913.

SUNDKLER, Bengt, and Christopher Steed. *A History of the Church in Africa*. Cambridge: Cambridge University Press, 2000.

TENGATENGA, James. *The UMCA in Malawi: A History of the Anglican Church 1861–2010*. Zomba, Malawi: Kachere, 2010.

TUCKER, Ansley. "The Historic Episcopate in Anglican Ecclesiology: The Esse Perspective." *Consensus: A Canadian Journal of Public Theology* 12, no. 1 (1986): 99–115. https://scholars.wlu.ca/consensus/vol12/iss1/7/

WARD, Kevin. "The First World War and Mission in the Anglican Communion." In *The First World War as a Turing Point: The impact of the years 1914–1918 on Church and Mission (with special focus on the Hermannsburg Mission) / Wendezeit Weltkrieg: Die Auswirkungen der Jahre 1914 - 1918 auf Kirche und Mission (unter besonderer Berücksichtigung der Hermannsburger Mission)*, edited by Frieder Ludwig, 105–127. Quellen und Beiträge zur Geschichte der Hermannsburger Mission und des Ev.-Luth. Missionswerkes in Niedersachsen 27. Berlin: Lit Verlag, 2020. https://www.lit-verlag.de/media/pdf/aa/ca/1f/9783643911377.pdf

WESTON, Frank. *The Case against Kikuyu: A Study in Vital Principles*. London: Longmans, Green, and Co., 1914. Digitized at https://anglicanhistory.org/weston/kikuyu1914.html

———. *The One Christ: An Enquiry into the Manner of the Incarnation*. London: Longmans, Green & Co., 1907.

———. *The Christ and His Critics: An Open Pastoral Letter to the European Missionaries of his Diocese*. London: Mowbrays, 1919.

———. *In Defence of the English Catholic*. London: Mowbray, 1923.

WESTON, Frank. *Ecclesia Anglicana: For What Does She Stand? An Open letter to the Right Reverend Father in God Edgar, Lord Bishop of St. Albans*. London: Longmans, Green, and Co., 1914 Digitized at https://anglicanhistory.org/weston/ecclesia_anglicana.html

———. *The Revelation of Eternal Love: Christianity Stated in Terms of Love*. Milwaukee, Wisconsin, USA: Morehouse, 1920.

———. *The Serfs of Great Britain: Being a Sequel to* The Black Slaves of Prussia. London: W. Knott, 1920.

WILLIAMS, Peter. "'Not Transplanting': Henry Venn's Strategic Vision." Chapter 6 in *The Church Mission Society and World Christianity, 1799–1999*, edited by Kevin Ward and Brian Stanley, 147–172. Studies in the History of Christian Mission. Grand Rapids, Michigan, USA: Eerdmans, 2000.

Finding the Kingdom of God in Africa

BOOK REVIEW ESSAY
Shaw, Mark, and Wanjiru M. Gitau. *The Kingdom of God in Africa: A History of African Christianity.* 2nd edition. Carlisle, Cambria, UK: Langham Global Library, 2020. Pp. xii + 368; maps. £19.99 (paperback).

Christine Chemutai CHIRCHIR

Kenya Highlands Evangelical University, Kericho, Kenya
christinechirchir6@gmail.com

Shaw and Gitau introduce the book with an illustration of wrestling to describe how Africans have worked hard to embrace the kingdom of God. Examining the statistics of Christian growth in Africa, one may be tempted to think that the wrestling match has ended and Christianity is triumphant. However, the story is more complex than that and the authors warn that such triumphalism would be out-of-place, as "millions of Africans still struggle with what it means to be both African and Christian" (2), "grappling with the person of Jesus Christ" (1). Continuing with the athletic metaphor, Shaw and Gitau discuss historiographical methods and approaches — "wrestling with history" (5–10). They compare five perspectives from which African Christian history have been examined — The Subjective Side of History, Missionary Historiography, Nationalist Historiography, Ecumenical Historiography, and The Perspective of World Christianity — and commit to follow the latter.

Next, the authors 'wrestle with the Kingdom', discussing the various ways that the Kingdom of God can be, and has been, understood. A major contribution of this book is its connecting what we may call 'kingdomology' with ecclesiology, exploring the relationship between differing understandings of the Kingdom of God with what the Church has looked like at different times and in different places. Do we understand the Kingdom as "the Providential and Theocratic Rule of God", "the Redemptive Rule of Christ", or as "the Promotion of Justice"? How we understand "Kingdom of God" necessarily impacts how we understand the nature of the Church. The book is divided into four parts each covering a different epoch of African history.

Part 1. The Imperial Rule of God: Beginnings to AD 600

During this time period, ecclesial understandings of *Kingdom of God* were

Christine Chemutai Chirchir
Finding the Kingdom of God in Africa
BOOK REVIEW ESSAY: *The Kingdom of God in Africa: A History of African Christianity*, **by Mark Shaw and Wanjiru M. Gitau**

understandably modeled on understandings of imperial rule by human kings and emperors. This section has three chapters —
- 2. The kingdom along the Nile: Christianity in Egypt to AD 640;
- 3. The City of God: Christianity in North Africa;
- 4. Kings of Glory: Christianity in Ethiopia and Nubia to AD 600

— beginning with a focus on northern Africa, describing Egyptian religion and culture and how these prepared the coming of Christianity. Elements in Egyptian culture and religion were similar to Christianity such as belief in the afterlife and traditional kings which were considered divine. The city of Carthage was home to Italian immigrants, Phoenicians, and native Africans, each with their languages and cultures. In Augustine's concept of the two cities, the pagan and the Christian, Carthage was a symbolic reminder of its inner cultures of darkness and light fighting for survival and supremacy. The story of the church's witness to the kingdom is a story of partial victories and mixed messages. Nubian and Ethiopian understandings of kingdom parallel the Kingship of Christ. The Nubian kingdom was the gateway between colonial coast — Egypt and North Africa had, of course, been colonized by Rome — and the African inland. It acted as a bridge between Rome and the reest of the African continent. The guardians of the gateway were the great kings of Nubia. This is reflected in their art, architecture, and literature where the king is regarded as semi-divine and a servant of the gods. Therefore, after Nubians embraced Christian faith, Nubian art depicts Christ as the royal bridge between the empire of Nubia and the heartland of heaven. This entire section shows how Christianity found a rich grounds in which to plant the seeds of Christianity.

Part 2. The Clash of the Kingdoms: Medieval African Christianity (600–1700)

Next, the authors examine competing kingdoms which offered allegiance to different kings in the following chapters:
- 5. The Kingdoms of Allah and Mungu — Islam and African Religion in the Middle Ages;
- 6. Crumbling Kingdoms — Nubian Collapse and Ethiopian Survival;
- 7. The Kingdoms of Christendom — The European Discovery of Africa, 1500–1700.

In this section, authors recount the coming of the Islamic religion, the presence of the African Religion, and the introduction of the European Christianity into the continent. They introduce the often-neglected histories of Christianity in Nubia and Ethiopia during this time period. Nubian Christianity thrived for a thousand years centuries before the coming of the Euro-American missionaries but then declined. The Ethiopians are descendants of Aksumites

Christine Chemutai Chirchir
Finding the Kingdom of God in Africa
BOOK REVIEW ESSAY: *The Kingdom of God in Africa: A History of African Christianity*, by Mark Shaw and Wanjiru M. Gitau

who are Semitic in culture and language, though their culture is authentically African and indigenous even though other Semites have Asian cultures.

Shaw and Gitau thus note that "Africa is a continent with a triple heritage. For thousands of years, she has been the meeting ground of Western, indigenous, and Semitic cultures. This triple heritage is particularly evident in the area of religion. Islam, Christianity, and African traditional religion are all deeply rooted in the African past" (83). But the implied equations that

Western = Christian, indigenous = ATR, and *Semitic = Islamic*

is overly facile and, of course, wrong. The Copts were the indigenous Egyptians. They are African, and neither Semitic nor western. The Nubians were Nilotic. The Ethiopians were mostly Semitic and Cushitic, depending on the ethnic group. But within the story of early Christianity, Egyptian (Coptic), Nubian, and Ethiopian Christianity represent Eastern cultures, not Western cultures. There is also a strong argument that Egyptian-Coptic, Nubian, and Ethiopian/Eritrean forms of Christianity are themselves an African traditional religion, with an older history than some ATRs are able to boast.

Thus there are *two separate* senses in which we can speak of Africa having a "triple heritage." First, culturally, Africa has been the meeting place between Western (Greek, Roman/Latin, and eastern European) cultures, indigenous African cultures (e.g, Coptic, Nilotic, Cushitic, Bantu) which includes some indigenous semitic cultures (e.g., Aksumite), and imported Arabic semitic culture (as well as imported Jewish culture, which at times has been especially important in Egypt and in what is now Ethiopia and Eritrea). Second, religiously, Africa has been the meeting place between non-Judeo-Christian traditional religions, Christianity, and Islam (though this leaves out the importance of Judaism in North Africa, Egypt, and Ethiopia + Eritrea). For clarity of narrative, Shaw and Gitau have perhaps oversimplified the picture. But they clearly demonstrate that throughout this period at times the Church struggled to survive, at times it seemed to die, and yet it has risen from the ashes and continued to grow.

Part 3. The Reign of Christ: African Christianity in the Eighteenth and Nineteenth Centuries

Now well into the modern period, the Church continued to wrestle with what it means for Christ to reign. The authors first explore the Christian struggle against (or at times acquiescence to) the evils of slavery, and then examine Christian history in three different regions of Africa through the lens of *kingdom*.

> 8. The Liberating Kingdom — The Crusade Against the Slave Trade;

Christine Chemutai Chirchir
Finding the Kingdom of God in Africa
BOOK REVIEW ESSAY: *The Kingdom of God in Africa: A History of African Christianity*, by Mark Shaw and Wanjiru M. Gitau

9. Kingdom and Community in West Africa;
10. A Kingdom Divided — South African Christianity;
11. The Violent Kingdom — East African Christianity.

After the eighth chapter's narration of the Church's struggle against the slave trade, chapter 9 recounts the settlement of freed slaves in Sierra Leon to begin an experiment in Christian community in Africa. They named the city Freetown, in hope that it would be a community where the liberating power of the gospel to break the chains of sin and slavery would be demonstrated. Chapter 10 opens with the story of the "scattering of kingdoms" in flight from the violent Zulu expansion and continues with a narrative of the spread of Christianity, "scattering its gospel as as widely as Shaka had scattered his spears" (184). The story of the gradual conversion of Moshoeshoe reminds us "that the clash of kingdoms during the early decades of the nineteenth century involved more than guns and spears" as "the arrival of the gospel of the kingdom in various forms represented another kind of kingdom clash between traditional concepts of kingship and the new concepts of Christendom and Christ's rule in one's heart" (184).

The authors then investigate South African Christianity which was divided by (supposed) racial differences. In the nineteenth century, South Africa experienced Christian revitalization movements in three contexts. Just as Shaka constructed the Zulu into a new nation, the Afrikaners developed into a distinct people, with the Afrikaner identity explicitly tied to the vision of the kingdom "as a Reformed Theocracy" (186). Opposed to the Afrikaner theocracy were vast numbers of evangelical missionaries who "understood the kingdom as the rule of Christ in hearts rather than trule of the elect on earth" (191), especially exemplified by the teaching and practice of revivalist Andrew Murray. The third context envisioned "the Kingdom as Justice," in which prophets of social culture fought against societal injustices, especially oppression based on racial theories just as apartheid.

More trouble was experienced within the Eastern Africa region. The authors characterize East African Christianity as violent during this time because "Christians were killed and engaged in killing to promote the faith" (211). Chapter 11 "seeks to tell the story of an East African Christianity that came in meekness and martyrdom only to end in militancy" (211), focusing on the story in what are now Ethiopia, Kenya, Tanzania, and Uganda. In Ethiopia, the European "kingdoms of Christendom represented by a militant Italy bent on colonial expansion almost destroyed a newly reunited" — and theocratically Christian — "Ethiopia." Ethiopia's successful resistance and victory enhanced "the legend of Ethiopianism" (216), ultimately inspiring many 'Ethiopian' AIC movements across Africa.

Christine Chemutai Chirchir
Finding the Kingdom of God in Africa
BOOK REVIEW ESSAY: *The Kingdom of God in Africa: A History of African Christianity*, by Mark Shaw and Wanjiru M. Gitau

Part 4. The Kingdom on Earth: African Christianity in the Twentieth and Twenty-First Centuries

This section recounts the influence of colonialism and the impact of the missionary movement in Africa.

12. Ambassadors of the Kingdom — The Missionary Factor in Colonial Africa;
13. Cities of Zion — Independent Christian Movements before 1960;
14. Christianity in Post-Independence Africa.

Ambassadors of the Kingdom investigates the successful work of the missionaries in colonial Africa. Where there was colonial control, there the church grew and expanded including establishment of social institutions such as schools and hospitals. Colonial protection acted like a magic wand in bring about conversions even though the presence of colonial power did not guarantee church growth. Where missionaries were perceived as helpful mediators between the indigenous people and a potentially beneficial foreign power, local response to missionary message was generally favorable. Political independence brought with it a challenge in the church movement also. This caused the rise of African Initiated (independent) churches. Christians decided to break away from the mainstream churches run by the missionaries. The final chapter tries to present lessons and reflections from the struggling African Christianity. Shaw and Gitau conclude by pointing out that the story of the African striving for genuine kingdom identity has universal significance.

Evaluation

Shaw and Gitau have given an excellent chronological presentation of the history of Christianity in Africa. While the first section of the book presents the life of African culture before the coming of Christianity, the entire book details the challenges and successes that Christianity has experienced as it has tried to permeate culture. The historical narrative given in the book is first rate and clearly summarizes major historical periods in detail. Every chapter presents a powerful presentation of the church as it wrestled with penetrating and changing the culture.

The book opens with the Ogbu Kalu's idea that the African story of Christianity focuses on the Church's struggle to bring Christianity to the poor. That in itself raises questions (poor in what? in spirit? in material wealth? in knowledge?) in the mind of the reader. However, the writers immediately explain that history is written from one of two perspectives, either objectively or subjectively. Similarly, reading also can be objective or subjective. Thus understandings about who "the poor" are will impact the answer to the question

Christine Chemutai Chirchir
Finding the Kingdom of God in Africa
BOOK REVIEW ESSAY: *The Kingdom of God in Africa: A History of African Christianity*, **by Mark Shaw and Wanjiru M. Gitau**

of how "the poor" responded to the gift of "the gospel of the kingdom" (4). Readers from a developed nation will probably have a different understanding than readers from a developing nation.

The authors offer a concise chronological presentation of the history of Christianity in Africa right from the inception of the Christianity in Africa. Though they do not sound optimistic that the Christian message will have lasting impact in the life of the African Church, they are not pessimistic but are warning against triumphalism. How can Christianity in any place or culture remain authentic? Throughout history, they note, "African Christians have discovered that reflecting the rule of Christ and his kingdom is often an elusive ideal never perfectly achieved by any of the real-world institutions that bear Christ's name" (17). This leads us to ask, 'for how long will African Christians wrestle with Christianity, if it is an elusive thing?' This takes us back to the introduction where the writers indicate that Africans were already religious people and the concepts found in the Christian message are related in some ways to the concepts found in the African traditional religion. This has made it possible for the Christian message to find a place in the life of the African person. The rich legacy of the African religious heritage is significant in shaping the understanding of African Christianity. The entire book is intent on showing the flow of the history of Christianity within the African Continent and how the African church has struggled to be effective witness to the one she worships. In every period in the history of the church, she has had to work hard to maintain balance and stay true to her God.

The Kingdom of God in Africa is beautifully written and throughout the work, the authors have presented clear summaries of people, places, and events. In summary, this contribution to the literature on African Christianity is a plus. The rich legacy of African Christian history has been limited to a few sources for so long time. My only wish for them is that as historians of African literature, to present a more discrete elaboration of the term 'poor', which is a theme of the book, and more fully address the weaknesses and strengths that are found in understanding the African Traditional religion in relation to Christianity. I find that there is much that the writers mention at the introductory section from the African perspective that should have been beneficial to the Christian religion, as they were part of the life of the African and also part of the Christian message. E.g., the idea as life after death as demonstrated in the Egyptian religion or the Divine King as seen through the life of Pharaoh. I believe if that if understood well, such may provide a link between the Christian religion and the African man. This is because the introductory points are very crucial in pointing out the direction of flow of history in the African context. If done well, this might give more room for an authentic Christianity to flourish in Africa. While the writers have pointed out that historiography can be done from an objective or

Christine Chemutai Chirchir
Finding the Kingdom of God in Africa
BOOK REVIEW ESSAY: *The Kingdom of God in Africa: A History of African Christianity,* **by Mark Shaw and Wanjiru M. Gitau**

subjective point of view, I believe they have presented an example of balanced historiography in *The Kingdom of God*. The Church in Africa is still wrestling with rooting the message of salvation, with adhering to the Kingdom of God.

Authentic Christianity may not be as elusive as the writers have suggested, but has found key points of entrance into African cultures and is changing cultures throughout history from the Nile Delta, down the Nile River and on to Southern Africa, and across the continent from West Africa to East Africa. With all the challenges that Christianity experienced and still experiences, it has survived for centuries in Africa. Different generations of Christians have struggled to maintain the Christian faith, as the writers have indicated in their historical narrative. The same spirit continues to permeate the African continent. With the few trivial cautions as mentioned above, I am very excited about this book with the contribution that is it makes to the history of Christianity in Africa. Both its subject matter and organization serve to make this text a 'must read' for students and non-students alike. The authors are excellent historians and I recommend this work unreservedly. It is time for the African student and pastor to commit to understanding the development of the history of Christianity — both how much has been done and how much still needs to be done. As the Sotho king Moshoeshoe realized in the early 1800s, "the message about heavenly kingdoms [has] enormous earthly implications" (184). There is a lot that is still necessary and that is waiting to be done for the kingdom of God to be sufficiently deeply rooted within the African Christian context.

La « contextéisation » théologique : Un nouveau paradigme en théologie contextuelle

ESSAI CRITIQUE DU LIVRE
Lygunda Li-M, Fohle. *Contextualisation aujourd'hui : Questions approfondies en théologie contextuelle.* Kinshasa : Fohle Legacy Publishing, 2023.

Lessi Traoré [1]

Université de Strasbourg, Strasbourg, France
traoles@yahoo.fr

Introduction

La *contextualisation* est un mot très bien connu en milieu chrétien et est partout présent de nos jours dans la réflexion théologique. Sans aucun doute, toutes les disciplines théologiques parlent de contextualisation à divers degrés. En réalité, la nature de cette contextualisation généralisée est différente d'une discipline théologique à une autre. Elle ne concerne pas seulement les éléments du texte étudié, mais prend aussi en compte ceux qui concernent l'actualité du théologien.

La contextualisation est un concept, sinon un paradigme théologique qui, aux yeux de Fohle Lygunda li-Mwangwela (désormais Fohle), doit être repensée. Dans ce livre, il propose un nouveau paradigme, comme alternatif à la contextualisation traditionnelle. L'objectif de cette recension est d'exposer le maillage argumentatif de ce concept. Les autres aspects du livre ainsi que des incohérences, jeux de mots et paradoxes réels internes au livre, inhérents à toute œuvre humaine, passeront sous silence, leurs enjeux étant jugés mineurs par rapport aux idées fondatrices de la « contextéisation ».

Deux articulations ponctuent cette recension. L'auteur mérite d'être connu, ce personnage doit être mis en lumière avec son œuvre gigantesque. À défaut de présenter toute sa production intellectuelle, travail très fastidieux au regard de la pléthore de ses écrits, le contenu de l'ouvrage fondateur de la « contextéisation » sera dévoilé. Un examen critique de la pensée de l'auteur est

---

[1] Lessi Traoré est Burkinabé.

Lessi Traoré
La « contextéisation » théologique : Un nouveau paradigme en théologie contextuelle
ESSAI CRITIQUE DU LIVRE: *Contextualisation aujourd'hui : Questions approfondies en théologie contextuelle*, par Fohle Lygunda Li-M

nécessaire, pour présenter les insuffisances des arguments avancés pour soutenir la « contextéisation », ce faisant, on insistera, au passage, sur des aspects positifs.

L'auteur et sa pensée

Dans le monde de la réflexion théologique, il n'est pas très courant de rencontrer, en lisant un ouvrage, de nouveaux concepts, encore moins de néologismes. L'ouvrage ici recensé s'inscrit dans cette rareté. L'auteur, son livre, et sa pensée retiennent l'attention.

Brève présentation de l'auteur

Fohle Lygunda li-Mwangwela est un nom qu'on ne peut plus ignorer aujourd'hui dans le milieu théologique aussi bien africain que hors d'Afrique. Couramment appelé le Professeur Fohle, cet homme atypique se démarque par sa foisonnante production théologique. Ce génie est né le 17 novembre 1963, dans le village de Malinda, dans la province orientale de Kisangani, en République Démocratique du Congo (RDC). Sa singularité est enrichie par sa facilité à parler plusieurs langues : topoke (sa langue maternelle), lingala, français, et anglais. Son cursus académique fut des plus ordinaires. Il eut son BAC théologique (BTh) en 1989, à l'Institut Supérieur de Théologie Evangélique de l'Ubangi (RDC) ; fut titulaire d'un Doctorat en Ministère (DMin), option : *Théologie de la mission et développement du leadership*, en 2009, à Asbury Theological Seminary, Wilmore, Kentucky, aux États-Unis ; doublé d'un *Philosophiæ doctor* (PhD), option : *Éducation missiologique : théologie de la mission, histoire de la mission et gestion de l'enseignement supérieur*, en 2016, au North-West University, en Afrique du Sud.

L'excellence de ses rendements dans ce parcours académique lui a valu plusieurs récompenses et bourses dont on ne peut rapporter le nombre exact. Le professeur Fohle se présente comme un homme très engagé et infatigable, épris pour des questions de la mission et de la formation académique. Véritable pasteur, son humilité n'a pas d'égale, il fait preuve de qualités humaines exceptionnelles. Il est l'auteur de plusieurs structures qu'il a fondées, dont il dirige certaines. Il enseigne dans plusieurs facultés et universités d'Afrique et dans le monde. Ses productions intellectuelles sont essentiellement missiologiques. La théologie contextuelle retient actuellement son attention, qui l'a conduit à offrir au monde théologique son ouvrage fondateur du concept de « contextéisation » : *Contextualisation aujourd'hui. Questions approfondies en théologie contextuelle*.

Contexte général de rédaction et structure de l'ouvrage

Tout est parti d'un ouvrage collectif intitulé : *Contextual Theology : Skills*

Lessi Traoré
La « contextéisation » théologique : Un nouveau paradigme en théologie contextuelle
ESSAI CRITIQUE DU LIVRE: *Contextualisation aujourd'hui : Questions approfondies en théologie contextuelle,* par Fohle Lygunda Li-M

and Practices of Liberating Faith (anglais : 'Théologie contextuelle : Compétences et pratiques d'une foi libératrice'), sous la direction de Sigurd Bergmann et Mika Vähäkangas, publié à Londres aux éditions Routledge en 2021, qui a suscité des discussions entre missiologues. L'auteur semble être interpellé par cette publication, qui l'a conduit à requestionner la contextualité de la théologie en Afrique francophone (chap. 1). Il entend participer aux débats internationaux sur la contextualisation en en proposant un nouveau paradigme. Il se pose la question fondamentale suivante, dont la réponse va donner une nouvelle direction à sa penser : Faut-il contextualiser la théologie comme hier ?

Dans cette problématique ainsi posée, apparait une remise en question de la traditionnelle contextualisation. Que reproche Fohle à cette contextualisation habituelle, qui a pourtant servi de modèle théologique pendant longtemps ? Elle porte probablement des aspects qui ne sont plus bénéfiques pour aujourd'hui. Fohle tentera de le démontrer dans son ouvrage, en proposant un nouveau modèle, qu'il baptise d'un nouveau nom, tout en gardant la racine linguistique commune : contexte. Son nouveau paradigme est expliqué dans ce livre fondateur : *Contextualisation aujourd'hui. Questions approfondies en théologie contextuelle.*

L'auteur organise sa pensée en trois grandes parties réparties entre plusieurs chapitres (25 en tout). On fera l'impasse sur l'étude spécifique de chaque chapitre, qui n'est pas indispensable pour cette recension. La première partie comporte sept chapitres, la deuxième onze chapitres et la dernière sept chapitres. On voit bien apparaître une parfaite symétrie dans la réflexion de l'auteur.

La première partie constitue un état des lieux de la contextualisation de la théologie en Afrique, en établit un bilan évaluatif, des thèmes tels que la culture africaine et la formation théologique sont longuement étudiées. L'auteur veut comprendre le degré d'enracinement de la contextualisation traditionnelle dans le milieu chrétien africain, mais aussi dans les milieux de productions intellectuelles où se forme la plupart des leaders religieux, lieux où on leur apprend à contextualiser. Les programmes académiques intéressent Fohle pour en faire un diagnostic complet. Cette démarche lui permet de déceler le véritable problème de la contextualisation théologique en Afrique, ce qui lui donne la possibilité de proposer un autre modèle de faire de la théologie contextuelle.

Dans la deuxième partie, l'auteur rend compte des discussions d'autres savants de la contextualisation, expose tour à tour les différents débats qui y sont menés et en tire les conséquences qui s'imposent. L'interprétation des Écritures semble retenir l'attention, détient une grande place, tout se joue là, dans la contextualisation autour de ces textes sacrés.

Lessi Traoré
La « contextéisation » théologique : Un nouveau paradigme en théologie contextuelle
ESSAI CRITIQUE DU LIVRE: *Contextualisation aujourd'hui : Questions approfondies en théologie contextuelle,* **par Fohle Lygunda Li-M**

Dans la dernière partie, l'auteur poursuit les discussions sur la contextualisation traditionnelle, entre dans son sanctuaire dans les chapitres 24 et 25, les plus long du livre, qui sont l'aboutissement de sa longue réflexion, pour proposer au monde sa définition de la *contextéisation*, son nouveau paradigme théologique. Toutes les conditions épistémologiques de ce concept y sont bien expliquées. Il ne manque pas, dans cette partie, du sens de la pédagogie, de définir la nature, le contenu et les sources de la *contextéisation*. Comment ce paradigme s'applique-t-il ? L'auteur y répond en proposant une méthodologie. Comme pour tout nouveau concept, Fohle est prolixe et très démonstratif, pour l'expliquer au monde.

Argumentation de l'ouvrage

La thèse est la suivante : *Le théologien africain dispose de toutes les ressources en propre, il est capable de créer par lui-même, en toute liberté et indépendance intellectuelles, de nouveaux cadres théoriques et concepts théologiques originaux (CT), la « contextéisation » lui sert de guide épistémologique.* Cette thèse met en présence deux rapports, d'une part, celui du théologien africain avec lui-même, et d'autre part, celui qu'il entretient avec la pensée occidentale. Tout réside dans ces deux types de rapports, la *contextéisation* y joue un rôle fondamental.

Pour expliquer ces deux types de rapports, Fohle a recours à la trilogie contextualité, contextuelle, et *contexteisation*, cette dernière qu'il oppose au concept de contextualisation, à laquelle il attache les cadres théoriques et concepts théologiques hérités mais importés (CTHI). Cette trilogie est ce à quoi doit aboutir la théologie africaine, qui a longtemps été, selon l'auteur, une théologie de contextualisation, c'est-à-dire d'adaptation, qui a toujours accordé la prééminence aux CTHI, une telle contextualisation devrait maintenant être dépassée.

La *contextéisation* réunit en elle le contextuel et la contextualité de la théologie, ces deux concepts l'expliquent. La *contextéisation* est connotée épistémologiquement, qui est un processus, une dynamique réflexive qui consiste à penser de nouveaux cadres conceptuels théologiques originaux (chap. 24, pp. 231–232). Cette réflexion épistémologique se déroule — et c'est en cela que l'auteur innove — dans le cadre fixé par quatre critères de la contextualité. Une théologie est dite contextuelle chez Fohle, lorsqu'elle répond à ces quatre critères : (1) elle émane d'un besoin réel du contexte concerné qui en définit la problématique, (2) répond effectivement à ce besoin réel, (3) est construite à partir des sources qui proviennent prioritairement du même contexte et composée suivant les catégories épistémologiques et philosophiques du contexte, (4) enfin se caractérise par une expression linguistique correspondant

Lessi Traoré
La « contextéisation » théologique : Un nouveau paradigme en théologie contextuelle
ESSAI CRITIQUE DU LIVRE: *Contextualisation aujourd'hui : Questions approfondies en théologie contextuelle*, par Fohle Lygunda Li-M

à celle des destinataires pour en faciliter la réception (chap. 3, pp. 52–53 ; chap. 15, p. 165 ; chap. 24, p. 237 ; chap. 25, p. 254).

Fohle est convaincu que le théologien africain possède tout ce qu'il faut pour établir des CT (chap. 22, p. 214 ; chap. 24, pp. 29–30 ; chap. 25, p. 267). Les différents écrits théologiques existants effectués par les Africains, les multiples et innombrables prédications, les procès-verbaux écrits et oraux des différentes réunions et consultations ecclésiales et théologiques, les rapports de colloques tenus par les Africains, etc., sont autant d'éléments qui peuvent constituer des sources de la réflexion en théologie contextuelle (chap. 5, pp. 70–71).

Le théologien africain doit partir de lui-même, de son milieu, de la réalité qu'il veut étudier, pour construire un discours théologique africanisé (DTA), qui est simplement dit dans des catégories conceptuelles africaines, selon une vision africaine du monde. Il doit dire Dieu en Africain, avec la pure pensée africaine, rester authentiquement africain pour parler de Dieu (chap. 21, p. 204). Ce DTA veut garder cette altérité africaine tout en dialoguant avec les autres pensées théologiques. La théologie contextuelle telle que présentée ne s'applique pas seulement à l'Afrique Fohle la veut universelle (chap. 15, pp. 167–168). Il pense qu'un théologien africain peut élaborer un discours théologique contextuel occidental même s'il est lui-même en Afrique, tout comme un Occidental peut articuler un discours théologique contextuel africain même s'il est lui-même en Occident. Le lieu d'élaboration ne rend pas nécessairement contextuelle une théologie. La contextualité théologique qu'il défend est mobile, transportable, et le théologien en est le véhicule.

Fohle voit dans les CTHI des colons de la pensée théologique africaine, qui pour lui constituent de véritables entraves à l'indépendance et à la liberté de penser du génie théologique africain (chap. 25, pp. 260–261, 263–266, 279–281). Ce qui explique que le théologien africain n'est pas en mesure de proposer des CT. Le contexte, le milieu de production du discours théologique occidental, est ici le facteur déterminant d'appréciation. Ce milieu occidental est affecté par Fohle d'un coefficient de prétention impérialiste. On comprend dès lors sa volonté de décoloniser l'esprit du théologien africain, à le conduire à se départir de ces CTHI, à faire confiance en lui-même, et à créer des CT à partir de la réflexion sur le contexte africain (chap. 25, pp. 272–273). La théologie contextuelle fohlienne ne clôt pas l'étude sur un phénomène, la contextualité théologique est pour lui un questionnement permanent sur un phénomène donné, pour en découvrir le maximum d'aspects possibles en fonction des contextes (chap. 25, p. 275).

L'interprétation des Écritures semble capitale pour la théologie contextuelle fohlienne au point qu'il lui consacre sept chapitres (chap. 9–15). Le rapport du

Lessi Traoré
La « contextéisation » théologique : Un nouveau paradigme en théologie contextuelle
ESSAI CRITIQUE DU LIVRE: *Contextualisation aujourd'hui : Questions approfondies en théologie contextuelle*, par Fohle Lygunda Li-M

théologien « contextéisateur » avec les Écritures se veut simple. Le lecteur doit être dépouillé de tous présupposés hérités, des préjugés intellectuels qui pourraient l'influencer dans son approche des textes bibliques (chap. 6, pp. 76–78). Il doit y réfléchir librement, sans aucune autre influence possible, l'individu se tient face aux textes bibliques avec ses propres présupposés. L'auteur définit ainsi une herméneutique pour l'exégèse contextuelle, qui met en face deux contextes et les entraîne à dialoguer. Fohle parle d'un va-et-vient entre ces deux contextes : du contexte biblique à celui du lecteur, et de celui du lecteur au contexte biblique (chap. 13 ; chap. 24, p. 232). Le théologien exégète contextuel ne puise dans aucune autre ressource que lui-même et son contexte pour interpréter le texte biblique. Pour lui, théologie biblique et exégèse biblique doivent aller de pair (chap. 6, p. 78).

À l'instar de la contextualisation, la *contextéisation* devient un paradigme théologique qui s'applique à toutes les disciplines théologiques. Fohle veut changer la manière traditionnelle de faire de la théologie, la répartition de cette science en plusieurs disciplines semble problématique à ses yeux. Il refuse le cloisonnement des disciplines théologiques, qu'il juge limitatif, il veut les décloisonner pour mieux mettre en exergue leur complémentarité (chap. 3, p. 54). Fohle est bien conscient de l'héritage théologique qui continue de façonner le paysage théologique en Afrique (chap. 8, pp. 105–112). Informé de la lutte, des revendications et dénonciations des pionniers, il veut les dépasser. Il ne prétend pas refonder la théologie, mais plutôt la repenser et la reformuler (chap. 8, p. 114).

La théologie qu'il promeut n'est pas qu'une théologie pour les Africains, elle est une théologie au service de l'Afrique et pour le monde (chap. 8, p. 114 ; chap. 15, pp. 167–168). Ce qui importe à ses yeux, qui est en réalité le nerf de son combat, est que le théologien africain réussisse à formuler par lui-même ses propres cadres conceptuels théologiques (chap. 8, pp. 114–116 ; chap. 24, pp. 29–30). Le théologien africain doit être à l'écoute de Dieu qui lui parle dans son contexte, doit être en mesure d'exprimer librement sa foi avec ses propres conceptions sans aucun recours à une conception étrangère. Ce faisant, en accordant une place importante au Saint-Esprit dans sa réflexion (chap. 22, p. 210), le théologien africain en viendrait à formuler une théologie vivifiante, qui s'oppose à la théologie mortifère (chap. 25, p. 251). Une théologie mortifère est celle qui détourne l'Église de sa vocation et la plonge dans le formalisme, tandis qu'une théologie vivifiante rend la foi vivante, active et fructueuse (chap. 25, pp. 251–253). La théologie vivifiante est marquée par un discours dont le contenu est non seulement compris par les destinataires, mais élaboré en tenant compte de leur contexte.

Lessi Traoré
La « contextéisation » théologique : Un nouveau paradigme en théologie contextuelle
ESSAI CRITIQUE DU LIVRE: *Contextualisation aujourd'hui : Questions approfondies en théologie contextuelle*, par Fohle Lygunda Li-M

Pour l'auteur, l'impact positif d'un discours théologique dépend de sa contextualité, c'est-à-dire qu'il est exprimé dans des réalités conceptuelles des destinataires. Le référentiel des destinataires commande la conception du discours. Les CTHI étant construits hors contexte des destinataires en présence, il n'est pas étonnant qu'ils aient un faible impact dans un contexte étranger à leur conception. Le discours théologique élaboré en milieu occidental est empreint du contexte occidental et semble inadéquat au contexte africain. L'auteur pense qu'un tel discours théologique construit avec ces CTHI conduirait à la mort. Seul un discours théologique construit en tenant compte des réalités conceptuelles des destinataires aurait un impact sur ces derniers, donc produirait la vie. La pensée de Fohle est cohérente dans l'explication qu'il donne pour enraciner son concept de *contextéisation*. Malgré tout, on peut observer quelques insuffisances dans ce système bien tissé.

Un regard critique sur l'ouvrage

L'analyse ici menée porte essentiellement sur quelques arguments, sur certains de leurs aspects. Elle consiste à soulever des éléments qui font figure de contrepoids ou qui n'ont pas été suffisamment approfondis par l'auteur. Les limites avancées dans cette section sont de nature pratique.

Critique des thèses avancées

L'auteur est sans doute animé de bonnes intentions dans l'articulation qu'il fait de son paradigme théologique. En recherchant une indépendance totale de la pensée notamment théologique africaine, il est porté par une volonté émancipatrice. De ce fait, son concept de *contextéisation* passe pour être un concept éminemment politique. Il est l'idée d'une lutte qui veut une autodétermination de la pensée théologique africaine. Ce néologisme en milieu théologique est un signal lancé pour une réforme en profondeur de la théologie, qui doit s'exprimer désormais au pluriel. Il ne devrait plus y avoir un critère universel de validation de la réflexion théologique à prédominance des CTHI.

Fohle travaille pour une égalité de la pensée et du respect mutuel dans le monde intellectuel théologique, s'oppose fortement à cette condescendance théologique des CTHI. Il est temps pour le théologien africain de prendre conscience de sa force intrinsèque et des ressources propres de son contexte qui peuvent et doivent lui permettre de créer des CT. La théologie africaine n'est pas à minimiser, elle a quelque chose à dire au monde, c'est au théologien africain de s'éveiller à cette réalité et de travailler à produire des CT qui soient à la hauteur des CTHI. L'échiquier mondiale de la théologie a longtemps été dominé par ces CTHI, les CT des théologiens africains doivent désormais entrer en concurrence avec ces derniers.

Lessi Traoré
La « contextéisation » théologique : Un nouveau paradigme en théologie contextuelle
ESSAI CRITIQUE DU LIVRE: *Contextualisation aujourd'hui : Questions approfondies en théologie contextuelle*, par Fohle Lygunda Li-M

Le processus de création des CT africains est porté par la *contextéisation* qui définit quatre critères selon lesquels doivent se dérouler les réflexions théologiques (cf. supra). La méthode fondamentale fohlienne est que le théologien africain s'abstienne de dialoguer en amont avec les CTHI et ne le fasse qu'en aval dans ce processus de création des CT. Cette méthode de *contextéisation* est désormais opposable à la méthode traditionnelle qui admet ce dialogue tout au long de la recherche. La promotion d'une nouvelle méthode de faire de la science n'est pas ici remise en question, c'est plutôt l'inadéquation de la méthode avec l'esprit de la lutte qui est mise en exergue. Comment peut-on juger de l'originalité d'un CT sans dialogue préalable en amont d'une recherche ?

En recherche théologique, il y aura toujours des aspects communs, indépendamment du contexte de leur formation, qu'il faut connaître en amont d'une recherche. C'est à partir de ces éléments, parmi lesquels peuvent figurer les CTHI, qu'on peut juger si la recherche est innovante, originale ou non, s'elle aboutira à la formation d'un quelconque CT. Ce principe est bien connu de Fohle, mais pour lui, le dialogue en amont se tient uniquement (peut-être prioritairement) avec les sources contextuelles, avec les productions issues des théologiens africains (cf. supra critère 3). Il décide de ramener ce dialogue avec les CTHI en aval de la recherche. Il pense qu'un tel dialogue en amont serait susceptible d'influencer le chercheur africain, en réduisant de facto sa lucidité, en lui faisant perdre toute liberté et indépendance intellectuelles. La création d'un CT issu d'une telle recherche serait compromise.

Une telle façon de procéder, originale soit-elle, a la vertu de priver le théologien africain d'informations très importantes, utiles pour sa recherche. Si la crainte d'influence des CTHI est justifiée en amont, cette même influence existe en aval. Le principe de la pensée, qui fait surgir des idées en mosaïque dans l'entendement humain, puisqu'il n'y a jamais qu'une seule idée présente à l'esprit, n'admet pas cette chronologie amont aval. Dans l'entendement humain, la pensée se déroule toujours dans l'instant présent. La pensée en amont se tient dans les mêmes conditions que la pensée en aval, et ne sont en réalité rien d'autre qu'une seule et même pensée, qui n'est pas à l'abri d'une influence. À cet égard, pour être cohérente avec elle-même, la *contextéisation* devrait aller au bout de sa logique pour écarter définitivement toutes les formes de CTHI pour s'assurer de l'originalité des CT, en refusant ainsi tout dialogue intellectuel avec toutes les formes de pensée, sauf celles contextuelles africaines. Une telle position reste arbitraire et méthodologiquement compromettante.

Tous les savoirs attestés sur un sujet donné, quel que soit le contexte de leur élaboration, au nom du principe de l'universalité de la science, ne doivent pas

Lessi Traoré
La « contextéisation » théologique : Un nouveau paradigme en théologie contextuelle
ESSAI CRITIQUE DU LIVRE: *Contextualisation aujourd'hui : Questions approfondies en théologie contextuelle*, **par Fohle Lygunda Li-M**

être écartés à aucun moment de la recherche. Elles la rendent fécondent et contribuent plutôt à la création de CT. Rien ne prouve qu'une réflexion n'est ni indépendante ni libre parce qu'elle est effectuée en association. Toute réflexion est par ailleurs associative et ne saurait empêcher une quelconque créativité. On peut tout autant réfléchir avec les CTHI tout en créant des CT. Les CTHI ne devraient pas être connotés négativement, ils ne portent en eux aucune velléité dominatrice, ce ne sont que des savoirs neutres, il n'y a aucun danger à réfléchir avec ces CTHI dès lors que l'esprit humain est capable de lucidité pour dissocier les éléments contextuels qui y sont attachés. Dépouillés de leurs éléments contextuels, les CTHI deviennent universels, et sont la propriété de l'humanité. Les rejeter mordicus, revient aussi à rejeter la science, à rejeter la rationalité. Les CTHI n'empêchent pas de réfléchir lucidement, rationnellement, sainement et africainement. Il ne faut surtout pas opposer une rationalité théologique africaine à une autre.

Au cours de sa réflexion, l'auteur fournit très peu d'exemples concrets sur les CTHI. On voit apparaître dans son ouvrage le concept de démythologisation de Bultmann. Peut-être que ce concept convient mieux à sa logique argumentative, l'explication qu'il en donne suffit à créer un doute vis-à-vis de tous les CTHI. Il reste particulièrement général sur ces CTHI, est étonnement silencieux au sujet de ceux qui, en réalité, conviennent bien au contexte africain, par exemples, ceux concernant la foi, le salut, le baptême d'eau, le travail, la charité, le don de soi, etc. Cette lecture sélective de ces CTHI est préjudiciable à sa démarche. Discerner dans les CTHI ce qui sied au contexte africain, revient à écouter et vivre selon le modèle apostolique (1Thessaloniciens 5. 21).

L'auteur fait preuve, pour une des rares fois, de nuance vis-à-vis des CTHI, dans la section qu'il consacre sur le développement de passer de la « théologie d'émerveillement à une théologie d'engagement » (chap. 22, p. 207). Il dépeint la situation actuelle des églises et de la théologie d'être une situation de photosynthèse, un contexte qui n'est plus celui de l'époque des missionnaires, une nouvelle réalité recomposée, qui nécessite, selon son expression, « de remettre en question *certains*[2] éléments épistémologiques appris selon le modèle d'ailleurs. . . . [et d'] apprécier les valeurs culturelles et épistémologiques locales afin d'en tirer la sève qui convient pour la formulation de . . . discours théologiques contextuels » (chap. 22, p. 210). Pourquoi concède-t-il enfin cette nuance ?

En vérité, elle ne peut se comprendre qu'au regard de ce qui précède dans son livre, où il reconnaît que des missionnaires occidentaux continuent encore

---
[2] La mise en valeur est de nous.

Lessi Traoré
La « contextéisation » théologique : Un nouveau paradigme en théologie contextuelle
ESSAI CRITIQUE DU LIVRE : *Contextualisation aujourd'hui : Questions approfondies en théologie contextuelle*, **par Fohle Lygunda Li-M**

aujourd'hui d'intervenir et d'implanter des églises en Afrique. Cette section s'adresse à cette situation pour signifier que les églises missionnaires actuelles sont implantées dans un contexte de photosynthèse. Les théologiens doivent, dans ce cas précis, « remettre en question *certains*[3] éléments épistémologiques appris selon le modèle d'ailleurs. ... [et d'] apprécier les valeurs culturelles et épistémologiques locales afin d'en tirer la sève qui convient pour la formulation de ... discours théologiques contextuels » (chap. 22, p. 210). La nuance ne concerne donc pas de fait toutes les églises africaines de façon générale. L'auteur reste fidèle à sa logique que ces CTHI, sans distinction aucune, sont des obstacles à l'élaboration d'une théologie contextuelle africaine authentique.

Il ressort tout au long du livre des affirmations à caractère évasif, qui suffisent pour l'auteur à fonder son concept (chap. 24, p. 234 ; chap. 25, p. 252). Les causes réelles qui fondent sa pensée demandent plus de preuves concrètes, l'auteur n'en donne à peine que quelques-unes, alors qu'il faudrait davantage en fournir et dépasser des procès d'intentions, quand on veut asseoir un concept noble comme celui de la *contextéisation*.

Est-il judicieux d'étendre la contextualité à tous les aspects de la théologie et de la vie chrétienne ? L'auteur semble montrer que tous les textes bibliques sont contextuels, en occultant au passage le caractère révélateur des Écritures. La contextualité universalisante l'affaiblit et la rend relative, sa portée n'est qu'en réalité réduite et ne s'applique finalement pas à tout le monde. N'est-il pas à cause d'une telle conception que la théologie africaine est dite contextuelle et marginalisée ? La contextualité fohlienne appliquée aux textes bibliques rend inopérant leur caractère révélateur, les prive de leur universalité, et rend leur message relatif. En suivant cette perspective, les textes bibliques finissent ainsi par ne plus rien dire au monde d'aujourd'hui.

Toute théologie est contextuelle, affirmation récurrente chez l'auteur, contextualité qui répond aux quatre critères qu'il a énoncés. Pourtant, il existe des théologies qui sortent de son maillage épistémologique, qu'on pourrait appeler de « théologies a-contextuelles », qui ne répondent ni au premier critère, ni au deuxième encore moins au troisième. Le quatrième critère est communicationnel, s'applique à toute forme de pensée. Il y a de ces théologies qui sont nées, non pas d'un quelconque besoin du contexte du théologien, donc ne solutionneront pas ce besoin, construites sur la base des sources disponibles sans aucune distinction, mais venant simplement d'un besoin personnel, d'une simple curiosité scientifique, d'un appel intérieur à explorer une thématique, un sujet, d'une expérience personnelle avec Dieu, etc. Certains des écrits de Boèce,

---

[3] La mise en valeur est de nous.

Lessi Traoré
La « contextéisation » théologique : Un nouveau paradigme en théologie contextuelle
ESSAI CRITIQUE DU LIVRE: *Contextualisation aujourd'hui : Questions approfondies en théologie contextuelle*, par Fohle Lygunda Li-M

d'Augustin, de Thomas d'Aquin, des réformateurs, etc., peuvent être rangés parmi ces théologies a-contextuelles, parce qu'on leur reconnaît un caractère universel, ils traitent des problématiques qui concernent tout le monde.

Un théologien africain qui développe une théologie a-contextuelle est appelé à réfléchir avec les CTHI dans ce domaine, qui ne constituent pas des entraves à sa liberté de penser et à son indépendance intellectuelle, cela ne l'empêcherait pas de créer des CT. Contextualité ou non, la création d'un CT ne devrait pas nécessairement être liée au contexte, mais plutôt au génie du chercheur. Toutefois, on peut admettre avec l'auteur que le contexte peut favoriser leur création. Au-delà de ces insuffisances argumentatives, existent des limites réelles à l'application de la *contextéisation*.

Limites de la « contextéisation »

On ne peut faire de la théologie contextuelle africaine sans des ressources bibliographiques conséquentes bien connues. Les travaux des théologiens africains, les discours tenus par des chrétiens africains, les colloques universitaires tenus par les théologiens africains, les comptes rendus des réunions ecclésiales africaines, etc., qui doivent servir de sources à la théologie contextuelle africaine sont tapis dans l'ombre. L'un des échecs de la contextualité de la théologie africaine viendra de son insuffisance en ressources bibliographiques doublée d'un manque en ressources financières et matérielles pour mener des recherches adéquates.

Les productions théologiques africaines ne sont pas suffisamment vulgarisées. Les ressources bibliographiques les plus disponibles, les plus vulgarisées sont celles produites selon des CTHI. Comme le dit un adage burkinabè : « On danse aux sons des tam-tams qui battent à côté ». Les tam-tams lointains de nos braves théologiens africains, comble du paradoxe, ce sont en réalité des tam-tams qui battent à côté, mais leurs sons semblent très faibles au point qu'on croit qu'ils proviennent de très loin. Ces sons ne peuvent pas participer aux festivités de la théologie africaine. En revanche, ce sont des tam-tams qui battent de très loin, qui réussissent à se faire entendre de très près, en Afrique. Voici le paradoxe africain, qui nécessite de travailler à inverser la tendance.

L'une des limites de la *contextéisation* réside dans les réticences auxquelles elle fera face, qui s'ajoutent au manque d'assurance en eux-mêmes de certains théologiens africains à produire des CT. Le plus grand défi sera de réussir à rallier les esprits à la cause de la théologie contextuelle. Ce défi ne pourra être relevé que lorsque les thématiques et les sujets abordés intéresseront vraiment à la fois le monde universitaire, pour qu'il les intègre dans son programme, que le lecteur lambda et le leader religieux, qui cherchent à se cultiver. La réception

Lessi Traoré
La « contextéisation » théologique : Un nouveau paradigme en théologie contextuelle
ESSAI CRITIQUE DU LIVRE: *Contextualisation aujourd'hui : Questions approfondies en théologie contextuelle*, **par Fohle Lygunda Li-M**

généralisée de ces théologies contextuelles africaines permettra de mesurer leur degré d'influence et suscitera un engouement en leur faveur. De tel défi s'inscrit naturellement dans un combat séculaire. Les pensées de certains théologiens, aujourd'hui considérées comme portant un caractère universel, qui occupent une place importante dans les programmes des facultés de théologie, ne se sont pas imposées d'un seul coup à la première production. C'est à la suite d'un long débat théologique que certaines pensées ont fini par s'imposer.

La *contextéisation* doit considérer le fait que certains théologiens africains ignorent ce que sont exactement les catégories épistémologiques et philosophiques de leur contexte (CEPC), pour deux raisons : d'une part, ils vivent dans un monde hybride, façonné par l'interculturalité et l'école, qui les éloignent de plus en plus de ces catégories, et d'autre part, en l'absence ou l'insuffisance des ressources bibliographiques contextuelles à leur disposition, ils ne peuvent pas constituer un capital de savoir sur ces CEPC pour former des CT. Face à une telle réalité, la *contextéisation* doit se réinventer.

Le dernier élément est d'ordre linguistique. La pléthore des langues vernaculaires africaines rend souvent difficile la communication. Il y a autant de groupes ethniques que de CEPC en Afrique, au point que l'Afrique se conjugue au pluriel. Comment construire un discours théologique qui s'inspire des CEPC d'une localité, qui soit compréhensible dans toutes les autres localités d'Afrique sans tomber dans la contextualisation traditionnelle (adaptation) ? Il faudrait ici exclure le quatrième critère, qui veut que le discours théologique contextuel soit exprimé dans des catégories linguistiques des destinataires. Quels destinataires, en ce qui concerne l'Afrique, d'autant plus qu'il y a en Afrique, au moins autant d'ethnies que de langues ? Peut-être que la solution viendrait du côté de la langue du colon. Si tel est le cas, alors apparait le paradoxe africain, la plupart des productions qui peuvent servir de sources pour le théologien *contextéisateur* d'Afrique francophone sont en anglais, y compris la majorité des productions intellectuelles de notre auteur, qui est issu d'un pays francophone. On est en droit de se demander si on est en présence d'un mythe ou de la réalité.

Conclusion

La *Contextualisation aujourd'hui : Questions approfondies en théologie contextuelle* du Professeur Fohle Lygunda li-Mwangwela, est un véritable texte fondateur, trace les linéaments d'un nouveau paradigme théologique qu'est la *contextéisation*. En lisant cet ouvrage, le lecteur se sent connecté avec l'esprit de l'écrivain qui parle avec toute la sincérité qu'on puisse trouver. Cette recension n'aura pas tout dit sur la compréhension de ce concept, qui fait son apparition

Lessi Traoré
La « contextéisation » théologique : Un nouveau paradigme en théologie contextuelle
ESSAI CRITIQUE DU LIVRE: *Contextualisation aujourd'hui : Questions approfondies en théologie contextuelle*, **par Fohle Lygunda Li-M**

et qui demande à être davantage élucidé par d'autres textes explicatifs de son fondateur ou de ceux qui seront épris de ce concept et acquis à cette cause. Cette œuvre ne pouvant être complètement recensée, il est du devoir de celui qui veut en savoir davantage de se rapporter directement à ce livre, qui lui parlera et qui corrigera probablement certaines des appréhensions à l'égard de ce concept, qui est un véritable apport substantiel dans le monde de la science théologique.

Theological 'Contextedization': A New Paradigm in Contextual Theology

BOOK REVIEW ESSAY
LYGUNDA LI-M, Fohle. *Contextualisation aujourd'hui : Questions approfondies en théologie contextuelle*. Kinshasa: Fohle Legacy Publishing, 2023.

Lessi TRAORÉ [1]

Université de Strasbourg, Strasbourg, France
traoles@yahoo.fr

Introduction

Contextualization is a well-known word in Christian circles and is everywhere present in theological reflection today. Without doubt, all theological disciplines speak of contextualization to varying degrees. In fact, the nature of this generalized contextualization differs from one theological discipline to another. It concerns not only the elements of the text under study, but also those that are relevant to the theologian's current situation.

Contextualization is a concept, if not a theological paradigm, which, in the eyes of Fohle Lygunda li-Mwangwela (henceforth Fohle), needs to be rethought. In this book he proposes a new paradigm as an alternative to traditional contextualization. The aim of this review is to set out the argumentative mesh of this concept. Other aspects of the book, as well as the inconsistencies, puns and paradoxes inherent in any human work, will not be discussed, as they are considered minor in relation to the founding ideas of *contextéisation*, a French neologism, or 'contexted-ization'.

Two points punctuate this review. The author deserves to be better known, and his gigantic body of work needs to be brought to light. While it would be tedious to present his entire intellectual output, given the plethora of his writings, the content of the founding work of 'contextedization' will be revealed. A critical examination of the author's thought is necessary, in order to present the inadequacies of the arguments put forward in support of 'contextedization', while at the same time emphasizing its positive aspects.

---

[1] Lessi Traoré is from Burkina Faso.

Lessi Traoré
Theological 'Contextedization': A New Paradigm in Contextual Theology
BOOK REVIEW: *Contextualisation aujourd'hui : Questions approfondies en théologie contextuelle,* by Fohle Lygunda Li-M

The author and his thought

In the world of theological reflection, it is not very common to come across new concepts, let alone neologisms, when reading a work. This book is one of those rare encounters. The author, his book, and his thinking are worthy of our attention.

Fohle Lygunda li-Mwangwela is a name that can no longer be ignored today in theological circles both within and outside Africa. Commonly referred to as Professor Fohle, this atypical man stands out for his prolific theological output. This genius was born on 17 November 1963, in the village of Malinda, in the eastern province of Kisangani, in the Democratic Republic of Congo (DRC). His uniqueness is enriched by his ability to speak several languages: Topoke (his mother tongue), Lingala, French, and English. His academic background was quite ordinary. He obtained his theological BAC (BTh) in 1989, from the Institut Supérieur de Théologie Evangélique de l'Ubangi (RDC); a Doctorate in Ministry (DMin) with a concentration in *Mission Theology and Leadership Development* in 2009, at Asbury Theological Seminary, Wilmore, Kentucky, USA; and finally a PhD in *Missiological Education* with a focus on *mission theology, mission history and higher education management,* in 2016, at North-West University, South Africa.

His excellent performance on this academic course has earned him several awards and scholarships, the exact number of which cannot be reported. Professor Fohle presents himself as a highly committed and tireless man, enamoured with issues of mission and academic training. A true pastor, his humility has no equal, and he displays exceptional human qualities. He is the founder and director of several structures. He teaches in several faculties and universities in Africa and around the world. His intellectual output is essentially missiological. Contextual theology is currently the focus of his attention, leading him to offer the theological world his seminal work on the concept of "contextedization" : *Contextualisation aujourd'hui. Questions approfondies en théologie contextuelle.*

General editorial context and structure of the book

It all started with a collective work entitled *Contextual Theology: Skills and Practices of Liberating Faith,* edited by Sigurd Bergmann and Mika Vähäkangas, published in London by Routledge in 2021, which sparked off discussions among missiologists. The author seems to be challenged by this publication, which has led him to reconsider the contextuality of theology in French-speaking Africa (chapter 1). He intends to participate in international debates on contextualization by proposing a new paradigm. He poses the following fundamental question, the answer to which will give a new direction to his

Lessi Traoré
Theological 'Contextedization': A New Paradigm in Contextual Theology
BOOK REVIEW: *Contextualisation aujourd'hui : Questions approfondies en théologie contextuelle*, by Fohle Lygunda Li-M

thinking: S hould theology be contextualized as it was yesterday?

This question poses a challenge to traditional contextualization. What is Fohle's criticism of this customary contextualization, which has long served as a theological model ? It probably has aspects that are no longer beneficial today. Fohle will attempt to demonstrate this in his book, by proposing a new model, which he christens with a new name, while retaining the common linguistic root: context. His new paradigm is explained in this seminal book: *Contextualisation Aujourd'hui: Questions approfondies en théologie contextuelle* ('Contextualisation Today: In-Depth Questions on Contextual Theology').

The author organizes his thinking into three main sections. each chapter, which is not essential for this review. The first part comprises seven chapters, the second eleven and the last seven. There is a clear symmetry in the author's thinking.

The first part takes stock of the contextualization of theology in Africa, drawing up an evaluative balance sheet, and examining at length themes such as African culture and theological education. The author aims to understand the extent to which traditional contextualization has taken root in African Christian circles, but also in the intellectual production environments in which most religious leaders are trained, places where they are taught to contextualize. Fohle's interest in academic programs lies in their comprehensive diagnosis. This approach enables him to identify the real problem of theological contextualization in Africa, which in turn enables him to propose an alternative model for contextual theology.

In the second part, the author reports on the discussions of other scholars of contextualization, outlining in turn the various debates involved and drawing the necessary conclusions. Interpretation of the Scriptures seems to hold a great deal of attention and space, and everything is at stake here, in the contextualization of these sacred texts.

In the final section, the author continues his discussion of traditional contextualization, entering its sanctuary in chapters 24 and 25, the longest of the book, which are the culmination of his long reflection, to propose to the world his definition of *contextedization*, his new theological paradigm. All the epistemological conditions of this concept are well explained. In this section on the meaning of pedagogy, he goes on to define the nature, content and sources of *contextedization*. How is this paradigm applied? The author answers this question by proposing a methodology. In his enthusiasm to explain this new concept, Fohle is very demonstrative though perhaps unhelpfully longwinded at times.

Argumentation of the book

Lessi Traoré
Theological 'Contextedization': A New Paradigm in Contextual Theology
BOOK REVIEW: *Contextualisation aujourd'hui : Questions approfondies en théologie contextuelle*, **by Fohle Lygunda Li-M**

The thesis is as follows: *The African theologian has all the resources at his or her disposal; he or she is capable of creating new theoretical frameworks and original theological concepts (TC) on his or her own, with intellectual freedom and independence; "contextedization" serves as an epistemological guide.* This thesis brings together two relationships: each African theologian's relationship with him or herself, and their relationship with Western thought. Everything lies in these two types of relationship, with *contextedization* playing a fundamental role.

To explain these two types of relationship, Fohle uses the trilogy contextuality, contextual, and *contextedization*, the latter of which he contrasts with the concept of contextualization, to which he attaches inherited but imported theoretical frameworks and theological concepts (TFTC). This trilogy is what African theology needs to achieve, since it has long been a theology of contextualization, i.e. of adaptation, according to the author, which has always given pre-eminence to TFTC, such contextualization should now be overcome.

Contextedization brings together the contextual and the contextuality of theology, and these two concepts explain why. Contextedization has an epistemological connotation, being a process, a reflexive dynamic that consists in thinking out new and original theological conceptual frameworks (chapter 24, pp. 231–232). This epistemological reflection takes — and this is where the author breaks new ground — within the framework set by four criteria of contextuality. For Fohle, a theology is said to be contextual when it meets these four criteria: (1) it emanates from a real need in the context concerned, which defines its problematic ; (2) it effectively responds to this real need ; (3) it is constructed from sources which come primarily from the same context, and is composed according to the epistemological and philosophical categories of the context; (4) finally, it is characterized by a linguistic expression corresponding to that of the addressees, to facilitate its reception (chapter 3, pp. 52–53; chapter 15, p. 165; chapter 24, p. 237; chapter 25, p. 254).

Fohle is convinced that the African theologian has what it takes to establish TCs (chap. 22, p. 214 ; chap. 24, pp. 29–30 ; chap. 25, p. 267). The various existing theological writings by Africans, the innumerable sermons, the written and oral minutes of various ecclesial and theological meetings and consultations, the reports of colloquia held by Africans, etc., are all elements that can constitute sources for reflection in contextual theology (chapter 5, pp. 70–71).

The African theologian has to start from himself, from his environment, and from the reality he wants to study, to build an Africanized theological discourse (ATD), which is simply articulated in African conceptual categories, according to an African worldview. He must speak of God as an African, with pure African thought, remaining authentically African to speak of God (chap.

Lessi Traoré
Theological 'Contextedization': A New Paradigm in Contextual Theology
BOOK REVIEW: *Contextualisation aujourd'hui : Questions approfondies en théologie contextuelle,* by Fohle Lygunda Li-M

21, p. 204). This ATD aims to preserve this African otherness while maintaining a dialogue with other theological thinking. Contextual theology as presented does not only apply to Africa — Fohle wants it to be universal (chap. 15, pp. 167–168). He believes that an African theologian can elaborate a Western contextual theological discourse even if he himself is in Africa, just as a Westerner can articulate an African contextual theological discourse even if he himself is in the West. The place of elaboration does not necessarily make a theology contextual. The theological contextuality he defends is mobile, transportable, and the theologian is its vehicle.

Fohle sees the TFTCs as colonizers of African theological thought, who for him constitute real impediments to the independence and freedom of thought of African theological genius (chap. 25, pp. 260–261, 263–266, 279–281). This explains why the African theologian is not in a position to propose TCs. The context, the milieu in which Western theological discourse is produced, is the decisive factor here. In Fohle's view, this Western milieu is affected by a coefficient of imperialist pretension. We can therefore understand his desire to decolonize the mind of the African theologian, to lead him to let go of these CTHIs, to trust in himself, and to create TCs based on reflection on the African context (chap. 25, pp. 272–273). Fohlian contextual theology does not close the study on a phenomenon; theological contextuality is for him a permanent questioning on a given phenomenon, to discover the maximum of possible aspects according to contexts (chap. 25, p. 275).

The interpretation of Scripture seems so central to Fohlian contextual theology that he devotes seven chapters to it (chapters 9–15). The 'contextualizing' theologian's relationship with Scripture is intended to be simple. The reader must be stripped of all inherited presuppositions and intellectual prejudices that might influence his approach to biblical texts (chapter 6, pp. 76–78). Without any other possible influence, the individual stands before the biblical texts with his or her own presuppositions. The author thus defines a hermeneutic for contextual exegesis, which brings two contexts face to face and brings them into dialogue. Fohle speaks of a to-and-fro between these two contexts: from the biblical context to that of the reader, and from that of the reader to the biblical context (chapters 13 and 24). The contextual theologian draws on no other resource than himself and his context to interpret the biblical text. For him, biblical theology and biblical exegesis must go hand in hand (chapter 6, p. 78).

Like contextualization, *contextedization* becomes a theological paradigm that applies to all theological disciplines. Fohle wants to change the traditional way of doing theology, as the division of this field into several disciplines seems problematic in his eyes. He rejects the compartmentalization of theological

Lessi Traoré
Theological 'Contextedization': A New Paradigm in Contextual Theology
BOOK REVIEW: *Contextualisation aujourd'hui : Questions approfondies en théologie contextuelle,* by Fohle Lygunda Li-M

disciplines, which he sees as limiting, and wants to break down the barriers between them in order to emphasize their complementary nature (chapter 3, p. 54). Fohle is well aware of the theological heritage that continues to shape the theological landscape in Africa (chapter 8, pp. 105–112). Informed of the struggle, the claims and denunciations of the pioneers, he wants to go beyond them. He does not claim to re-found theology, but rather to rethink and reformulate it (chap. 8, p. 114).

The theology he promotes is not just a theology for Africans, it is a theology at the service of Africa and for the world (chapter 8, p. 114 ; chapter 15, pp. 167–168). What is important to him, and in fact the crux of his struggle, is for the African theologian to succeed in formulating his own theological conceptual frameworks (chapter 8, pp. 114–116 ; chapter 24, pp. 29–30). The African theologian must listen to God who speaks to him in his own context, must be able to express his faith freely with his own conceptions, without recourse to any foreign conception. In so doing, by giving the Holy Spirit an important place in his thinking (chapter 22, p. 210), the African theologian would come to formulate a life-giving theology, which is opposed to mortifying theology (chapter 25, p. 251). A mortifying theology is one that diverts the Church from its vocation and plunges it into formalism, whereas a life-giving theology makes faith alive, active and fruitful (chap. 25, pp. 251–253). Life-giving theology is characterized by a discourse whose content is not only understood by those to whom it is addressed, but also developed with their context in mind.

For the author, the positive impact of a theological discourse depends on its contextuality, i.e., it is expressed in the conceptual realities of the addressees. The addressees' frame of reference dictates the design of the discourse. Since TFTCs are constructed outside the context of the recipients in question, it's not surprising that they have little impact in a context foreign to their conception. The theological discourse elaborated in a Western environment is imbued with the Western context and seems inadequate to the African context. The author believes that such a theological discourse constructed with these TFTCs would lead to death. Only a theological discourse constructed with the conceptual realities of the recipients in mind would have an impact on them, and thus produce life. Fohle's thinking is coherent in the explanation he gives to ground his concept of *contextedization*. Despite this, we can observe a few shortcomings in this well-woven system.

A critical look at the work

The analysis here focuses on a few of the arguments, on certain aspects of them. It consists in raising elements which act as counterweights or which have not been sufficiently explored by the author. The limitations outlined in this

Lessi Traoré
Theological 'Contextedization': A New Paradigm in Contextual Theology
BOOK REVIEW: *Contextualisation aujourd'hui : Questions approfondies en théologie contextuelle*, by Fohle Lygunda Li-M

section are of a practical nature.

Constructive insights

The author's articulation of his theological paradigm is undoubtedly well-intentioned. In seeking total independence for African theological thought in particular, he is driven by a desire to emancipate. As a result, his concept of *contextedization* comes across as eminently political. It is the idea of a struggle for the self-determination of African theological thought. This neologism in theological circles is a signal for an in-depth reform of theology, which must henceforth be expressed in the plural. There should no longer be a one-size-fits-all criterion for validating TFTC-dominated theological thinking.

Fohle works for equality of thought and mutual respect in the theological intellectual world, and strongly opposes the theological condescension of the TFTC. It's time for the African theologian to become aware of his intrinsic strength and the resources of his own context, which can and must enable him to create TCs. African theology is not to be minimized, it has something to say to the world, and it's up to the African theologian to wake up to this reality and work to produce TCs that measure up to TFTC. The world theological scene has long been dominated by these TFTCs, and the TCs of African theologians must now compete with them.

The process of creating African TCs is driven by *contextedization*, which defines four criteria according to which theological reflections must take place (see above). The fundamental Fohlian method is that the African theologian refrains from dialoguing upstream with the TFTCs and only does so downstream in the process of creating the TCs. This method of *contextedization* is now opposed to the traditional method, which allows dialogue throughout the research process. The promotion of a new way of doing science is not in question here, but rather the inadequacy of the method with the spirit of the struggle. How can one judge the originality of a TC without prior dialogue upstream of the research?

In theological research, there will always be common aspects, irrespective of the context of their formation, which need to be known upstream of a search. It is on the basis of these elements, which may include the TFTC, that we can judge whether the research is innovative, original or not, whether it will lead to the formation of any kind of TC. This principle is well known to Fohle, but for him, the upstream dialogue takes place solely (perhaps primarily) with contextual sources, with productions from African theologians (see above, criterion 3). He decides to bring this dialogue with the TFTC back downstream from the research. He believes that such an upstream dialogue would be likely to influence the African researcher, reducing de facto his lucidity and causing him to lose all intellectual freedom and independence. The creation of a TC

Lessi Traoré
Theological 'Contextedization': A New Paradigm in Contextual Theology
BOOK REVIEW: *Contextualisation aujourd'hui : Questions approfondies en théologie contextuelle,* **by Fohle Lygunda Li-M**

based on such research would be compromised.

This kind of approach, original though it may be, has the virtue of depriving the African theologian of very important information, useful for his research. If the fear of TFTC influence is justified upstream, the same influence exists downstream. The principle of thought, which gives rise to a mosaic of ideas in the human mind, since there is never just one idea in the mind, does not allow for this chronology upstream. In human understanding, thought always takes place in the present moment. Upstream and downstream thoughts are in fact one and the same, but not immune to influence. In this respect, to be coherent with itself, "contextedization" would have to go to the end of its logic and definitively rule out all forms of TFTC in order to ensure the originality of TCs, thus refusing any intellectual dialogue with all forms of thought, except African contextual ones. Such a position is arbitrary and methodologically compromising.

In the name of the principle of the universality of science, all knowledge attested on a given subject, whatever the context in which it was developed, must not be excluded from research at any time. Rather, they make it fruitful and contribute to the creation of TC. There is nothing to prove that just because something is done in association, it is neither independent nor free. All thinking is associative and cannot prevent creativity. It is just as possible to reflect with the TFTC while creating TCs. There's no danger in thinking with them, as long as the human mind is lucid enough to dissociate the contextual elements attached to them. Stripped of their contextual elements, TFTCs become universal, and are the property of humanity. To reject them outright is to reject science and rationality. The TFTC do not prevent us from thinking lucidly, rationally, healthily and African-style. Above all, we must not pit one African theological rationality against another.

In the course of his reflection, the author provides very few concrete examples of TFTC. Bultmann's concept of demythologization appears in his work. Perhaps this concept suits his argumentative logic better, but the explanation he gives is enough to create doubt about all TFTCs. He remains particularly general about these TFTCs, and is astonishingly silent about those which, in reality, are well suited to the African context, for example, those concerning faith, salvation, water baptism, work, charity, self-giving and so on. This selective reading of the TFTC is detrimental to his approach. To discern in the TFTC what is appropriate to the African context is to listen and live according to the apostolic model (1Thess 5:21).

For one of the few times the author shows nuance with regard to the TFTC, in the section he devotes to the development of moving from a "theology of wonder to a theology of commitment" (chapter 22, p. 207). He depicts the

Lessi Traoré
Theological 'Contextedization': A New Paradigm in Contextual Theology
BOOK REVIEW: *Contextualisation aujourd'hui : Questions approfondies en théologie contextuelle,* by **Fohle Lygunda Li-M**

current situation of churches and theology as one of photosynthesis, a context that is no longer that of the missionary era, a new recomposed reality, which requires, in his words, "questioning *certain*[2] epistemological elements learned from elsewhere.... [and to] appreciate local cultural and epistemological values in order to draw from them the appropriate sap for the formulation of ... contextual theological discourses" (chapter 22, p. 210). Why does he finally concede this nuance?

In truth, it can only be understood in the light of what precedes it in his book, where he acknowledges that Western missionaries are still intervening and planting churches in Africa today. This section addresses this situation to mean that today's missionary churches are planted in a context of photosynthesis. Theologians must, in this case, "question *certain*[3] epistemological elements learned from the model elsewhere. ... [and to] appreciate local cultural and epistemological values in order to draw the appropriate sap for the formulation of ... contextual theological discourses" (chap. 22, p. 210). This nuance does not, in fact, apply to all African churches in general. The author remains true to his logic that these TFTCs, without distinction, are obstacles to the development of an authentic African contextual theology.

Throughout the book, evasive statements are made, which the author considers sufficient to justify his concept (chapter 24, p. 234; chapter 25, p. 252). The real causes on which his thinking is based require more concrete evidence, and the author gives barely any, whereas more should be provided, and we should go beyond trials of intent, when we want to establish a noble concept such as *contextedization*.

Is it wise to extend contextuality to all aspects of theology and Christian life ? The author seems to show that all biblical texts are contextual, overlooking the revelatory character of Scripture. Universalizing contextuality weakens it and makes it relative; its scope is only actually reduced and ultimately does not apply to everyone. Is it not because of such a conception that African theology is said to be contextual and marginalized? Fohlian contextuality applied to biblical texts renders their revelatory character inoperative, deprives them of their universality, and renders their message relative. From this perspective, biblical texts end up saying nothing to today's world.

All theology is contextual, as the author repeatedly asserts, a contextuality that meets all four of his criteria. And yet, there are theologies that fall outside his epistemological mesh, that could be called 'a-contextual theologies', that

---

[2] Emphasis added.
[3] Emphasis added.

meet neither the first nor the second criterion, let alone the third. The fourth criterion is communicational, applying to all forms of thought. Some of these theologies are born, not from any need in the theologian's context, and so will not solve that need, built on the basis of available sources without any distinction, but coming simply from a personal need, from a simple scientific curiosity, from an inner call to explore a theme, a subject, a personal experience with God, and so on. Some of the writings of Boethius, Augustine, Thomas Aquinas, the Reformers, etc., can be ranked among these a-contextual theologies, because they are recognized as universal, dealing with issues that concern everyone.

An African theologian who develops an a-contextual theology is called upon to reflect with the TFTC in this field, which do not constitute impediments to his freedom of thought and intellectual independence, this would not prevent him from creating TCs. Contextuality or not, the creation of a TC should not necessarily be linked to context, but rather to the genius of the researcher. However, we can agree with the author that context can encourage their creation. Beyond these argumentative shortcomings, there are real limits to the application of *contextedization*.

Limits to 'contextedization'

Contextual theology in Africa cannot be done without substantial, well-known bibliographical resources. The works of African theologians, speeches given by African Christians, university colloquia held by African theologians, proceedings of African ecclesial meetings, etc., which should serve as sources for African contextual theology, are lurking in the shadows. One of the failures of African theological contextuality will come from its lack of bibliographical resources, coupled with a lack of financial and material resources to carry out adequate research.

African theological productions are not sufficiently popularized. The most widely available and popularized bibliographical resources are those produced by TFTC. As the Burkinabe saying goes: "We dance to the sounds of the tom-toms beating next door." The far-off tom-toms of our brave African theologians, with the height of paradox, are in fact tom-toms beating next door, but their sounds seem so faint that we believe they come from far away. These sounds cannot be part of the festivities of African theology. Instead, tom-toms beating from far away manage to be heard up close, in Africa. This is the African paradox, and we must work to reverse the trend.

One of the limits of *contextedization* lies in the reluctance it will encounter, coupled with the lack of self-confidence of some African theologians in producing TCs. The greatest challenge will be to succeed in rallying minds to the cause of contextual theology. This challenge can only be met when the

Lessi Traoré
Theological 'Contextedization': A New Paradigm in Contextual Theology
BOOK REVIEW: *Contextualisation aujourd'hui : Questions approfondies en théologie contextuelle*, by Fohle Lygunda Li-M

themes and topics addressed are of genuine interest both to the academic world, so that it can integrate them into its curriculum, and to the lambda reader and religious leader, who are seeking to cultivate themselves. The widespread reception of these African contextual theologies will enable us to measure their degree of influence and create a craze in their favor. Such a challenge is naturally part of an age-old struggle. The thoughts of certain theologians, now considered to have a universal character and occupying an important place in the curricula of theology faculties, did not impose themselves on the first production all at once. It was only after a lengthy theological debate that certain ideas came to the fore.

Contextedization must take into account the fact that some African theologians do not know exactly what the epistemological and philosophical categories of their context (EPCC) are, for two reasons: on the one hand, they live in a hybrid world, shaped by interculturality and the school, which distances them more and more from these categories, and on the other, in the absence or inadequacy of contextual bibliographical resources at their disposal, they cannot build up a capital of knowledge on these EPCC to form TCs. Faced with such a reality, *contextedization* has to reinvent itself.

The final element is linguistic. The plethora of African vernacular languages often makes communication difficult. There are as many ethnic groups as there are EPCCs in Africa, to the point where Africa is conjugated in the plural. How can we construct a theological discourse that draws on the EPCC of one locality, and is comprehensible in all other localities in Africa, without falling into traditional contextualization (adaptation)? The fourth criterion, that contextual theological discourse be expressed in the linguistic categories of the addressees, should be excluded here. Who are the addressees in Africa, especially as there are at least as many ethnic groups as there are languages? Perhaps the solution lies in the settler's language. If this is the case, then the African paradox becomes apparent: most of the works that can serve as sources for the 'contextualizing' theologian in French-speaking Africa are in English, including most of the intellectual works of our author, who comes from a French-speaking country. This begs the question: is this myth or reality?

Conclusion

Contextualisation Aujourd'hui. Questions approfondies en théologie contextuelle by Professor Fohle Lygunda li-Mwangwela is a truly seminal text, tracing the lineaments of a new theological paradigm that is *contextedization*. In reading this work, the reader feels connected to the spirit of the writer, who speaks with all the sincerity one can muster. This review will not have said everything about the understanding of this concept, which is just emerging and

Lessi Traoré
Theological 'Contextedization': A New Paradigm in Contextual Theology
BOOK REVIEW: *Contextualisation aujourd'hui : Questions approfondies en théologie contextuelle*, **by Fohle Lygunda Li-M**

needs to be further elucidated by other explanatory texts from its founder or those who will be enamored of the concept and won over to the cause. As this work cannot be completely surveyed, it is the duty of those who want to know more to refer directly to this book, which will speak to them and which will probably correct some of their apprehensions with regard to this concept, which is a truly substantial contribution to the world of theology.

Peregrinatio
Migrants and Migration in Christian History

BOOK REVIEW ESSAY
Hanciles, Jehu J. *Migration and the Making of Global Christianity*. Grand Rapids, Michigan, USA: Eerdmans, 2021. Pp. xvii + 361. US$47.99, £36.99.

Joshua Robert BARRON

ORCID: 0000-0002-9503-6799
ACTEA, Nairobi, Kenya
Joshua.Barron@ACTEAweb.org

*For [Christians], any foreign country is a motherland,
and any motherland is a foreign country.*
— "Epistle to Diognetus" (qtd, 141)

To put it plainly, the mission of God starts on the margins.
— Jehu J. Hanciles (126)

Jehu Hanciles has produced a magisterial text which should be widely read. The book belongs "to the growing list of monographs that provide a historical study of global Christianity" which provides a selective and "illustrative rather than comprehensive" treatment of its subject (6). Hanciles's

> central aim is to assess key episodes and major historical transitions in the history of Christianity that demonstrate the pivotal impact and profound implications of human mobility for the cross-cultural and translational expansion of the Christian faith. Foremost attention is given to the initial Christian encounter with non-Christian peoples or the spread of Christian ideas and practices into non-Christian contexts, and also to missionary encounters that reflect or illustrate expanding global linkages and escalating movement. (6–7)

While he necessarily limits his scope, this text is more comprehensive than

Joshua Robert Barron
Peregrinatio: Migrants and Migration in Christian History
BOOK REVIEW ESSAY: *Migration and the Making of Global Christianity,*
by Jehu J. Hanciles

standard treatments of Christian history.[1]

Hanciles convinces this reader that no biblical theology can be complete without a theology of migration. "Migration and displacement" are, of course, "firmly at the heart of Israel's origins as a nation" (106), the Sinai covenant "lays a theological foundation for thinking about migration as inextricably connected to a life of faith or being a people of God" (107), and a "view of Yahweh as a God of the migrant-foreigner framed Israel's religion" (109). We should not be surprised, then, to find that understanding migration is central to understanding Christian history as well. Hanciles demonstrates that "recurrent migrant movement of individuals and groups … provided central impetus for the spread of the Christian message and the establishment of Christian communities," both within and far beyond the bounds of the Roman Empire. He emphasizes that "*every Christian migrant is a potential missionary*!" (1, 418) and repeats "all migrants are potential missionaries" (29).

Conceptual Overview

Following his Introduction, Hanciles begins with a "Conceptual Overview" composed of three chapters:
1. Migration in Human History: A Conceptual Overview
2. Migration and the Globalization of Religion: Understanding Conversion
3. Theologizing Migration: From Eden to Exile

In the first chapter he provides the historical context of the biblical narratives and of early Christian history. He also identifies four types of migration — "home-community migration", "colonization", "whole-community migration", and "cross-community migration" (21–23). Similarly he describes four types of migrants (note well that these categories do not overlap with the previous ones) — settlers, sojourners, itinerants, and invaders (26) — and introduces the roles which each type of migrant has played in Christian history. It would be interesting to evaluate various groups of contemporary missionaries within this framework. Historically, Paul arguably alternated between sojourner and itinerant. Most missionaries today are sojourners, although a few are settlers and a few are itinerants. Some, of course, have had the colonizing mindset of invaders, seeking to control. But migrants were often the unsung missionaries, as frequently "Christian *witness* was a matter of *with-ness*" (149).

---

[1] Hopefully books written from World Christianity perspectives like this one, Dale T. Irvin and Scott W. Sunquist's *History of the World Christian Movement* (Orbis Books; vol. 1, 2001; vol. 2, 2012), and David W. Kling's *A History of Christian Conversion* (Oxford: Oxford University Press, 2020) will set a new standard.

Joshua Robert Barron
Peregrinatio: Migrants and Migration in Christian History
BOOK REVIEW ESSAY: *Migration and the Making of Global Christianity,*
by Jehu J. Hanciles

Historical Assessment

The second part of the book, chapters four through ten, offers a historical assessment of Christian history in different regions and eras though the interpretive lens developed in the first three chapters:

4. Christianization of the Roman Empire: The Immigrant Factor
5. Frontier Flows: The Faith of Captives and the Fruit of Captivity
6. Minority Report: From the Church in Persia to the Persian Church
7. Christ and Odin: Migration and Mission in an Age of Violence
8. To the Ends of the East: The Faith of Merchants
9. Gaining the World: The Interlocking Strands of Migration, Imperial Expansion, and Christian Mission
10. Beyond Empire

In the early generations of Christianity within the Roman Empire, growth of the faith within "the higher social classes" took place "mainly through the efforts of women" (146). While we are not wrong to laud the work of famous missionaries and writing theologians, it was ordinary "face-to-face encounters" of people on the move throughout their days which "were essential for evangelism" (147).

Hanciles demonstrates that "migration played a key role not only in Christianity's expansion but also, and by implication, in its theological development" (179). Today there are many Christians, perhaps primarily in North America, who are trapped in a bubble of monocultural myopia, unaware of that Christian experience, thought, and theological expression form rich multicultural and multilingual tapestry. Until recently, Western scholarship has been guilty of a "willful amnesia about the unparalleled missionary expansion of Christianity" across Asia (402). That expansion was so great that the Mongol catholicos of the Church of the East in the 1200s and 1300s "exercised ecclesiastical sovereignty" over a far greater territory than did the Roman pope in the same period (403). Christianity has never been merely an affair of the Roman Empire or of Europe.

In medieval Europe, "Christian missions were chiefly initiated by [migratory] monks and monarchs" (291). Yet frequently "the spread of Christianity" into new areas has "rested on the actions of migrant actors and owed nothing to imperial ties or formal missionary enterprise" (193). Christian history outside of realms where Christianity was granted imprimatur by the state, and especially across Asia, clearly demonstrates that "state sponsorship of political power is by no means a requirement for the successful spread of religion

Joshua Robert Barron
Peregrinatio: Migrants and Migration in Christian History
BOOK REVIEW ESSAY: *Migration and the Making of Global Christianity*,
by Jehu J. Hanciles

across cultural frontiers" as "the spread of Christianity in Asia was wholly dependent on migration and the missionary capacity of Christian migrants" (321).

Conversion in Christian History

There is little which could be improved in this book without increasing either its scope or its length. The discussion on conversion in the second chapter could perhaps be strengthened by engagement with Hanciles's late mentor Andrew Walls's distinction between conversion and proselytization[2] and with David Kling's recent monograph, *A History of Christian Conversion*.[3] Lacking that, in other chapters of the book "proselytization" and "conversion" seem to be used interchangeably.[4] Strikingly, however, while "proselytization" is frequently used with reference to movement into the Christian faith, when movement into Islam is discussed only "conversion" and "convert" is used. This is significant because while someone may truly convert to Islam, entry into Islam is *inherently* a form of proselytization, due its absolutization of Arabic culture and language: Islam lacks the translatability principle that is crucial to Christianity. Hanciles correctly notes that "conversion is central to Christianity, and the concept is laden with notions of radical change" and that consequently "the Christian faith, in sharp contrast to the various primal or ancestral religious systems it encountered throughout the world, demanded" — and still demands,

---

[2] See Andrew F. Walls, "Converts or Proselytes? The Crisis over Conversion in the Early Church" *International Bulletin of Missionary Research* 28/1 (2004): 2–6; Walls, "Worldviews and Christian Conversion," chapter 11 in *Mission in Context: Explorations Inspired by J. Andrew Kirk*, edited by John Corrie and Cathy Ross, 155–166 (Farnham, England: Ashgate, 2012); and Walls, "Proselytes or Converts: Gospel and Culture in the New Testament," in *World Mission in the Twenty-First Century*, ed. Kwang Soon Lee, 81–90 (Seoul: Center for World Mission, Presbyterian College and Theological Seminary, 2005). I have built on Walls's theme in my "Conversion or Proselytization? Being Maasai, Becoming Christian," *Global Missiology* 18, no. 2 (April 2021): 12 pages. http://ojs.globalmissiology.org/index.php/english/article/view/2428

[3] David W. Kling, *A History of Christian Conversion* (Oxford: Oxford University Press, 2020). To be fair to Hanciles, *Migration and the Making of Global Christianity* would have been already under production before Kling's volume was released. Hanciles does engage with many of Walls's other contributions as well as with Kling's ideas on conversion in his earlier "Conversion to Christianity," Chapter 27 in *The Oxford Handbook of Religious Conversion*, edited by Rambo R. Lewis and Charles E. Farhadian, 598–631 (Oxford: Oxford University Press, 2014).

[4] To be fair to Hanciles, the confusion between conversion and proselytization is as common as it is problematic, both in the literature and (perhaps consequently) in popular understandings.

Joshua Robert Barron
Peregrinatio: **Migrants and Migration in Christian History**
BOOK REVIEW ESSAY: *Migration and the Making of Global Christianity,*
by Jehu J. Hanciles

we should note — "exclusive allegiance" (60).[5] But this allegiance is to Christ, not to the Jewish culture and Aramaic and Greek languages of the Apostles. Hanciles cogently engages with "the 'translation principle' propounded by … Lamin Sanneh and Andrew Walls" (67). Over several pages (67–73) he discusses this translatability and in that context explicitly states Wallsian understandings of conversion and culture:

- "Gentile converts to faith did not have to adopt the norms and traditions of Judaism to become followers of Christ. Rather, their conversion required the Christian message to be expressed in the ideas and concepts of the Hellenistic cultural and religious environment they belonged to" (69);
- "crossing cultural frontiers is not only a perquisite for the spread of the Christian movement; it is also the means whereby the worldwide community of faith increasingly experiences the fullness of the gospel" (70).

He later explores at length translatability in terms of migration and mobility (128–137). While admitting it unlikely that the early church was free from the ethnocultural prejudices of the its hosting cultures, Hanciles observes that ancient Christianity affirmed all cultures and thereby "minimized the indignities of immigrant existence" (166). Similarly his observation that "there is no indication that the Goths who became Christian ceased to be Goths" clearly points to a conversionary model involving "successful cross-cultural transmission of the Christian message" (204) rather than a proselytizing model. Consequently his apparent conflation, elsewhere in the book, between conservation and proselytization is both surprising and disappointing. But in over 400 pages, that is my only complaint.

Conclusions

Hanciles has convincingly argued his missiological thesis that throughout Christian history "migration was inseparable from mission" (329). This book has convinced me that any Christian theology or missiology which lacks a robust theology of migration is incomplete. *En route,* Hanciles's engagement with the sources is masterful yet he maintains epistemic humility throughout the text. He successfully "debunks the centuries-old view that the global spread of the Christian faith is largely the work of institutional entities (ecclesiastical or political) and their trained agents" (8). No one who reads this book can

---

[5] Matthew W. Bates develops the importance of allegiance as the center of New Testament πιστις (*pistis,* 'faith') in his *Salvation By Allegiance Alone: Rethinking Faith, Works, and the Gospel of Jesus the King* (Grand Rapids, Michigan: Baker Academic, 2017).

Joshua Robert Barron
Peregrinatio: Migrants and Migration in Christian History
BOOK REVIEW ESSAY: *Migration and the Making of Global Christianity*,
by Jehu J. Hanciles

continue to think that Christianity is a 'European religion' or 'the white man's religion.' Noting that "within the Jesus movement no faithful individual or group should be mistreated simply because they were stranger-outsiders" (127), Hanciles implicitly calls the church today — which often ignores biblical calls to welcome and protect migrants — to repentance.

This book cogently makes the case that "successful cross-cultural missionary outreach requires translation and cultural adaptation to facilitate transmission and appropriation" (251). The more effectively that the Christians practice such translation and adaptation, the more deeply rooted the local church is able to become. Hanciles shows that "human migration has played an indispensable role in the cross-cultural spread of the Christian faith principally because migrants who are Christian inevitably fulfill a missionary function in their encounters with non-Christian peoples and societies" (269). In so doing, he implicitly challenges contemporary Christians to similarly fulfil their own missionary function. There is a sense in which all Christians are strangers and aliens in the world (cf. Heb 11:13, 1 Pet 2:11). Hanciles reminds us that "the rise of Christianity as a world movement has been through the agency and activity of" migrant Christians, individuals and communities, who are "living as strangers and outsiders in foreign lands" (420).

Tolle lege.

Contemporary Christology in Africa: Evangelical Perspectives

BOOK REVIEW ESSAY
Reed, Rodney L., and David K. Ngaruiya, eds. *Who Do You Say That I Am? Christology in Africa*. ASET Series 6. Carlisle, Cumbria, UK: Langham Global Library, 2021. Pp. xv + 678. £25.99 (paper); US $25.99 (Kindle).

Diane B. STINTON
ORCID: 0000-0003-0541-8863
Regent College, Vancouver, Canada
dstinton@regent-college.edu

The title of **Rodney Reed** and **David Ngaruiya**'s edited work, *Who Do You Say That I Am?*, clearly recalls Jesus's question to Peter (Matt 16:15), reiterated in this text as "arguably the most important question in all of human history" (15). The subtitle, *Christology in Africa*, not only locates the context for this volume, but also reflects the fundamental conviction that Jesus's question is addressed to every individual in every age and every locale. Acknowledging the plurality of titles and names for Jesus in the Bible and throughout the history of Christianity, Reed articulates rationale for the present publication in the need for "appropriately contextualizing the response to Jesus's question" as an "absolutely indispensable prerequisite for evangelism, mission and discipleship" (15). Against the backdrop of common claims that the Western missionaries proclaimed Jesus as being "much too Western" (16), thereby accounting for the assumed shallowness of Christianity across Africa, this work highlights African Christians' attempts "to identify a Jesus who speaks their language and speaks into their contexts" (15). The overall purpose of the book is to contribute to the ongoing debates regarding contemporary Christology in Africa, and to do so from evangelical perspective. From the outset of the project, it is established that contextualization requires a careful balance between describing Jesus in the thought forms that are meaningful to African audiences, while also ensuring that any proposals for African Christology are theologically consistent with biblical teaching.

What strikes the reader initially is the sheer magnitude of this anthology of current essays on African Christology, demonstrating the ongoing significance of the subject. At double and triple the length of other volumes in the Africa Society of Evangelical Theology (ASET) series, this volume offers twenty-four chapters from selected papers presented at the 2020 ASET conference in Kenya.

Diane B. Stinton
Contemporary Christology in Africa: Evangelical Perspectives
BOOK REVIEW: *Who Do You Say That I Am ?*, ASET 6,
edited by Rodney L. Reed and David K. Ngaruiya

With only seven women authors featured, the proportion of gender representation does not align with the predominantly female demographics of African Christianity. Nonetheless, it is crucial that these women scholars' perspectives are disseminated, and it is hoped that their representation will continue to grow within ASET and its publications. The volume is further enriched by the range of authors from various church traditions and locations, including several African countries (e.g., Kenya, Uganda, Zambia, South Africa, Ghana, and Nigeria), the UK, and the US.

The volume is divided into four parts: Part 1, "Christ in the Bible"; Part 2, "Christ in Theology and Church History"; Part 3, "Christ in Praxis"; and Part 4, "Tributes to the Late Professor John S. Mbiti," who passed away in 2019, prior to the ASET Conference. Given the length and complexity of this work, this review will restrict itself to outlining selected chapters as illustrative of the wider content.

Unsurprisingly for an evangelical society, the greatest number of papers fall within Part 1, "Christ and the Bible." Eight authors examine specific passages or concepts from the New Testament (NT), including the Gospels and Epistles, in relation to cultural and contemporary sociopolitical realities in Africa. For example, **Timothy J. Monger** offers "**An East African Perspective on Jesus as Revealer of the Father through His Use of the Friend at Midnight Parable as a Means for Teaching Powerful Prayer (Luke 11:1–13).**" He argues that Swahili versions of the NT that translate the Greek term *anaideia* as "persistence" or "importunity" create "a misunderstanding of the parable and a denial of its potency" (48). Instead, from his analysis of the historical and literary context of the parable in Luke's Gospel, with its focus on hospitality, Monger states the term is better rendered "avoiding shame" (48). He then interprets the parable from the perspective of an African village with an honor-shame culture akin to that of Jesus's original audience, explaining that the ultimate reason the sleeper in the parable rises is to avoid shame, not only for the friend knocking at midnight but for the entire village. On this basis, he outlines East African cultures' contributions to interpreting this parable, with implications for understanding Jesus's revelation of the Father, for prayer, and for recovering hospitality as "a great strength of East Africans" and as central to the mission of God (67–68).

From the NT Epistles, **Elizabeth W. Mburu** focuses on "**Exploring the Multidimensional Nature of Christology in Galatians through the Lens of an African Hermeneutic.**" Noting that certain limitations in Western Christianity have "stunted the growth" of Christianity in Africa, Mburu draws upon recent gains in African theology to highlight the multidimensionality of the Christian faith (89). That is, it is both universal in nature and context-specific in

Diane B. Stinton
Contemporary Christology in Africa: Evangelical Perspectives
BOOK REVIEW: *Who Do You Say That I Am ?*, ASET 6,
edited by Rodney L. Reed and David K. Ngaruiya

expression, as is the theology developed globally across time. Mburu then examines the concept of multidimensionality in relation to the person of Christ, employing an African intercultural hermeneutical approach to elucidate aspects of Christology in Galatians. This African hermeneutic, which Mburu herself develops elsewhere,[1] entails a "four-legged stool" method of discerning parallels between "the biblical text and context and the Kenyan context" (90). She applies this method to outline several Christological emphases in Galatians which are resonant with African cultures and worldviews: first, Christ as the liberator of humankind in the spiritual and physical realms. Mburu asserts,

> The African worldview, in which many live in fear of demonic forces, witchcraft, evil spirits, curses, and so forth, has been confronted and overturned by Christ. We no longer need to perform protective rituals, consult witchdoctors, healers and spirits, buy "anointed" items at exorbitant prices or revert to those aspects of our culture that contradict Christianity. (100)

Second, Christ is the unifier of the church, overcoming human hostilities based on ethnicity, gender, socioeconomic status, and political persuasion. Third, he is the victor over sin, with all its ramifications, and fourth, Christ is the truth, vying against any false teaching such as the prosperity gospel. Finally, Christ is the curse-bearer, which carries deep relevance for African contexts in which belief remains strong in the power of curses and in traditional means of addressing them. From this intercultural dialogue between Galatians and African contexts, Mburu draws implications for African Christians in terms of their identity as African believers and their understanding and practice of faith.

Part 2, "Christ in Theology and Church History," offers seven chapters ranging from Christological developments in the early church, with implications for African Christianity today, to contemporary contextualized images of Jesus. This section in particular demonstrates the "tensions" in Africa, both in Christological method and content, "among Christian traditions with respect to how each conceives the person of Christ" (277). Some advocate a return to the expressions of classical Christology formulated in the apostolic church and in the patristic era. For example, **Henry Marcus Garba** sets forth **"The Unitive Understanding of the Person of Christ in Cyril of Alexandria's Christology and Its Relevance for Contemporary African Christianity."** He highlights the significant contribution made by Cyril of Alexandria in maintaining the union of Christ's divine and human natures, "which are inseparably united, yet without mixture, loss of separate identity, or transfer of properties or attributes" (271). Garba identifies Cyril's unitive understanding

---

[1] Elizabeth Mburu, *African Hermeneutics* (Carlisle, Cumbria, UK: Langham Publishing, 2019).

Diane B. Stinton
Contemporary Christology in Africa: Evangelical Perspectives
BOOK REVIEW: *Who Do You Say That I Am ?*, ASET 6,
edited by Rodney L. Reed and David K. Ngaruiya

of the person of Christ as "the peak of the process of Christological reflection" (260), with relevance for Christianity today in the call to reaffirm this mainstream tradition of orthodoxy and to guard against any language or thought deemed to diverge from this tradition. He cautions that many modern African theologians who have sought to reinterpret Christology by proposing images from African tradition "have gone beyond the norm of using biblical images to define Christology" (277). He concludes with the imperative to appropriate an historical approach to understanding Christ's identity for a renewed appreciation of longstanding orthodoxy that will enhance unity in Christ.

Similarly, **John Michael Kiboi** focuses on Christological method in his chapter, "**Who Are You for Us, Yesu Kristo? Christological Confessions of the Early Church in Contemporary Africa**." The crux of the debate lies in the relevance of ontological Christology (dealing with the person of Christ) in relation to functional Christology (dealing with the work of Christ). Acknowledging that all theology is contextual, **Kiboi** traces the Christological controversies in the early church and the patristic era, noting the influence of Greco-Roman philosophies in the confessions of the first four ecumenical councils: Nicaea (325), Constantinople (381), Ephesus (431), and Chalcedon (451). Within these cultural contexts, theologians developed philosophical, speculative, and ontological approaches to Christology that addressed the critical needs of their time in relevant ways. The problem, as Kiboi points out, is that contemporary African theologians commonly critique these classical, ontological approaches to Christology as producing "an intellectual, abstract Christology that is irrelevant to functional realities" in Africa (287–288). In turn, Kiboi critiques functional approaches as "producing a functional Christology that is not orthodox – that is, it does not uphold the apostolic Christology . . . articulated by the church councils" (288). He therefore argues for a "a revelation from above—a top-down ontological approach" (305), "whose end product upholds both the ontological and functional Christologies in balance" (288) so that it will remain orthodox but also relevant to African realities.

However, other authors in this volume demonstrate greater openness to functional Christologies for the sake of communicating the identity and significance of Christ meaningfully within African contexts. **E. Okelloh Ogera** presents "**Jesus Christ as Ker: Toward an African High Priest Christology**." Drawing upon the rationale for inculturation Christologies from scholars like Justin Ukpong, Ogera states that "the theological task consists of rethinking and re-expressing the original Christian message in an Africa cultural milieu" (316). On this basis he proposes the concept of *Ker* (high priest) among the Luo people of Western Kenya as a Christological motif that is suitable for introducing Jesus in this context. He develops a functional analogy between this Luo high priest

Diane B. Stinton
Contemporary Christology in Africa: Evangelical Perspectives
BOOK REVIEW: *Who Do You Say That I Am ?*, ASET 6,
edited by Rodney L. Reed and David K. Ngaruiya

figure and Jesus as high priest in the Bible, explaining those parallels that elucidate Christ while also stressing how Christ supersedes the human figure. He analyses both the potential benefits and the liabilities of this Christological image, noting that "*Ker* Christology, being a functional Christology, also emphasizes the humanity of Jesus over his divinity, creating a Christology that is too immanent at the expense of the transcendent Christ" (326). Despite such limitations, Ogera nonetheless insists that *Ker* is an effective Christological image within the Luo community.

Thandi Soko-de Jong not only affirms "**African Images of Christ,**" but examines the image of Christ as healer which is prevalent in African theology and experience. Specifically, she conducted field research in Blantyre, Malawi, on faith narratives of evangelical African Christians who suffer illnesses that are treatable but not yet curable (e.g., diabetes, HIV). Aside from the content of her findings, which challenge assumptions from the global church about Pentecostals in Africa necessarily adhering to the prosperity gospel, Jong's study is noteworthy for its methodological stance of deep inquiry into African believers' experience of Christ. So, from the primarily philosophical, ontological approaches of classical Christology to the more functional approaches of recent inculturation and liberation christologies, to the empirical methods employed to explore and analyze the "lived christologies"[2] of African believers, the field of African Christology continues to flourish with rich content expressed through a range of methodologies.

Part 3 of this volume, "Christ in Praxis," is considerably briefer with only four chapters: one on visual Christology, one on the lordship of Christ in relation to mission, and, notably, two on Jesus in relation to Islam. **Billy Chilongo Sichone** writes the final chapter on "**Jesus in Islam: Meaning and Theological Implications for Christian-Muslim Engagement.**" Intending his inquiry for lay Christians who are often unaware of the high place accorded to Jesus (*Isa*) in the Qur'an, **Sichone** examines Muslim perceptions of *Isa* and draws out implications for Christian theology and ministry. A central argument challenges Muslims' common assumption that the prophet *Isa* in the Qur'an is the same person as Jesus in the Bible, outlining fundamental Christian doctrines about Jesus that are rejected within Islam. **Sichone** therefore urges believers to study Islam carefully, to engage constructively with Muslims about Christian

---

[2] The term "lived christologies" has gained currency since African theologians such as John Mbiti distinguished between "oral theology (in contrast to written theology), from the living experiences of African Christians. It is theology . . . from the pulpit, in the market place, in the home as people pray or read and discuss the scriptures." John S. Mbiti, *Bible and Theology in African Christianity* (Nairobi: Oxford University Press, 1986), 229.

Diane B. Stinton
Contemporary Christology in Africa: Evangelical Perspectives
BOOK REVIEW: *Who Do You Say That I Am ?*, ASET 6,
edited by Rodney L. Reed and David K. Ngaruiya

faith.

Finally, Part 4 provides five "Tributes to the Late Professor John S. Mbiti" from senior theologians. While **Reed** comments that "these may be largely unrelated to the theme of the book" (17), in fact their very presence and content are deeply significant. For among the pioneering African theologians, it was Mbiti who proclaimed in 1968 that "African concepts of Christology do not exist."[3] Lamenting this lacuna, he urged his fellow African theologians to develop theological reflection on four "pillars": (1) the Bible, as the final authority in religious discourse, (2) the theology of the older churches, especially Christian tradition in Europe, (3) the traditional African world, encompassing indigenous thought-forms and religious concerns, and (4) the living experience of the church in Africa, including the African Independent Churches (AICs).

It is noteworthy that over fifty years later, this volume presents a new generation of theologians who continue to fill that gap in Christological reflection in Africa. Moreover, they do so along the lines that Mbiti recommended, to varying degrees. Altogether, these essays certainly demonstrate the first pillar regarding the fundamental authority of Scripture in Christological reflection, with a key strength being the serious attention given to the biblical revelation of Christ in relation to contemporary realities in Africa. The second pillar of Christian tradition features to a lesser extent, with some authors examining Christological developments in the patristic, Reformation, or modern missionary eras and their implications for African Christianity today.

With respect to the third pillar, most of the essays identify and reflect Christologically on issues related to the traditional and contemporary African world, including socio-cultural and religious thought-forms and practices. For example, in addition to various issues mentioned previously in this review, **Telesia K. Musili**, in "**Marital Infidelity through an African Women's Christological Heremeneutic: A Dramatized Rereading of the Narrative of the Woman Caught in Adultery (John 7:53–8:11)**," highlights the notorious injustices African women commonly face. She draws upon Mercy Oduyoye's attempts, together with those of the Circle of Concerned African Women Theologians, to "challenge the oppression of women through sexism, racism, colonialism, neocolonialism and androcentric tendencies" in Africa (32–33). Musili therefore affirms "the relational, experiential and liberating traits of Jesus" that African women's Christologies have advanced in their attempt to

---

[3] John S. Mbiti, "Some African Concepts of Christology," in *Christ and the Younger Churches*, edited by Georg F. Vicedom (London: SPCK, 1972), 51.

Diane B. Stinton
Contemporary Christology in Africa: Evangelical Perspectives
BOOK REVIEW: *Who Do You Say That I Am ?*, ASET 6,
edited by Rodney L. Reed and David K. Ngaruiya

foster "hope and transformation" (33). In contrast to this in-depth focus on African realities in relation to the biblical text, **Gift Mtukwa**, in "**Paul's Use of Μιμηταί and Its Relationship to His Christology**," offers sound biblical scholarship, yet without citing a single African source and only minimally addressing the implications of his argument for African Christianity today. Similarly with the fourth pillar, there are varying degrees of engagement with the life of the African church, with particular strengths including the qualitative study mentioned above, regarding African believers' experiences of Jesus as healer, as well as those addressing African women's christologies. It is not that every Christological reflection is obliged to evidence all four of Mbiti's recommended pillars; rather, the observation is intended to note the sources and methods these evangelical theologians employ in their individual and communal scholarship.

Given the breadth and richness of this anthology of essays on Christology, there are further aspects to commend. Fundamentally, throughout the volume and even within those proposals for contextualized African Christologies, there is a recurring affirmation of the humanity and divinity of Christ as the two non-negotiables of any valid expression of Christology (318). Moreover, these authors together present compelling evidence for how African perspectives enhance our reading of Scripture and our understanding of the identity and significance of Christ. While discerning and eschewing negative aspects of African cultures, the authors encourage consideration of positive aspects that shape African Christian identities, such as "a respect for the elderly, family values, hospitality, a sense of community, and appreciation of the arts, or nuanced spiritism" (111).

Another commendable feature is the attention given to the "lived" nature of African Christologies. While noted briefly above, it is worth citing **Lydia Chemei**, who points out this feature of African women's Christologies. In "**Embracing Hybridity in Imaging Christ for Egalitarian Church Leadership through a Rereading of John 4:1–42**," Chemei notes how the Samaritan woman encountered Jesus in the ordinary, everyday task of drawing water from the well. She relates this to African women who also "experience Christ in the common daily endeavors that characterize their lives" (81), citing Douglas Waruta that for these women, "faith is not expressed through creedal formulations or theological statements but in a day-to-day encounter with the challenges of life."[4] An additional contribution from these African women theologians, including **Chemei** and **Mburu**, lies in the distinct hermeneutical frameworks

---

[4] Douglas W. Waruta, "Who Is Jesus Christ for Africans Today? Prophet, Priest, Potentate," in *Jesus in African Christianity*, edited by J. N. K. Mugambi and L. Magesa (Nairobi: Acton Publishers, 2003), 45.

Diane B. Stinton
Contemporary Christology in Africa: Evangelical Perspectives
BOOK REVIEW: *Who Do You Say That I Am ?*, ASET 6,
edited by Rodney L. Reed and David K. Ngaruiya

proposed for African Christology.

A final commendation regards the missional dimension of African Christology, made explicit in **Alistair I. Wilson**'s chapter, "'**Missionaries Did Not Bring Christ to Africa – Christ Brought Them' (Bediako/Mbiti): Christ's Lordship in Mission in African Theology**." Where this vital theme has been overlooked or underrepresented in African Christologies to date, Wilson draws valid attention to it in a stimulating chapter. In so doing, he demonstrates, along with his fellow authors, the ongoing nature of Christological discourse represented in this volume.

Since the process of interpreting Christ in Africa continues, there are aspects of the present volume that could be enhanced. For example, relatively little attention is devoted to oral and vernacular expressions of Christology, so fundamental to African Christianity. Moreover, certain expressions of methodology could be further clarified, such as a survey being undertaken among East African people and qualitative answers cited, yet without sufficient delineation of the survey method employed (53). In addition, some statements could be further nuanced, such as the assertion that "even though affirmations such as the Nicene Creed originated in an African context, they may not be immediately viewed as relevant in twenty-first-century Africa" (89).[5] It is also contestable that "reconstructive Christologies, in twenty-first-century Africa, have become the dominant motif" (93). And not all interpreters of African Christianity may agree with the decidedly negative depictions given in places, for example that "much of Kenyan Christianity is an apostate Christianity in which 'the true sense of values is so corrupted that sin has become an ally of sorts — sanitized, cleansed, absolved,' normalized, 'and accommodated'" (103–104).

Yet these very questions and divergent perspectives manifest the ongoing nature of Christological discourse in Africa and invite further participation in it. This text provides indispensable reading for theologians, pastors, and educated lay people who seek to deepen their knowledge of and love for Christ, not only those in Africa but around the world. With the tremendous contribution of Christological reflections in this volume, no doubt John Mbiti would be pleased.

Watafutao elimu wako njiani kwa mungu.
(Swahili proverb: The seekers of knowledge are on the path of God.)

---

[5] Alternate views are expressed within this volume, as well as in a more recent publication by Langham Literature: Isuwa Y. Atsen, *A Tapestry of Global Christology: Weaving a Three-Stranded Theological Cord* (Carlisle, Cumbria, UK: Langham Academic, 2022).

Division and Unity

BOOK REVIEW ESSAY
Kalu, Ogbu U. *Divided People of God: Christian Union Movement in Nigeria: 1875–1966*. Foreword by James I. McCord. Lagos: NOK Publishers, 1978. <u>Reprint edition</u>: Austin, Texas, USA and Ibadan, Nigeria: Pan-African University Press, 2018.

Okuchukwu Venatus AKPE

ECWA Theological Seminary, Igbaja, Nigeria
Chukllinic@gmail.com

Ogbu U. Kalu (1942–2009), a Nigerian theologian, was his generation's doyen of African Christian historiography. This re-publication of *Divided People of God: Church Union in Nigeria: 1875–1966*, first published in 1978, offers a fresh perspective on "history as interpretation" and on why the historians' commitment to facts, accuracy, objectivity, and balance in his or her endeavor remains an essential component of sound historiography.[1] This commitment is also beneficial to the church as it grapples with understanding the present in light of the past, and in its quest to navigate the future in light of the present.

Kalu's *Divided People of God* brings to the fore the unfolding journey and complexities involved in the emerging hope of a potential church union in Nigeria. The combination of divisions between European and American Protestant denominations, Protestants and Roman Catholics, competing missionary agencies, and the rising plethora of AICs[2] had resulted in a diverse and disunited tapestry of Christianity in Nigeria. In this context of different church bodies in Nigeria, with competing organizational polities, interests, ecclesial rivalries, and differing internal and external factors, Kalu uses a cohesive historical-theological approach to incisively unearth the beginning of the journey of church union in Nigeria. He explores the emergence of the idea of union by foreign mission agencies as an effort to face the challenges of the

---

[1] Ogbu U. Kalu, *Clio in a Sacred Garb: Essays on Christian Presence and African Responses, 1900-2000* (Asmara, Eritrea: Africa World Press, 2008), 12.

[2] Editors' note: i.e., African Indigenous Churches, Africa Independent Churches, or African Initiated Churches.

Okuchukwu Venatus Akpe
BOOK REVIEW: *Divided People of God: Christian Union Movement in Nigeria: 1875–1966*, by Ogbu U. Kalu

mission field, further development of this idea by missionary-founded churches through numerous consultations, and its eventual failure due to irreconcilable differences in 1965.

Chapters 1 and 2 highlight the impulse and path to union primarily inspired by the famous Edinburgh Conference of 1910. Kalu points to these developments in phases.

1. Discussions by the Presbyterian, Methodist, and Qua Iboe Missions over boundary agreements in the mission field;
2. A 1911 missionary conference, initiated by the Presbyterians, focusing on more practical issues;
3. An invitation extended by the Presbyterians, Primitive Methodists, Niger Delta Pastorate, and Qua Iboe Mission in 1923 to the Yoruba Mission (Anglican), the Wesleyans, Dutch Reformed Church, SIM, etc.

The first proposal towards church union was introduced at a 1926 missions conference. Kalu notes the difficulties caused when the missionary agencies who were still in full control of the churches in Northern Nigeria drew back from participation in the proposed union, choosing to uphold the boundaries of the civil administration. Further attention is given to the refusal of the Southern Baptists to participate, and the withdrawal of SUM (Sudan United Mission) and QIM (Qua Iboe Mission) in 1947 (34).

In Chapter 3, Kalu presents a theological appraisal of the then-contemporary theologies of unity. He justifies *one-ness* as Jesus's intention for his church. Drawing from the Bible and other credible sources, the author emphasizes the distinctness and mystery of the Christian church regardless of its several denominational extractions "as a community of faithful people sustained by the mysterious indwelling of Christ and by the gift of the Holy Spirit to the glory of God" (59). Thus, he spotlights a glaring weakness evident in the consultations on union which led to the eventual fallout in plans as "preserving their traditions as opposed to speaking to find how as Africans the reality of God revealed in Jesus Christ could be realized among them in their particular situation" (72). More so, he prescribes the "common clan structure" peculiar to Africans as a better paradigm of the nature of bonds that should bind us over denominational representation that ends in possible rivalry.

Chapter 4 critiques the proposed constitution for the Church Union in Nigeria and its specifics, which comprise doctrine and confession, worship and liturgy, ministry and polity, and the unification of the ministry. Referred to as *The Scheme of Church Union in Nigeria*, it stood as the proposed and final ratified constitution to guide the proposed Church Union in Nigeria comprised of the Methodist, Anglican, and Presbyterian churches. The author indicts the consultations' extreme focus on organizational problems, leaving out more

Okuchukwu Venatus Akpe
BOOK REVIEW: *Divided People of God: Christian Union Movement in Nigeria: 1875-1966*, by Ogbu U. Kalu

important issues such as mission and worship. In addition, he highlights each party clinging to their foreign heritage for the fear of absorption despite acknowledging a dynamic conception of unity (86).

Chapters 5 and 6 highlight the fallout of the union inauguration as planned, the aftermath in salvaging the situation responsible for the fallout, and recommendations for the future by the author. In this light, the author asserts that the collapse was a commentary on the predicament of the church in Nigeria and was a symptom of theological failings (135). This assertion leaves me, as a twenty-first-century reader and a Nigerian Christian, with an important question: Do the presence of existing fellowships of churches — i.e., the Christian Association of Nigeria, Christian Council of Nigeria, and the Pentecostal Fellowship of Nigeria — portray a true vision of unity as Christ desires (John 17:21–23) in light of their inception, vision, public representation, and its prophetic role?

Evaluation

Kalu is to be commended for his lucid argumentative approach, accurate historical interpretation and representation, and unambiguous use of language. He helpfully offers practical recommendations for future consultations, objective critique, contextual relevance, and sound theological grounding. Kalu has succeeded in filling a gap in the history of missions in Nigeria and addressed a theological failing. The book could perhaps be stronger if it had more engagement with other ecclesiastical camps, such as the early Pentecostal churches outside the Protestant churches, in light of the idea of attempted union. For example, the indigenous churches such as the Aladura churches were only mentioned in passing with first contact with them after the unfortunate postponement (35). A more robust discussion on the peculiarity of the Indigenous churches' unique Christian expression based on its proximity to the African worldview remains to be explored. The emphasis of Pentecostal churches on the Spirit could help to emphasize the role of the Spirit in facilitating and executing organic unity beyond human tethers. More so, such engagement with AICS and Pentecostal churches could have served in corroborating his African-drawn "common clan structure" nature of bond required for proper dialogue over safeguarding denominational ties, since the indigenous churches offer a more indigenized expression of the Christian faith.

Conclusion

Though the first edition was published forty-six years ago, this 2018 reprint of Kalu's *Divided People of God* offers much to emerging twenty-first century Nigerian Church leaders grappling with the idea of Church union and ecumenism in light of biblical injunction. Contemporary Nigeria has a plethora of church traditions, all of which have a need to reconsider modes of negotiation, the dangers of sentimental denominational attachment, conflict management, the necessity for contextual authenticity, attentive communication, and grassroots engagement in building a united ecclesiology faithful to the Nigerian context. Kalu helpfully offers appropriate lessons that remain pertinent today. Furthermore, Kalu reminds us of the need for repentance and renewal as an essential component toward forging an organic united front, in response to Jesus's vision for the Church (John 17:21) and towards fulfilling his mission. *Divided People of God* presents an interesting perspective on the history of missions in Nigeria, exploring importance and praxis of Christian unity.

AFRICAN CHRISTIAN THEOLOGY
vol. 1, n° 2 (2024) 412–429

Experiencing Salvation in Africa

BOOK REVIEW ESSAY
Reed, Rodney L, and David K. Ngaruiya, eds. *Salvation in African Christianity*. ASET Series 8. Carlisle, Cambria, UK: Langham Global Library, 2023. Pp. xv + 416. £24.99.

Raphael Akhijemen IDIALU

ORCID: 0000-0001-5538-7319
Methodist Theological Institute, Sagamu, Nigeria
idialuraphael@gmail.com

Introduction

The Africa Society of Evangelical Theology (ASET) is an academic society with pan-African (both from across the continent and from the Diaspora) and international membership. The best papers presented at the annual ASET conferences, after the usual peer review process, are subsequently published in an edited volume in the ASET Series.[1] *Salvation In African Christianity* explores understandings and expectations of salvation in general and in the African context specifically, as an effort to answer the age-long question, "What must I do to be saved?" The contributors and editors are to be commended for the strength of the presented data, critical assessment of that information, clarity of arguments, and presentation of ideas.

Review and Analysis

This book warrants a short review of each chapter, based on its content, style, clarity, and effectiveness, as well as the continuity and coherence of the chapters in relation to the book's objective. All twenty chapters in this book are

---

[1] The ASET Series so far includes: 1. *Christianity and Suffering: African Perspectives* (2017), 2. *African Contextual Realities* (2018), 3. *Governance and Christian Higher Education in the African Context* (2019), 4. *God and Creation* (2019), 5. *Forgiveness, Peacemaking, and Reconciliation* (2020), 6. *Who Do You Say That I Am? Christology in Africa* (2021), 7. *The Holy Spirit in African Christianity* (2022), and 8. *Salvation in African Christianity* (2023).

Editors' note: vol. 6 in the ASET Series is reviewed in this issue of this journal and vol. 7 in the ASET Series was reviewed in vol. 1, no. 1. ASET vol. 9, on ecclesiology in Africa, is due to be published in late 2024.

Published with license by ACTEA | DOI: https://doi.org/10.69683/ttjx1k78
© Raphael Akhijemen Idialu, 2024 | ISSN: 3006-1768 (print); 3007-1771 (online)
This is an open access article distributed under the terms of the CC BY 4.0 license.

valuable, but seven especially captured my attention.

Stand-out chapters

Chapter 18

"**Salvation and the Problem of Negative Ethnicity and Schism in the Church in Kenya: Towards an *Ubuntu* Salvation Theology**" by **Jackline Makena Mutuma** & **John M. Kiboi** — both at St Paul's University (Limuru, Kenya) — is exceptional! This is especially so in the light of their use of Ubuntu Salvation Theology as a template for understanding of salvation in African Christianity. In spite of 80% of Kenyans identifying as Christian (as of 2019), it is baffling to note that there is a significant presence of negative ethnicity in the Church in Kenya. Individualism, negative ethnicity, and denominationalism undermine the very values that both Christianity and African *ubuntu* espouse. The authors deem negative ethnicity and schism as twin dangers to the effective impact of Christianity in Africa. Negative ethnicity is the manipulation of ethnic identities for personal gains and interests. It injures, frustrates, ridicules, and demeans people and groups. Effects of negative ethnicity and schism include animosity, tyranny of numbers, oppression of minorities, discrimination, ethnic violence, and exclusion by members of the dominant community. This is also present in the Church. Ecumenism attempts to curtail this menace and bring peace and unity to the Church but has failed to foster the needed ecclesial unity and peace. A lasting panacea may be Ubuntu Salvation. Ubuntu represents a sense of humanity and togetherness, emphasizing the eminence of being human, ethical theory, and relational cosmology. These are reflected in African communitarian philosophy, human dignity and interrelatedness, commonality, and vital force. Salvation in the light of *ubuntu* includes wholeness in the physical, social, and psychological aspects of the human being, thereby offering healing for the negative ethnicity and schism that have caused division and pain in the African society and Church.

Chapter 11

"**Critical Analysis of the Doctrine of Adoption through the Honor and Shame Paradigm**" by **Kenosi Molato**, a researcher at SHINE Africa Project (Gaborone, Botswana), is an exciting and insightful read. The treatment of the concepts of adoption and the honour/shame dynamic concerning salvation is beautiful. He takes a dynamic step in reconstructing a doctrine of adoption from the Western perspective to look at it through the lens of the African honour and shame paradigm, arguing that *adoption* was a different conception in the OT than it is today. Traditional western interpretations understand adoption as the means whereby a believer is transferred from a status of alienation from God to a position of acceptance and favour with God or as the process of the redeemed becoming sons and daughters of God. Alternatively,

Raphael Akhijemen Idialu
Experiencing Salvation in Africa
BOOK REVIEW ESSAY: *Salvation in African Christianity,*
edited by Rodney L. Reed and David K. Ngaruiya

the concept of honour and shame is more about preserving the honour and integrity of a person, family or community.

Adoption is not a new idea. In the first century, the practice of adoption was common. In Greco-Roman culture, the family encompassed the more than the 'nuclear family' but included the wife and husband, unmarried children, slaves, freedmen, and foster children. If a man did not have a male child to carry the family name, a male child might be adopted. The adoptee would have the full rights of a natural born heir. The term Paul uses for adoption, *huiothesia,* is an honour term, emphasising the state of honour believers have in Christ. It is a place of dignity, a position in which believers are dignified to appropriate their privileges in Christ. Rather than being a place of maturing to sonship, believers are placed in this position because of their allegiance to Christ. In this way, the shame orientation that believers in African societies experience is dealt with. So, there is a sharp distinction between the understanding and practice and the process of adoption as practised in the early Greco-Roman world and Paul's use of the concept of adoption of believers in Christ.

Chapter 16

"**Emerging Soteriological Issues in African Christianity in the Light of Resurgent African Cultures: The Practice of Ancestral Debts**" by **Kamau Thairu** was quite exciting and a bit ridiculous; ridiculous not in a negative way, but I was just wondering how people can have such belief of ancestors causing havoc because they are allegedly owed debts by their living family members. So, the chapter is insightful and worth reading. **Kamau** notes that "recently among the Agĩkũyũ community of Kenya, there has been a campaign to abandon Christianity and return to 'culture'" (308). In response to this, he argues that there have been practices in the Kenyan community which demand revisiting concepts of salvation and the extent of its impact in ordinary lives of people. More importantly, it has stirred apathy towards missionary Christianity. This apathy, built on the premise that missionary Christianity is a tool for colonisation and the demolition of African culture, is a bane to African Christianity.

A prevalent concept among the teachings among Christians in Central Kenya is the practice of *thiiri wa ngomi,* meaning, the payment of ancestral debts. Oppositions to these teachings assert that Christ's redemptive work has satisfactorily paid all debts including those of the ancestors. Proponents of ancestral debts argue that because of these debts, the ancestors visit the living with calamities such as *mirimu* (e.g., malaria, typhoid, cholera), *ndwari* (e.g., cancer, diabetes, arthritis), or failed businesses as a punishment. If a man fails to pay the dowry of his wife and his parent-in-law dies without receiving the payment of the dowry, they can come back for the man and his family. It is even

Raphael Akhijemen Idialu
Experiencing Salvation in Africa
BOOK REVIEW ESSAY: *Salvation in African Christianity*,
edited by Rodney L. Reed and David K. Ngaruiya

argued that the prevalence of alcoholism, juvenile delinquency, divorce, and the like are attributed to debts owed by the ancestors. In response to this practice, understanding the scope of Christ's redemptive work in revelaton, ruling, and reconciliation is important. Jesus Christ revealed the Father, a ruler who sits on God's glorious throne, and he reconciles humanity to God. In Agĩkũyũ understanding of sin, sin is ontological and social. Communal calamities are considered as results of sin. The Agĩkũyũ believe that the dead can see the living because they live among the living even though they are not seen. However, the Bible teaches that the dead cannot see the living, and hence they cannot demand for any payment for any debt. Also, since they do not need the things of the physical world to survive in the world of the spirit, paying physical debts becomes irrelevant. While some may see "the claim by Christians that Christ's work at the cross has paid ancestor debts" as appropriate contextualization, **Kamau** argues that this "is misinformed and a misappropriation of Christ's work" (322).

Chapter 5

"**Household Conversions in Acts and Their Significance for House-to-House Evangelism in Africa**" by **Isaac Ampong**, a Ghanian serving as Pastor for Youth and Families at St. Paul's Anglican Church, Tervuren, Belgium, is also an excellent chapter. **Ampong** begins his chapter with a beautiful story of his experience of his conversation with a woman who said that she would ask her husband first whether they should place their trust in Jesus Christ and accept the message of salvation, and that if her husband decided to convert to Christianity, she would follow and if he refused, then she would not. **Ampong** argues in the chapter that the conversion of the head of the household functions as a catalyst in the conversion of others in the household. He also posits that the Greco-Roman cultures share some similar values with African culture and and thus Christians in Africa can employ similar strategies for household conversions. **Ampong** borrows Nock's now-classic definition: "conversion is the reorientation of the soul of an individual, his deliberate turning from" what is wrong to what is right.[2] In the NT, conversion, repentance, penitence, and faith are strongly connected. Matthew Michael, the Nigerian biblical scholar and theologian, sees conversion as "repentance from sin and exercising of faith in Christ Jesus" (76).[3] This is the view of most Christians. **Ampong** lists several key examples from Acts, including the conversion of the Philippian jailer and his household (16:25–34), Cornelius and his household (10:1–11:18), Lydia and

---

[2] Citing Arthur Darby Nock, *Conversion: The Old and New in Religion from Alexander the Great to Augustine of Hippo* (London: Oxford University Press, 1933), 7.

[3] Citing Matthew Michael, *Christian Theology and African Traditions* (Eugene, Oregon, USA: Resource Publications, 2013), 178.

Raphael Akhijemen Idialu
Experiencing Salvation in Africa
BOOK REVIEW ESSAY: *Salvation in African Christianity*,
edited by Rodney L. Reed and David K. Ngaruiya

her household (16:11–15); Crispus and his household (18:8). He argues that within a household, in the ancient Roman context families typically shared a single religious adherence. In this context, conversion may not be genuine for every member of the family. However, the biblical witness of conversion narratives demonstrates "that the other members of the household were not compelled . . . to follow the *paterfamilias* in his conversion" (87). Some catalysts for conversion as identified by **Ampong** include preaching, miracles, crisis points and the conversion of the *paterfamilias* (head of the family). Because of similaries of culture and of conversion catalysts in the New Testament era and in contemporary Africa, the significance of the conversion of the head of the family for the conversion of the family as a whole is a strategy that African Christianity should adopt for effective result is house-to-house evangelism.

Chapter 19

"**An All-Embracing, Contextual, Challenging, Now and Not Yet Salvation for Ugandan Rural Communities**" by **Timothy J. Monger** is a classic! You could feel the author in the work. His application of the survey and reports from the survey give readers a sense of nearness to the rural communities of Uganda, and what they understand to be their expectation of salvation. His chapter is situated in the context of some rural communities in Uganda, communities that have been ravaged by colonialism, civil war, HIV/AIDS, poverty, climate change, food insecurity, social breakdown, and domestic violence. What type of salvation message can be preached to these kinds of people? These people witnessed internal displacement, and when they returned to their land, they were destitute their land remained untended, and farming skills had been lost. Children becoming orphans due to HIV/AIDS and civil war. In the midst of all these, what type of salvation message do they need?

The author seeks to discover how local churches can offer an authentic, vibrant, and powerful salvation for Ugandan rural communities. Rural communities of Gulu, Kitgum, Lira, and Masindi were used in the research. The result from this research in these rural communities shows that war, famine, diseases, death, hopelessness, struggle for education, low literacy, lack of basic needs, land grabbing, laziness, alcoholism, lack of knowledge, witchcraft, injustice and lack of infrastructure are some of the challenges of these rural communities. The respondents feel that becoming God-fearing, ability to support family, having business opportunities, good local ecosystem, purposeful life, good relationship with God and neighbours, having personal freedom, and joy and wholeness in the community will go a long way to restoring life in the community and engendering the salvation that is needed in the community. What true and relevant salvation then can the Ugandan Church offer these rural communities? They are to offer a salvation that reflects the following, among others:

Raphael Akhijemen Idialu
Experiencing Salvation in Africa
BOOK REVIEW ESSAY: *Salvation in African Christianity*,
edited by Rodney L. Reed and David K. Ngaruiya

1. Living God's story — understanding God's purpose in creation, vision of the new creation, the role of God's people in participating in his story.
2. That God reigns here — the vibrant connection between salvation and the kingdom of God. This salvation reminds the people of God's presence in their midst.
3. Holistic salvation — a salvation that embraces the spiritual and the physical, the personal and the communal, and the creational and the economic, affecting the whole life of a person.
4. Salvation for the downtrodden and marginalised — a salvation that reaches the most disadvantaged.
5. Embracing the Cross and leading sacrificially — salvation that recognises the Cross and places it at the centre of salvation and the work of Christ on the Cross, admonishing people to lead sacrificially.
6. Salvation for those different from us — salvation that breaks down tribal, ethnic, social, religious, economic, and other barriers.
7. Salvation is the beginning of a new chapter and the hope of all things made new — the salvation of new beginnings, instilling an unbreakable hope for the best which is yet to come is undeniably a powerful salvation.

Monger clearly demonstrates that the Church in Uganda can do something for the restoration of the rural communities mentioned in the chapter.

Chapter 17

"**Finding New 'Alphabets' for Proclaiming Salvific Faith in Africa**" by **Julius Kithinji**, who teaches at St Paul's University (Limuru, Kenya) and **Pauline K. Mwaura**, a minister in the Presbyterian Church of East Africa. stands out for me because of the catchy nature of the topic of the chapter. I was intrigued by what the authors mean by "alphabets." They use the image as a metaphor for effective proclamation of the gospel, arguing that a search for "new 'alphabets'" is necessary because many African Christians have remained at the level of confession of faith without corresponding practice of that faith, demonstrating that the contemporary African Church's alphabet is tired and worn out, and thus ineffective in the proclamation of the gospel of salvation — there were no sufficient "alphabets" for the proclamation of the gospel in Africa.

The call for a new and contemporary alphabet for the proclamation of the gospel is necessitated by the lack of depth in the state of growth of Christianity in Africa. The rise of secularism also calls for an alternative hermeneutics of proclamation in the African Church. There is a need to also look at the prevailing agitation for the ordination of gay priests, solemnisation of gay marriages, and perversion of sexual orientations. The issue of *mburi cia kiama* among Agĩkũyũ and *njuri nceke* among the Ameru advocates for oathing that undermines the gains of Christianity in Africa are other concerns. (The gĩGĩkũyũ and Meru phrases refer to traditional rituals which many Christians consider to be tied to idolatrous practice.) There is also a rapid increase in deliberate single motherhood, believed to be occasioned by *Mipango ya kando* ("side and unofficial marriages and secret marriages," 331), which is another area of concern related to relaxed sexual morals which lead to untold challenges in the family. There are consequences of sticking to worn-out alphabets. Giving preference to elders at the expense of the youth had led to the young people disengaging from the Church. This is especially sad for Africa which is regarded as a youthful continent. A continuation of this trend means that the future of youthful activeness in the Church is bleak. The alphabet of coziness is another worn-out alphabet that needs to be changed. This alphabet gave rise to the relaxed teaching of the scriptures. The proposed new alphabet includes the creation of a Pentecost community. For the authors, *Pentecost* is different from *Pentecostalism*. Pentecost is the fusion between the Holy Spirit and humanity, "producing a new dimension of living and Christian witness" (335). Pentecostalism "raises the danger of circularity" (335), whereby it contests against other Pentecostal communities, instead of winning souls to God. Another alphabet of note is that that speaks directly to religio-ethnicism. Africa of today is challenged with religio-ethnic issues, even within the Church. This has to be arrested. In current African Christianity, the alphabet of intentional scriptural and contextual discipleship is imperative for the Church to have any impact on the African continent.

Chapter 15

"**The Logical Implication of Trinitarian Exclusivism**" by **Joseph B. Onyango Okello**, a Kenyan teaching at Asbury Theological Seminary (Orlando, Florida, USA), is the most difficult to understand due to the philosophical nature of his approach to the treatment of the topic. The author's style of writing is quite clear, but philosophy is philosophy! He examines a major exclusive claim in Christianity — that Jesus is the only salvific way to God the Father.

Within contemporary African contexts, this has generated a key challenge to the evangelistic enterprise: What is the fate of the unevangelised? There are three primary positions: exclusivism, pluralism, and inclusivism. Exclusivism holds that the only way to the Father and eternal life is through the acceptance of Jesus Christ as your Lord and Saviour; there is no other way to God. Religious pluralism maintains that all religions are salvifically valid, and hence, all adherents of all religions will be saved, indeed. Inclusivism maintains the centrality of Christ but asserts that anonymous Christians exist in other religions. **Okello** discusses the implications of Trinitarian exclusivism, drawing on the logic of Thomas Aquinas and thus ultimately of Aristotle. He offers a view that "humans who reject Jesus Christ will be condemned because a rejection of God is a rejection of Jesus Christ and a rejection of Jesus Christ is also a rejection of God" (305). He concludes with a call to the evangelistic enterprise.

Raphael Akhijemen Idialu
Experiencing Salvation in Africa
BOOK REVIEW ESSAY: *Salvation in African Christianity,*
edited by Rodney L. Reed and David K. Ngaruiya

Other chapters

Chapter 1

Jamie Viands is a scholar in Biblical Studies at Africa International University (Nairobi, Kenya). In **"Jeremiah 29:11: Rightly Applying an Old Testament 'Salvation' Text,"** he brings expertise in Biblical exegesis and knowledge of Hebrew to bear in his analysis of Jeremiah 29:11 — "'For I know the plans I have for you,' declares the LORD, 'plans to prosper you and not to harm you, plans to give you hope and a future'" (NIV-1984) —positing that Jeremiah 29:4–23 was a letter to the Jews in exile. The major thrust of the chapter is his concept of "Hopeful Future." He argues that the text was for a future hope, a kind of eschatological expectation, and not for the present nor those experiencing challenges in their lives. Even though the author argues that the text is not directly for individual Christians today, he admonishes that the text is "profitable" and applicable in various ways, hence, he identified six different ways of understanding the text. These are:

1. God has promised a hopeful future — but this is a long-term hope that is beyond our lifetime.
2. God's good plan for us is primarily focused on spiritual realities, not material things.
3. The promise of a hopeful future is only for those who call upon the Lord.
4. God's plans are for his collective people, not our individualistic plans for ourselves
5. God's plans point to the gracious character that believers experience in Christ.
6. The letter and text serve as a warning to false prophets of imminent prosperity.

Though this is a good chapter, Viands should have looked for a better way of applying this popular text in contemporary African Christianity. The exegesis of the text is sound, but the application and affirmation of its relevance for contemporary African Christianity is lacking.

Chapter 2

Daniel M. Mwailu examines **"Concepts of Righteousness and Salvation in African Perspectives: An Assessment of Biblical and African Understandings of Salvation in African Christianity."** Mwailu is a Senior Lecturer in Theology and Biblical Studies at Africa Nazarene University (Ong'ata Rongai, Kenya). He posits that the biblical idea of salvation depicts three aspects: rescue from danger, rescue from harm, and rescue from death. From the perspectives of African Traditional Religions (ATRs), he argues that salvation is ritualistic and utilitarian in nature, which he said is similar to that of

Hinduism. In Islam, salvation is obtained in submission to Allah. He notes Tokunboh Adeyemo's claim that "in the three major monotheistic religions — Judaism, Christianity and Islam — salvation is achieved by submission" (25).[4] According to the Mwailu, salvation is from sin and evil through repentance by purification and rituals. In all of the efforts at achieving salvation, it is only God who can give salvation. An interesting part of the chapter is his treatment of what evil or sin is in some African contexts. For example, for the Nuer people (South Sudan, western Ethiopia), an evil act is not evil if it is not punished. For example, if a man sleeps with another man's wife, it is not evil if they are not found out by the society that forbids it. So, this means that if an evil is not discovered, it is not evil. This is quite different from the views of the New Testament and of African Christianity. Another interesting perspective of evil is that it is hierarchical. It is believed that those who are at the top of the hierarchy cannot commit sin or do evil. God and leaders in the community are seen in this light. The chapter is an interesting one. However, the author should have engaged more with the concept of righteousness and salvation rather than focusing on the concepts of sin and evil in an African context.

Chapter 3

Micah Onserio Moenga, a lecturer at Pan Africa Christian University (Nairobi, Kenya), discusses **"Salvation — Prosperity or Poverty? An Assessment of African Pentecostal Christianity."** Themes of prosperity and poverty are ubiquitous in African Christianity today. **Moenga** argues these are central to the theologies and preaching of Pentecostal Christianity in Africa, with special emphasis on poverty, diseases, prosperity, and victory. Reviewing "scholarly concepts of salvation and prosperity" (32), he highlights Ghanaian scholar J. Kwabena Asamoah-Gyadu's understanding of salvation as transformation and empowerment, healing and deliverance, and prosperity and success; a transformation of our human situation to that which is in sync with reality. According to Sandra Barnes, **Moenga** reports, for many black megachurches, salvation is godly living that results in both economic and non-economic benefits. **Moenga**'s treatment of the biblical concept of salvation reveals that salvation is basically deliverance — emancipation from the oppression inflicted on one by enemies, as was the case with the Israelites. So salvation is deliverance from danger or harm. This was the case of the Exodus of the Israelites from Egypt. In the NT, in the story of Jesus and Zacchaeus, salvation is found with the imparting of pardon. In **Moenga**'s treatment of

---

[4] Mwailu cites Tokunboh Adeyemo, *Salvation in African Tradition* (Nairobi: Evangel, 1979; revised edition, 1997); and Tokunboh Adeyemo, "Ideas of Salvation," *Africa Journal of Evangelical Theology* 16, no. 1 (1997): 67–75.

Raphael Akhijemen Idialu
Experiencing Salvation in Africa
BOOK REVIEW ESSAY: *Salvation in African Christianity*,
edited by Rodney L. Reed and David K. Ngaruiya

Psalm 51 in the story of the confession of David, it is repentance and forgiveness that ensure the joy of salvation. In Pauline soteriology, **Moenga** emphasizes the place of transformation as a sign of salvation in one's life. In summary, salvation is holistic, involving physical, spiritual, and social dimensions. Therefore, it is imperative to consider these three dimensions in the treatment of soteriology. On the whole, **Moenga** presents a simple and lucid concept of salvation for the understanding of the average reader.

Chapter 4

Kyama Mugambi, at the time of publication a researcher at the Centre for World Christianity, Africa International University (Nairobi, Kenya) but currently at Yale Divinity School (New Haven, Connecticut, USA), explores "'Jesus Is My Personal Saviour': Engaging Evangelical Themes of Individual Salvation in African Communal Contexts." For Mugambi, evangelical theology has prioritized individualistic interpretations of salvation. This individualistic interpretation of salvation implies that soteriology is predicated on the individual's conversion experience. This individualistic approach to conversion by Africans arose from their contact with Western missionaries through preaching and discipleship. According to Mugambi, conversion is central to salvation. This conversion is hinged on God's love as expressed in Jesus Christ. A justification for the individualistic approach to conversion is the personal contextual nature of its experience. Conversion differs from one person to the other, and so, many see it as personal as it is always different from that of the next person. However, in some African communities, salvation is more or less seen from a communal perspective rather than from a personal one.

Chapter 6

"A Pauline Theology of Justification and Its Implications for Ecclesiology in Kenya amid Ethnic Divisions: An Exegesis of Galatians 2:11–21" — by **Danson Ottawa Wafula** of the Africa Centre for Apologetics Research (Kenya) and **Edwin Mwangi Macharia** of African International University (Nairobi, Kenya) — identifies some of the challenges the African Church faces. These include the proliferation of false teaching, divisions over ethnicity, and syncretism. Circumcision, as understood by the Jews, was a sign of the covenant between God and the children of Abraham. A closer look at this covenant relationship reveals the traditional conflict between the children of Abraham and those that were not. In Paul's polemic on the issue of justification, however, he argued that for those who believed in Christ through faith, the demarcation between them and the Gentiles was removed. There was no longer any distinction. **Ottawa Wafula** and **Macharia** discuss the relationship between faith in Christ and the works of the law; being dead to the law and being alive in God (Gal 2:19). Being dead to the law means not being under the restrictions of

Raphael Akhijemen Idialu
Experiencing Salvation in Africa
BOOK REVIEW ESSAY: *Salvation in African Christianity*,
edited by Rodney L. Reed and David K. Ngaruiya

the law because he is crucified with Christ so that he may live to God. In Galatians 2:20–21, a key result of justification is the dying to self which produces life. It is the new life that one gets when he is dead to self and the law. So, in ensuring justification, the ground for justification is ultimately the work of Christ and secondly the believer's union with Christ. What is learned in Galatians is applicable to the African context of the Church, especially as it relates to ethnic divisions. The writers insist that Paul's argument regarding the coming together of the Jews and Gentiles through the work of Christ be adopted to solve our own ethnic divisions and propose that the concept of *Ubuntu* be adopted by African Christians to stem the tide of ethnic divisions in the Church in Africa. Our understanding of justification should affect how we relate to people in the faith, seeing them as brothers and sisters.

Chapter 7

In **"Past, Present, and Future: Paul's View of Salvation in the Thessalonian Correspondence," Gift Mtukwa** — from Zimbabwe but teaching at Africa Nazarene University (Ong'ata Rongai, Kenya) — explores what salvation entails from the Shona (Zimbabwe) perspective through the lens of Paul's letters to the Thessalonians. The chapter uses African biblical hermeneutics to determine whether salvation is in the past, present, or future. For salvation to be fully understood in the African context, it must be relevant to the various realities that make up Africa such as disease, racism, poverty, ignorance, oppression, hatred, war, tribalism, insecurity, economic hardship, etc. In the Shona worldview, salvation is not only in the afterlife but also in the here and now. To them, salvation should be anthropocentric, affirming life. *Ruponeso* is the Shona word for salvation, and it can mean 'to give birth', 'to sustain life', 'to rescue', or 'to deliver a baby'. This is akin to the Akan soteriological concept which has to do with the protection and preservation of life, both physical and spiritual, from evil-doers like witches. Among the Shona, *chivi* is what salvation saves people from. *Chivi* is a sin — anything that threatens the life and general well-being of human beings and communities. Salvation in this sense results in harmonious relationships in the communities. Among the Shona, the idea of a saviour who died to save humanity is non-existent, even though the idea of sacrificing oneself for others is present. From the Thessalonian correspondence, salvation denotes 'healing from disease', 'safe travel', and 'protection in times of trouble' (1 Thess 1:9b–10). It is also used to denote deliverance from sin and ultimate deliverance when one is saved to enter eternal bliss with Christ at the end of life. In 1 Thessalonias 5:8–10, salvation is futuristic and eschatological. The use of 'the day of the Lord coming in a time no one knows' is a pointer to this, and so warns everyone to be on guard. 2 Thessalonians is also eschatological. In the soteriological synthesis, salvation as seen from the Shona perspective is mainly in the present. Thus, its futuristic meaning is not as dominant as that in Paul's correspondence to the Thessalonians. True Christian salvation ought to be holistic because Jesus provided spiritual salvation and physical and emotional healing. Salvation in Shona and the general African perspective does not offer eternal salvation, but this can only be seen in the atoning work of Jesus Christ.

Chapter 8

Moses Iliya Ogidis, a minister with Evangelical Church Winning All (ECWA) in Nigeria currently working on a PhD in New Testament at St Paul's University (Limuru, Kenya), addresses the challenge of infertility that confronts marriages in some African homes in **"How Can Women Be Saved? A Reinterpretation of 1 Timothy 2:15 within a Nigerian Context."** Even though the text is not directly about infertility, **Ogidis** cleverly weaves infertility into his interpretation. Infertility is seen as an involuntary childlessness that affects couples culturally, socially, religiously, and psychologically. This reality is said to affect couples in most African nations. While childlessness may not be a big issue in some other nations of the world, it is a big issue in Africa. Infertility can safely be classified as a pandemic that kills joy and peace in families. Most women with this challenge avoid social events and gatherings where children are present.

Situating the concept of infertility in the text, Moses notes that most scholars understand 'being saved through childbearing' as "the physical preservation of the [mother's] body during" the labor and delivery of childbirth (142). An alternative and christological interpretation suggests that it is through Mary's *teknogonías* ('childbearing') of Jesus — that is, through Jesus himself — that women will be saved. But **Ogidis** laments the exclusion of women who may not have the ability to give birth from this interpretation. Such women may be medically infertile or have an infertile husband or may have had reproductive organs removed due to health complications. The challenge for the Church in Africa is that reading this text in the context of infertility requires reading against the grain of historical interpretation. **Ogidis** admonishes that the text should be read in "its multidimensional context" (149) to include women's infertility. Some scholars share his opinion. In conclusion, the idea of "being saved through childbirth" needs to be interpreted through the "hermeneutics of life" (133, 135, 136, 149, 150) to enhance the lives of women who cannot conceive. This inclusive approach will be of great help to the church in Africa in incorporating women who cannot conceive into the mainstream of the life of the Church and society.

Chapter 9

Henry Marcus Garba, another ECWA (Nigeria) pastor and a PhD candidate (World Christianity) at Africa International University (Nairobi,

Raphael Akhijemen Idialu
Experiencing Salvation in Africa
BOOK REVIEW ESSAY: *Salvation in African Christianity*,
edited by Rodney L. Reed and David K. Ngaruiya

Kenya) considers the ongoing revelance of the African patristic era for African Christianity today in **"Understanding the Soteriological Conceptualization of the Early Church Fathers: An Exploration of the Legacy of Athanasius and Its Relevance to Africa Christianity."** The early Church had to grapple with many issues and heresies. The personality of Christ was among the thorniest of all. Additionally, the issue of salvation also confronted the Church. Athanasius, born around AD 293 in Egypt, was among the most important to tackle these challenges. He was probably ethnically Coptic (ancient Egyptian) rather than from the Greek upper class. **Garba** passes on the urban legend that Athanasius was referred to as "a black dwarf," suggesting that he was dark-complexioned (161).[5] He trained under Bishop Alexander while serving as a secretary to that patriarch. There are three categories of patristic and medieval soteriology – redemption, sanctification, and deification. The soteriology of Athanasius was founded on the theological meaning of deification and its implications. The soteriology of deification is about participation, which speaks of salvation as sharing God's incorruption and personal communion between the persons of the Trinity. Deification therefore means adoption, and not absorption. He posits that we are adopted by God, and not absorbed into Him. Athanasius argued that the nature of the fallen human race must be changed for salvation to be realized and that salvation is only possible through Christ. Athanasius also views salvation as restoring and recreating God's original intention for human existence. Athanasius argues strongly for the Incarnation as necessary for human salvation. This is where deification comes in. Salvation is inconceivable without deification which Athanasius sees as the personal encounter of the believer with God and His work of grace, whereby believers experience communion with God and are regarded as children of God. The soteriological contribution of Athanasius is also against the Arians' subordinationism which denied the Trinity and its soteriological implication for humanity. Athanasius

---

[5] Editors' note: the earliest known reference to Athanasius as a 'black dwarf' is in 1984: Justo L. González, *The Story of Christianity*, vol. 1: *The Early Church to the Dawn of the Reformation* (New York: HarperSanFrancisco, 1984), 199. This was retained in reprint edition (Peabody, Massachussets: Prince Press, 1999), 173–174. However, González did not provide any citation. Inumerable other historians, including one of this journal's editors, have searched fruitlessly to find any primary source reference to Athanasius as a 'black dwarf.' When this was brought to González's attention, he checked his notes but was unable to find any information. Thus in the revised and updated second edition (New York: HarperOne, 2010), González removed this error. Here, Garba cites Mark Ellingsen, *African Christian Mothers and Fathers: Why They Matter for the Church Today* (Eugene: Wipf & Stock, 2015), 130. Ellington, however, fails to provide any citation except to a blogpost that actually points out González's error.

Raphael Akhijemen Idialu
Experiencing Salvation in Africa
BOOK REVIEW ESSAY: *Salvation in African Christianity,*
edited by Rodney L. Reed and David K. Ngaruiya

argued that Christ is not *like* God, but rather *of the same essence and substance with* God. From the African perspective, Africans have always believed in God before the advent of Christianity, but when the missionaries came, they brought the concept of the Son of God who is also God, and who brings salvation. But misunderstandings of salvation abound. However, the practice of inculturation, indigenization, and contextualization have helped Africans to understand soteriology from African perspectives. For Athanasian soteriology to be understood properly in Africa, there is a need for a collaborative dialogical reflection on soteriology in the language of Athanasius's soteriology, in appropriate response to the contemporary needs of African Christianity.

Chapter 10

The place of sacrifice in the religious worldview of Africans cannot be overemphasised. In African Christianity, it holds a prime place in the hearts of adherents and the same holds for traditional religions. In Christianity, the sacrifice of Christ for the salvation of humanity is significant. However, some critics have taken the sacrifice of Christ with a pinch of salt, arguing that it holds little or no value in explaining the meaning of atonement in Western contexts. **Samuel K. Bussey** addresses these issues in **"The Sacrifice of Christ in African Perspective: A Contribution to the Atonement Debate."** He notes that African scholars such as John Ekem, Edison Kalengo, and Mercy Oduyoye have challenged such western interpretations in five important ways:

	Western interpretation	vs	African interpretation
1.	Metaphorical approach		Dialogical Approach
2.	Focus on ritual sacrifice		Focus on both ritual sacrifice and self-sacrifice
3.	Reduction of sacrifice to moral self-giving		emphasis on multiple themes
4.	Association of sacrifice and death		Strong association of sacrifice with life
5.	Focus on understanding and articulation		deep concern for worship and everyday life

Some modern theological interpretations argue that the death of Christ, while effective for our atonement, was only an example of moral self-giving. This understanding diminishes the atoning work of Christ and renders it incapable of truly saving humanity from sin. In the Luo context (Kenya, Uganda, Tanzania), sacrifice is seen as a means of removing a barrier or curse from the life of an individual or community, not just a practice of 'satisfaction' or 'penal substitution' as it is understood in many Western contexts.

In contrast to this, **Bussey** highlights contributions from the aforementioned African theologians, making use of several methods: dialogical

Raphael Akhijemen Idialu
Experiencing Salvation in Africa
BOOK REVIEW ESSAY: *Salvation in African Christianity*,
edited by Rodney L. Reed and David K. Ngaruiya

exegesis, intercultural/cross-cultural hermeneutics, intertextual dialogue, and applied hermeneutics. These scholars aregue that Christ's sacrifice should be understood in terms of gift, atonement, substitution, covenant, and communion. Oduyoye notes the sacrifice of women in the Church in Africa. She sees the story of sacrifice from within the narrative of liberation, making women's experiences the starting point for her dialogical typological account of sacrifice. In light of African theological contributions, **Bussey** argues that western reductions of sacrifice to mere moral self-giving should be discarded for the rich African dialogical concept of sacrifice, and finally, sacrifice should also be seen from a robust ecclesial perspective in liturgy and communion.

Chapter 12

Joseph Mavulu, a minister in the Africa Inland Church who teaches at International Leadership University (Nairobi, Kenya), attempts to proffer "**A Balanced Approach to Understanding the Concept of Salvation in Contemporary African Christianity.**" For him, salvation is the deliverance of humankind by religious means from sin or evil, an attempt that strives towards restoring humans to their truest state which leads to eternal blessedness. Western theologians seem to classify grace into common grace and saving grace. Common grace is about good health, rain, children, prosperity, protection from danger and evil, provision of general well-being and the like by God. Saving grace is the salvation that brings people to spiritual salvation, the saving of their souls. By this approach, it seems the provisions of physical blessings are not part of holistic salvation for humanity.

In the Old Testament, the concept of salvation, associated with the Hebrew term *yesha* and its cognates, means to bring to a spacious environment where one is at ease, free to develop without hindrance. Metaphorically speaking, it conveys the sense of freedom from limitations and factors that constrain or confine. Within ATRs, salvation refers to physical wholeness, protection from dangers or anything that is in opposition to the general well-being of humanity. This is almost the same understanding as in African Christianity, as we see in the works of John Mbiti and Henry Mugabe. In African cosmology, salvation is not individualistic, but collective, communal, and corporate. Another important factor in varied African perspectives of salvation is the influence of the prosperity gospel, which sees salvation in very practical terms which must manifest in general well-being, good health, and material prosperity. According to some prosperity gospel proponents, one is not truly saved unless free from what prevents the enjoyment of physical and spiritual wholeness.

In achieving a balanced understanding of the concept of salvation, **Mavulu** finds a study of Mark 5:35 useful, where Jesus tells a woman that her faith has healed her and commands her to go in peace and be whole. **Mavulu** argues that

Raphael Akhijemen Idialu
Experiencing Salvation in Africa
BOOK REVIEW ESSAY: *Salvation in African Christianity,*
edited by Rodney L. Reed and David K. Ngaruiya

this statement is more than a dismissal formula. It means to go as one restored to a proper relationship with God. It can also mean wholeness. So, even though this woman was healed physically from her sickness, her healing also had a spiritual dimension. From this text, it is clear that Jesus was and is not only interested in the physical well-being of people but also in their spiritual well-being. So, a balanced salvation must focus on both the spiritual and the spiritual dimensions of the life of individuals.

Chapter 13

David K. Ngaruiya, an Associate Professor at International University (Nairobi, Kenya), offers an **"An Exploration of Understanding Seven Dimensions of Salvation in African Christianity."** He examines salvation from seven dimensions in African Christianity using two selected African churches:

1. Salvation from God's wrath
2. Eschatological Salvation
3. Salvation form sin
4. Salvation from being lost
5. Salvation from physical ailments
6. Salvation from life's pollution
7. Salvation from danger

Ngaruiya finds a point of convergence between salvation from the perspective of ATR and the Lukan expression of salvation. To the general view that salvation in ATR is primarily the physical well-being of people, this chapter adds a geographical dimension to the salvation in African understanding. People seek refuge in times of danger or challenges in sanctuaries such as sacred mountains, caves, shrines, or rocks. These can also be places for sacrifice. Two additionals aspect of salvation are its historicity and spirituality.

Building on traditional African concepts of salvation — such as the Annang (Nigeria) concept of *edinyanga* which encompasses movement from danger to a state of safety, being free from physical attack, safety from sources of harm, flourishing in a safe environment, harmonious relationships with others, and acting in ways which bring salvation — and the Gospel of Luke's concern that salvation necessarily includes the transformation of human life, forgiveness of sin, healing from diseases and release from any kind of bondage, with an added emphasis on the social issues of the poor, **Ngaruiya** recognizes that salvation is multidimensional. Insights from African cultures and religions can help African Christians recover or retain this holistic understanding of salvation. ATRs, however, are not the panacea that some claim — ATRs can be idolatrous and tend to minimize the perspective of the Kingdom of God.

From the case studies reviewed in this chapter, **Ngaruiya** offers three proposals and one observation for African Christians. The African Church, while not neglecting the spiritual aspect of salvation, needs to be deliberate in teaching a holistic salvation. Evangelists (and pastors) in African churches need training in how to proclaim a holistic gospel while safeguarding themselves from prosperity gospel that is harmful. Discipleship needs to reflect that the gospel is holistic. Understanding the concept of salvation in ATR helps with contextualisation of the gospel. An understanding of these seven dimensions of salvation vis-à-vis the position of the scriptures on the same is imperative for a balanced African Church

Chapter 14

Philemon Ongole, Overseer of Deliverance Churches in Eastern Uganda, continues the theme of **"Holism in Salvation."** Holism in the context of salvation means the impact of salvation on the whole life of a human being. Justification and faith are key in the understanding of salvation in the context of this chapter. As has been seen from previous chapters, there is a tendency to impose an unbiblical dichotomy onto reality: secular or sacred, physical or spiritual, cultural/political or ecclesiastical, private or public, holy or unholy, what is for God or what is for the world, religious or not religious. Holism is important because God's restorative programme in the salvation of humanity does not leave out some aspects of human life. Salvation reaches all areas of human life. Holism also extends the view of the experience of God's kingdom values in Africa. This is the experience of the dynamic reign or kingly rule of God in the sphere in which the rule is experienced. Even though this understanding could be futuristic, it has been inaugurated by Jesus Christ. A challenge in the understanding of holism is that African have a strong attachment to their culture, values, and lifestyles. These can result in syncretism, whereby believers have Christian faith but also engage in traditional beliefs that are not supported by the Scriptures, Some of which lead to immorality, idolatry, or ancestor worship. Second, a great deal of influence comes from the West into Africa. Some of these lead to aspects of postmodernism which disregard the truth of God. African believers still need much of discipleship to help them navigate these tricky paths. In conclusion, holism is a profound Christian truth that should be taken with all seriousness because salvation is holistic biblically, theologically, and practically.

Chapter 20

Kevin Muriithi Nereba, another lecturer at St Paul's University (Limuru, Kenya), embarks on **"An Exploration of Pentecostal Theology and Praxis of Salvation in Kenya."** He identifies three key themes in Pentecostal theology: dominion (creation mandate), empowerment (charismata in the Christian life), and present wholeness (over-realized eschatology). Pentecostal theology in the

Raphael Akhijemen Idialu
Experiencing Salvation in Africa
BOOK REVIEW ESSAY: *Salvation in African Christianity,*
edited by Rodney L. Reed and David K. Ngaruiya

Kenya context has been identified with its belief in personal transformation, informal liturgy, fluidity, and dynamism. It utilises a holistic worldview approach which connects the doctrine of salvation to the doctrines of creation, pneumatology, sanctification, and eschatology. Avoiding a dualistic understanding of Christian life that can weaken Christian life, it sees salvation as the recovery of the mandate of humanity given at creation and the possibility of well-being in this life. From this perspective, it tries to mitigate African realities coloured by corruption, poverty, and inadequate public health care systems. Theology must maintain a dialogical engagement between local worldviews and biblical theology. In African contexts, Christian theology must not overemphasize African traditional worldviews through an overbearing focus on African cosmologies. Allowing biblical worldview and theology to inform its understanding and practices, pentecostal theology can be enriched by viewing salvation within the broader scope of the Spirit's work in creation, sanctification, and consummation. In all, Pentecostal theology, when properly harnessed, will do a lot for good for African Christianity and the African society at large.

Conclusion

My overall impression is that *Salvation In African Christianity* is a must-read for churches, seminaries and Departments of Theology in African Universities. Its key messages and its value to the intended audience are well communicated in the chapters. My rating for the book is an A+, and my recommendation is that this Book should be made accessible in both soft and hard copies to everyone. However, I admonish the editors that in subsequent series, they should endeavour to ensure that contributors are more representatively spread across Africa, covering the north, east, west and south. This particular volume concentrated more on East Africa, and particularly on Kenya.

Women in Ordained Ministry

BOOK REVIEW ESSAY
Nkesiga, Diana Mirembe. *Woven in Spirals: The Journey of an African Woman to the Priesthood*. Kampala, Uganda: Beta Inspiration, 2019.[1]

Francis OMONDI

ORCID: 0000-0003-0650-4595
Oxford Centre for Religion and Public Life;
Canon, Anglican Church of Kenya
francis.omondi@ocrpl.org

Rev. Canon Diana M. Nkesiga was asked, "Do women go into full-time ordained ministry?" *Woven in Spirals* is her response, answering this question not in academic abstraction but through her narrated lived experience. The book opens with high drama. The ordination of Diana Mirembe Nkesiga to the Anglican priesthood signalled a thawing position on the ordination of women in the Church of Uganda, which had her in the frozen states of 'church worker' and deacon. She recounts, "I rose off my knees, as a priest of the church" to the gentle whisper of Rev. Canon Ernest Kibuuka, as he loosened her stole over her shoulders from the right side where it had hung since 1991, "*hmm, mwana wange, ekibo bakiluka nga kyetolola*" (Luganda: 'hmmm, my child, a basket is woven in spirals') (2–3). These words remain an apt depiction Diana's journey.

While her clergy brothers arrived at priesthood in two years, it took her five, and with drama when the time came. The Rt. Rev. Misaeri Kauma invited her back to Uganda from South Africa to be ordained as a priest, but the function stalled because the bishop retired that year. Diana narrates the agony of the in-between, awaiting the new Bishop Samuel Balagadde Sekadde to restart the process of ordaining a woman to pastoral ministry on his terms. She quips, "The spirals weaved during this time have been both deep and wide, and I want to believe colourful!" (7).

Diana narrates the discovery of identity and calling through the lens of her upbringing and family lineage. She was the secondborn of Edward Hugo Sematimba Barlow, the Kabanyolo University Farm manager, and Mary Nantongo a teacher. Like most teenagers, Diana had an identity crisis expressed

---

[1] Editors' note: A Kindle reprint edition is available from Quiet Garden Publishing, 2021.

Francis Omondi
Women in Ordained Ministry
BOOK REVIEW ESSAY: *Woven in Spirals: The Journey of an African Woman to the Priesthood*, **by Diana Mirembe Nkesiga**

in a change of name. Although her parents named her *Mirembe*, meaning 'peace' or 'freedom' in Luganda, she explains, "I changed to using my middle name Diana, as a typical teenager and through peer pressure, so that God could have the pleasure of redeeming the goddess of hunting" (12).

A teenager during Idi Amin's reign, Diana shared her country's apocalyptic angst. She discusses the uncertainty and unpredictability of life in Uganda, an era characterized by fear, accentuated by the 1977 murder of Archbishop Janani Luwum. Meanwhile, this pulsating anxiety nudged her to God. With the Gayaza Christian community, as they implored for divine intervention, she explains "the teachers organized the first-ever official night of prayer . . . The decision by the Christian staff helped us remain anchored to Christ and kept us returning to the staff for answers" (14). Later at Gayaza High School, as a young teacher, Diana claims, "I encountered what would spiral me onto the road to ordination" (14).

She later realized that this impulse for ordained ministry draws from deep wells. Church service ran deep in Diana's family line. Her great-grandfather Mikka Makamba Ssematimba, who despite being a confidant to Kabaka (King) Mwanga of Buganda, was an ardent Christian who pushed his family to serve God. Mikka took part in translating the gospel of John into Luganda. Her grandfather, John Barlow, prayed that one of his five sons would take up ordained ministry. Although not one of John's sons took clerical orders, his granddaughter Diana's vocation fulfilled this desire.

After graduating from Kyambogo National Teacher Training College, Diana recounts her unsettlement, as she began a teaching career at Gayaza Girls. She returned to the scene of her extraordinary encounter with God at age fourteen, an experience which changed her and transformed "a shy, awkward teen, with low self-esteem, into a courageous individual who felt loved and valued" (15). Here, her leadership was birthed.

Her experience as assistant chaplain counselling many young girls assaulted during the war to oust Iddi Amin in 1979, confronted her "with a pain and injustice I had never faced" (16). Their ordeal, including sexual assault, rape, and other brutality, horrified and made her angry. In seeking answers, Diana was exposed to experiences of extreme prejudice, injustice, and inequalities against the female gender. She thought training in theology would answer her questions.

Her thought of joining theological training caused unease in her confidants. She describes their reluctance thus, "I got prompts like, 'Isn't it about that time you got married?' Or remarks like, 'Do women go into full-time ordained ministry?' 'This is an unchartered territory for women, isn't there a safer option?'" (17). Some in her family worried about that she would remain

Francis Omondi
Women in Ordained Ministry
BOOK REVIEW ESSAY: *Woven in Spirals: The Journey of an African Woman to the Priesthood*, by Diana Mirembe Nkesiga

unmarried. Despite lukewarm support, she enrolled at Bishop Tucker Theological College (BTTC, today Uganda Christian University) in 1986. Rather than answering all of her questions, theological training brought new ones to Diana. She struggled for the first time with gender issues, and it is here that her identity struggles were heightened. Here too was her first encounter with the face of HIV-AIDS, laying the ground for her later ministry in South Africa. Diana had to learn to fight for equality.

Diana discusses her entry into theological school, class of '86, in chapter 4 and what became of her classmates in chapter 8. When she joined BTTC, twenty-nine years had passed since Florence Septume Njangali had become the first woman student to enroll in any Ugandan theological college. Nkesiga writes, "Three decades later, nothing had changed, except that the exclusion had become more sophisticated, more subtle, and the opportunity felt more like window dressing" (19).

The Church of Uganda (Anglican), then, and the college remained "unconvinced by the theological debate supporting women's training for ordination" (20). Thus, any woman walking through the gates of BTTC as a student felt the "unspoken disapproval" (20). Diana and Florence Adong were the only ladies in a class with eighteen men. Although the two ladies were not physically banished to study on the veranda as Rev Florence Njangali had been twenty-nine years before, Diana's exclusion meant that she "sat alone in the front row . . . like an alien treated with suspicion with no one daring to sit next to me" (25). She discusses a woman's experience in a male-dominated bible school, particularly being the subject of debate in between lectures. Diana sensed her presence was an unwanted intrusion. But this eventually changed.

This class of '86 became the crucible which forged Diana into a warrior with a unique sense of "love, justice, righteousness, sin and suffering" (65). She credits Dr Amos Kasibante for shaking them out of holding simple assumptions about life into deeply probing issues. She discusses her successful class, a rare group of graduates serving in extraordinary circumstances who became high-calibre clergy for the church.

The college experience had made Diana an open and assertive woman which caused disquiet among the church leadership. Even though the attitudes towards women in ministry shifted positively at the time of Diana's graduation, at least in the college, this book reveals a different story with church ministry. As she prepared for her final exams, she recounts a disturbing episode: "I learned that the two clergy from Namirembe Diocese, my sending diocese, were being prepared for ordination in secret before the set date" (29). She confronted the ordaining bishop asking: "Why was this very important religious rite being brought forward to such a peculiar time? And why I was being omitted from

Francis Omondi
Women in Ordained Ministry
BOOK REVIEW ESSAY: *Woven in Spirals: The Journey of an African Woman to the Priesthood*, **by Diana Mirembe Nkesiga**

being part of the process?" (29). She was not given a straight answer, but that December, while the men of her class were ordained as deacons, she was commissioned as a 'Church Worker', a designation never given to a male minister, which she calls in this book, "an undefined role created to displace the women who desired to join full-time ministry" (30).

In August 1989, Diana married a former classmate at BTTC, Rev Dr Solomon Nkesiga. Being married, she observes, did not shield her from discrimination in the diocesan service. She soon noted that her pay was half the salary of fellow tutors, despite having better qualifications, a holder of a bachelor's degree in divinity (BD) and a diploma in education. She enlisted Solomon to confront this discrimination and appealed to Bishop Kauma who resolved the issue.

The practice of commissioning women as 'Church Workers' was dropped in 1990 when the Church of Uganda unanimously accepted that women could be ordained deacons and priests. Until then, only the diocese of Kigezi under Bishop Festo Kivengere ordained women to the diaconate and priesthood. Kigezi ordained its first female priest in 1983. Because of the principle of autonomy of dioceses, Kigezi was free to order its own diocesan affairs, thereby become the first diocese in Uganda to approve the ordination of women. The diocese of Namirembe, where Diana would be ordained, resolved to ordain women into the diaconate in 1991, eight years after the Kigezi diocese had ordained its first women to the priesthood.

This cleared the way for Diana to be added to the ordinand list for new deacons in 1992. However, her name was quietly withdrawn on the discovery of her pregnancy. A pregnancy debate ensued, degenerating into "... women being unclean through their menstrual cycle, Leviticus 15:19–33, and therefore unable to celebrate Holy Communion" (32). She aptly challenges these positions, mounting a convincing defense in this book. Diana contends, "All these are man-made exclusions etched in the day's culture" (33). In her struggle against the exclusion of women in the church over the years, she won many male compatriots, as acknowledged in her book. These men supported and aided her ministry, foremost among them is her husband, Rev Dr Solomon Nkesiga, her cheerleader and one who shared her frustration. But she was finally ordained as a deacon before the end of 1992.

If one imagined that the Church of Uganda's institutions, such as BTTC or the dioceses, a cut above the preclusion of women in ministry, Diana chronicles subtle exclusion in South Africa. Solomon and Diana went to South Africa at the end of 1992, which was a high drama for Diana (41–51). Whereas Solomon was absorbed in immediate deployment, Diana had to wait. The irony is that South Africans and her fellow Ugandans, serving in the same diocese at Ugie in

Francis Omondi
Women in Ordained Ministry
BOOK REVIEW ESSAY: *Woven in Spirals: The Journey of an African Woman to the Priesthood,* **by Diana Mirembe Nkesiga**

South Africa's Eastern Cape, championed the delays and exclusion she experienced. Though denied full recognition of her vocational calling, she continued faithfully in active Christian service. She describes this time of active waiting:

> As I waited for both acceptance and deployment, I served in the community as an HIV-AIDS activist, mobilizing schools and business owners, partnering with the hospital, local chiefs, health workers and pastors raising awareness at the family planning clinics and in the churches. I knew how to keep myself busy. For me AIDS was a serious battle, one we had to take by the horns. It was a life and death situation, and I would fight it to the very last. (40)

She was called back to Uganda briefly in 1994 when she was ordained as a priest. But back in South Africa, her ecclesial status was largely ignored. Until she represented the Port Elizabeth diocese at the all-black post-apartheid Anglican clergy conference in Johannesburg, she remained obscure. Diana had often been "bypassed for minor reasons like my tribe, my gender, my nationality or my forthrightness" (50). And with no explanation her name was withdrawn from being made a canon even though the bishop had prepared her. Over this and more, she concluded: "I was not only a woman, but a foreigner, I suppose, being an unrecognized missionary didn't count much. The exclusions go on and on, and the spiral spins deeper and deeper, but the ministry and service continue" (51). Then at the 1995 conference in Johannesburg, Archbishop Desmond Tutu arranged for her to celebrate the Eucharist, and the archbishop was the first to receive from her. A picture published of her with the archbishop at the conference marked a turning point for her vocational career.

For its adventure, Solomon urged Diana to mark her tenth year of priesthood with a thanksgiving Service. She had been serving as a teacher, but with a missionary designation as supporting priest to Solomon at St Agnes Church in the parish of Swartkops River Valley, Port Elizabeth in South Africa. She reflects on this stage of her journey, including her 28 November 2004 speech during the service.

Diana holds a mirror to the Church, questioning our attitudes towards 'the other'. As her journey began, not with the glamorous prospect of the vocation, but with the calling to be God's servant, in the *Woven in Spirals*, Canon Diana is calling us to dare to open our ears to the Lord who calls our attention to the people around us. In this book, Diana has demonstrated that women are called to full-time ministry. When we, like her — whether men or women —respond to the impulse to serve God, we may discover our hidden talents. Since God calls women, men must ordain them!

CALL FOR PAPERS
Nicaea at 1700: Roots and Branches in African Christianity

For the majority of Christians around the world, the Nicene Creed of 325 and the Nicene-Constantinopolitan Creed of 381 remain normative. But many dismiss Nicene articulations of Christian faith as a corrupted hellenization of Christianity. Calls to *de-hellenize* Christianity are as common as calls for decolonization. Historian Robert Louis Wilken revisits the value of this ancient contextual theology:

> The notion that the development of early Christian thought represented a hellenization of Christianity has outlived its usefulness. ... a more apt expression would be the Christianization of Hellenism ... Christian thinking, while working within matters of thought and conceptions rooted in Greco-Roman culture, transformed them so profoundly that in the end something quite new came into being.[1]

Similarly, Kenyan biblical scholar Andrew M. Mbuvi affirms the validity of the historical hellenization both on its own terms and as a model to be followed in other contexts.[2] Yet Mugambi's complaint that Nicene trinitarian jargon of 'persons' — and presumably of *homoousia* and *homoiousia* as well! — is so foreign to African contexts as to be simply unhelpful is fair.[3]

Nonetheless, from Athanasius (c. 296 – 373) and Augustine (254–430) to Yared the Melodist (500s) of Aksum in the patristic era, to medieval Coptic and Nubian and Ethiopian Christian communities, to millions of contemporary Christians from Angola to Zimbabwe, the Creed is not mere western dogma but an *African* doxology which arises not from philosophical speculation but from lived experience of God in Christ. Moreover, the Nicene Creed was *not* created from the top down — the attendees represented a suffering people who had just emerged from a period of intense persecution at the hands of Empire — and the Creed arose as an ecumenical and global expression of a lived faith.

To mark the seventeenth centennial of the Nicene Creed in 2025, **African Christian Theology** 1, no. 2 (September 2025) will be a themed issue: "Nicaea at 1700: Roots and Branches in African Christianity." Submissions on this theme that fall within the scope of the journal should be received by Easter 2025 (20 April 2025). Submission guidelines are available on the journal's website. Submissions may be made online or sent to submissions@AfricanChristianTheology.org

---

[1] Robert Louis Wilken, *The Spirit of Early Christian Thought: Seeking the Face of God* (New Haven, Connecticut, USA: Yale University Press, 2003), xvi–xvii.

[2] Andrew M. Mbuvi, *African Biblical Studies: Unmasking Embedded Racism and Colonialism in Biblical Studies* (London: T&T Clark, 2023), 123.

[3] Jesse N. K. Mugambi, *African Christian Theology: An Introduction* (Nairobi: East African Educational Publishers / Heinemann Kenya, 1989; reprint edition: Nairobi, Acton Publishers, 2002), 7.

APPEL À CONTRIBUTIONS
Nicée à 1700 ans : Racines et Branches dans le Christianisme Africain

Pour la majorité des chrétiens dans le monde, le credo de Nicée de 325 et le credo de Nicée-Constantinople de 381 restent normatifs. Mais nombreux sont ceux qui rejettent les articulations nicéennes de la foi chrétienne comme une hellénisation corrompue du christianisme. Les appels à la *déshellénisation* du christianisme sont aussi fréquents que les appels à la décolonisation. L'historien Wilken revient sur la valeur de cette ancienne théologie contextuelle :

> L'idée selon laquelle le développement de la pensée chrétienne primitive représentait une hellénisation du christianisme a fait son temps. ... une expression plus appropriée serait la christianisation de l'hellénisme ... La pensée chrétienne, tout en travaillant sur des sujets de pensée et des conceptions enracinés dans la culture gréco-romaine, les a transformés si profondément qu'en fin de compte quelque chose de tout à fait nouveau a vu le jour.[4]

De façon similaire, le bibliste kenyan Andrew M. Mbuvi confirme la validité de l'hellénisation historique à la fois en tant que telle et en tant que modèle à suivre dans d'autres contextes.[5] Pourtant, la plainte de Mugambi selon laquelle le jargon trinitaire nicéen des « personnes » — et vraisemblablement aussi de *l'homoousia* et de *l'homoiousia* ! — est tellement étranger aux contextes africains qu'il n'est tout simplement pas utile.[6]

Néanmoins, depuis Athanase et Augustin jusqu'à Yared le Mélodiste d'Axoum à l'époque patristique, en passant par les communautés chrétiennes médiévales coptes, nubiennes et éthiopiennes, jusqu'aux millions de chrétiens contemporains de l'Angola au Zimbabwe, le Credo n'est pas un simple dogme occidental, mais une doxologie *africaine* qui découle non pas de la spéculation philosophique, mais de l'expérience vécue de Dieu dans le Christ. En outre, le Credo de Nicée n'a *pas* été créé du haut vers le bas — les participants représentaient un peuple souffrant qui venait de sortir d'une période de persécution intense aux mains de l'Empire — et le Credo est apparu comme l'expression œcuménique et mondiale d'une foi vécue.

Pour marquer le dix-septième centenaire du Credo de Nicée en 2025, ***Théologie Chrétienne Africaine*** 1, n° 2 (septembre 2025) portera sur : « Nicée à 1700 ans : Racines et Branches dans le Christianisme Africain ». Les soumissions correspondant au champ d'application de la revue doivent être reçues avant Pâques 2025 (20 avril 2025). La ligne éditoriale est disponible sur le site web de la revue. Les contributions peuvent être soumises en ligne ou envoyées à submissions@AfricanChristianTheology.org

---

[4] Robert Louis Wilken, *The Spirit of Early Christian Thought: Seeking the Face of God* (New Haven, Connecticut, États-Unis : Yale University Press, 2003), xvi–xvii ; notre traduction.

[5] Andrew M. Mbuvi, *African Biblical Studies: Unmasking Embedded Racism and Colonialism in Biblical Studies* (London : T&T Clark, 2023), 123.

[6] Jesse N. K. Mugambi, *African Christian Theology: An Introduction* (Nairobi : East African Educational Publishers / Heinemann Kenya, 1989; reprint edition : Nairobi, Acton Publishers, 2002), 7.

CONVITE DE ARTIGOS
Nicéia a 1700 anos: Raízes e Ramos do Cristianismo Africano

Para a maioria dos cristãos em todo o mundo, o Credo Niceno de 325 e o Credo Niceno-Constantinopolitano de 381 continuam a ser normativos. Mas muitos rejeitam as articulações nicenas da fé cristã como uma helenização corrompida do cristianismo. Os apelos à *des-helenização* do cristianismo são tão comuns como os apelos à descolonização. O historiador Robert Louis Wilken revê o valor desta antiga teologia contextual:

> A noção de que o desenvolvimento do pensamento cristão primitivo representou uma helenização do cristianismo ultrapassou a sua utilidade. . . . uma expressão mais adequada seria a cristianização do helenismo . . . O pensamento cristão, embora trabalhando em matérias de pensamento e concepções enraizadas na cultura greco-romana, transformou-as tão profundamente que, no final, surgiu algo muito novo.[7]

De forma semelhante, o biblista queniano Andrew M. Mbuvi afirma a validade da helenização histórica, tanto nos seus próprios termos como um modelo a seguir noutros contextos.[8] No entanto, a queixa de Mugambi de que o jargão trinitário niceno de 'pessoas' — e presumivelmente também de *homoousia* e *homoiousia* ! — é tão estranho aos contextos africanos que simplesmente não é útil, é justa.[9]

No entanto, desde Atanásio e Agostinho até Yared o Melodista de Axum, na época patrística, passando pelas comunidades cristãs medievais coptas, núbias e etíopes, até aos milhões de cristãos contemporâneos, de Angola ao Zimbabué, o Credo não é um mero dogma ocidental, mas uma doxologia *africana* que surge não da especulação filosófica mas da experiência vivida de Deus em Cristo. Além disso, o Credo Niceno *não* foi criado de cima para baixo — os participantes representavam um povo de sufrimento que tinha acabado de sair de um período de intensa perseguição às mãos do Império — e o Credo surgiu como uma expressão ecuménica e global de uma fé vivida.

Para assinalar o décimo sétimo centenário do Credo Niceno em 2025, **Teologia Cristã Africana** 1, nº 2 (setembro de 2025) será uma número temática: "Nicéia a 1700 anos: Raízes e Ramos do Cristianismo Africano." Os trabalhos sobre este tema que se enquadrem no âmbito da revista devem ser recebidos até à Páscoa de 2025 (20 de abril de 2025). As normas de submissão estão disponíveis no sítio Web da revista. As submissões podem ser feitas em linha ou enviadas para o meu endereço submissions@AfricanChristianTheology.org

---

[7] Robert Louis Wilken, *The Spirit of Early Christian Thought: Seeking the Face of God* (New Haven, Connecticut, Estados Unidos,: Yale University Press, 2003), xvi–xvii; nossa tradução.

[8] Andrew M. Mbuvi, *African Biblical Studies: Unmasking Embedded Racism and Colonialism in Biblical Studies* (London: T&T Clark, 2023), 123.

[9] Jesse N. K. Mugambi, *African Christian Theology: An Introduction* (Nairobi: East African Educational Publishers / Heinemann Kenya, 1989; reprint edition: Nairobi, Acton Publishers, 2002), 7.

CALL FOR PAPERS

Center of Biblical Studies, Research, and Development
West African Advanced School of Theology, Owerri, Nigeria

First Annual International Hybrid Conference 2024

The Bible, African Spirituality, and Post-Modernity
4–6 December 2024
10:00 am
WAAST Conference Hall / Online

Abstracts of not more than 200 words and correspondence should be sent to cbibsrd@gmail.com. Abstracts are invited to be submitted on any of the following subthemes:

- The Role of the Bible In Contemporary African Sociocultural Identity
- Intersections of Tradition and Modernity
- Intersection of Biblical Hermeneutics & African Traditional Beliefs
- African Traditional Beliefs & Biblical Narratives
- Decolonization of Biblical Interpretation
- Postmodern Challenges to Religious Identity
- Liberation Theology in African Contexts
- Syncretism & Hybrid Spiritualities
- Ecological Perspectives in African Spirituality
- Media, Technology, and Sacred Narratives
- Technological Literacy in Pastoral Education and Formation
- African Diaspora and the Resilience of Spiritual Identity
- Ethics and Morality in Postmodern African Spirituality
- Pluralism & Religious Tolerance
- Post-Modern Critiques of Biblical Authority in African Contexts

Abstracts should be of not more than 200 words and submitted single-spaced in Times New Roman, size 12 font. If the abstract is accepted, paper submissions should be no more than twelve pages in length, double-spaced, Times New Roman, size 12 font.

Deadline for submission of abstract: 10 November 2024

Conference Fees: ₦ 15,000 (in person), ₦ 10,000 (virtual), ₦ 5,000 (PG students)
   Bank: UBA | Account Name: WAAST | Account No.: 1007369206
   Deposit receipts should be forwarded to WhatsApp contact 08066269954 (Nigeria)

Submissions and inquiries: cbibsrd@gmail.com

CALL FOR PAPERS

Yale-Edinburgh Group on World Christianity and the History of Mission

2025

Christianity, Democracy, and Nationalism

28–30 May 2025
Universidade Mackenzie, São Paulo, Brazil
Submission deadline: 15 December 2024

The 2025 Yale-Edinburgh Conference invites papers that interrogate the relationship between democracy, nationalism, Christian communities, and the Christian faith around the world. We especially welcome historical case studies exploring the relationship of Christian bodies with changing sociopolitical circumstances; ethnographies that illuminate the religious and cultural imaginaries of Christian communities and their lived realities; theological interrogations into the politicisation of Christian religion; comparative studies highlighting patterns of interactions between religious communities, democratisation, and nationalism; and any other pertinent topics.

For more details, see https://www.cswc.div.ed.ac.uk/2024/09/yale-edinburgh-2025-call-for-papers/

Send your name, affiliation, and 250-word abstract by 15 December 2024 using this form: https://forms.gle/6dDtQqNLzBGSSzDi9

Proposed abstracts and papers may be submitted in English, Portuguese, and Spanish.

CONVITES DE ARTIGOS

Grupo de Yale-Edimburgo sobre o Cristianismo Mundial e a História da Missão

2025

Cristianismo, Democracia, e Nacionalismo
28–30 maio 2025
Universidade Mackenzie, São Paulo, Brazil
Prazo de apresentação: 15 dezembro 2024

A Conferência de Yale-Edinburgh de 2025 convida à apresentação de comunicações que questionem a relação entre democracia, nacionalismo, comunidades cristãs e a fé cristã em todo o mundo São especialmente bem-vindos estudos de casos históricos que explorem a relação dos corpos cristãos com as circunstâncias sociopolíticas em mudança; etnografias que iluminem os imaginários religiosos e culturais das comunidades cristãs e as suas realidades vividas; interrogações teológicas sobre a politização da religião cristã; estudos comparativos que realcem padrões de interação entre comunidades religiosas, democratização e nacionalismo; e quaisquer outros tópicos pertinentes.

Para mais informações, consultar https://www.cswc.div.ed.ac.uk/2024/09/yale-edinburgh-2025-call-for-papers/

Envie o seu nome, filiação e um resumo de 250 palavras até 15 de dezembro de 2024 utilizando este formulário: https://forms.gle/6dDtQqNLzBGSSzDi9

Os resumos e artigos propostos podem ser apresentados em inglês, português, e espanhol.

BOOK NOTE REVIEW

Amevenku, Frederick Mawusi, and Isaac Boaheng. *Biblical Exegesis in African Context*. Series in Philosophy of Religion. Malaga, Spain: Vernon Press, 2021. Pp. xvi + 120. US$37 (Hardback); $24 (paperback); $57 (e-book).

Anthony SMITH

Pioneer Bible Translators, Nile Africa Region
anthony.smith@pioneerbible.org

The stated purpose of *Biblical Exegesis in African Context* is to "guide African readers on how they can interpret the Bible within the socio-cultural context of Africa and apply it appropriately to their lives" (xi). *Exegesis* is here defined as "an interactive process of interpretation in which readers seek the meaning of the text in its original context," while *hermeneutics* is described as "applying the results of exegesis to contemporary contexts" (1). This is in keeping with much contemporary discussion of exegesis and hermeneutics. After a brief overview of exegesis in the first chapter, the authors use the following five chapters to examine various steps in the exegetical process, from textual analysis to literary and socio-rhetorical analysis. The next three chapters provide specific application of biblical exegesis to the African context. Chapter 7 considers the history and *status quaestionis* of African Biblical Studies (ABS). Mother-tongue biblical hermeneutics is the subject of chapter 8. Chapter 9 turns to the role of women in African church leadership and a brief study and application of 1 Corinthians 14:34–35 and 1 Timothy 3:1–7. The book concludes with a brief summarizing conclusion. Each chapter is well organized and includes review questions to aid in study. A bibliography and topical index are also included.

It must be stated at the outset this is a valuable and useful contribution to the growing body of biblical study aids focused on the African context. Of course there is a wide variety of African contexts which are difficult to generalize. Both authors are from Ghana. However, I found nothing in the book which seems overly focused on a West African context to the exclusion of the rest of the continent. The exegetical principles and methodology provided in the first half of the book are not exceptional; the material found here can be found in any of a dozen other exegesis textbooks. This is good. Such methods have been well-honed throughout the modern period of biblical studies. However, I am aware of no other textbook which combines a concise yet thorough treatment of

Anthony Smith
BOOK REVIEW: *Biblical Exegesis in African Context,*
by Frederick Mawusi Amevenku and Isaac Boaheng

methodology with such specific and useful application to African context. For this, the authors are to be praised.

Beyond use as an exegetical textbook, this volume is worthy of consideration if only for the historical review and analysis of ABS and mother tongue exegesis. Here the authors provide a meaningful justification for this field of study and analyze the field under a series of historical stages which are quite useful for students new to the field. In considering a method of mother tongue exegesis, the authors suggest the student discuss the use of the concept in their own language and culture as well as consult other mother-tongue speakers for additional insight (89). I can think of no better way to initiate the integration of serious biblical exegesis and application in African contexts. In my consultations with African Bible translators, we use a similar method for understanding and contextualizing foreign concepts.

I am surprised such a *crux interpretum* as 1 Timothy 2:11–15 was not included in the discussion of the role of women in ministry. Also, a short list of suggested readings for each chapter would have been helpful. Finally, considering the intended use of the book, a more affordable e-book or kindle version would be immensely beneficial.

BOOK NOTE REVIEW
Kigame, Reuben. *Essays in African Christianity and Theology.* Eldoret, Kenya: Posterity Publishers, 2023.

Francis OMONDI

ORCID: 0000-0003-0650-4595
Oxford Centre for Religion and Public Life;
Canon, Anglican Church of Kenya
francis.omondi@ocrpl.org

Reuben Kigame's ideas in this book were initially developed as submissions of his doctoral assignments on emergent issues in African Christianity and theology. Kigame addresses these emerging issues from multi-disciplinary perspectives in the thirteen chapters of this book. He ventures into areas including decolonizing African theology, African identity, and LGBTQI controversy.

Decolonizing African Christianity is central in Kigame's book, discussed in nine out of the thirteen chapters. In Kigame's view, decolonization should interest theology and all disciplines. He shares the decolonization thoughts of Prof Ndlovu-Gatscheni Selebo and Kwasi Wiredu,[1] prioritizing three domains where colonization has most affected African thinking. These include *epistemicide*, which shuns indigenous knowledge, *lingucide*, where the colonizers' language replaced the local vernacular, and *culturecide*, which demotes the values and local way of life while promoting [foreign] 'civilization'. To decolonize African theology, Kigame proposes emancipating it from the empire's influence in literature, philosophy, education, architecture, music, medical science, and history. He deals with these in chapters 4, 5, 6, 7, and 8. For him, Christians are better off studying theology in African institutions, with contextualized theological instruction. The primary decolonization example in Kigame's essays is indigenized Christianity, as explained in chapters 7 and 8. He discusses indigenized African Christianity in Kenya in chapter 4, including the Africa Israel Nineveh Church in Vihiga County (western Kenya), the *Roho* churches among the Luhya and Luo peoples of western Kenya, and the *Akurinu*

---

[1] Kwasi Wiredu, "Toward decolonizing African Philosophy and Religion," *African Studies Quarterly* 1, no. 4 (1998): 17–46, https://asq.africa.ufl.edu/wp-content/uploads/sites/168/Vol-1-Issue-4-Wiredu.pdf

Francis Omondi
BOOK REVIEW: *Essays in African Christianity and Theology,*
by Reuben Kigame

(aka Holy Ghost Church of East Africa) in central Kenya among the Agĩkũyũ people.

True to the spirit of the interdisciplinary approach, Kigame acknowledges and analyses earlier African proponents of decolonization. He especially mentions Ngugi wa Thiong'o's concept of using vernacular rather than English,[2] and Okot P'Bitek's call to purge African Christian Christianity of Greek influences.[3] Although Kigame rides on the African writers' conception of decolonization, their deriding of the Christian faith appalls him. He first, as a Christian apologist, protests the way post-colonial literature presented Christianity as colonial and un-African. He then defends Christianity from undue criticism by positioning Christianity as a universal faith.

By employing historical and hermeneutical responses, Kigame refutes claims that Christianity is not an African faith and disagrees with the categorization of Christianity as a Western religion. For Kigame, St Luke's writing attests that Christianity came into Africa in the first century and, therefore, was deemed an African faith. Kigame calls for an AFRICENTRIC interpretation of Christianity as a global faith, a departure from the misleading Eurocentric Christianity, and sees no reason to reject the rich Christian Heritage of Africa based on a distorted interpretation of historical facts.

Kigame's genius is his engagement of African identity through the African musical genre; this is only natural as Kigame himself is a well-known Kenyan musician. He takes the Congolese musician Verckys's number "*Nakomitunaka*" (Lingala for 'I ask myself') to set the identity dialogue.[4] Verckys directs his questions to God, as his ultimate arbiter, and engages his *négritude* by questioning culture and colonization, both socio-political and theological. In his music, Verckys addresses the themes of *négritude* identity, the decolonization of Christian symbolism, and the place of *négritude* in biblical theology. Verckys questioned the portrayal of Adam and Eve and the angels and Saints of the Church as white, while our ancestors, Satan, and evil as portrayed as black. Kigame interprets Verckys's question as decolonizing skin colour, which gave notoriety to black negativity. In Kigame's analysis, Verckys was deconstructing the Christian missionary symbols that undermined African

---

[2] Ngugi wa Thiong'o, *Decolonising the Mind: The Politics of Language in African Literature* (Nairobi: Heinemann Kenya, 1981).

[3] Okot p'Bitek, *African Religions in Western Scholarship* (Nairobi: Kenya Literature Bureau, 1971).

[4] Georges Kiamuangana Mateta (1944–2022) performed under the *nom d'arte* "Verckys." "Nakomitunaka" was released on a 1973 album by Verckys and Orchestre Vévé.

Francis Omondi
BOOK REVIEW: *Essays in African Christianity and Theology*,
by Reuben Kigame

identity. Hence, Kigame calls for divesting Christian symbols of misleading excesses.

In Chapter 11, Kigame wades into the LGBTQI discourse. He opens it with an anecdote which exposes his bias: the story of a 20-year-old lady who, Kigame claims, made a moral decision to ditch a homosexual lifestyle for a heterosexual marriage. This revealed Kigame's persuasion that the conditions listed as LGBTQI were biological (bisexual and transgender), but the remaining were lifestyle and social alternatives. He claims long periods of isolation in one gender context allowed for the LGBTQI condition and that people discovered being gay during their imprisonment or unisex primary and high school. For Kigame, the concern for LGBTQI is to be seen in terms of whether its associated behaviors are sin or not. He considers the use of terms like 'inclusion' and 'exclusion' as a coverup for promoting sexual orientation ideology. While he opposes ostracization of gay people, at a personal level, and urges for their support in society as fully equal citizens, he does not extend this support to the church where his interest lies. For Kigame, the LGBTQI question presents the Church worldwide with a crisis, although he conceives a possibility of the church owning the crisis while staying faithful to the scriptures, hence the "Judean Solution" by loving homosexuals and not condoning their practices (328–329). He recommends a balance between obeying scriptures in denouncing homosexuality as a sin and extending mercy to those involved. The Anglican church can love homosexuals by leading them to abstain from perversions and nudging them to reform. He further recommends barring them from partaking in the Eucharist.

Kigame's postulation on decolonizing African Christianity is too blunt for failing to anchor his reasoning on a coherent definition. Lumping three key themes together — resistance to colonialism, indigenization, and neo-colonialism in decolonization — obscured aspects of theology needing attention. Nonetheless, through these essays, Kigame opens the door for scholars in African Christianity and theology, to probe further the notions of colonization and decolonization, of coloniality and decoloniality. These terms, claim Maldonado-Torres,[5] are becoming key terms for movements that challenge the predominant racialized, religious, liberal, and neoliberal politics and religion of today.

---

[5] Nelson Maldonado-Torres, "Outline of Ten Theses on Coloniality and Decoloniality, Caribbean Studies Association (2016), 2.
https://caribbeanstudiesassociation.org/docs/Maldonado-Torres_Outline_Ten_Theses-10.23.16.pdf

BOOK NOTE REVIEW

Ayuk, Ayuk Ausaji. *African Theology of Missions.* Foreword by Blayne C. Waltrip. Port-Harcourt, Nigeria: Zumafind, 2023. Pp. xii + 143. ₦9,600.00

Kent Michael SHAW, I

Southeastern University, Lakeland, Florida, USA
kentmshaw@gmail.com

Introduction

Dr Ayuk, a Nigerian missionary in the Philippines, presents a compelling argument for an *African Theology of Missions*. His perceptive and imaginative theological praxis emerge from a lived experience as an African. Written from this lens, it provides a prototype for a missions theology globally. Arising from the African landscape, an exploration of inculturation and contextualization is a recurring theme throughout this work. These concepts are not defined by lines of demarcations; however, they are applicatory to the missionary, the student of missions, and the missiologist.

This examination explores the global significance of African theology in shaping missions practice. Dr Ayuk argues that African theology reflects and challenges issues confronting present-day Africans. The questions posed seek to understand salvation, worldview, ancestors, tribalism, and life as an African.

Overview

Each chapter is inscribed with a biblical motif for implementing an African theology of missions. Ayuk possesses a vast comprehension of theology, missions, and practice, which surfaces in each section. Ayuk tactfully addresses the oblivious lack of sensitivity suffered by some western missionaries and compares this to the Apostle Paul's missional appropriations. Paul demonstrates that the gospel is adaptable to all cultures and not monolithic in approach and function. As exegeted by the author, the Apostle's teaching depicts a prescription of assimilating into differing ethnic groups with the apprehension of cultural demeanors. Practitioners of mission in Africa from North America and Europe should intentionally grapple with cultural adaptation without undue suspicion. This analysis must take into consideration traditions and societal norms prior to the implementation of Christian tenets. Dr Ayuk proposes a paradigm shift to inclusivity of religious altruism, Indigenous integration, perpetual discussions, and the alleviation of bias. These enactments

Kent Michael Shaw I
BOOK REVIEW: *African Theology of Missions*,
by Ayuk Ausaji Ayuk

will create sustainable systems for the success of each missionary worker.

African Theology encapsulates traditions, understandings of indigenized religious discipline, and theology from an African perspective. This theological rubric expands God's intimate understanding of the African continent revealed to his people. Dr Ayuk's articulation of African theology speaks to matters and questions from the sacred text. He uniquely affirms this school of thought and encourages African Christians to embody their ethnocultural heritage. *An African Theology of Missions* answers distinct questions and confers the author's understand of God's response.

Another vital aspect of this intriguing research is the educational insight provided by the author. He affirms the significant premise that theological educators should draw upon the worldview of their students and targeted ethnic groups. This component creates a space to inquire how one views their society, practices their values, and expresses expectations. Therefore, these underpinnings foster contextualization, sensitivity, and efficacy in the educational methodology. Together, this course of action will allow dialogue and theologizing that remains contextualized, thus equipping the pupil with indispensable tools of preparation.

Evaluation

These pages contain pivotal details and findings for an African Theology of Missions in contemporary times. Importantly, these themes are answered with insightfulness and a contextual framework. Appraising the twelve chapters and placing them in four categories articulates an established pedagogy for a theology of missions. Through the first three chapters, a well-defined position on theology and mission is detailed. Chapters four, five, and six illustrate African theology reflective of literature and constructive cultural systems. The contents in chapters seven, eight, and nine divulge inside beliefs and juxtapose the writings of Chinua Achebe's literary work with African Missions Theology. Equally important are the remaining chapters that promulgate a biblical basis for African Theology, implications for theological education, and applied strategies.

Conclusion

African Theology of Missions is a consequential text for the study of missiology. As a missiologist, Dr Ayuk delineates his interpretation of a missions theology constructed for the African continent. Through Ayuk's assessment, a theological delineation of missiological implementations formed for Africa emerges. This book serves as an enduring conveyor of inculturation, contextualization, Christianity rooted in African soil, and missions theology.

www.ingramcontent.com/pod-product-compliance
Lightning Source LLC
Chambersburg PA
CBHW050848230426
43667CB00012B/2196